Managing Bodily Injury Claims

Managing Bodily Injury Claims

James R. Jones, CPCU, AIC, ARM
Director of Claims Education
American Institute for CPCU/Insurance Institute of America

Junie Maggio, RN, BSN, CCM
Case Management Specialist
Overland Park, KS

Medical Editor
Barry Gustin, MD, MPH, MA
Medical Director
American Medical Forensic Specialists, Inc.
Berkeley, CA

Second Edition • Ninth Printing

American Institute for Chartered Property Casualty
Underwriters/Insurance Institute of America
720 Providence Road, Suite 100
Malvern, Pennsylvania 19355-3433

© 2001

American Institute for Chartered Property Casualty Underwriters/Insurance Institute of America

All rights reserved. This book or any part thereof may not be reproduced without the written permission of the copyright holder.

Unless otherwise apparent, examples used in AICPCU/IIA materials related to this course are based on hypothetical situations and are for educational purposes only. The characters, persons, products, services, and organizations described in these examples are fictional. Any similarity or resemblance to any other character, person, product, services, or organization is merely coincidental. AICPCU/IIA is not responsible for such coincidental or accidental resemblances.

This material may contain Internet Web site links external to AICPCU/IIA. AICPCU/IIA neither approves nor endorses any information, products, or services to which any external Web sites refer. Nor does AICPCU/IIA control these Web sites' content or the procedures for Web site content development.

AICPCU/IIA specifically disclaims any implied warranties of merchantability or fitness for a particular purpose. No warranty may be created or extended by sales representatives or written sales materials.

AICPCU/IIA materials related to this course are provided with the understanding that AICPCU/IIA is not engaged in rendering legal, accounting, or other professional service. Nor is AICPCU/IIA explicitly or implicitly stating that any of the processes, procedures, or policies described in the materials are the only appropriate ones to use. The advice and strategies contained herein may not be suitable for every situation.

Information which is copyrighted by and proprietary to Insurance Services Office, Inc. ("ISO Material") is included in this publication. Use of the ISO Material is limited to ISO Participating Insurers and their Authorized Representatives. Use by ISO Participating Insurers is limited to use in those jurisdictions for which the insurer has an appropriate participation with ISO. Use of the ISO Material by Authorized Representatives is limited to use solely on behalf of one or more ISO Participating Insurers.

Second Edition • Ninth Printing • November 2007

Library of Congress Control Number: 2001089876

ISBN 978-0-89462-147-5

Foreword

The American Institute for Chartered Property Casualty Underwriters and the Insurance Institute of America (the Institutes) are independent, not-for-profit organizations committed to expanding the knowledge of professionals in risk management, insurance, financial services, and related fields through education and research.

In accordance with our belief that professionalism is grounded in education, experience, and ethical behavior, the Institutes provide a wide range of educational programs designed to meet the needs of individuals working in risk management and property-casualty insurance. The American Institute offers the Chartered Property Casualty Underwriter (CPCU®) professional designation, designed to provide a broad understanding of the property-casualty insurance industry. CPCU students may select either a commercial or a personal risk management and insurance focus, depending on their professional needs.

The Insurance Institute of America (IIA) offers designations and certificate programs in a variety of disciplines, including the following:

- Claims
- Commercial underwriting
- Fidelity and surety bonding
- General insurance
- Insurance accounting and finance
- Insurance information technology
- Insurance production and agency management
- Insurance regulation and compliance
- Management
- Marine insurance
- Personal insurance
- Premium auditing
- Quality insurance services
- Reinsurance
- Risk management
- Surplus lines

You may choose to take a single course to fill a knowledge gap, complete a program leading to a designation, or take multiple courses and programs throughout your career. No matter which approach you choose, you will gain practical knowledge and skills that will contribute to your professional growth and enhance your education and qualifications in the expanding insurance market. In addition, many CPCU and IIA courses qualify for credits toward certain associate, bachelor's, and master's degrees at several prestigious colleges and universities, and all CPCU and IIA courses carry college credit recommendations from the American Council on Education.

The American Institute for CPCU was founded in 1942 through a collaborative effort between industry professionals and academics, led by faculty members at The Wharton School of the University of Pennsylvania. In 1953, the American Institute for CPCU merged with the Insurance Institute of America, which was founded in 1909 and which remains the oldest continuously functioning national organization offering educational programs for the property-casualty insurance business.

The Insurance Research Council (IRC), founded in 1977, helps the Institutes fulfill the research aspect of their mission. A division of the Institutes, the IRC is supported by industry members. This not-for-profit research organization examines public policy issues of interest to property-casualty insurers, insurance customers, and the general public. IRC research reports are distributed widely to insurance-related organizations, public policy authorities, and the media.

The Institutes strive to provide current, relevant educational programs in formats and delivery methods that meet the needs of insurance professionals and the organizations that employ them. Institute textbooks are an essential component of the education we provide. Each book is designed to clearly and concisely provide the practical knowledge and skills you need to enhance your job performance and career. The content is developed by the Institutes in collaboration with risk management and insurance professionals and members of the academic community. We welcome comments from our students and course leaders; your feedback helps us continue to improve the quality of our study materials.

Peter L. Miller, CPCU
President and CEO
American Institute for CPCU
Insurance Institute of America

Preface

This second edition of the text includes a new chapter that addresses the diagnosis, evaluation, and treatment of psychological injuries and conditions. Because of the increase in the frequency and severity of mental injury claims today, workers compensation and liability claim representatives need to understand the fundamental characteristics, causes, and treatment of common psychological injuries.

This text is one of two for the Associate in Claims (AIC) 34 course. The goal of this text is to provide some guidance on how to meet the changing needs of injury claim management. Although many of the techniques and studies included in this text are related to workers compensation claims, the information and case studies presented in this text can be applied to all bodily injury claims. The purpose of this text is not to be a reference on anatomy and trauma issues. Numerous sources serve this purpose. Instead, the purpose of this text is to offer a process and framework for managing injury claims that claim professionals can apply to their everyday work life. We hope this text serves this purpose for you.

Following the precipitous climb in medical costs, insurers, consumers, and legislatures realized that financial resources are limited and action was required to control injury claim costs and the subsequent rise in insurance premiums. Legislation was enacted that permitted medical management, especially in workers compensation and automobile personal injury protection (PIP) benefits. Claim professionals who manage bodily injury claims must ensure that only reasonable and necessary claims are paid while providing fair compensation to injured parties. The challenge of managing injury claims compared to managing property claims is that each claim involves an injured person with a unique set of medical, psychological, emotional, and financial circumstances that are difficult to evaluate. Consequently, claim professionals need claim management sophistication to deal with serious injury claims.

Some of the techniques that have proven effective in managing medical expenses in group health insurance, such as physician networks, fee schedules, and disability management, are now being applied to casualty losses. Unfortunately, some health-care organizations have cut costs at the expense of patient care and have depersonalized health-care services. This behavior has led to increased litigation, regulation, and legislation, especially in the group health-care industry. In the casualty industry, the objective is to control *overall* costs, which frequently means that more aggressive or expensive medical treatments are used to control the nonmedical costs such as pain and suffering, lost wages, permanent disfigurements, and permanent disabilities; therefore, there is less pressure in the casualty industry to reduce medical expenses, but the potential for controls to become abusive still exists. Claim professionals dealing with casualty claims must understand not only the techniques for managing injury claims, but also the need to treat injured parties as individuals who have emotional as well as financial needs. To reduce complaints, contentiousness, and litigation, claim professionals must learn to use their compassion. Treating injured parties with respect and dignity is not inefficient or costly but rather an essential part of good injury claim management.

This text begins with an explanation of the need for injury claim management and an overview of injury claim management techniques. The text then describes the specific ways that claim professionals can evaluate injuries and treatments and how these injuries create impairments and disabilities. Following this discussion is an explanation of how rehabilitation and disability management is used to mitigate the consequences of injuries. One chapter is devoted to understanding low back injuries in casualty claims because of their prevalence and costs in the casualty insurance industry. The purpose of the three case study chapters is to allow students to see how the concepts of injury claim management are applied, to see how various compensability and disability management issues are handled, and to understand the anatomy and trauma issues for injuries commonly encountered in casualty claims.

Several people should share credit for this text because of their influence on our personal and professional development. With deep appreciation, we acknowledge the following people who helped to form the philosophies, strategies, and knowledge that we carry with us each day:

John Robinson and Tom Wilson, who instilled the commitment to proper investigation and documentation in claims

Virginia Sewing, RN, MA, CCM, who gave sage advice on keeping the role of nurse case consultants out of claim payment issues

Gloria Blackmon, RN, CBSN; Carolyn Jensen, RN, BSHCM; Kathleen E. King, RN, BSN, CLNC; Vickie L. Milazzo, JD, RN, MSN; and Suzanne P. Smith, RN, EdD, FAAN, for their encouragement and support

We would like to thank Dr. Barry Gustin who took time from his busy schedule as Medical Director of the Berkeley-based American Medical Forensic Specialists to serve as medical editor for the text.

We would like to thank the following individuals who contributed valuable feedback as reviewers of this text:

Wayne Browne, CPCU

Ken Brownlee, CPCU, ARM

Joanne Ebert, BSN, M.S.

John Eckley, CPCU

James A. Franz, CPCU, AIC, ARM

William Gawne, CPCU

Eric Giesy, CPCU

Lisa Hiney, AIC

Mark Hofer, CPCU, AIC

Delores Hynes, RN

Dianne M. Johnson, RN, BSN

Christian LaChance, CPCU, CLU

Janet-Lynn McLeary, CPCU, CLU

Kathleen J. Robison, CPCU

Glen Salka, AIC, ARM, SCLA

Jerry Searles, CPCU

Kord Spielman

Sandra Thomas, CPCU, AIC, AIM

David Weaver, CPCU, ARM

Although this text is new, we remain grateful to all of the contributing authors of the textbook *Medical Aspects of Claims*. Their work provided the foundation for several sections of this text. We would especially like to thank Beth Brown, RN; Francis X. Comella, Jr., CPCU, CLU, ChFC; Jonathan H. Gice, CPCU, CRC, CIRS; Cathy Y. Hamby; Lee Levin, RN, CRC; Suzanne Switzer, RN; and Minh D. Vu, CPCU.

We thank the members of the AIC Advisory Committee, who helped to marshal resources for this project and who provided insight and suggestions. Finally, we thank all of the students and course leaders who took time from their busy schedules to give us constructive feedback on the AIC 34 course. We encourage this feedback and extend an invitation to students and course leaders to make comments on this text so that we may constantly improve our course material.

For more information about the Institutes' programs, please call our Customer Support department at (800) 644-2101, e-mail us at customersupport@cpcuiia.org, or visit our Web site at www.aicpcu.org.

James R. Jones

Junie Maggio

Contents

1 Bodily Injury Claim Management — 1-1
Reasons for Managing Bodily Injury Claims — 1-2
Techniques for Managing Bodily Injury Claims — 1-12
Managed Care in Casualty Claims — 1-26
Managed Care in Workers Compensation — 1-26
Employer Liability Related to Managed Care in Casualty Claims — 1-33
Summary — 1-35

2 Injury and Treatment Evaluation — 2-1
Issues in Medical Treatment — 2-2
Medical Documents — 2-22
Expert Assistance — 2-33
Summary — 2-43

3 Impairment and Disability — 3-1
Definitions of Impairment and Disability — 3-2
Determination of Disability — 3-14
Overcoming Disability — 3-20
Summary — 3-29
Appendix — 3-31

4 Rehabilitation — 4-1
Overview of Rehabilitation — 4-1
The Practice of Physical/Psychosocial Rehabilitation — 4-4
The Practice of Insurance Rehabilitation — 4-9
Parties to the Insurance Rehabilitation Process — 4-13
The Insurance Rehabilitation Process — 4-18
Summary — 4-38

5 Low Back Injury Claims — 5-1
Challenges of Handling Back Injury Claims — 5-2
Anatomy of the Spine — 5-6
Back Injuries and Conditions — 5-10
Diagnostic Testing for Back Injuries — 5-20
Treatment of Low Back Pain — 5-27
Tying It All Together — 5-33
Case Study—Low Back Injury Claim — 5-34
Appendix 5-A — 5-39
Appendix 5-B — 5-46

I Introduction to Case Studies — I-1
The Case Construction — I-1
Preparation for Case Studies — I-2
Approaching the Cases — I-7
Fraud and Insurance Abuse — I-8

6 Medical Investigation Process (The Arm Injury) — 6-1
Claim Process — 6-1
Medical Investigation — 6-4
Case Conclusion — 6-23
Case Evaluation — 6-23

7 Investigation of Causation (The Hip and Lower Extremities) — 7-1
Medical Investigation — 7-2
Anatomy, Trauma, Treatment, and Disability — 7-16
Case Conclusion — 7-22

8 Assessing Treatments and Disability (The Knee Injury) — 8-1

Knee Injuries — 8-2
Disability Related to Knee Injuries — 8-9
Case Conclusion — 8-12

9 Psychological Injuries and Conditions — 9-1

Psychological Response to Physical Injury — 9-2
Evaluation of Psychological Injury Claims — 9-5
Treatment — 9-25
Challenges in Handling Psychological Injury Claims — 9-29
Glossary — 9-31

Index — I

Chapter 1

Bodily Injury Claim Management

Bodily injury claims in casualty insurance can fall under any of the following types of coverage:

- Automobile medical payments coverage
- Automobile personal injury protection (PIP) plans
- Automobile liability coverage
- Automobile uninsured/underinsured motorists coverage
- Premises medical payments and liability coverage
- Product liability coverage
- Medical malpractice coverage
- Workers compensation/employers liability coverage

Bodily injury claims represent hundreds of billions of dollars and affect the lives and livelihoods of millions of people each year. Exhibit 1-1 compares the distribution of health-care costs in casualty claims among different lines of insurance.

These claims can be extremely traumatic experiences for insurance consumers, and the way these emotionally charged claims are handled can affect the reputations of the insurance company and even the industry as a whole.

Numerous techniques exist for managing bodily injury claims. Their purpose is to ensure that limited insurance resources are not wasted through unnecessary treatments, excessive medical bills, or fraud. However, legitimate claims must be paid. Any claim professional who uses injury management techniques as a basis for avoiding compensation for legitimate claims is acting unethically, and any claim professional who uses techniques inappropriately by failing to understand how to implement them or by failing to consider the unique characteristics of each injury is acting unprofessionally. Ronald E. Gots, M.D., Ph.D., explains the legitimacy and purpose of managing bodily injury claims in his statement of the principles of medical utilization review (these techniques are discussed in detail later in this chapter):

> The basic two underlying principles of medical utilization review are that the providers of care cannot be the sole arbiters of what care is to be provided and that modern medical practice is predicated upon sound principles. In regard to the former, those who pay must have a say. Pertaining to the latter, there are right and wrong ways to evaluate and manage patients. In a similar vein, there are also expensive and less expensive ways to provide medical care and expensive does not always mean better.[1]

Exhibit 1-1
Estimates of Casualty Health-Care Costs by Line of Insurance

Line of Insurance	Percentage of Health-Care Costs for Each Line
Workers compensation	42.0%
Personal automobile (medical payments, uninsured motorists, and liability)	40.6
General liability (and products liability)	8.8
Commercial auto	5.8
Medical malpractice	1.7
Homeowners and farmowners medical payments/liability	1.1

Insurance Services Office, "Health Care Costs in the Property and Casualty Insurance Industry" (New York: ISO, 1993).

The purpose of this text is to help claim professionals (claim representatives, medical support personnel, and claim consultants) to understand injury management techniques and how they can most appropriately be used in casualty claims. This chapter provides an overview of some of those techniques.

Claim representatives who have no medical training should not be involved in determining whether tests or treatments should be given but should act as a member of a team of professionals, including medical consultants and treating physicians, who are involved in injury management. The specific role of the claim representative is described in Chapter 2 and illustrated in the case studies in Chapters 6 through 8.

Reasons for Managing Bodily Injury Claims

The main reasons for the development and implementation of techniques for managing bodily injury claims are as follows:

- Medical costs that are increasing more rapidly than the Consumer Price Index
- Population changes
- Insurance fraud and buildup
- Cost shifting

Insurers that can deal with these changes by using injury management strategies will have a competitive advantage. Consequently, claim professionals who understand how to use these strategies appropriately will be valued employees.

Higher-Than-Average Medical Costs

U.S. health expenditures have grown enormously in the past two decades. In 1996, spending for health care reached over $1 trillion, compared to $247 billion in 1980. By 1998, health expenditures represented 14 percent of the gross domestic product (GDP), compared to 9 percent in 1980[2] and 7.4 percent in 1970. The U.S. currently has the highest level of health expenditures, as measured by percentage of GDP, of the industrialized nations. Health-care expenditures in the United Kingdom, Japan, and France are 6.7 percent, 7.3 percent, and 9 percent of those countries' GDPs, respectively.[3] In the U.S., managed care has helped to bring the medical inflation rate closer to the overall rate,[4] but since 1985, increases in medical care expenses have consistently outpaced the annual increases in the Consumer Price Index (CPI), as shown in Exhibit 1-2.

Exhibit 1-2
Comparison of the CPI Inflation Rate and the CPI Medical Care Inflation Rate

Year	Average Inflation Rate	Medical Care Inflation Rate
1985	3.6%	6.3%
1986	3.1	7.5
1987	3.6	6.6
1988	4.1	6.5
1989	4.8	7.7
1990	5.4	9.0
1991	4.2	8.7
1992	3.0	7.4
1993	2.6	5.9
1994	2.8	4.5
1995	3.0	3.5
1996	2.3	2.8

United States Department of Commerce, Statistical Abstract of the United States 1998 (Washington, DC: Department of Commerce, 1998), Table 772, p. 489.

The ratio of medical costs to total bodily injury claim costs (which include wage loss, disability, and general damages) varies according to claim type. The following approximate percentages show the significance that medical costs have on overall injury claim payments.[5] Medical costs represent:

- 50 percent of workers compensation payments
- 28 percent of automobile liability payments
- 78 percent of personal injury protection (PIP) payments
- 19 percent of general liability payments

Although medical costs are only a portion of the overall bodily injury claim, significant increases in medical costs ultimately affect all bodily injury claim payments. The exact effects of the increase in medical costs on the cost of liability claims cannot be measured. In the past twenty years, many other factors have also played a role in increasing liability claim costs; they include the medical malpractice crisis, changes in society's perceptions of legal liability, changes in tort laws, and experiments with the no-fault concept. Nevertheless, as medical expenses increase, so does the value of a liability claim. Therefore, the cost of liability claims, like the cost of health care, has been increasing faster than inflation in general. Furthermore, an increase in medical expenses is likely to make it easier for tort thresholds to be exceeded, thus reducing whatever effectiveness the no-fault system might have provided. In addition, the scope and duration of medical treatment often directly affect the scope and duration of an injured person's disability.

Aside from general inflation, the rise in health-care costs can be attributed to the following factors:

- Innovations in and spread of medical technology
- Hospital capacity
- The medical malpractice insurance crisis
- Lack of cost controls in casualty claims
- Physician surplus

As indicated in Exhibit 1-2, the medical inflation rate has been declining in more recent years. A major reason for this decline has been the proliferation of managed care organizations. Their effect will be discussed later in this chapter.

Innovations in and Spread of Medical Technology

Every year advances are made in medical diagnostic and therapeutic equipment. Largely because of extraordinary advances in miniaturization of diagnostic and surgical instruments and computer technology, medical services are now delivered on a highly sophisticated technological level. The use of diagnostic techniques such as magnetic resonance imaging (MRI), computerized transaxial tomography (CT) scans, and ultrasound has become routine. Although patients undeniably benefit greatly from these new technologies, those benefits have been expensive.

When physicians bear the high cost of the equipment as part of their private office overhead, they want to make greater use of the equipment in order to realize a return on their investment. New technology is therefore expensive in two ways. First, the equipment itself is costly. Second, a physician's attempt to recoup his or her purchase cost through increased use passes the cost on to patients. In this way, the technology essentially increases the cost of medical services by generating treatment when none may be needed.

Despite physicians' use, the cost of advanced technology is most evident in increased hospital costs. Hospitals typically own and operate high-technology equipment. It is common for all hospitals in a given area to acquire new technology without careful analysis of the rate at which it will be used. Thus, all hospitals in a given geographic area may own and operate the same new equipment, and all of them may be underusing the equipment. The cost of the excess equipment must be factored into the per patient charge or into each hospital's general overhead.

Hospital Capacity

A hospital's plant and equipment represent an enormous investment. This cost must be recovered through the charges to each patient. The overhead costs of a hospital are relatively fixed. Thus, the more patients a hospital serves, the less its per-patient overhead cost is. Conversely, hospitals that are not fully used must spread their overhead among existing patients, increasing the per-patient cost. Unfortunately for the sake of hospital rates, hospital utilization declined during the 1970s and 1980s, especially in private, for-profit hospitals, whose occupancy rates fell from 72.2 percent in 1970 to 51 percent in 1987. After numerous hospital closings and mergers, the occupancy rate had climbed back to 66 percent by 1994.[6]

The Medical Malpractice Insurance Crisis

A large increase in the number of medical malpractice lawsuits and in the amounts awarded occurred in the mid-1970s. Medical malpractice insurance premiums increased accordingly, even to the point of driving some physicians away from high-risk practices, such as obstetrics and gynecology. Medical malpractice insurance became a significant addition to the cost of providing medical care. In 1974 the tort costs for malpractice was $0.9 billion; by 1997 this figure had risen to $12.7 billion.[7] This additional cost is passed on to consumers through higher fees.

The threat of a medical malpractice lawsuit has altered the way physicians provide services, encouraging them to order more diagnostic tests and perform more costly procedures. Such practices are called defensive medicine because they are performed as much to protect the physician as to cure the patient. Defensive medical practice causes unnecessary utilization of medical services throughout the medical system. It is impossible to quantify exactly how much treatment is unnecessary and defensive. The cost of the malpractice threat may therefore be greater than the direct costs of malpractice insurance and payments.

Lack of Cost Controls in Casualty Claims

Insurance has undoubtedly contributed to medical inflation by taking away both the health-care provider's and the patient's incentive to control costs. Payments for medical services have traditionally been made retrospectively (after services have been provided) on an itemized fee-for-service basis. An expectation of 100 percent reimbursement provides little incentive for suppliers to control costs.

In addition, medical services have been viewed as different from other consumer products and services, for which consumers are able and willing to exercise bargaining power. Society, for the most part, views health care as a right rather than a commodity. Cost of service has therefore not been a primary concern.

Patients' lack of medical knowledge also causes indifference to cost control. The highly technical nature of health care restricts patient participation in the decision-making process. After the initial decision to seek a physician's help, the average person relies almost completely on the physician's judgment to determine and order appropriate types of service.

Patients' Disincentives To Control Treatment

A patient whose treatment is fully insured will not usually second-guess a physician's orders for tests or a course of treatment. Most patients feel that money is no object when their health is involved.

As a result, many health insurers require copayment by the insured. The copayment provision is typically about 20 percent, forcing the patient to bear some expense of every treatment. Both the government and private industry have implemented cost control strategies, including incentives for patients to moderate their use of the health-care system by sharing part of the costs. Cost control changes that have proven effective in group health plans have only recently begun to be implemented in casualty insurance.

Workers compensation insurance and liability insurance do not include copayment provisions. Thus, assuming that liability and coverage are clear, a patient being reimbursed by casualty insurance can expect every dollar of treatment expense to be covered. Claim representatives in casualty insurance cannot expect claimants to make suggestions about controlling treatment, but must expect to moderate treatment themselves.

Multiple Uncontrolled Treatments

In complicated cases, a patient may visit several different physicians for consultation or treatment. In those cases, the referrals to other physicians should be made by a single controlling physician familiar with the entire case. However, claimants often see numerous physicians, none of whom may know of or communicate with one another. In addition to being an abuse of the system, this practice is incorrect medical treatment. Such situations usually arise because the claimant or his or her attorney is controlling treatment. Claim representatives should always resist reimbursing such treatment until a single physician is controlling the case.

Physician Surplus

The number of physicians has been growing at a rate of 1.5 times that of the general population. In the United States, there is currently an overall surplus of 125,000 physicians (although many rural areas are underserved). The rate of physicians per 100,000 population grew from 168 in 1970 to 239 in 1996.[8] The Council on Graduate Medical Education (COGME) conservatively estimates that this rate will grow to 298 by the year 2020.[9] One unknown variable in the projected surplus of physicians is how managed care will affect the number of people interested in becoming physicians.

Because of the technical nature of medical services, an increase in the supply of physicians tends to cause a simultaneous increase in demand for services. In most markets, suppliers have no control over demand, and an increase in supply leads to a reduction in price as a result of competition. This is not so with medical services. Doctors have substantial control over the amount of treatment patients receive. Even with fewer patients per physician, physicians will not necessarily lose revenue if they can generate more revenue per patient. When there is a surplus of physicians, there is pressure to increase utilization. Physicians, rather than patients, generally determine how many follow-up visits a patient makes, whether the patient must undergo surgery, and whether the patient is to be cared for in a hospital rather than at home.

Population Changes

In addition to escalating medical costs, the need for managing bodily injury claims is increasing because of changes in the population.

As the baby boom generation ages and as life expectancy increases, the U.S. population has experienced an upward shift in its age composition, coupled with a surge in teenagers (the children of baby boomers). The effect of this shift on medical costs has so far been modest, but it will become greater in the next century. These changes could lead to overall increases in bodily injury claims requiring claim representatives to develop the skills to manage these claims.

Some important changes in the overall population that could affect claims are as follows:

- In 1998, there were thirty-five million people over sixty-five years old (up four million since 1990). The median age of the population of the United States has increased five years since 1980.
- The number of workers in the fifty-five-to-sixty-four-year-old age group will increase by an estimated 49.6 percent from 1995 to 2005 (see Exhibit 1-3).
- The number of young drivers will increase as the "boomlet" (children of the baby boomers) generation begins driving.

Exhibit 1-3
Age Changes in the Civilian Workforce

	Number of People in Workforce (in millions)				Percent Increase/Decrease	
Age Group	1980	1990	1995	2005 (projection)	1980-1995	1995-2005
16-19	9.4	7.8	7.7	8.6	−18.1%	11.7%
20-24	15.9	14.7	13.6	15.3	−14.5	12.5
25-34	29.3	36.0	34.2	30.5	16.7	−10.8
35-44	20.4	32.2	35.8	35.9	75.5	0.0
45-54	16.9	20.2	25.2	34.5	49.1	37.0
55-64	11.9	11.5	11.9	17.8	0.0	49.6
65+	3.1	3.5	3.8	4.4	22.6	15.8

United States Department of Commerce, Statistical Abstract of the United States 1998 (Washington, DC: Department of Commerce, 1998).

The Aging Population

As people age, they are more likely to develop arthritis and cumulative trauma problems (more than $20 billion is currently spent each year on cumulative trauma claims). One study predicts that 18 percent of the population will have arthritis by 2020. Workers with arthritis make 34 percent more work-related claims.[10] The effects will be especially noticeable in workers compensation. The recovery period from an injury is longer for older people. The median number of lost workdays rises with age, from four days for workers twenty-four and under, to six days for workers thirty-five to forty-four, up to ten days for workers over sixty-five.[11] This increase will obviously affect worker compensation indemnity payments and the wage loss portion of liability claims, and this trend makes disability management more important than ever.

People over fifty-five, also have a higher incidence of nonspecific diagnosis, chronic ailments that are not accident-related. This type of diagnosis will complicate compensability decisions by claim representatives, who will have to distinguish between accident-related injuries and injuries caused by the normal aging process. Nurse case managers will play an invaluable role in assisting claim representatives with this evaluation.

Exhibit 1-4 shows the increasing number of workers with disabilities in the workforce as the population ages. Unfortunately, workers with disabilities are 36 percent more likely to be injured on the job.[12]

An aging population also affects where people live, the type of housing they choose, their health-care needs, their buying patterns, and legislation. All of these can affect claims. A growing number of assisted living facilities are being built to accommodate the needs of older people. Liability exposures will increase as a larger percentage of the population move out of their own homes (where they have no

Exhibit 1-4
Disabilities by Age

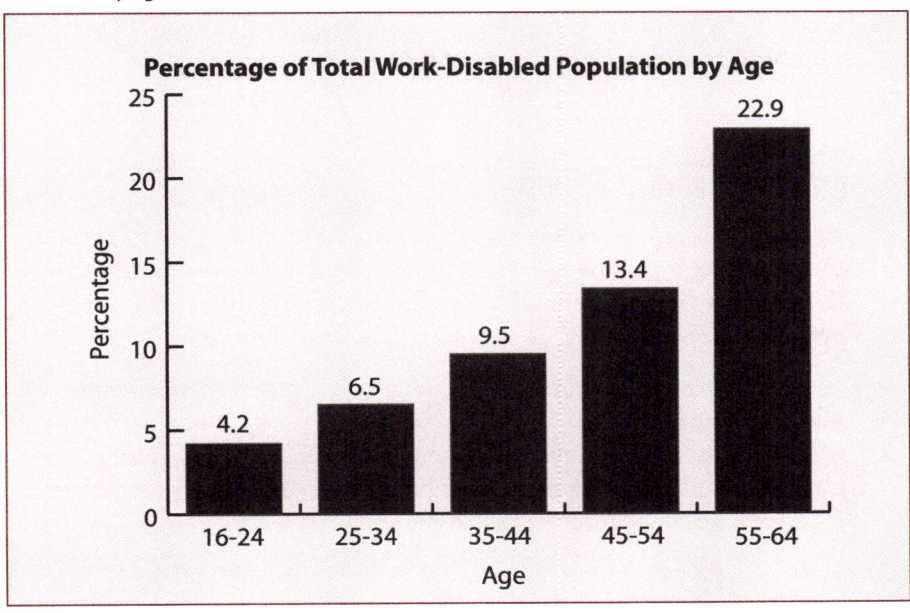

"Workers With Disabilities at Higher Risk for Injuries," *Journal of Commerce*, December 30, 1997, p. 8A.

liability exposure against themselves) and into assisted-living facilities (where they represent challenging liability exposures to the facility). Many experts are expecting these types of claims to dramatically increase over the next decade.

Younger Drivers

At the other end of the age spectrum is an increase in the number of teenagers, the children of the baby boomers. In 1998, there were 19 million people in the fifteen-to-nineteen-year-old age group. Younger drivers tend to have more accidents than older, more experienced drivers. One especially disturbing trend is the increase in the rate of fatalities for sixteen-year-old drivers. Exhibit 1-5 depicts this trend.

Exhibit 1-5
Fatalities for Sixteen-Year-Old Drivers

Year	Fatalities (per 100,000 16-year-old drivers)
1985	26
1990	30
1995	32
1996	35

Insurance Institute for Highway Safety.

The reason for the increased rate is not known. Teenage drinking and driving has actually declined in recent years. Some experts speculate that the increased fatality rate could be related to increased time spent driving or the mismatch in the sizes of vehicles now on the road. This mismatch is increasing as more people purchase light trucks, vans, and sport utility vehicles, while others are driving smaller, fuel-efficient cars. Whatever the cause, there will be an increased need for skills in managing bodily injury claims.

Insurance Fraud and Buildup

Insurance fraud refers to the fabrication of insurance claims. **Buildup** refers to exaggerating losses from a real accident and taking advantage of insurance benefits. Fraud and buildup in bodily injury claims can be performed by claimants, their health-care providers, and lawyers.

According to the Insurance Research Council, 36 percent of automobile bodily injury claims and 21 percent of personal injury protection (PIP) claims involve fraud or buildup. Excess payments as a result of fraud and buildup are estimated to be between 17 and 20 percent of total injury claims, representing as much as $6.3 billion in 1995. The number of bodily injury (BI) claims made for every 100 auto property damage (PD) claims has grown from just over 22 in 1987 to just over 29 BI claims in 1994. The cultural acceptance of fraud varies widely by region in the United States. This difference cannot always be explained by the differences in laws. In California, for example, 55 out of 100 auto PD losses led to BI claims. In Philadelphia, 78.5 BI claims are paid for every 100 PD claims; across the state in Pittsburgh, 18 BI claims are paid per 100 PD claims.[13] Differences in cultural norms and values among the communities are likely contributors to the differences in claim-making behavior. Insurers operating in areas of high fraud and buildup need to have claim representatives who are well-trained in evaluating and managing bodily injury claims.

Self-referral, a form of provider abuse, is the practice of physicians referring patients to clinics in which the physicians have an economic interest. The Journal of the American Medical Association published statistics showing that rehabilitation and physical therapy clinics owned by doctors, on average, have nearly 50 percent more visits per patient than facilities not owned by doctors. Patients referred by doctors with interests in the rehabilitation centers or physical therapy clinics were found to have up to 45 percent more visits than patients referred by doctors without an interest in the facilities. Patient care did not increase, however; patients referred to doctor-owned facilities received only about half as many minutes of treatments as patients who were treated at independent facilities. Physician-owned facilities generated 30 to 40 percent more revenue per patient.[14] The same self-referral abuse occurs with diagnostic imaging equipment owned by doctors. One study conducted in California in 1992 concluded that self-referrals accounted for $356 million in unnecessary workers compensation medical costs.[15] Legislators and some physician groups who disagree with the practice are trying to stop this form of abuse. Claim representatives will need to understand how to use treatment guidelines to help control this problem. The use of treatment guidelines will be covered in more detail in the case studies at the end of this text.

Within the range of acceptable medical practice, physicians have a choice between conservative and aggressive treatment. There are powerful financial and legal incentives for physicians to be biased towards aggressive treatment. Obviously, the more a physician treats, the more he or she earns. In addition, the fear of malpractice suits causes many physicians to diagnose and treat to the maximum for their own protection. Finally, many physicians seem to choose an aggressive approach because some of their patients expect it. These patients expect action from their physicians, not mere reassurances that they "will be fine."

When medical care is completely insured, physicians tend to justify putting their patients' expectations and their own interests above an insurer's. Indeed, some physicians go beyond aggressive treatment and knowingly abuse insurance. In light of their own and their patients' interests, some physicians have no problems justifying this abuse.

Cost Shifting

The vast majority of health-care costs are paid by health insurers, government programs, or directly by patients. Casualty insurers pay only a small percentage of health-care costs. As a result, payment sources other than casualty insurers have been much more sensitive to increasing costs and have been far ahead of casualty insurers in the use of cost-containment techniques. Their success in containing costs has resulted in shifting some costs to casualty insurers. For this reason, claim professionals involved in casualty claims must learn to use the same cost-containment techniques to avoid being taken advantage of by providers.

Cost shifting is the charging of higher fees to payment sources that impose fewer controls. Payment sources that impose substantial controls and regulations will not accept whatever costs the medical provider happens to generate. Costs not covered by a regulated payment source may be shifted to a relatively unregulated source, such as workers compensation and liability insurance. As more payment sources become regulated, health-care providers are increasingly pressured to shift costs to the few remaining unrestricted payment sources. For example, as inpatient hospital costs are increasingly controlled, hospitals have shifted costs to outpatient and ancillary services that are less closely controlled.[16]

Hospitals and physicians have been increasingly diligent in searching for a connection between their treatments and a work-related or other kind of accident.[17] To the extent that such a connection exists, it is perfectly legitimate for charges to be directed to the applicable insurer. Whenever insureds are treated for accidental injuries, health insurers now routinely ask them about any connection to auto or work-related accidents. In some cases, they make such inquiries for every type of treatment. Before such inquiries became routine, health insurers were undoubtedly paying for a great number of accidents that casualty insurance should have covered.

Unfortunately, pressure from regulated payment sources (such as health insurers) may lead physicians and hospitals to exaggerate the connection between their treatment and a work-related or another kind of accident.[18] In order to receive as much compensation as possible for their services, physicians and hospitals may report that, for example, an injury of unclear or unknown origin was suffered on the job, thereby involving the patient's workers compensation insurance instead of the patient's health insurance. Unless the workers compensation insurer suspects that the injury was not work-related and investigates the case, the workers compensation insurer will be responsible for reimbursing costs that the patient's health insurer probably should have been responsible for reimbursing. Because the pressure on physicians and hospitals from health insurers to control costs can lead to increasing costs for casualty insurers, claim representatives must explore ways to contain the costs of all the claims they handle.

Techniques for Managing Bodily Injury Claims

The **injury claim management equation**, the basis on which injury claims are managed, is as follows:

Price of services × Use of services = Total cost of health-care services

Traditionally, managing bodily injury claims has mainly involved techniques for managing the amount of settlement payments, retrospectively, after medical expenses were incurred. In this approach to injury claim management, fees are controlled by audits, and treatments are reviewed after they have been performed. Retrospective management of injury claims is sometimes the only approach available in a casualty claim in which the parties are in an adversarial relationship. In the early 1980s, health-care insurers began to implement techniques to control the fees charged by providers prospectively by prearranged fee schedules. Casualty insurers have adapted some of these techniques to help manage bodily injury claims, especially workers compensation and PIP claims. These fee control techniques are valuable, but in casualty claims, unlike in health insurance plans, treatment fees are only a portion of the overall costs. The greater portion of bodily injury claims relates to claimants' wage loss and general damages. These nonmedical injury costs are often tied to the disability suffered by the claimant.

Managing injury claims for casualty insurers involves an increasing variety of techniques that address injury, disability, and treatment utilization as well as techniques for controlling fees. These techniques involve managing the frequency and type of medical treatment; managing the extent of disability through aggressive treatment, return-to-work programs, and rehabilitation; and managing overall injury costs through loss control methods. These techniques require intervention before or during a claimant's medical treatment. Exhibit 1-6 illustrates a continuum of approaches to bodily injury claim management.

Exhibit 1-6
The Continuum of Approaches to Managing Bodily Injury Claims

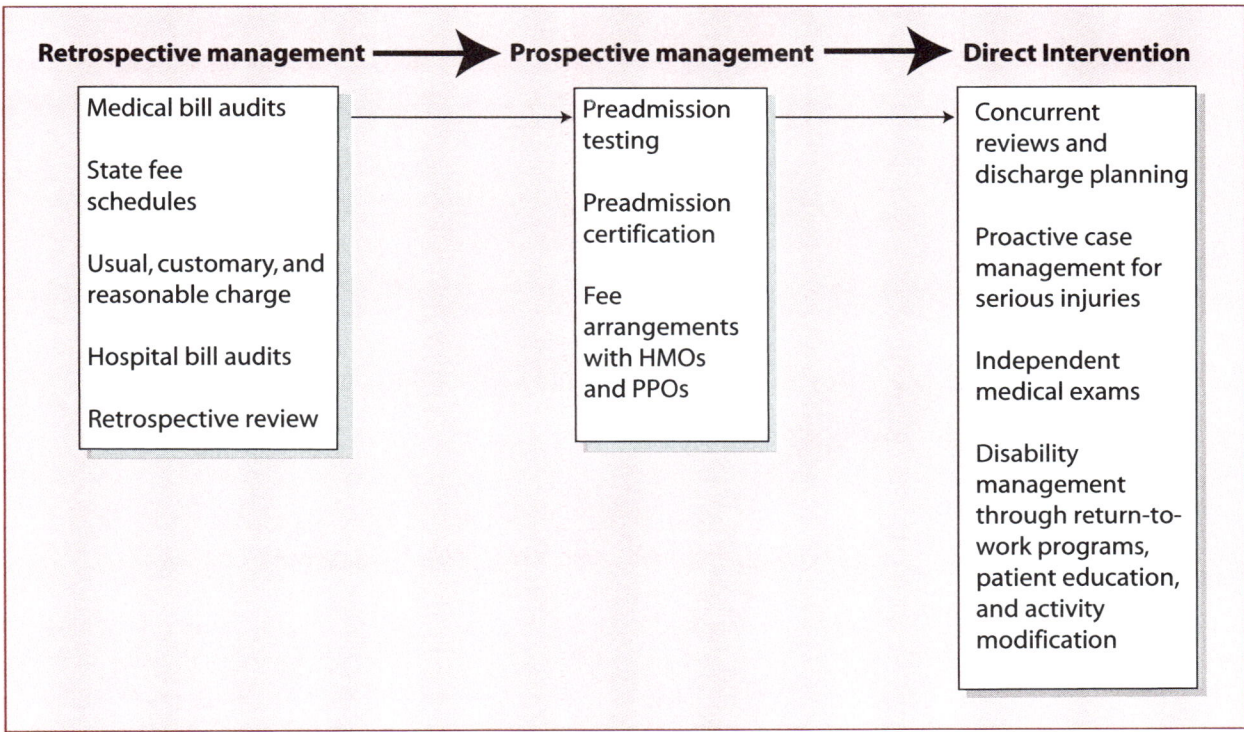

Opportunities for implementing managed care techniques are expected to grow. In workers compensation insurance, an increasing number of states now permit employers to choose doctors for their injured employees. This change permits employers and their insurers to implement a broader variety of techniques. More states are also permitting limited tort options with PIP plans that allow insurers to implement some form of managed care. On first-party claims, some insurers now offer a form of managed care for first-party automobile medical coverage. Because managed care techniques are likely to increase in casualty claim practice, casualty claim professionals need to become familiar with these techniques.

To make these techniques more understandable, the text breaks them into three broad categories based on the timing of the approach taken. The three approaches are retrospective, prospective, and direct intervention. **Utilization reviews (URs)** can be any technique that evaluates the necessity, frequency, and costs of treatments. Utilization reviews include methods that fall into all three categories.

Retrospective Management of Injury Claims

The most basic approach to managing bodily injury claims is the **retrospective management** approach. The main techniques of this approach are as follows:

- Medical bill audits
- State fee schedules
- Usual, customary, and reasonable charge
- Hospital bill audits
- Retrospective review

These claim management techniques are used after a claimant has undergone treatment. The main weakness of the retrospective approach is that it cannot stop unnecessary costs or overbilling; it can only identify unnecessary costs or overbilling after the fact. Traditionally, retrospective techniques have been used with complicated, unusual, or high-dollar cases. Today, peer reviews and fee audits are being conducted in more routine injury claims.

Medical Bill (Fee) Audits

Medical bill audits are a fundamental tool of medical cost containment. In a **medical bill audit**, bills from health-care providers are analyzed to ensure that proper services are being billed and that the charges for such services are appropriate. Medical bill audits can detect services not provided, services not provided in the manner or scope indicated, and redundant services. Medical bill audits can also identify improper charges by comparing charges to rates that are considered proper. Medical bill audits can be performed through the use of state fee schedules or through usual, customary, and reasonable charges.

State Fee Schedules

Fee schedules are a form of price control introduced by the federal government in the early 1970s. These schedules, as adopted by Medicare, allowed fees to rise with a cost index. Thereafter, the states developed fee schedules in workers compensation. As of 1998, forty-two states were using some form of fee schedule in workers compensation cases to limit the fees charged by physicians and sometimes hospitals.

Most **state fee schedules** are based on a relative value scale. Services are measured in terms of number of units, with a predetermined price per unit. The effect of a fee schedule is to establish fixed relative values for medical service and treatments. A few states use a modification of Medicare or Medicaid schedules. For example, Pennsylvania's fee schedule for workers compensation is 112 percent of Medicare. Although generally not overly restrictive, state fee schedules limit the amount that health-care providers could otherwise charge in an unrestricted market.

Health-care providers' compliance with fee schedules is advantageous to insurers. In addition, studies have reported that bills audited against state fee schedules can result in savings, ranging from 10 percent to 15 percent, that would not be realized if health-care providers had not complied with fee schedules.[19]

The use of fee schedules has become increasingly routine in workers compensation claim handling. Insurers can easily train their personnel to audit bills against fee schedules or can refer the work to outside bill auditing firms. These firms can usually review bills by computers programmed with the fee schedules of every state and locale.

The effectiveness of fee schedules can be limited. Alone, they do not control the degree of health-care use. Medical providers can theoretically make up any lost revenue caused by fee schedules by increasing the amount of services because the fee schedule concept does not address the necessity of treatments. Nonetheless, not using fee schedules means that an insurer may be paying for both excessive charges and excessive health-care use. Fee schedules should be used as a first step in any cost-containment program. Increasingly, bill auditing services also analyze the frequency and duration of treatment in addition to comparing charges to fee schedules.

Usual, Customary, and Reasonable Charge

A common criterion for fee schedules is the **usual, customary, and reasonable charge (UCR)**. Among other limitations, health insurance contracts almost invariably limit reimbursement to the UCR, which limits fees to the local reasonable prevailing rates. Usual, customary but unreasonable charges should be rejected. The UCR standard is not written into casualty insurance contracts, but it is still important in casualty claims. The law itself provides that reimbursement for medical services should be limited to UCR amounts. Casualty claim representatives can refuse to pay unusual or unreasonable charges. Independent fee auditing services can provide advice about UCR amounts.

Hospital Bill Audits

Hospital bill audits are also performed to ensure the appropriateness of charges. The services billed by the hospital are compared to what the physician ordered and to what was actually performed. The objective of these audits is to identify billing errors such as duplicate charges and charges for services not rendered.

Firms specializing in cost containment perform hospital bill audits. Nurses at those firms use computers to review billing charges against hospital records, often conducting on-site audits at the hospitals. Audit services may be charged at a fixed fee, at a percentage of the bill, at a percentage of savings, or per line on a bill. Hospital bill audits typically produce savings of about 5 percent.[20] Larger savings usually come from larger bills, which have a greater potential for billing errors.

Hospital bills should be selectively audited. The decision to audit is based on criteria established by insurers and may include the dollar amount of bills (such as those above $5,000), length of stay (such as three days or more), and hospital reputation. Bills showing disproportionate charges from certain departments may be audited, with the focus only on the department in question. Most cost-containment service firms provide a free preliminary screening of bills considered for audit to assess whether an audit is likely to yield savings.

Like fee schedules, hospital bill audits do not address the issue of necessity of treatment. As hospitals continue to improve their billing procedures to prevent errors, hospital bill audits can be expected to become less necessary. In response, bill auditing services have adopted and begun to offer utilization review services.

Retrospective Review

If a review of all records and bills fails to resolve questions about the cause of injury and appropriateness of treatment, a review by an independent medical consultant should be considered. Frequently, there may be disputes over the type of treatments provided. In this situation, a medical consultant may be asked to provide an opinion about those treatments. This process is called a retrospective review.

A **retrospective review**, sometimes called a records review, is a **peer review** (review of a medical provider by another medical provider practicing in a similar discipline). The retrospective reviewer does not usually see the claimant but rather bases his or her review on what is documented in the claim file. The purpose of a retrospective review is to examine any of the following:

- The relationship between the injury and the known facts of the accident
- The relationship between the treatment and the injury claimed
- The necessity of ongoing medical treatment

The consultant submits a report giving an opinion about the medical questions asked. The conclusions should be based as much as possible on objective evidence. For an individual claim, these reviews are less authoritative than other review techniques, such as independent medical exams, because retrospective reviews are conducted without the benefit of examining the patient. Unfortunately, in some disputed claims, a retrospective review is the only technique available. Retrospective reviews are most effectively used to help spot trends and identify areas or providers that have excessive charges.

Other types of peer reviews are conducted to examine only the issues of treatment fees, treatment frequency, and treatment duration. The two most common peer reviews are chiropractic reviews and physical therapy reviews. (Chapter 2 will explain how to arrange peer reviews.) These peer reviews are typically based on generally accepted treatment guidelines to determine whether the treatments were appropriate.

Treatment guidelines (called treatment protocols in some states) are developed through research of numerous health-care providers to establish common protocols for treatment or therapy. These guidelines show, in effect, the most efficient treatment for a given condition and the typical progress that the patient can expect in uncomplicated cases. The guidelines are based on what is currently possible and being performed by practitioners. If, for example, it has been determined that more than three types of treatment in one visit yield no additional benefit, then the guidelines would recommend against more than three treatments. A provider would need to provide an acceptable reason for deviation from the guidelines in order to be paid for the additional treatment. The guidelines are not intended to eliminate a clinician's judgement, but providers should be expected to explain deviations. Guidelines should not be based on financial objectives. The purpose of these guidelines is not to ration or reduce care, but rather to minimize waste and inefficiency, thereby making the best use of limited insurance dollars.

As of 1998, twenty-one states had developed formal treatment guidelines for workers compensation. Many states now have treatment guidelines for automobile no-fault medical benefits. New Jersey, for example, has a specified care path (with specific treatment guidelines) for injuries such as soft tissue injuries to the neck and back.

The manner in which claim representatives use these reviews and health-care management guidelines will be discussed in more detail in Chapter 2 and in the case studies at the end of the text.

Treatment guidelines are still controversial. One part of the controversy can be attributed to disagreements about the goals of medical treatments. There are basically two types of care:

1. **Palliative care**, the goal of which is to relieve pain for the patient
2. **Restorative care**, the goal of which is to restore functional abilities to the patient

Terminal cancer patients provide a classic example of the use of palliative care. They may be given treatments and medication whose sole purpose is to relieve their pain. No one is likely to dispute the need for this palliative care even though it may not enhance the patient's ability to function. However, if a patient is suffering from arthritis and receives physical treatments that solely reduce back pain without any restorative benefits, the palliative care is suspect and unlikely (at some point) to be compensable. Health-care providers disagree as to when and to what extent physical treatments should be given for palliative purposes if they are not helping to restore a range of motion or increase a patient's functional abilities.

Most of the evaluation of treatment described later in this text is based on research on restorative goals because the subjective nature of pain makes palliative care results difficult to measure. Some states have specifically addressed these differing views of care in their treatment guidelines. New Jersey, for example, specifically excludes palliative care in its automobile no-fault statutes by expressly stating that it is not "medically necessary" treatment.[21]

Treatment guidelines can also act as a prospective form of injury cost management because they are developed before treatment is given. Unlike many of the fee agreements described in the next section, however, treatment guidelines are still disputed by some health-care providers, and many health-care practitioners are unaware of their details. For these reasons, guidelines are still applied retroactively in many cases, which might change in the future.

Prospective Management of Injury Claims

Prospective management refers to management techniques implemented before treatment occurs. When possible, prospective management is preferable to retrospective management because setting guidelines before services have been rendered is more effective than disputing services after they have been rendered. Not all casualty claims can be prospectively managed, but a growing number of them can. Examples of prospective management techniques include obtaining preapproval for specific medical care before it occurs, planning the best use of hospital stays before admission, and negotiating agreed fees with physicians before medical services are provided.

Preadmission Certification

Preadmission certification (also referred to as preadmission review or preadmission screening) is a form of prospective review; it is a process of establishing preapproval for hospital admission or surgery. Preadmission certification can prevent unnecessary treatment and suggest alternative treatment. More money is spent on hospital care than on any other element of health-care spending. Some hospitalizations are unnecessary because the treatment is unnecessary and in other cases because the treatment, although necessary, can be provided on an outpatient basis.

Second opinions are common in preadmission certification. Claim personnel in workers compensation have long practiced preapprovals of surgeries and requests for second opinions. Second opinion consultations often cause the patient to reconsider the proposed surgery. Frequently, the need for surgery depends on how painful or disabling the condition is to the patient. In those cases, the patient must decide whether the problems caused by the condition are sufficient to justify the risks of surgery. For example, back surgery for disk problems or degenerative conditions is usually optional. The patient can choose to live with the symptoms or to have surgery, which includes such risks as surgical scars and adhesions that can cause the problem to be as severe as it was before the surgery. Often through the process of obtaining a second opinion, the patient decides how bearable or unbearable his or her problems are.

Preadmission Testing

In the past, when patients were scheduled for surgery, they were often admitted to the hospital a day of two before the operation to have diagnostic tests administered. But these same tests can be performed on an outpatient basis, saving the expense of the hospital room. Testing before admission is a popular form of prospective management.

From 1980 to 1995, hospitalization admissions declined 26 percent as outpatient services increased 77 percent.[22] Prospective management such as **preadmission testing** is one reason for this trend.

Fee Arrangements

Under the traditional **fee-for-service (FFS) system**, the health-care provider sets its fee, and the insurer or patient pays it after the service is rendered. This system requires additional administration costs for auditing the fees, as was discussed earlier. An alternative approach to managing treatment costs is for the treatment payers to prearrange agreed fees before service is provided. This is a prospective approach.

These prospective fee arrangements were introduced with the formation of preferred provider organizations (PPOs) and health maintenance organizations (HMOs). In their simplest forms, PPOs and HMOs are mainly financing arrangements that provide treatment at discounted rates to insurers. However, as these forms have evolved, they have begun to address the costs related to overuse as well as excessive fees.

Preferred Provider Organizations

A **preferred provider organization (PPO)** is a medical provider or a group of medical providers organized to offer services at a discount in exchange for a high volume of referrals. The term preferred provider reflects the relationship of the health-care organization to its source of referrals. The health-care organization is preferred, or chosen, over other organizations. The primary advantage to insurers of PPOs is their willingness to negotiate fixed fees at a discount for all types of services. The discounts are usually 10 to 20 percent off the fee schedules or UCR amounts. PPOs typically have utilization control measures within their network to control costs and help realize a profit. Large employers that can generate a large volume of referrals from employees and their dependents have especially benefited from PPOs.

PPOs can be formed by physicians, hospitals, joint ventures of physicians and hospitals, insurance companies, or cost-containment firms. Insurers (and self-insurers that are large enough) and other producers of health care can enter into PPO arrangements directly or through a third-party cost-containment service firm.

The typical PPO arrangement includes four types of important parties: (1) the health-care providers who offer a service to PPO participants; (2) the PPO organization that creates the PPO arrangement; (3) the employer or insurer that refers participants to the PPO health-care providers; and (4) employees or insureds and their dependents who obtain health services through the PPO. In many PPO arrangements, the health-care providers, the employer, or the employer's insurer owns and controls the PPO organization. In other cases, the PPO is a separate for-profit organization.

PPOs, or employers and insurers using PPOs, negotiate various sorts of fee discounts. The most common arrangement for hospital services is to establish a fixed per-diem charge at a rate below that paid by indemnity-type insurance plans. For other health services, especially physician services, PPOs arrange a percentage discount from the fee usually paid by indemnity insurance plans. Percentage discount arrangements offer less certainty of savings. The "usual" fee, from which discounts are calculated, may be fictional in the sense that it is rarely, if ever, paid by any party. Thus, the "discount" fee may be as high as any other.

PPOs do not insure health-care services for participants for a flat annual fee; therefore, they do not bear the risk that the health-care needs of its participants will be greater than expected. The PPO does not provide the health care directly; rather, it acts as a broker by arranging discounts with select health-care providers. PPOs pass along to employers and their insurers all actual costs based on the discounted fees. Employers or their insurers must create incentives such as deductibles or copayments for employees and their dependents to use the health-care providers in the PPO network.

PPOs have become increasingly popular arrangements for workers compensation in states in which the employer has the right to select the treating physician. Without the right to select the physician, the employer and its insurer cannot guarantee any particular volume of claims, and PPOs become impractical.

Health Maintenance Organizations

Health maintenance organizations (HMOs) contract with health-care providers to establish a health-care network. Unlike PPOs, HMOs generally do not cover services by providers who are not part of the network. HMOs claim to have two advantages over traditional FFS plans:

- They can better control the quality of care by selecting only the most qualified providers.
- They can negotiate fees for the services provided.

HMOs are popular with health insurers because their costs are predictable. The HMO or the provider bears the risk that participants may need more health care than expected. The HMO commits to provide all care needed by its participants in exchange for a fixed fee per year from the insurer. In 1980 there were 235 HMOs in the United States with an enrollment of 9 million people. By 1997 the enrollment had climbed to over 46 million people in 651 HMOs across the country.[23]

Overutilization affects the HMO's profitability. In an HMO, a primary physician acts as a "gatekeeper" in controlling utilization. Participants who join an HMO obligate themselves to go through the gatekeeper physician when seeking care. HMOs emphasize preventive medicine based on the premise that early detection of health problems will result in treatment that is briefer and less costly. Thus, HMOs manage health care as well as costs.

HMO payments to providers can be structured in several ways. A discounted-fee-for-service payment structure pays providers a certain percentage of their normal fee. The providers accept the discounted fees in exchange for a larger, more stable patient base. In this type of HMO, the HMO—not the provider—bears the financial risk. All providers in the organization receive the same reimbursement rate regardless of whether they are cost-conscious or charge higher fees than others. One way HMOs address the problem of higher-than-average fees is to set fee schedules for medical procedures and services. In this type of HMO, the providers have no incentive to control the patients' use of health-care services.

Another HMO payment structure is called capitation. About 62 percent of HMOs use this payment structure.[24] With capitation, the HMO prepays the medical providers a flat amount based on the number of members in a specified period, typically on a monthly basis. In this arrangement, the provider is paid the same amount each period regardless of how often the patient is seen or how costly the treatment is. HMOs that use a capitation payment structure bear a relatively fixed amount of financial risk. Most of the risk is passed on to the providers, so the providers have an incentive to contain medical costs.

Some HMOs may also pay providers on a salary basis. Providers under this type of payment structure sometimes receive performance-based bonuses.

Certain PPOs have become more active in health-care management through arrangements such as gatekeeper physicians and restrictions on which physicians may be seen. Furthermore, most HMOs allow participants to choose their own primary physician by paying an additional fee. As PPOs respond to employer pressures and accept some financial risks of excessive treatment, and as HMOs allow a wider choice of physicians, the distinction between HMOs and PPOs may become less clear.

Only recently have HMOs been used in casualty claims. This involvement will be discussed in the section on managed care in casualty claims in this chapter.

Direct Intervention Techniques

Direct intervention approaches encompass various techniques for injury management that take place while the patient is still undergoing treatments and/or suffering a disability. These techniques range from traditional techniques such as concurrent reviews to more recent disability management techniques. Direct intervention techniques include:

- Concurrent reviews
- Independent medical exams
- Medical case management
- Disability management

Concurrent Reviews

The purpose of **concurrent reviews** is to monitor the appropriateness of inpatient services and length of hospital stay. Concurrent review can also help to determine whether a doctor's orders are being followed. As with precertification, concurrent reviews can provide information about alternative treatments. For example, concurrent reviews might show that the type or amount of physical therapy is inappropriate or that generic drugs could be used instead of brand-name drugs.

Discharge planning, usually part of concurrent reviews, is the process of establishing a program for the type and amount of treatment after the patient is discharged from the hospital. Patients discharged from hospitals frequently need nursing home care, intravenous drug therapy, physical therapy, oxygen, antibiotics, or follow-up doctor services, all of which should be planned.

Determining the need for and the length of a hospital stay is one of the most valuable aspects of concurrent review. Patients should not be hospitalized unless they cannot practically receive appropriate care outside a hospital. They should not be hospitalized merely for the doctor's convenience—many patients are admitted and discharged on dates that suit the doctor's schedule rather than dates indicated by medical necessity. Analyzing the length of stay has resulted in substantially shorter periods of hospitalization than were common fifteen to twenty years ago.

Independent Medical Examination

An **independent medical examination (IME)** has a limited and specific definition in the medical community. It includes a brief review of the patient's history and treatment to date, and a physical examination of the patient. The purpose of the examination is to help the physician make a medical determination as to causation, current physical impairment, and the need for present or future treatment.

An IME is done selectively as a reaction to a dispute rather than in an ongoing manner. However, an IME is an important technique for intervention in managing injury claims. The insurer's ability to intervene with an IME is easier with first-party insurance claimants than with third-party liability claims. Most medical insurance policies provide, as a condition of the contract, that the insurer may obtain a medical examination of the injured party as many times as it deems necessary. In third-party tort claims that become the subject of a lawsuit, at least one IME can be secured as part of the discovery procedure, often after the claimant has completed most of his or her medical treatments. In many cases, even before suit is filed, plaintiff attorneys will allow the insurer to perform an IME if doing so helps to conclude the claim.

For example, an IME could be used in a claim involving a scar revision (a medical procedure to improve the appearance of scarred skin) for a person who suffered a cut to the arm. The treating physician may indicate that the revision is needed but may be far from definitive in the recommendation. In this situation, an IME may be helpful both for resolving the claim and for helping the patient plan his or her future medical care. The IME is essentially a second medical opinion.

In many cases, however, claim representatives need an IME as well as a retrospective review to resolve a claim. For example, a claim might involve a soft tissue injury with what appears to be unnecessary or unreasonable treatment, or treatment at a greater frequency than would be expected for the injury. This condition along with an allegation of continuing disability and need for treatment may require an IME with retrospective review.

Nevertheless, an IME has benefits not available from a retrospective review alone. The most obvious is that, unlike the retrospective reviewer, the independent examiner has an opportunity to examine the injured person. This examination provides information that may be the basis for a prognosis and determining the necessity of future treatment. The independent medical examiner also has an opportunity to evaluate the injured party as a witness if the case goes to litigation. This aspect of the IME is critical because an experienced medical examiner can provide insight as to whether the injured party is overreacting or exaggerating and as to how this will come across to a jury. Chapter 2 will discusses the advantages and disadvantages of IMEs and how claim representatives should arrange them.

Medical Case Management

Case management is a UR technique that early on identifies potentially long-term claims and ensures that the case is managed properly. Long-term and catastrophic claims result in the highest level of waste in the form of duplicate testing and unnecessary services and result in the highest costs. Good planning can prevent wasteful and unnecessarily costly procedures.

Serious disabling injuries can require medical care that costs tens of thousands of dollars per year and continues for the life of the patient, often thirty or forty years. The total expected cost of such cases can often exceed $1 million. The patient must therefore receive necessary and appropriate care in the most cost-effective manner. Case managers are experts in coordinating such care. With a high level of commitment to the patient, they do not settle for inadequate or inferior care, but work to ensure that patients receive the best appropriate care.

A case manager's most important function is to determine in what setting a patient can best receive care. If practical, the patient's home is the most desirable location. Most patients are much more physically and psychologically comfortable at home than at other locations. However, the patient's home is not a feasible place for care if the patient's needs create too great a burden for the patient's family. Case managers interview the patient, the patient's family, and the doctors to determine whether home care is feasible.

When a patient must be institutionalized, case managers are experts at selecting the most appropriate facility. For example, certain rehabilitation centers specialize in serving victims of brain trauma. Chapter 2 will describe the specific tasks and types of case management.

Disability Management

Disability is a loss or reduction of a person's capacity to meet personal, social, or occupational demands. Disability management is a broad term for techniques used to help reduce the disability of an injured person. The nature and determination of disability will be discussed in Chapter 3, along with ways to overcome permanent disabilities.

Rehabilitation, another type of disability management, includes techniques for minimizing an injured person's disability and will be covered in detail in Chapter 4.

Other examples of disability management can be as simple as patient education. The role of patient education in reducing disability will be discussed in Chapter 5 on low back pain.

In workers compensation, disability management involves return-to-work programs that accelerate the person's ability to return to a productive role. Activity modification and return-to-work initiatives are popular techniques for achieving this goal.

Activity Modification

After patients' initial visits, physicians in many cases simply tell injured patients to stay home and rest for days or weeks until the injury heals and the disability is gone. This approach is unnecessary for most claims if the injured person's job can be modified. In some cases, as with back injuries, the traditional approach might actually worsen the patient's condition. A more common-sense approach is for providers to be involved in modifying an injured person's activities.

In the broadest sense, physicians' recommendations about work restrictions are a form of treatment because inactivity can postpone and limit recovery for many patients. Appropriately designed, modified activity that allows individuals to remain on the job while they fully recover can enhance the patient's recovery. In this way, **activity modification is a form of injury management**. Activity modification is aimed at allowing patients to continue enough physical activity to avoid complete disability while maintaining a tolerable comfort level.

In recommending activity modifications, physicians should obtain from the employer a description of the physical demands of the patient's job. Jobs that include heavy or repetitive lifting, total body vibration, or unusual postures or postures held over long periods of time or activities such as twisting, bending, and prolonged sitting may need to be altered or avoided. Doctors need to determine these tasks and explain how jobs can be modified appropriately.

In workers compensation claims, physicians should ideally establish activity goals based on a claimant's job requirements that will enable the person to return to work as soon as possible. These goals can be very important as a way of keeping the person focused on improvements and returning to full functional status at work.

Despite the potential benefit of modified work to patients and employers, many union contracts still do not permit individuals to return to work until they have reached complete recovery under the often misguided belief that they are protecting their workers from re-injury or permanent disability. These misconceptions have been overcome at several companies through employee education. However, many union contracts still have wording that takes the decision of when the employee can return to work out of the doctor's hands. Claim representatives and nurse case managers need to be aware of these contracts when trying to manage workers compensation claims.

Return-to-Work Initiatives

Return-to-work initiatives are essential to good disability management in workers compensation. Employers and/or their insurance carriers often use nurse case managers to monitor treatment and make sure that the claimant's health concerns are addressed. Claim complications often arise from injured parties feeling ignored or uncertain about their care. In the workers compensation setting, the patient, the doctor, the patient's employer, and the insurance company are all trying to achieve the same goal—helping the patient recover and return to work.

A good return-to-work program involves the following components:

- Early identification of atypical, long-duration cases
- Quick intervention to coordinate care
- Setting return-to-work expectations
- Use of treatment and disability guidelines

A recent study found that 82 percent of employers surveyed stated that they used early return-to-work programs as one of their cost-containment initiatives, but most injured workers reported that no one ever discussed return-to-work programs with them while they were off work. The results of this study illustrate the gap between what employers believe they are doing and what actually occurs.[25]

Individuals who have persistent, disabling pain may benefit from physical therapy, pain clinics, work-hardening, occupational therapy, or antidepressant medication (because of the psychological component of back injury claims). These will be discussed later in the text. Exhibit 1-7 illustrates the importance of returning claimants to work. Although most workers with low back pain return to work in about two weeks, others, with the same diagnosis, do not. As the length of time grows longer, the likelihood of the employee's returning to work diminishes.

Employer supervisors, as well as claim professionals, can be trained to recognize potentially serious problems that may seem minor so that employee care is not delayed. If an employee is required to miss workdays, supervisors should maintain frequent contact with the worker. This contact helps prevent the worker from feeling alienated. The supervisor can also assist the treating doctor in planning activity modification plans. The supervisor is often the person who knows best what the employee could still do to remain productive. The insurance company should be kept informed of the individual's progress by maintaining contact with the injured worker and the employer or nurse case manager.

Exhibit 1-7
Time to Return to Work With Low Back Pain

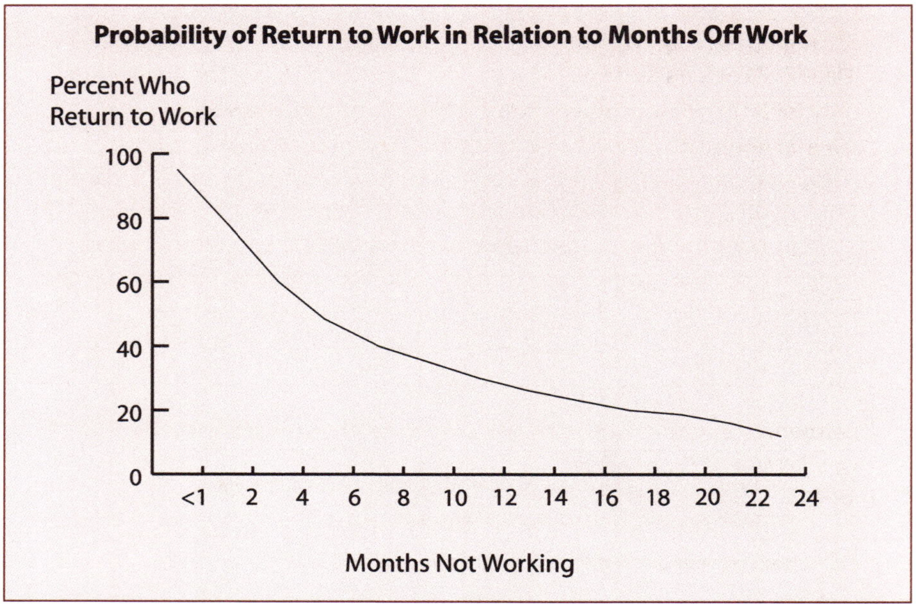

Probability of Return to Work in Relation to Months Off Work

[Graph: Percent Who Return to Work (y-axis, 0–100) vs Months Not Working (x-axis, <1 to 24). Curve starts near 95% at <1 month and decreases to approximately 12% at 24 months.]

William E. Fordyce, Back Pain in the Workplace (Seattle, WA: International Association for the Study of Pain, 1995), p. 21.

Managed Care in Casualty Claims

To most people, managed care means HMOs and PPOs because most people are familiar with them. In casualty claims, these structured forms of managed care were, until recently, seldom used and for that reason were not considered the only forms of managed care. Managed care in its broadest sense includes any technique for containing injury costs. Under this broader definition, managed care already exists in some form for every kind of casualty claim.

Some institutional forms of managed care such as HMOs and PPOs are used in workers compensation because several states permit employers to direct employees to selected physicians, at least for some limited period of time. However, even states in which employees can choose their own physicians have had success in getting employees to go to selected PPOs or HMOs, especially if they have a reputation for prompt, quality care.

This section will examine how HMOs and PPOs are used primarily in workers compensation, though there may be opportunities to use them in other types of claims now and in the future.

Managed Care in Workers Compensation

The use of managed care techniques in workers compensation continues to grow. Exhibit 1-8 shows the results of a 1993 Towers Perrin Survey of 1,050 companies. The top ten managed care techniques are listed.

Exhibit 1-8
Managed Care Used in Workers Compensation

Managed Care Technique Used in Workers Compensation	Percentage of Companies Surveyed Using the Technique
Safety initiatives/injury prevention	85%
Case management	84
Return-to-work program	78
Utilization review	70
Medical bill audits	68
Vocational rehabilitation	66
Claim administration audits	61
Fee schedule compliance	60
Precertification of medical treatment	57
Use of HMOs, PPOs, or other managed care network	50

Source: Towers Perrin, Regaining Control of Workers Compensation Costs: The Second Biennial Towers Perrin Report, 1993.

Not every state permits the use of all of these techniques. As of 1998, twenty-seven states had a formal program allowing some form of managed care networks for injured workers. Ten states gave employers full control of the choice of physicians for injured workers, and another twenty-one states permitted limited control, often through the use of a state-certified managed care organization. Forty-two states used fee schedules to limit what providers could charge. Case management was formally permitted in twelve states, and utilization reviews were permitted or mandated in at least twenty-five states. Although the use of treatment guidelines was not popular when the survey was conducted in 1993, by 1998 twenty-one states had developed treatment guidelines, especially related to low back injuries. The treatment guidelines in some of these states mirrored the federal Agency for Health Care Policy and Research Guidelines discussed in Chapter 5. The implementation of managed care networks (HMOs and PPOs) is the most complicated technique but the one that has the greatest potential to influence costs. Exhibit 1-9 shows the results from one study comparing the costs of unmanaged workers compensation claims to managed workers compensation claims.

Differences Between Group Health and Workers Compensation Systems

Before discussing how HMOs and PPOs can be implemented in casualty claims, it is helpful to understand how workers compensation differs from group health insurance. PPOs and HMOs have thrived in

Exhibit 1-9
Comparison of Managed and Unmanaged Workers Compensation Claims

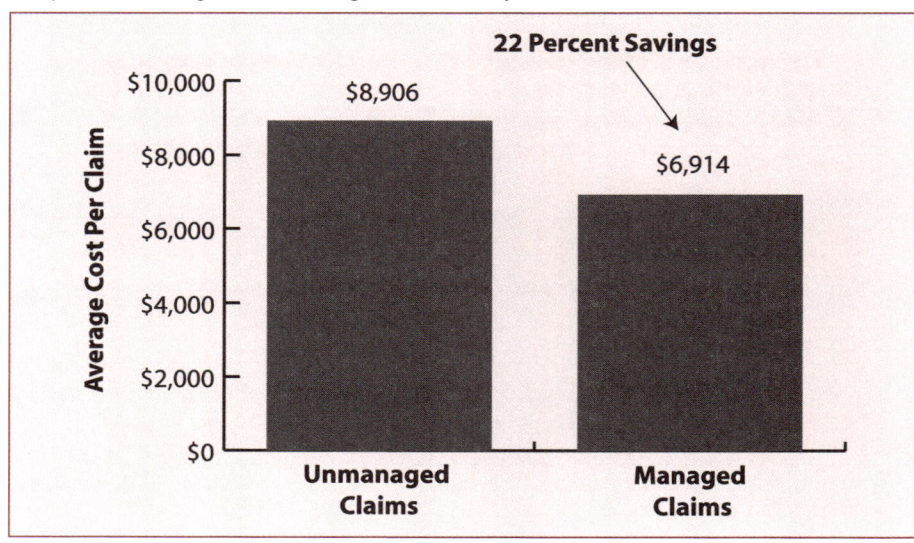

Maddy Bowlins, "Measuring the Financial Impact of Workers Compensation Managed Care," *Journal of Workers Compensation*, vol. 5, no. 3, Spring 1996, p. 38.

group health insurance, but several important differences make their use in workers compensation more challenging. Despite the challenges posed by these differences, employers and their insurers have found ways to overcome them.

One difference is that workers compensation sources collectively account for only a minor percentage of health-care expenditures and have a limited voice in how money is spent. When HMOs or PPOs are used in workers compensation, the discount rates on fees are usually not as significant as with group health plans. As described earlier, HMOs (or the providers working for them) bear the financial burden of medical costs. If medical costs exceed what was anticipated, HMOs must absorb the loss. HMOs are willing to accept this risk in group health insurance because group health insurance relies on highly predictable, large numbers of patients. The law of large numbers makes the injuries and illnesses more predictable and therefore more tolerable. Workers compensation injuries are less predictable, because projections for workers compensation injuries rely on smaller numbers of people. With workers compensation is a possibility of lifetime benefits. Group health insurance plans usually have some cap. Unlike group health care, workers compensation is regulated by a patchwork of various state guidelines. Keeping up with the individual state guidelines increases administrative overhead.

HMOs typically have a gatekeeper to help control costs. The gatekeeper is usually a doctor chosen by the patient beforehand. In workers compensation, there may be no similar gatekeeper. Only about half of the states permit employers to choose providers for their injured employee; many employers in those states opt not to choose providers.

Diagnosis and treatment philosophies differ between the two systems. Containing medical costs is the goal in group health insurance; containing overall costs, including lost wage costs, is the goal of workers compensation. These different goals lead to different treatment philosophies. Group health treatment is conservative, and returning the patient to work is not a main concern. Workers compensation treatments take more of a sports-medicine approach. Treatments may be more aggressive (and sometimes more expensive) than group health treatment because the overall goal is to return the person to work as soon as possible. Group HMO doctors do not always understand this difference. To illustrate the difference, Exhibit 1-10 compares back treatment between workers compensation and group health providers in California. Providers who are familiar with both systems claim that a philosophical difference is the main cause for the difference in treatment. The overall effect in the workers compensation treatment approach appears to be more treatment but shorter treatment duration than group health treatment.[26]

Exhibit 1-10
Back Injury Treatment

Measure	Workers Compensation Average	Group Health Average	Percentage Difference
Visits	12.24	9.94	23.1%
Procedures	28.11	15.54	80.9
Procedures per visit	2.26	1.54	48.7
Visits per week	2.19	.88	148.9
Treatment duration (weeks)	11.76	24.56	−52.1

California Workers Compensation Institute.

In group health insurance, the cause of an injury is irrelevant. In workers compensation, the cause of the injury is crucial to compensation. How can employers direct employees to doctors if they are not sure the claim is compensable? This situation requires agreements up front that all parties understand, so that the injured worker is not delayed in receiving care while the insurance issue is pending.

Implementing Managed Care in Workers Compensation

Despite the challenges, managed care is successfully implemented in workers compensation. The results of managed care and the exact method of implementation vary by state and by employer.

Workers Compensation Managed Care Results

From 1982 to 1991, workers compensation indemnity and medical payments increased from $13.8 to $39.2 billion in the United States.

Between 1992 and 1993, these costs declined by $1.8 billion.[27] Rates of increase have leveled off since then. The reduction in the growth is believed to be related to the use of managed care techniques.[28]

Numerous studies indicate that managed care is effective. Florida, Ohio, New York, and Oregon all conducted statewide studies. Florida conducted the most comprehensive study on the effect of changing workers compensation from fee-for-service to managed care networks. The Florida study combined two pilot projects, an HMO pilot and a PPO pilot. The results of the HMO pilot were as follows:

- A 58 percent reduction in medical costs
- A 64 percent reduction in indemnity costs
- A total reduction of 54 percent after adjusting for the added administrative costs of the HMOs

The cost savings were attributed to a 15 percent health-care provider fee discount, less hospitalization, shorter hospital stays, fewer treatments, less expensive types of treatments, and a quicker return-to-work time. Although most claimants were satisfied with their care under the HMO, the number of claimants who expressed dissatisfaction was almost twice that of those who were dissatisfied under the traditional fee-for-service system (34 percent versus 18 percent).

The results under the PPO pilot were not as dramatic as with the HMO participants. The PPO had on average a 23 percent reduction in cost; however, the percentage of claimants expressing dissatisfaction with the PPO care (20 percent) was similar to those under the traditional system (18 percent).[29] Oregon reported a 27 percent cost reduction with the use of managed care organizations.[30] New York announced that it had reduced workers compensation costs by 25 percent by expanding the use of managed care networks (mainly PPOs) in treating work-related injuries. Insurers in Ohio reduced premiums by 10 percent based on Ohio's experience with managed care networks.[31] The Ohio managed care program produced surprising satisfaction ratings. Employee satisfaction increased under the managed care program. This increase was attributed to faster care and reduced paperwork.[32]

Managed Care Networks in Workers Compensation

Managed care networks are mainly, but not exclusively, used in states that permit employers to choose providers or managed care networks for injured employees.

Exhibit 1-11 shows the three general ways that employers structure arrangements for care to injured employees. The third arrangement, using **managed care organizations (MCOs)**, is the one most often considered "workers compensation managed care."

An MCO arrangement begins with a managed care organization that manages and coordinates claims with a team of specialists. The MCO usually does not provide care but just coordinates the medical aspects of workers compensation claims with employers, providers, or insurers and contracts with a medical network (typically a PPO) to provide treatment. The treatment network has a group of providers with good credentials who understand the need for returning patients to a productive status as soon as possible.

Exhibit 1-11
Employer Arrangements With Providers for Workers Compensation Care

Informal Arrangement	Direct Arrangement	Arrangement with Managed Care Organization (MCO)
The employer, its insurer, or both suggest health-care providers to injured workers, but employees ultimately retain the right to choose their own provider.	The employer, its insurer, or both contract directly with health-care providers. The employer establishes and manages the details of the managed care program.	The employer, its insurer, or both contract with a managed care organization that establishes and manages the details of the managed care program.

Typically the managed care organization has an account manager who works with the employer. Some MCOs arrange for on-site assessments with a loss prevention specialist who examines workplace hazards and develops safety programs with the employer. The MCO has case managers (usually consulting nurses) who intervene early in the claim by acting as a liaison between the network provider and the employer or its insurer's claim representatives. The network provider treats the worker and advises the case manager on work restrictions and injury prognosis. The case manager works with the claim staff of a third-party administrator (TPA) or insurance company. The claim representative sets reserves, investigates compensability problems, calculates wage loss payments, and works with the employer to return the injured worker to work.

A good MCO will have a quality provider network, effective case managers, significant fee discounts, and expert utilization reviewers. The advantages of using a good MCO are as follows:

- Prompt access to medical care
- Prompt referrals to specialists for medically necessary services
- Active case management
- Earlier return to work
- Effective coordination among all parties (employers, providers, and insurers)
- Quality assurance through monitored care and formal selection process

When employers have arrangements with MCOs, employees are usually given cards with phone numbers to call in case of injury at work. The employee or supervisor calls the MCO, who directs the employee to a provider. Neither the employee nor the employer needs to worry about finding an approved, conveniently located provider.

MCOs must choose network providers that meet criteria established by the state in which the employer conducts business. Exhibit 1-12 contains the criteria that New York established for workers compensation PPOs.

Exhibit 1-12
New York Criteria for Workers Compensation PPOs

Preferred Provider Organizations

Legislation enacted in July 1996 allows employers and insurers to use PPOs to treat injured workers. Under the new law, employers have 30 days of control over employees' choice of physician. The state approved the first PPOs under this new program on Sept. 30, 1997.

Any plan or entity with the ability to establish a network of medical providers to treat all services covered under workers' compensation law may apply for PPO certification. Provider networks must have a full panel of specialists with a good geographic distribution for their planned service areas.

No insurer or employer shall have any financial interest in the PPO.

PPOs applying for certification must submit:

- Names and addresses of members of the governing body of the PPO that will be responsible for policies, management, quality assurance, utilization review and all other operations;
- Certification of Incorporation and bylaws, an independently audited financial statement, and demonstration of character, competence, experience and community standing of top officials in the PPO;
- Selection standards for participating providers;
- Names and credentials, authorization to treat workers' compensation cases, licensing and certification requirements, and description of any final dispositions of professional misconduct for each provider;
- Names and credentials, authorization to treat workers' compensation cases, licensing and certification requirements, and description of any final dispositions of professional misconduct for each provider;
- Description of times, places and manner of providing services under the PPO;
- Procedures for ongoing quality assurance;
- Procedures for utilization review;
- Procedures for dispute resolution; and
- A description of how the PPO will meet the provider network criteria requirements.

Network Criteria

PPOs in urban counties must have at least one acute care hospital within the county and at least two other acute care hospitals available in contiguous counties. Rural counties should contain an acute care hospital for claimants within 40 miles of the claimant's worksite or home. If this is not available in the PPO, then the claimant has the right to be treated at the nearest acute care hospital.

The PPO must ensure that at least five medical or healthcare providers in each area of specialization required or offered will be made available in each county to claimants, or document alternative arrangements.

Access to Care

PPOs must ensure access to emergency care 24 hours a day. PPOs shall ensure access to initial treatment for all non-emergency care within 48 hours. PPOs shall develop and ensure a system through which employees may obtain information on a 24-hours-a-day basis regarding the availability of medical services and emergency services. PPOs shall develop and require provider adherence to treatment standards and protocols. PPOs shall maintain a return-to-work program in conjunction with the employer, treating physician and carrier to facilitate the return of injured workers to the workplace.

Choice of Provider

PPOs must make claimants aware of their right to opt out of PPO care and seek medical treatment outside the PPO. The right to opt out is per injury.

The employee may seek medical treatment from a provider outside of the PPO network only after 30 days from the date of the initial visit to a PPO provider.

The employer has the right to require a second opinion from a provider within the PPO.

The PPO shall permit the claimant to choose treatment for an occupational disease from the New York State Occupational Health Clinics Network.

Provider Reimbursement

PPOs shall not be required to reimburse for provider services in accordance with the provider fee schedules authorized by workers' comp law. Inpatient hospital fees are not negotiable, but are tied to Medicaid rates.

Utilization Review

Workers' compensation PPOs that have utilization review programs certified by the American Accreditation HealthCare Commission/URAC are exempt from compliance with the state utilization review law.

Jane Anderson, *State by State Laws and Regulations on Workers Compensation Managed Care* (Alexandria, VA: Capitol Publications, 1998), p. 48.

Managing Other Kinds of Injury Claims

Although workers compensation claim representatives have a greater ability to influence outcomes than the claim representatives handling automobile bodily injury or other casualty claims, claim representatives handling claims under automobile medical payments coverage and personal injury protection should not simply become bill processors. With increased limits of medical payments coverage and a growing number of injury management resources, the bill-processing approach is outdated and costly for insurance companies and their insureds. Claim representatives in all areas need to learn to manage claims better by taking advantage of available resources. Insurers can use nurse case managers and educational materials to help achieve those objectives.

Employer Liability Related to Managed Care in Casualty Claims

Managed care in casualty claims is a recent development, so no well-defined body of law exists for determining employer liability related to managed care. As managed care develops, state legislatures and courts will begin to address the issue of employer liability for managed care. Based on traditional theories of liability, claim representatives can anticipate where liability exposures are likely to be found.

The more directly the employer is involved with the treating physician, the higher is the risk for liability. Employers that have informal arrangements but allow employees the ultimate right to choose their own doctors would have the lowest risk. Employers that establish and manage a network of providers would have the highest risk. If the employer manages the details of the providers and is supposed to monitor provider treatment, courts may find that the provider is acting as an employee of the employer and hold the employer liable.

Provider selection is another area of potential exposure. If, for example, the employer selects providers that do not have the appropriate credentials and give inferior care (in exchange for discounts to the employer), the employer might be liable for negligent selection. Courts have already held employers liable for not adequately investigating the backgrounds of their providers.[33] Employers who work through MCOs have an additional layer to protect them and would likely have less exposure.

The timing of injury management also affects the likelihood of liability. Retrospective reviews have the lowest risk because the treatments have already been provided. However, in the prospective and direct approaches, the liability risks are higher. If, for example, a preadmission certification or a nurse case manager's decision causes a treating physician not to provide care, the employer might be held liable for medically inappropriate decisions. This form of liability already exists in group health insurance cases.[34] For this reason, nonmedically trained claim representatives should never make treatment decisions on nonroutine cases without the guidance of medical consultants. Even medically trained experts must use caution when their recommendations run counter to those of a patient's treating physician.

Employers must also be careful about what they write and say about the providers. For example, if an employer wants to convince employees to use a particular network in order to receive fee discounts, the employer might make or suggest promises that the network providers cannot keep. Employees who have unusual disabilities or health problems may need specialized care not available through the providers selected. If the employee relies on the employer's recommendation and seeks treatment with the recommended providers only to find they cannot help the employee, the employer might be held liable for misrepresentation.

Liability in the use of managed care techniques will continue to evolve. Employers and their insurers can take some measures to reduce the risk of liability. Following is a list of suggestions for employers and their insurers:

- Train all claim personnel to know their limits and role in managing injury claims

- Provide personnel with adequate supervision and guidance
- Do not become involved in managing or controlling physicians
- Adhere to established guidelines
- Do not make exaggerated or ambiguous claims about network health-care providers
- Do not lose track of the goals of managing injury claims (eliminate waste, inefficiency, fraud, and buildup without adversely affecting the health care of claimants)

Although the trends in workers compensation managed care have so far shown remarkable reductions, insurers and employers should not believe that the trend will continue indefinitely. One temptation for casualty insurers in a competitive soft market is to set premiums based on the expectation of continually declining costs. Casualty insurers should study the results of the group health insurance industry to see that, eventually, after waste and inefficiency have been eliminated, costs flatten. At that point, the only way to continue to achieve reductions is to ration or reduce the quality of care. This approach obviously has ethical and political pitfalls. Some critics claim that part of the backlash against some group health plans is the perception that the quality of care is now being compromised. To avoid overly strict regulation and adverse legislation, casualty insurers must avoid sacrificing quality care to injured claimants in pursuit of injury management.

Summary

Managing bodily injury claims is the responsibility of all claim professionals. Injury management must be performed ethically and with professionalism. The reasons for the increasing need for injury management techniques are escalating medical costs, population changes, insurance fraud and buildup, and cost shifting.

Injury management techniques fall roughly into three categories: retrospective, prospective, and direct intervention. The retrospective approach includes medical and hospital bill audits, state fee schedules, UCR, and retrospective reviews.

Prospective reviews occur before treatment is given. Examples of prospective treatments include preadmission certification, preadmission testing, and fee arrangements (PPOs and HMOs).

The direct intervention approach requires involvement while the claimant is still undergoing treatment. Examples of this approach include concurrent reviews, independent medical exams, medical case management, and disability management (activity modification and return-to-work programs).

The implementation of managed care techniques offers challenges but huge potential rewards. Managed care has been most successfully implemented in workers compensation, but all lines of insurance offer opportunities to implement new injury management techniques.

Chapter Notes

1. Ronald E. Gots, "Workers Compensation: The Last Bastion of Open Medical Checkbook," *Journal of the International Association of Industrial Accident Boards*, Summer 1987, p. 36.
2. United States Department of Commerce, *Statistical Abstract of the United States 1998* (Washington, DC: U.S. Department of Commerce, 1998), Table 164, p.118.
3. Statistical *Abstract of the United States 1998*, Table 1349, p. 833.
4. Statistical *Abstract of the United States 1998*, Table 772, p. 489.
5. Insurance Research Council, *Medical Cost Containment in Casualty Claims* (Oak Brook, IL: Insurance Research Council, 1990), p. 8.
6. United States Department of Commerce, *Statistical Abstract of the United States 1996* (Washington, DC: U.S. Department of Commerce, 1996), p. 127.
7. Insurance Information Institute, *Property and Casualty Insurance Fact Book*, 1997, p. 56.
8. Statistical *Abstract of the United States 1990*, p. 131.
9. Neal Vanselow, M.D., "Physician Workforce: Issues for American Medical Centers," American Association of Medical Colleges, December 2, 1996, World Wide Web: http:/www.aamc.org/about/progemph/fullrdoc.htm p. 2 (25 January, 1999).
10. Medical Consultants Northwest, "Issues of Injury," Spring 1996, vol. 10, no. 1, p. 1.
11. Massachusetts Safety Council, "Up-to-Date," July 1998 (Braintree, MA: Massachusetts Safety Council, 1998), p. 1.
12. "Workers With Disabilities at Higher Risk for Injuries," The Journal of Commerce, December 30, 1997, p. 8A.
13. Insurance Research Council, *Trends in Auto Injury Claims—Part I*, (Wheaton, IL: Insurance Research Council, 1995), p. 26.
14. Statistics from *The Journal of the American Medical Association*. Cited in Sally Roberts, "Self-Referrals Increase Health-Care Costs," Business Insurance, November 2, 1992, pp. 3, 28.
15. Roberts, p. 29.
16. Jerry Geisel, "Insurers, UR Firms Target Rising Outpatient Claims," *Business Insurance*, May 20, 1989, p. 10.
17. Jeffrey Harris, "Workers Compensation: Business As Usual May Mean Going Out of Business," *NCCI Digest*, vol. IV, no. III, October 1989, p. 35.
18. Gots, p. 36.
19. Gots, p. 37.
20. Gots, p. 37.
21. New Jersey Automobile Insurance Plan N.J.A.C. 11.3-4.2.
22. *Statistical Abstract of the United States 1997*, Table 185, p. 129.
23. *Statistical Abstract of the United States 1998*, Table 187, p. 128.
24. Marion Merrell Dow Inc., *Managed Care Digest*, HMO Edition, vol. 8, 1994, p. 12.
25. Gallup Organization, CIGNA Integrated Care, "CIGNA Integrated Care/Gallup Survey of Employee Experiences with Disability and the Benefit Process," April 1998, p. 7.

26. Stephanie D. Esters, "Managed Care Seen As Key to Cutting WC Costs," *1997-1998 Workers Compensation Managed Care Sourcebook* (New York: Faulkner and Gray, 1997), p. 77.
27. National Foundation for Unemployment and Workers Compensation, Research Bulletin: Fiscal data for state workers compensation system, 1982-1991 (Washington, DC: National Foundation for Unemployment and Workers Compensation, December 1993).
28. Edward Bernacki, M.D., and Sahn Tsai, Ph.D., "Managed Care for Workers Compensation: Three Years of Experience in an Employee Choice State," *Journal of Occupational and Environmental Medicine*, vol. 38, no. 11, 1996.
29. Research and Oversight Council on Workers Compensation, State of Texas, "Managed Care and Workers Compensation: A Review of Research," *1997-1998 Workers Compensation Managed Care Sourcebook*, p. 44.
30. Oregon Department of Consumer and Business Services, "Managed Care in the Oregon Workers Compensation System," December 1995.
31. William L. Newkirk, M.D., FACPM, "Managed Care Workers Compensation: An Overview," *1998 Workers Compensation Managed Care Sourcebook*, p. 2.
32. Jim Samuel, "Ohio Managed Care Plan Surprises with Improved Satisfaction Ratings," *Workers Compensation Managed Care*, vol. 6, no. 12, December 1998, p. 1.
33. Harrell v. Total Health Care, 781 S.W. 2d 58 (MO 1989).
34. Wickline v. State of California, 239 Cal. Rptr. 805, 741 P.2d 613 (Cal. 1987), and Wilson v. Blue Cross of Southern California, 222 CAL. APP 3d 660, 271 Cal. Rptr. 876 (Calif. Ct. of Appeal 1990).

Chapter 2
Injury and Treatment Evaluation

A critical evaluation of a claimant's medical treatment is one of the most challenging tasks facing claim representatives. Claim representatives are not physicians, yet they must be able to understand and evaluate injury claims well enough to determine whether a claim is owed and how to find assistance in evaluating nonroutine injury claims. This chapter describes how claim representatives perform the task of evaluating medical treatment.

As part of this evaluation, claim representatives must determine whether an insured event caused the claimant's injury or condition. Unlike health insurance that covers virtually all medical conditions regardless of cause, casualty insurance covers only injuries and conditions caused by a specific insured event, such as a work-related accident, an automobile accident, or an accident on certain premises. Having determined the cause of an injury or condition, the claim representative must then evaluate the necessity and appropriateness of treatment. Many claim representatives do not feel confident about performing this evaluation, yet they cannot abandon their responsibility by simply assuming that physicians will provide only the necessary treatment. Experience shows that physicians have incentives to overtreat. Claim representatives must also be satisfied that the suggested future course of treatment is appropriate and that the overall control of the claimant's treatment is adequate.

The decision to handle a case alone or to request assistance is one of the most crucial choices a claim representative must make. Claim representatives can use specific criteria to identify cases requiring additional or expert assistance. But because claim representatives handle most cases alone, they must be knowledgeable about medicine and medical practices in order to be successful.

In all cases, the claim representative bases the evaluation on medical bills, records, and reports. Claim representatives must therefore be familiar with the preparation, contents, maintenance, and significance of those documents. By selecting and procuring the documents essential to resolving a case, claim representatives can make the best decisions in the most efficient manner.

The evaluation of certain cases requires additional or expert assistance. Experts can independently review medical records and examine the claimant. Claim representatives must understand the services offered by experts in order to hire the most appropriate expert service and to obtain the information needed to conclude the claim.

Issues in Medical Treatment

Any claimant is entitled to be compensated for *no more than* reasonable and necessary treatment for injuries and conditions caused by an insured event. Even when liability and coverage for the insured event are clear, claimants are not entitled to compensation for unnecessary treatment, unreasonable treatment (in amount or cost), or treatment for injuries and conditions not related to the insured event. The application of this concept of compensation to specific cases can be complex, and it is the claim representative's responsibility to ensure that compensation is appropriately provided. In order to do so, the claim representative must (1) verify the cause of the injury, (2) confirm the necessity of proposed treatment, (3) assess the need for further treatment, and (4) identify and control complex claims.

Verification of Cause

Casualty insurance, such as workers compensation, auto, or general liability, covers only injuries or conditions caused by an insured event. However, claimants or their physicians commonly submit medical bills and reports for problems not caused by insured events. This error is generally not intentional, but the result of ignorance or thoughtlessness. Still, claim representatives should be aware that documents might be submitted for problems that are completely unrelated to the insured event, for problems that are chronic, or for problems that occur after the insured event but that were not caused by it.

Unrelated Problems

At any given time, a significant percentage of the population has some sort of medical problem. Some of those people become involved in accidents that result in insurance claims. If they are injured in accidents, they are likely to seek treatment for both their accidental injuries and their pre-existing problems from the same physician. Because many physicians are indifferent about who pays them, all billings are likely to be directed to a casualty insurer if patients notify them of an insurer's involvement.

Because of the prevalence of pre-existing medical problems, claim representatives should always determine the nature of the patient's complaint and the physician's treatment before paying bills for office visits. Similarly, claim representatives must understand the purpose of diagnostic and laboratory tests to know whether they are related to injuries suffered in an insured accident.

Chronic Problems

Chronic medical conditions, like unrelated pre-existing problems, are not usually caused by accidental injuries. Many claim representatives mistakenly believe that chronic and acute both mean bad or severe. In the context of medicine, chronic means ongoing or frequently recurring, and acute means sudden or recent.

Claim representatives must carefully investigate any condition described as, or known to be, chronic. Joint problems, especially in the spine, knees, or hips; osteoporosis; arteriosclerosis; diabetes; and arthritis are all common chronic problems. Indeed, claim representatives should suspect that chronic problems might be involved in any prolonged case unless the injuries are obviously caused by an accident.

It is often alleged that a chronic condition has been aggravated by an accident. An exacerbation of a pre-existing problem is compensable, but with certain limitations. Once the condition has returned to its pre-injury status, it is no longer compensable. Likewise, an exacerbated chronic problem is no longer compensable if the natural course of that pre-existing condition would eventually have made it just as bad.

Intervening Problems

Some injured claimants begin to recover and then reinjure themselves. Those subsequent injuries are known as intervening problems or injuries. The insurer responsible for the original injury should not pay for the intervening injury unless it was an unavoidable consequence of the first injury. Intervening injuries are typically caused by independent accidents that often result from the claimant's negligence or some other uninsured cause. A claim for treatment for an intervening injury may be submitted for compensation along with a claim for treatment for the original injury. Unless the claimant admits that he or she has had a subsequent injury, such injuries can only be detected through careful reading of the medical records. Claimants are usually forthright about the cause of an injury with their treating physician.

Need for Correct Diagnosis

A correct diagnosis is crucial for determining the cause of a claimant's injury. Unless the nature of a claimant's problem is known, its cause cannot be known. Claim representatives should not accept a statement that refers only to symptoms, such as headache or back pain, as a diagnosis. Innumerable medical conditions can cause such symptoms.

Diagnosis is crucial, but physicians need not establish the diagnosis with 100 percent certainty. Successful and appropriate medical treatment can be based on a presumptive, or working, diagnosis. A presumptive or working diagnosis is a condition believed by the physician to be the most likely cause of the patient's symptoms. Unless the failure to treat any other possible causes would endanger the patient, treating on the basis of a presumptive diagnosis is good medical practice. The alternative is to run expensive and nearly endless diagnostic tests.

Any physician who seems to be avoiding making a diagnosis should be required to provide a working diagnosis. Any physician who is providing treatment without at least a working diagnosis is operating outside the bounds of accepted medical practice.

Exhibit 2-1 provides a list of situations that require additional investigative activity to confirm that the injury is accident-related and suggested investigative activities for those situations.

Exhibit 2-1
Investigative Issues Related to Causation

Investigative Issues and Suggested Activities for Resolution	
Investigative Issues	**Suggested Activity**

Issue: Time Discrepancies
Late Reporting
There is a significant delay between the date of the occurrence and the date an injury was claimed, or
The Injury Worsened Dramatically
The injury worsened suddenly after an extended period of time during which it was stable.
Examples:
• First report of the injury occurs two months after the date of accident.
• Four months after the claimant finishes treatment for a neck injury, treatment begins again.
	1. Determine whether there is a reasonable explanation for the difference.
	2. Review all statements, police reports, and medical documents to confirm that there was no mention of an injury earlier.
	3. Notify injured party about the discrepancy in dates and explain that relatedness must be determined before payment is made.
	4. Write provider and ask:
	• How did the accident cause the injury?
	• Why didn't the injury show up earlier?
	• Why did the injury worsen after such a long time?
	5. Investigate intervening cause.
	  a. Index claimant to check for recent injury claims.
	  b. Request statement from claimant asking specifically about recent events.
	  c. Obtain medical documents (including pharmacy and family doctor records) checking for recent activity.

	d. Write provider and ask whether intervening injury occurred. If so, ask: • Was the intervening injury an unavoidable consequence of this injury? • Why was the intervening injury an unavoidable consequence of this injury? • Based on the original and intervening injuries, how long will the claimant need to reach maximum medical improvement (MMI)?
Issue: Facts Don't Match the Injury There is a significant difference between the injury claimed and the circumstances of the accident. *Examples:* • Person is claiming a torn rotator cuff injury, but the impact to the car was minor. • Person claiming a fractured hip says she slipped but did not fall.	1. Review all statements and documents to determine whether some unusual fact would explain the discrepancy. **Example:** Person was turned in an awkward, vulnerable position when the car was struck. 2. Check for a discrepancy in injury claimed and diagnostic codes. If a discrepancy is found, investigate it. 3. Investigate the possibility of a prior condition. **Example:** A person with a history of back problems blames all problems on a recent accident.
Issue: Diagnosis Problems Codes don't match the injury claimed. There's a discrepancy between the HCFA-1500/UB-92 ICD-9 diagnostic codes and the injury claimed. *Examples*: UB-92 hospital bill shows 924.11, contusion of lower limb, but the patient is claiming a neck injury. Diagnosis is unclear. The diagnosis describes only signs and symptoms (such as headaches, pain, etc.), and not the nature and cause of the condition.	1. Review all medical records to see whether the discrepancy is explained in the clinical data. 2. Write health-care provider and ask: a. Why there is a discrepancy between the patient's diagnosis and the injury claimed. b. For a corrected diagnosis if the original diagnosis was wrong. 3. Advise the claimant of the discrepancy and explain that payment cannot be made until the problem is resolved. 4. If the diagnosis is unclear: a. Write and ask the health-care provider for a clear diagnosis. b. Write and ask the health-care provider for a differential diagnosis to rule out other possible conditions that have similar symptoms. c. Write and ask the provider for a "rule-out" diagnosis.

Continued on next page.

Issue: Prior Conditions	

There is a preexisting injury or preexisting chronic condition.
 	
Examples:
• A person who has an athletic injury to the knee sustains a knee injury from a slip and fall.
• An elderly person is claiming cardiac problems after an auto accident.
• Person with diabetes mellitus has an injury that heals slowly.
	1. Index claimant for prior injury claims. Check the claimant's background.
	2. Obtain all pertinent medical documents (including pharmacy and family doctor records). Check for recent activity. Check for prior similar medical history.
	3. Write provider and ask:
	  • What are the history and nature of the claimant's pre-existing conditions?
	  • How did the accident aggravate the pre-existing condition?
	  • To what degree did the accident aggravate the pre-existing condition?
	  • Would the current problem have occurred in the natural course of the pre-existing condition?
	  • How long will it take the claimant to return to pre-accident status?

Depending on the investigative issues and the provider response, many of these issues may require contact with the consulting nurse to arrange for an IME or retrospective or peer review. Surveillance and background checks should be considered on any related issues.	

Medical records will be covered in detail later in this chapter, but some specific medical records not mentioned there should be considered if it appears that claimants are not being forthright about the cause of the injury. The medical records used for discovering alternative causes of injury are as follows:

- Family doctors' records
- Obstetric/gynecological (OB-GYN) records
- Pharmacy records
- Employment and school records
- Personal financial records

These records may sometimes be obtained only by subpoena in the discovery process of a lawsuit, but they should be considered. The records of family doctors are probably the best source of information about pre-existing conditions and previous accidents and injuries. Family doctors are not normally involved in the litigation process, and their records are usually objective, accurate, and honest. OB-GYN records can be important sources of information for alternative causes of carpal tunnel syndrome and back pain. Pharmacy records are a good source for finding information about previous providers and previous prescriptions for prior accidents and illnesses. School records are good for identifying psychological and behavioral problems that pre-date a given accident that is now being blamed for the claimant's psychological and behavioral problems. Employers often keep good records in personnel files about prior injuries and illnesses. Personal bank statements can be used to verify payments of past medical expenses and to identify health-care providers when the claimant fails to recall these facts.

Diagnostic Tests

Technology is increasing the variety of diagnostic tests available to health-care providers in determining the cause of an injury or disease. The following diagnostic tests are tests with which claim representatives must be familiar.

X-rays (sometimes called radiographs or roentgenograms) are the oldest, most widely available, and least expensive imaging techniques. Plain film X-rays are one-dimensional pictures of the comparative densities of the areas of the body through which the X-rays have been passed. Broken bones are normally diagnosed by X-ray. But even if the examination reveals no injury and X-rays show no abnormality, it does not necessarily mean that no injury or abnormality is present. It only means that the films did not show the abnormality. The position of the patient, the position of the abnormality, and the quality of the X-ray may make it impossible for the abnormality to be seen.

X-rays cannot accurately detect soft-tissue damage, and they are not as good as other imaging techniques in determining anatomical defects in the back. X-rays were once considered routine; however, the routine use of X-rays is no longer considered appropriate in the mainstream medical community because it unnecessarily exposes patients to radiation.

Tomography involves taking many X-rays at various angles. **Computerized tomography scans (CT scans)** involve taking a series of X-rays at various angles and converting these images into digital codes that the computer interprets and reproduces on a video screen. CT scans can provide high-resolution images without the visual interference found in standard X-rays. The most successful uses of CT scans have been in the diagnosis of problems with the brain and spine.

The most common types of CT scans are as follows:

- CAT (computerized axial tomography) scans
- CTT (computerized transverse axial tomography) scans

Some radiographic tests use contrast agents, which are dyes that are injected into an area of the body to enhance the detail of the X-ray image and provide a two-dimensional picture. Myelography is an example of this kind of test. A myelogram involves the injection of radio-opaque dye into the spinal column. The dye settles in the spinal column so that X-rays can outline the spinal cord and nerves. The invasive nature of using contrast agents and their sometimes unpleasant side effects are the major disadvantages of this type of test.

Magnetic resonance imaging (MRI) uses a combination of a huge super-conductive magnet, electromagnetic waves, and a sophisticated computer system to create very detailed images of the body's interior.

Unlike conventional X-rays and CAT scans, the MRI does not use radiation. It is not stopped by dense bone and can create images on any plane—vertically, horizontally, and diagonally.

The electromyogram (EMG) uses electricity to diagnose problems. In an EMG, electrodes are inserted into muscle. The muscle's own electrical activity is projected onto a computer screen. The EMG can identify nerve damage by monitoring the electrical activity in the muscle. The EMG is accompanied by nerve conduction tests that determine how motor and sensory impulses move through nerve roots. This is an invasive procedure that is not typically used by itself to make a diagnosis.

Thermography maps any variations in temperature on the surface of the skin. The skin's dissipation of excessive internal body heat is regulated through the autonomic nervous system. Diagnosing with thermography is based on the presumption that asymmetrical temperature patterns on the skin indicate pathology of an underlying soft tissue. However, physiological studies have shown that the surface temperature of the body is not uniform, symmetrical, or consistent from time to time. It can also be affected by numerous external factors. Thermographic results should not be relied on as objective findings because they are not widely accepted in the medical community.

Necessity of Treatment

Liability for treating injuries caused by an insured event is limited to necessary treatments. To be sure that treatments are necessary, claim representatives must be familiar with the usual treatments and treatment alternatives for various conditions.

Usual Treatment

Claim representatives handling injury claims become familiar with the usual treatment for injuries and conditions that they see regularly. Most experienced claim representatives recognize the usual treatment for muscular strain and sprain, broken bones, lacerations, and joint problems. As a result, they can detect a course of treatment that appears unusual or excessive, such as the administration of drugs for conditions that might not be related to the drug, or treatment for muscle strain that lasts for months.

For injuries and conditions with which they are unfamiliar, claim representatives should consult medical reference resources or an expert. Most experts can quickly determine whether the nature or extent of treatment in a given case seems unusual.

The *Merck Manual* (seventeenth edition, 1999) presents information about the diagnosis and treatment of injuries and diseases. It is published by Merck & Co., Whitehouse Station, New Jersey. Exhibit 2-2 contains information from the *Merck Manual*.

Exhibit 2-2
Sample Information from *The Merck Manual*

175 / TRAUMA OF THE HEAD

Head injury causes more deaths and disability than any other neurologic condition before age 50 and occurs in > 70% of accidents, which are the leading cause of death in men and boys < 35 yr old. Mortality from severe injury approaches 50% and is only modestly reduced by treatment.

Damage may result from skull penetration or from rapid brain acceleration or deceleration, which injures tissue at the point of impact, at its opposite pole (countrecoup), or diffusely within the frontal and temporal lobes. Nerve tissue, blood vessels, and meninges can be sheared, torn, or ruptured, resulting in neural disruption, intracerebral or extracerebral ischemia or hemorrhage, and cerebral edema. Hemorrhage and edema act as expanding intracranial lesions, causing focal neurologic deficits or increased intracranial swelling and pressure, which can lead to fatal herniation of brain tissue through the tentorium or foramen magnum. Skull fractures may lacerate meningeal arteries or large venous sinuses, producing epidural or subdural hematoma. Fractures, especially at the skull base, can also lacerate the meninges, causing CSF to leak through the nose (rhinorrhea) or ear (otorrhea) or bacteria or air to enter the cranial vault. Infectious organisms may reach the meninges via cryptic fractures, especially if they involve the paranasal sinuses.

Symptoms, Signs, and Diagnosis

Concussion is characterized by transient posttraumatic loss of awareness or memory, lasting from seconds to minutes, without causing gross structural lesions in the brain and without leaving serious neurologic residua. Patients with concussion rarely are deeply unresponsive. Pupillary reactions and other signs of brain stem function are intact; extensor plantar responses may be present briefly but neither hemiplegia nor decerebrate postural responses to noxious stimulation appear. Lumbar puncture is generally contraindicated in cases of head trauma unless meningitis is suspected and should be performed only after appropriate x-rays or imaging studies.

Postconcussion syndrome commonly follows a mild head injury, more often than a severe one. It includes headache, dizziness, difficulty in concentration, variable amnesia, depression, apathy, and anxiety. Considerable disability can result. The part played by brain damage is unclear. The postconcussion syndrome is more common in patients with a premorbid neurotic disposition. However, studies suggest that even mild trauma can cause neuronal damage. Although this situation lends itself to malingering and fraud with the hope of compensation, many patients have legitimate complaints. The benefits of drug or psychiatric treatment are uncertain.

Cerebral contusions and lacerations are more severe injuries. Depending on severity, they are often accompanied by severe surface wounds and by basilar skull fractures or depression fractures (see also TEMPORAL BONE FRACTURES in Ch. 85). Hemiplegia or other focal signs of cortical dysfunction are common. More severe injuries may cause severe brain edema, producing decorticate rigidity (arms flexed and adducted, legs and often trunk extended) or decerebrate rigidity (jaws clenched, neck retracted, all limbs extended). Coma, hemiplegia, unilaterally or bilaterally dilated and unreactive pupils, and respiratory irregularity may result from initial trauma or internal brain herniation and require immediate therapy. Increased intracranial pressure, producing compression or distortion of the brain stem, sometimes causes BP to rise and pulse and respiration to slow (Cushing's phenomenon). Brain scans may reveal bloody CSF; lumbar puncture is usually contraindicated.

Nonpenetrating trauma is more likely to affect the cerebral hemispheres and underlying diencephalon, which are larger and generally more exposed, than the brain stem. Thus, signs of primary brain stem injury (coma, irregular breathing, fixation of the pupils to light, loss of oculovestibular reflexes, diffuse motor flaccidity) almost always imply severe injury and poor prognosis.

Thoracic damage often accompanies severe head injuries, producing pulmonary edema (some of which is neurogenic), hypoxia, and unstable circulation. Injury to the cervical spine can damage the spinal cord, causing fatal respiratory paralysis or permanent quadriplegia. Proper immobilization should be maintained until stability of the cervical spine has been documented by appropriate imaging studies.

Continued on next page.

> **Acute subdural hematomas** (blood between the dura mater and arachnoid, usually from bleeding of the bridging veins) and **intracerebral hematomas** are common in severe head injury. Along with severe brain edema, they account for most fatalities. All three conditions can cause transtentorial herniation with deepening coma, widening pulse pressure, pupils in midposition or dilated and fixed, spastic hemiplegia with hyperreflexia, quadrispasticity, decorticate rigidity, or decerebrate rigidity (due to progressive rostral-caudal neurologic deterioration). CT or MRI scans can usually identify operable lesions. Surgical excision of large lesions may be lifesaving, but posttraumatic morbidity is often high.
>
> **Chronic subdural hematomas** may not produce symptoms until several weeks after trauma. Although early diagnosis (2 to 4 wk after trauma) may be suggested by delayed neurologic deterioration, later diagnosis can be overlooked because of the time lapse between trauma and the onset of symptoms and signs. Subdural hematomas are more common in alcoholics and patients > 50 yr, in whom the head injury may have been relatively trivial, even forgotten. Increasing daily headache, fluctuating drowsiness or confusion (which may mimic early dementia), and mild-to-moderate hemiparesis are typical. In infants, chronic subdural hematomas can cause head circumference to enlarge, suggesting hydrocephalus. MRI scans are diagnostic; CT scans are less consistently so.

From *The Merck Manual of Diagnosis and Therapy,* Edition 17, pp. 1427-1430, edited by Drs. Mark H. Beers and Robert Berkow. Copyright 1999 by Merck & Co., Inc., Whitehouse Station, NJ. Used with permission.

The Medical Disability Advisor (third edition, 1999) provides information on the common treatments/prognosis of injuries and gives general guidelines on the duration of disabilities resulting from a given injury. The book was published by Reed Group, LTD, in Boulder, Colorado. Exhibit 2-3 contains sample information from *The Medical Disability Advisor.*

Exhibit 2-3
Sample Information From *The Medical Disability Advisor*

Brain Injury
850-854.19

WHAT IS IT?

Brain injury occurs when the tissues of the brain suffer an acute injury that results in temporary, chronic or permanent damage. Brain injury can result in loss of body movement (paralysis), weakness of muscles (paresis), abnormal muscle stiffness and movements (spasticity), memory loss (amnesia) or impairment, loss of consciousness, coma, personality changes, blindness, seizures or disruption of various chemical processes of the body. Causes of brain injury are traumatic such as can result from motor vehicle accidents, gunshot wounds, falls or any other blow to the head and non-traumatic, including strokes from blood clots or broken blood vessels, or tumors of the brain itself or of the tissues surrounding it.

HOW IS IT DIAGNOSED?

History can reveal a motor vehicle accident or fall. The individual (or individual's family members) may report signs of confusion, disorientation or the individual may have been found unconscious. Other symptoms can include headaches, nausea and vomiting, loss of muscle control, muscle weakness, paralysis, blurred vision, dizziness, impaired memory, anxiety, irritability, decreased concentration, insomnia, sleepiness or seizures. Past medical history can reveal episodes of seizures, personality changes, frequent falls or loss of control of normal movements. There may also be a history of alcohol or drug use.

Physical exam: Vital signs may reveal a slow pulse (bradycardia), elevated blood pressure, and the breathing pattern may be irregular. The size of the pupils may be large, tiny or uneven. There may be involuntary eye movements, or restriction of voluntary movement. Drooping of one side of the face is a classic sign that indicates damage to the nerves of the face. Reflexes can be overactive (hyperreflexia). The head and neck may be bruised and swelling. There may be blood in the ear and behind the eardrum, and the individual may show signs of hearing difficulty. Speech can be slurred or absent (aphasia). The individual may show a lack of normal sense of smell. There may be signs of memory failure.

Tests will include x-rays, CT scans, and MRI of the head and neck. Lab tests include blood chemistry tests. Drug and alcohol screens may be performed. A brain wave test electroencephalogram (EEG) may be useful in some cases where seizures are noted.

HOW IS IT TREATED?
Most cases usually require close observation of the individual's vital signs such as pulse, respiration, and blood pressure. The pupils and reflexes should be checked and memory tests should be administered for one to two days. More severe cases may require immediate surgical intervention to relieve pressure on the brain from swelling and bleeding (subdural hematoma). Drugs that decrease brain swelling, control seizures, or lower blood pressure may also be used.

WHAT MIGHT COMPLICATE IT?
Complications might include previously diagnosed or undiagnosed medical conditions such as bleeding disorders, high blood pressure, seizures, drug or alcohol use.

WHAT IS THE PREDICTED OUTCOME?
In most cases, the prognosis is excellent. In severe cases, the outcome may be permanent disability or death.

WHAT ARE POSSIBLE WORK RESTRICTIONS AND ACCOMMODATIONS?
In mild or less severe cases, a worker might temporarily need shorter work hours or more frequent breaks. Time off from work for ongoing rehabilitation and treatment may be necessary.

In severe cases, persons may be left with permanent and/or mental impairment that prevents them from doing previous duties. Accommodations may need to be made so that the workplace is wheelchair accessible.

WHAT ELSE MIGHT IT BE?
Metabolic disorders such as diabetes or hypothyroidism, meningitis, drug and alcohol abuse, or misuse of prescription drugs.

WHO ARE THE APPROPRIATE SPECIALISTS FOR TREATMENT, REFERRAL, OR INDEPENDENT EXAMINATION?
Neurologist, neurosurgeon, internist, physiatrist, and psychiatrist.

Continued on next page.

> **WHAT ARE THE FACTORS THAT MIGHT INFLUENCE LENGTH OF DISABILITY?**
> Factors that influence length of disability are age, severity of injury, and the person's willingness and ability to follow a treatment plan.
>
> **WHAT IS THE EXPECTED LENGTH OF DISABILITY?**
> Mild concussion. Disability may be permanent with severe concussion.
>
> | Job Classification | Minimum Expectancy | Optimum | Maximum Expectancy |
> |---|---|---|---|
> | SEDENTARY WORK | 2 DAYS | 7 DAYS | 21 DAYS |
> | LIGHT WORK | 2 DAYS | 7 DAYS | 21 DAYS |
> | MEDIUM WORK | 2 DAYS | 7 DAYS | 21 DAYS |
> | VERY HEAVY WORK | 2 DAYS | 7 DAYS | 21 DAYS |

Reprinted with permission from *The Medical Disability Advisor: Workplace Guidelines for Disability Duration*, 3d ed. (1997), Presley Reed, MD. © Reed Group, Ltd. Boulder, CO, (800) 347-7443. All rights reserved.

Redundancy of Treatment

Certain treatments essentially repeat other treatments. This problem is particularly common in chiropractic and physical therapy treatments (both of which are addressed at greater length in Chapter 3).

Tests can also be redundant. Imaging tests such as X-rays, CT scans, and MRIs serve a similar purpose. Multiple imaging tests may sometimes be necessary when identifying the abnormality or structure in question is difficult. However, claim representatives are entitled to an explanation as to why the original imaging or other testing was not satisfactory.

As in determining the necessity of treatment, a claim representative's experience, certain reference works, and expert consultants can help to identify redundant treatment.

Alternative Treatment

In many cases, a claimant can be treated in an alternative manner that is much less expensive and equally medically sound. Patients and their physicians may not consider alternative treatments if existing treatment is fully insured. For example, one medically sound alternative in many cases is to do nothing, or more precisely, to defer treatment while the physician simply follows the progress of the condition. The human body has a remarkable ability to heal itself. Much of the treatment provided by physicians does nothing more than relieve symptoms, with the real cure coming from the body itself. Although the alternative of doing nothing is often appropriate, claim representatives should only maintain that a particular treatment is unwarranted if they have solid expert support.

Because hospitalization is expensive, claim representatives should review alternatives. Hospitalization should be avoided when possible.

Many conditions that were once treated only in hospitals or that required long hospital stays are now treated on an outpatient basis. Likewise, many forms of long-term treatment can be performed at home rather than in an institution. Utilization review (UR) and case management experts, discussed in Chapter 1, can provide excellent consultation services regarding alternative treatments.

Further Treatment

Unless a patient has fully recovered or reached a maximum level of medical improvement, further treatment should be expected. Claim representatives generally find that controlling future treatment is more effective than criticizing past treatment. However, controlling further treatment requires a clear statement of a treatment plan from the treating physician and careful analysis of any disability statements by the treating physician.

Treatment Plan

A physician should always have a plan for a patient's future treatment. Otherwise, the treatment will be largely haphazard and, as a result, may be ineffective. A claim representative should be aware of this plan. In communicating the plan to the claim representative, the physician reveals when he or she expects the treatment to conclude, what the expected results are, and when alternatives will be considered if the current treatment does not produce results. Making these statements also forces the physician to think through the course of treatment and to justify any treatment that exceeds what was expected in nature or duration.

With certain medical conditions, the physician can express future outcomes only in terms of probability. The claim representative cannot insist that the physician be more definite when it is impossible to do so. A physician who describes the expected outcome as uncertain should nevertheless be able to identify the possible outcomes and the treatments that would be expected with each.

Disability Statements

As explained in Chapter 3, a physician cannot make a meaningful statement about disability without knowing the physical demands of the patient's job. This is especially true for statements about future disability. Meaningful statements about future disability should include descriptions of specific impairments that the patient is expected to suffer and their duration.

Identification and Control of Complex Claims

Claim representatives evaluate medical treatment for most cases on their own because most cases are too small to justify the expense of expert assistance. Furthermore, the medical treatment in most cases is legitimate and need not be analyzed by an expert. When the issues are relatively straightforward, in-house medical references may be sufficient to confirm payment for a claim. In many simple cases, payment can be made strictly on the basis of an itemized bill without supporting medical records. In more complicated cases, extensive medical records, including clinical and institutional records, are required before an informed decision as to what is payable can be made. In still other cases, a claim representative may need a medical consultant or an independent medical examiner to clarify the situation.

Many injury claims presented for reimbursement can be handled on the basis of a loss report and a standardized bill for services from the medical provider. A high percentage of injury claims, both first party and liability, involve minimal treatment over a brief period of time and are entirely legitimate. Because the volume of injury claims handled by one claim representative can be very high, and because most of these claims are for small amounts, a claim representative must separate the cases requiring extensive investigation from the cases that can be handled with minimal investigation and documentation. One of the occupational hazards of claim handling is the tendency to become cynical about the legitimacy of injury claims. Cynicism may be justified in a few cases, but the vast majority of claims presented for reimbursement are simple, straightforward cases that can be resolved quickly by appropriate payment.

Even many serious injuries are straightforward. For example, a loss report may indicate that the injured person sustained a fracture of the femur. During an interview, the claimant said that he was taken to the hospital, where a surgical procedure was performed to repair the fracture. The claimant is currently casted and walking with crutches. Physician and hospital billings substantiate the claim and the extent of the injury. The only questions not yet resolved concern the probability of a functional impairment and whether these functional limitations will create a disability for the patient. A request of the attending physician to address these questions and to provide support for his or her findings with documentation from the medical record might complete the investigation.

One of the most important functions of a claim representative is to identify cases that must be evaluated with additional assistance. Such cases typically involve serious or complex injuries and a significant financial exposure for the insurer. Early involvement of experts is essential for effective medical management. Thus, claim representatives must be thoroughly familiar with the criteria used by their insurers to identify serious cases.

For cases handled by one claim representative, the claim representative must rely on his or her knowledge of medicine, medical practices, and medical cost containment. Many claim representatives receive no special training in these areas and must educate themselves or accept the claimant's case at face value.

As an insurance professional, the claim representative must investigate and verify injury claims and learn to ask the appropriate medical questions. A claim representative is not a physician or a medical expert, but an insurance expert whose role is to develop adequate information in a reasonable period of time in order to make timely payment of bona fide claims and to resolve all others.

The typical criteria used to identify serious cases are type of injury, dollar amount, and medical complexity. In addition, claim representatives must be aware of cases that may be complex because of potential exaggeration. In well-run claim operations, supervisors and managers play a significant role in screening cases. In addition to the serious cases identified below, which typically require careful investigation and documentation, claim representatives should develop a means of identifying claims whose causes and treatments may be dubious.

Identification by Type of Injury

Certain types of injuries are known to be serious or troublesome to insurers. Some insurers consider all injuries of a certain type to be serious and require them to be brought to the attention of supervisors, managers, or outside experts. Some examples follow:

- Quadriplegia or paraplegia
- Amputation (other than fingers and toes)
- Loss of sight or hearing
- Third-degree burns over more than 15 percent of the body
- Brain trauma
- Joint replacements

The advantage of using the type of injury as a criterion for identifying serious cases is that it is not ambiguous. Claim representatives will always know whether to handle a case on their own as soon as they know the nature of the injury. The disadvantage of this criterion is that some serious cases may not be listed and might therefore be overlooked until it is too late. For example, cases of low back pain are usually not serious, but some can develop into claims for permanent total disability.

Identification by Dollar Amount or Length of Disability

Some claim departments require claim representatives to involve supervisors, managers, or experts whenever the case appears to be worth more than a certain dollar amount. A variation of this procedure is to require all cases expected to involve a certain length of disability to be referred. That is, cases involving more than four weeks of disability, for example, or cases involving any disability at all may have to be referred. Identifying serious cases by dollar amount or length of disability is the most common criterion used in claim departments. Most cases that would be identified by type of injury would also be identified as serious on the basis of dollar amount or length of disability.

To be effective, this identification criterion must be applied early in the case. Claim representatives must be able to accurately and diligently project dollar exposures. Claim representatives using this criterion use the same mental process as is used in reserving a claim. The reserve should represent the amount expected to be spent on the case. Accurate reserves should result in the accurate identification of cases needing more assistance. The advantage of this approach to identifying serious cases is that it does not exclude seemingly ordinary injuries with a significant dollar exposure.

Identification by Medical Complexity

Some insurers require claim representatives to refer any case in which the claim representative is not familiar with the nature of the injury or treatment. Identification by medical complexity is advantageous because it provides a standard that differs by claim representative depending on the knowledge of each claim representative. Ideally, this system would help to identify only cases needing referral.

The drawback of this criterion is that it requires claim representatives to recognize what they do not know. In addition, in many cases, the claim representative understands almost all of the case, but not everything. Some cases that should be referred are therefore not referred.

Identifiers of Exaggerated Claims

Some common characteristics indicate the need for additional medical investigation. The presence of one or more of these characteristics in a given claim is not conclusive proof that the injury claim is exaggerated. But the more there are of these characteristics, the more thorough the investigation should be:

- An aggravated pre-existing condition that under normal circumstances requires long-term continuing medical care (diabetes or arthritis, for example).
- An injury or the severity of an injury that seems inconsistent with the facts of the loss or the physical evidence—for example, a serious neck injury allegedly caused by an automobile accident with little or no damage to either vehicle.
- Problems characterized only by subjective reports. Injuries such as strain or sprain, anxiety or depression, or an ill-defined syndrome (a collection of symptoms) require the claim representative to request extensive records of the physician's findings in order to help identify the extent of the medical problem.
- Certain personality types who view trauma and especially minor injuries as a way of drawing attention to themselves and receiving care from a medical provider. The needs of these individuals are almost impossible to meet, and their claims are often characterized by long letters, daily phone calls about minor details, and an exaggerated willingness to discuss all aspects of the injury and treatment.
- The use of unusual or controversial medical treatment such as acupuncture, rolfing, or deep massage, or treatment coupled with

prescriptions for medical appliances that appear excessive for the injury involved, such as at-home whirlpool baths, transcutaneous electrical nerve stimulation (T.E.N.S.) units, or special support beds and mattresses for routine back or neck sprains. (Chapter 5 will discuss T.E.N.S. units in detail.)
- Involvement of legal representation.
- Redundant diagnostic testing as in the use of X-rays, followed by a CT scan, thermograms, and eventually an MRI, each with negative results, and often associated with extensive laboratory tests and electronic testing such as EEGs and EKGs.
- The presence of certain injuries such as sprains or strains, especially of the neck and back, or other soft tissue injuries that seem resistant to healing; the presence of conditions such as temporomandibular joint syndrome (TMJ), thoracic outlet syndrome, post-traumatic stress disorder, carpal tunnel syndrome, or any psychological or psychiatric disorder that appears to be inconsistent with the severity of the injury.
- Accidents involving injuries to multiple parties who have identical injuries, the same medical provider, and the same attorney.
- Legal liability. In general, claimants who are not negligent might profit most by exaggerating their claims in order to increase the amount of recovery.
- Individuals who may be subject to seasonal layoffs, such as construction workers or farm laborers, who may exaggerate injury claims when the time of year at which they expect to be laid off approaches.

Exhibits 2-4 and 2-5 list the indicators of casualty fraud and workers compensation fraud, respectively.

Claim representatives must remember that these circumstances are simply indicators. No injury claim should be denied or compromised simply because of the presence of one or all of these indicators. These indicators simply mean that additional medical investigation is needed before the claim can be concluded.

Involvement of Supervisors and Managers

In any well-run claim operation, claim representatives are not the only personnel involved in deciding which cases require additional assistance. Supervisors regularly review files and should spot cases that claim representatives should not be handling alone. A supervisor should know each claim representative's level of expertise and is responsible if the claim representative continues handling a serious case.

Managers are responsible for establishing criteria for case referral and for selecting outside experts for the claim department. The experts should be interviewed to determine their skills, staffing, claim philosophy, and fees. Managers are also responsible for communicating the claim department's needs to each expert service.

Exhibit 2-4
Indicators of Casualty Fraud

National Insurance Crime Bureau
10330 South Roberts Road
Palos Hills, Illinois 60465
708-430-2430

Indicators of Casualty Fraud
Detection--The First Line of Defense

Most claims are legitimate, but many are inflated or fraudulent. Therefore, it is appropriate for the adjuster to review all claims for possible fraud. Determining the "fraud probability" of any claim is facilitated when the adjuster is familiar with various fraud indicators.

These indicators, or fraud possibility factors, should help isolate those claims which merit closer scrutiny. No one indicator by itself is necessarily suspicious. Even the presence of several indicators, while suggestive of possible fraud, does not mean that a fraud has been committed. Indicators of possible fraud are not evidence that fraud has occurred.

All suspicious claims, though they may have to be paid for lack of conclusive evidence of fraud, should be referred to NICB.

General Indicators of Insurance Fraud

Note: Adjusters should familiarize themselves with the following general indicators of insurance fraud which may apply to more than one type of fraud scheme. After review of the general indicators, the adjuster can then refer to the more specific fraud categories which follow.

It should be noted that the following categories of fraud are separated merely to facilitate understanding of that type of fraud. However, multiple forms of fraud may appear in a single claim. For example, in a slip and fall products liability claim, there may also be evidence of both medical and lost earnings fraud.

- Claimant or insured is excessively eager to accept blame for an accident, or is overly pushy or demanding of a quick, reduced settlement.
- Claimant or insured is unusually familiar with insurance terms and procedures, medical, or vehicle repair terminology.
- One or more claimants or insured list a post office box or hotel as address.
- All transactions were conducted in person; claimant avoids using the telephone or the mail.
- The kind of accident or type of vehicles involved are not typical of those seen on a regular basis.
- Claimant threatens to go to an attorney or physician if the claim is not quickly settled.
- Claimant is a transient or out-of-towner on vacation.

Indicators of Automobile Accident Schemes

- Either no police report or an over-the-counter report for an accident resulting in multiple injuries and/or extensive physical damage.
- Accident occurred shortly after one or more of the vehicles were purchased or registered, or after the addition of comprehensive and collision coverage to the policy.
- Insured has a history of accidents within a short period of time on one policy. Index returns indicate an active claim history.
- Insured has no record of prior insurance coverage although damaged vehicle was purchased much earlier than inception of policy and date of loss.
- Expensive, late model automobile was recently purchased with cash (no lienholder).
- Attorney's lien or representation letter is dated the day of the accident or soon after.

Indicators of Auto Physical Damage Fraud

- Serious accident with expensive physical damage claim but only minor, subjectively diagnosed injuries, with little or no medical treatment.
- Despite expensive damage claims, the claimant vehicle remains drivable. Often, there are no towing charges for removing vehicle from the scene of the accident.
- Claimant vehicle was struck by a rental vehicle soon after the rental had occurred.
- Claimant vehicle is not to be repaired locally, but driven or shipped out of state for repair.
- All vehicles in a reported accident are taken to the same body shop.
- Claimant vehicles are not readily available for independent appraisal.
- Reported accident occurred on private property near residence of those involved.
- Claimant vehicle is repaired before the damage can be inspected.
- Claimant vehicle is parked in a way or at a location that makes inspecting the damage difficult.

Indicators of Medical Fraud/Claim Inflation

- Three or more occupants in the claimant or "struck vehicle"; all of them report similar injuries.
- All injuries are subjectively diagnosed, such as headaches, muscle spasms, traumas, and others.
- Medical claims are extensive, but collision is minor with little physical damage to vehicles.
- All of the claimants submit medical bills from the same doctor or medical facility.
- Medical bills submitted are photocopies of originals.
- Summary medical bills are submitted without dates and descriptions of office visits and treatments, or treatment extends for a lengthy period without any interim bills.
- Vehicle driven by claimant is an old "clunker" with minimal coverage.
- Insured, even though legally liable for accident, is adamant that claimants were responsible for accident, indicating that the insured may have been "targeted" by the claimants.
- Claimants retain legal representation immediately after the accident is reported.
- Minor accident produces major medical costs, lost wages and unusually expensive demands for pain and suffering.
- Past experience demonstrates that the physician's bill and report, regardless of the varying accident circumstances, is always the same.
- Treatment prescribed for the various injuries resulting from differing accidents is always the same in terms of duration and type of therapy.
- Medical bills indicate routine treatment being provided on Sundays or holidays.

Indicators of Lost Earnings Fraud

- Employment information is for an unknown business, often with a post office box for address, or a street address in a residential area.
- Business telephone number is connected to an answering machine or answering service.
- Lost earnings statement is handwritten or typed on blank paper, not business letterhead.
- Claimant started employment shortly before accident occurred, or is self-employed.
- One or more elements of claim is questionable: e.g. length of absence, rate of pay, income incompatible with claimant's residence.
- Efforts to verify lost wage statement with employer raise doubts about employer's legitimacy or about the actual employment of the claimant.

Slip & Fall and Food/Products Liability

- Use of a prop, i.e. broken glasses, broken dental plate, etc. to support or inflate the claim.
- Presence of an overly enthusiastic witness at the scene of the incident.
- No supporting evidence of foreign or contaminated substance; claimant threw food out and has only the can, box or wrapper.

Copyright © 1992 National Insurance Crime Bureau. All rights reserved.

Exhibit 2-5
Indicators of Workers Compensation Fraud

National Insurance Crime Bureau
10330 South Roberts Road
Palos Hills, Illinois 60465
708-430-2430

Indicators of Workers' Compensation Fraud
Detection--The First Line of Defense

Most claims are legitimate, but many are inflated or fraudulent, and the adjuster should review all claims for possible fraud. These indicators, or fraud possibility factors, should help isolate those claims meriting closer scrutiny. No one indicator by itself is necessarily suspicious. Even the presence of several indicators, while suggestive of possible fraud, does not mean that a fraud has definitely been committed. Indicators are "red flags" only, not actual evidence.

The Claimant, Prior Claim History and Current Work Status

- Employee is disgruntled, soon-to-retire, or facing imminent firing or layoff.
- Employee is involved in seasonal work that is about to end.
- Employee took unexplained or excessive time off prior to claimed injury.
- Employee takes more time off than the claimed injury seems to warrant.
- Employee is nomadic and has a history of short-term employment.
- Employee is new on the job.
- Employee is experiencing financial difficulties and/or domestic problems prior to submission of claim.
- Employee recently purchased private disability policies.
- Employee changes physician when a release for work has been issued.
- Employee has a history of reporting subjective injuries.
- Review of a rehab report describes the employee as being muscular, well tanned, with calloused hands and grease under the fingernails.
- First notification of injury or claim made after employee is terminated or laid off.
- Disputes the average weekly wage due to additional income (i.e. cash, per diem and/or 1099 income).
- Has several other family members also receiving workers' compensation benefits or other "social insurance" benefits, i.e. unemployment.
- Demands quick settlement decisions or commitments.
- Demands quick payments for medical providers, etc..
- Is unusually familiar with workers' compensation claim handling procedures and laws.
- Is consistently uncooperative.
- Surveillance or "tip" indicates that the totally disabled worker is currently employed elsewhere.
- Employee has submitted substantial material misrepresentation on the employment application.
- Employee comes to office for delivery of benefit checks, avoids use of U.S. Mail.
- Employee refuses to allow visits or rehabilitation at home or specifies plenty of warning time prior to a visit.
- Employee participates in contact sports or physically demanding hobbies.
- After injury, employee is never home or spouse/relative answering phone states the employee "just stepped out," or may have to contact him/her by pager.
- Return calls to residence have strange or unexpected background noises which indicate that it may not be a residence.
- Employee protests about returning to work and never seems to improve.
- Employee cancels or fails to keep appointment, or refuses a diagnostic procedure to confirm an injury.
- Employee complains to carrier's CEO or executive management at home office to press for payment.

- Social Security number provided does not belong to employee.
- Applicant refuses or cannot produce solid or correct identification.
- Employee's family member(s) know nothing about the claim.

Circumstances of the Accident

- Accident occurs late Friday afternoon or shortly after the employee reports to work on Monday.
- Accident is not witnessed, or witnesses to the accident conflict with the applicant's version or with one another.
- Employee has leg/arm injuries at odd time, i.e. at lunch hour.
- Fellow workers hear rumors circulating that accident was not legitimate.
- Accident occurs in an area where injured employee would not normally be.
- Accident is not the type that the employee should be involved in, i.e. an office worker who is lifting heavy objects on a loading dock.
- Accident occurs just prior to a strike, or near the end of probationary period.
- Employer's first report of claim contrasts with description of accident set forth in medical history.
- Details of accident are vague or contradictory, have inconsistencies, are not credible.
- Incident is not promptly reported by employee to supervisor.

Medical Treatment

- Diagnosis is inconsistent with treatment.
- Physician is known for handling suspect claims.
- Treatment for extensive injuries is protracted though the accident was minor.
- "Boilerplate" medical reports are identical to other reports from same doctor, do not identify by gender or get gender wrong.
- Workers' compensation insurer and health carrier are billed simultaneously; payment is accepted from both.
- Summary medical bills submitted without dates or descriptions of office visits.
- Medical bills submitted are photocopies of originals.
- Extensive or unnecessary treatment for minor, subjective injuries.
- Treatment directed to a separate facility in which the referring physician has a financial interest (especially if this is not disclosed in advance).
- Referral for treatment/testing to facility close to referring facility.
- Injuries are all subjective, i.e. pain, headaches, nausea, inability to sleep.
- Treatment dates appear on holidays or other days that facilities would not normally be open.
- Employee is immediately referred for a wide variety of psychiatric tests, when the original claim involved trauma only. These claims usually present with vague complaints of "stress."
- Inappropriate expensive medical equipment prescribed for minor injury.
- Alleged injury relates to a pre-existing injury or health problem.

The Claimant's Attorney

- Attorney becomes involved early in the claims process.
- Attorney is known for handling suspicious claims.
- Attorney lien or representation letter dated the day of the reported incident.
- Attorney threatens further legal action unless a quick settlement is made.
- Attorney inquires about a settlement or buy out early in the life of the claim.
- Employee initially wants to settle with insurer, but later retains an attorney with increased subjective complaints.
- High incidence of applications from a specific firm.
- Pattern of occupational type claims for "dying" industries, i.e. black lung, asbestosis; wholesale claim handling by law firms and multiple class action suits.
- Same doctor/lawyer pair previously observed to handle this kind of injury.
- Employee receives all mail by and through his attorney.

Copyright © 1992 National Insurance Crime Bureau. All rights reserved. Revised 10/1994 & 10/1996

Medical Documents

The claim process for injury cases has a beginning (the report of loss) and an ending (payment, denial, or compromise), but the intermediate steps vary depending on the type and complexity of the claim. As indicated in Exhibit 2-6, the claim representative must at each step judge the adequacy of documentation. If the medical documentation is adequate, the claim can be concluded. If it is not, the claim representative should continue to gather medical evidence until all questions have been answered.

Exhibit 2-6
Claim Verification Process

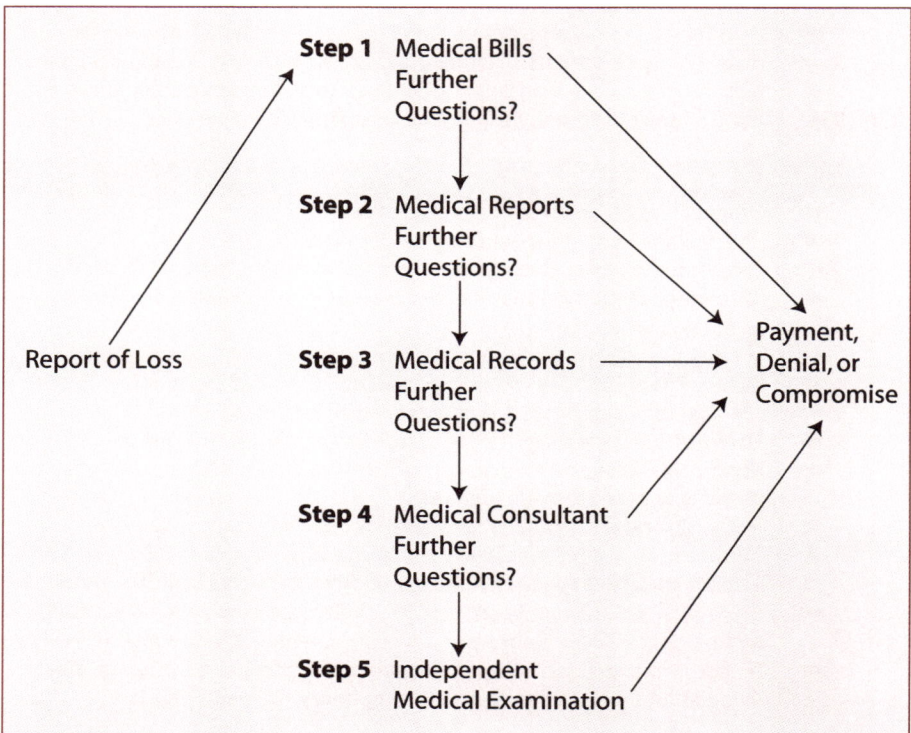

Medical records are fundamental to the investigation and documentation of medical and injury claims. The compensability of a claim often hinges on obscure or deeply buried information in the medical records. Claim representatives or medical consultants must sometimes pore through volumes of medical documents in order to piece together the information they need to make a decision on compensation. Claim representatives cannot rely on claimants to give accurate accounts of their treatment since so many claimants do not pay attention to, or do not understand, their treatment. As a result, medical records are the primary acceptable evidence of medical treatment.

The types of medical records described in this section are the basic tools used to determine the validity of an injury claim and what is owed on the claim. Medical bills and records can also guide the investigation. These records may clarify whether the loss is covered and can provide information concerning how the loss occurred. These documents often include a statement from the victim about how the injury occurred, and the claim representative can rely fairly heavily on the truth of these statements since they are made shortly after the injury while memories are still fresh and since they are made for the purpose of obtaining treatment.

Medical records can provide clues to unrelated or pre-existing conditions, and they can indicate prior admissions to the same treating facility. Blood-alcohol levels and the presence of other substances in the body are also often documented in these records. This section explains the purpose of and standards for medical records, identifies and describes the types of medical records used in a claim investigation, and explains the importance of and considerations related to obtaining these records.

Purpose of and Standards for Medical Records

Medical records, medical reports, clinical notes, and medicolegal reports offer different types of information for a claim review. Professionals from different medical disciplines prepare these records, and each type of document has a unique role in the care and treatment of an injured patient. To understand the relevance of these documents in the claim review process, the claim representative must recognize that these documents offer objective as well as subjective information. Claim representatives can better understand the contents and organization of medical records when they understand the purpose of and standards for preparation of such records.

Purpose of Medical Records

A **medical record** is any document that identifies the patient and the health care and services provided to the patient. It is a collection of information written by the health-care professional responsible for the patient's care pertaining to the patient's health, including past and present personal and familial histories and past and present illnesses or injuries and treatments. A medical record is legally viewed as official proof that specific patient services were provided.[1] The term record, as defined for purposes of the Federal Privacy Act of 1974, means tangible or documentary record.[2] The purpose of this record is to document and plan current patient care. The kind and amount of information to be included are dictated by what is essential to resolve a medical problem or to prevent future problems.

Medical records are the health-care provider's means of communicating to other health-care professionals. They also help health-care providers to organize their observations. The information in a medical record should be objective and concise.

Health-care providers must follow numerous requirements in preparing a medical record. The record must document the course of care and treatment and demonstrate appropriateness of care, provide sufficient information to establish a fair fee for service, and provide data needed to protect the legal interests of the patient, the medical provider, and any health-care facility at which the medical services were provided. The records may also help to educate other health-care professionals, provide data to expand the body of medical research and development, and possibly identify diseases that threaten public health.

Standards for Preparation of Medical Records

Health-care professionals should learn the scope, necessity, and value of accurate record keeping and report writing in their undergraduate and graduate education. A technician, whether involved in laboratory research or in taking X-rays, is taught to record the procedure and identify when it was done and by whom, and to describe the steps followed to ensure the quality of the procedure. Nurses are taught to document their observations, the treatment they provide, and the patient's response to that treatment. They also document information reported to other attending health-care providers concerning patient progress or problems.

Textbooks explain the administration of medical records; the value and use of medical records; the development, content, and maintenance of medical records in various institutional settings; the forms and designs of authorizations for disclosure of information; the nomenclature and classification systems; and the legal aspects of medical records.[3] In graduate and postgraduate training, students are further educated in recording and reporting information specific to the needs of a given discipline or specialty. Medical education stresses the need for detail in reporting the treatment provided and as proof of service rendered.

Health-care professionals are state-licensed and have a responsibility to work within their scope of practice as determined by state statute or code. The scope of practice describes the areas of treatment a professional is licensed to provide; it also requires each provider to bear the responsibility for maintaining records.

Types of Medical Documents

The most common medical documents are bills, clinical notes, reports, hospital records, and records from other institutions.

Medical Bills

Once an injury claim has been presented, a standard coded, itemized medical bill provided by the health-care facility or medical provider is the first document required for verification of the claim. There are various forms of bills, ranging from handwritten notations on a physician's prescription pad to refined and standardized formats in which each procedure or treatment is given a code specifying the diagnosis and itemizing the services rendered.

Many health insurers, Medicare, Medicaid systems, and workers compensation insurers require standardized billing on a UB-92 (hospital billing form) or HCFA-1500 (physician billing form). Examples of both billing forms and the importance of their format are explained in Chapter 6, and annotated examples are shown in that section of the text. The Health Care Financing Administration (HCFA) developed these forms to provide details of medical services provided for insurance reimbursement purposes. Coded and itemized bills in a standardized format should be obtained for all injury claims as a first step in a logical system of proper claim verification. The information contained in standardized bills may be sufficient to conclude a minor claim, but medical bills are not clinical documentation.

Clinical Notes

Clinical notes are a collection of the health-care provider's observations, examination, work-up, and treatment. Clinical notes should include an extensive review from the initial visit, the findings of any outside diagnostic services, and a detailed description of the plan of treatment. The notes should provide data that can be used to verify the cause or severity of an injury or illness. The clinical notes also refresh the provider's memory on subsequent visits. The provider can rely on previous notes to decide what questions to ask the patient, to determine what symptoms to observe, and to plan for any possible changes in the treatment. This type of record keeping helps the provider to control the treatment.

Medical Reports

A medical report may be a part of the total medical record or a summary of the information within the medical record. As part of the medical record, a report summarizes one aspect of treatment. For example, it may detail a surgical procedure, describe a specimen sent to the lab for a pathology evaluation, or state the progress of a patient in a physical therapy session.

Medicolegal reports are prepared by the health-care provider for an attorney, a claim representative, or an industrial commission. They describe the injury, the patient's current physical and mental condition, and the expected outcome of the patient's treatment. The report is used in negotiating a settlement, and it may also be the basis for further medical and legal research in a malpractice case. Medicolegal reports also summarize a case for health-care providers before deposition or trial. These reports are not intended to provide all details of a case, but should summarize a case, concluding with the provider's opinion. Even with a medicolegal report, a claim representative may need to review the complete medical records to verify details in a report.

A **narrative report** is similar to a medicolegal report in that the provider summarizes the course of treatment and states a diagnosis. Narrative reports are generally written for other health-care providers and are usually accompanied by supporting documentation from the medical record. A narrative report may also be written for an insurer in support of a claim of injury or a claim by the provider for a fee for service, or to substantiate the need for services provided.

To complete any of these reports, the provider's signature and date of review and approval must be included. Completing a report with a statement that reads "dictated but not read" indicates that the provider may or may not agree with the report content. A signature, on the other hand, makes the provider accountable.

Exhibit 2-7 summarizes the types of information in medical reports.

Exhibit 2-7
Information in a Medical Report

Summary Report Form	
Patient Name	Physical Examination
Address	Height/Weight
Age	Body System Review
Date of Injury	Description of Injury
Facts of the Accident	Current Medical Treatment
Past Medical History	Consultations
Current Medical History	Level of Functional Impairment/ Restrictions
Laboratory/X-Ray Findings	Prognosis

Because all medical reports are essentially written from memory by the attending medical provider, all elements of a report (illustrated in Exhibit 2-7) must be included in the body of the report. If elements are missing, the claim representative should continue to investigate the case by securing the clinical or hospital records and clarifying any questionable areas in the medical reports.

Hospital Records

Hospital records detail the care and treatment of the patient while in the hospital. Such records are evidence of what the hospital is accomplishing.[4] Licensure and accreditation requirements mandate that hospitals maintain records at a specified level of completeness and accuracy. Hospitals are also required to control the dissemination of such information. These requirements and guidelines are established by the Department of Health and Human Services, the Joint Commission on Accreditation of Hospitals, and state law and/or regulations. The Joint Commission on Accreditation of Hospitals (JCAH) is a voluntary organization. Although voluntary, JCAH standards are as influential with hospitals as are state and federal regulations. The JCAH has specific standards regarding the contents and maintenance of medical records. The JCAH requires records to be maintained for all patients, and that the records be detailed enough for physicians to provide continuing care or consultations or to assume the care of the patient, and to permit utilization review and quality assessment activities.[5] The JCAH also specifically requires all medical records to contain the following information:

- Identification data
- Medical history
- Report of physical examination
- Diagnostic and therapeutic orders
- Evidence of informed consent
- Clinical observations, including progress notes, consultations, and opinions
- Reports of procedures and tests
- Conclusion at end of hospitalization or treatment[6]

The flow of medical information in hospital records begins in the hospital's admissions office. When a patient is admitted, the first and most essential forms are completed. This part of the process provides the administrative data needed to identify the patient and assigns a patient identification number or hospital number that will be used on all medical records for the patient throughout the hospital stay.

The nursing service develops and maintains a chart on which all pertinent medical information is recorded. The chart is kept at the nursing station on the floor where the patient is staying. The admitting physician is responsible for compiling the history and performing the physical examination. Other physicians may be called in for consultation or additional care and treatment. All health-care providers involved in the case record on the chart their findings and services provided. This system provides easy access to pertinent information for all health-care providers involved with the patient.

When the patient is discharged, the file is sent to the medical records department for storage. Any subsequent reports are sent to the medical records department to be combined with the existing record. Exhibit 2-8 illustrates the flow of medical information within the hospital system.

Claim representatives should know what records might be included in a patient's chart so that relevant information can be obtained during the claim review process. Claim representatives should be able to clarify which records they need because if they request the entire record, they will receive unnecessary information. In addition, delivery of the information will be delayed because of the time required to reproduce an entire file. Furthermore, copy charges for records by a hospital are usually by the page.

Exhibit 2-9 lists the records and reports that may be available from a medical chart along with the information contained in each.

Other Medical Records

The emergency room is considered an outpatient facility. Depending upon the hospital's policy, the emergency care records may or may not be included in the inpatient hospital chart.

Exhibit 2-8
Medical Chart Records

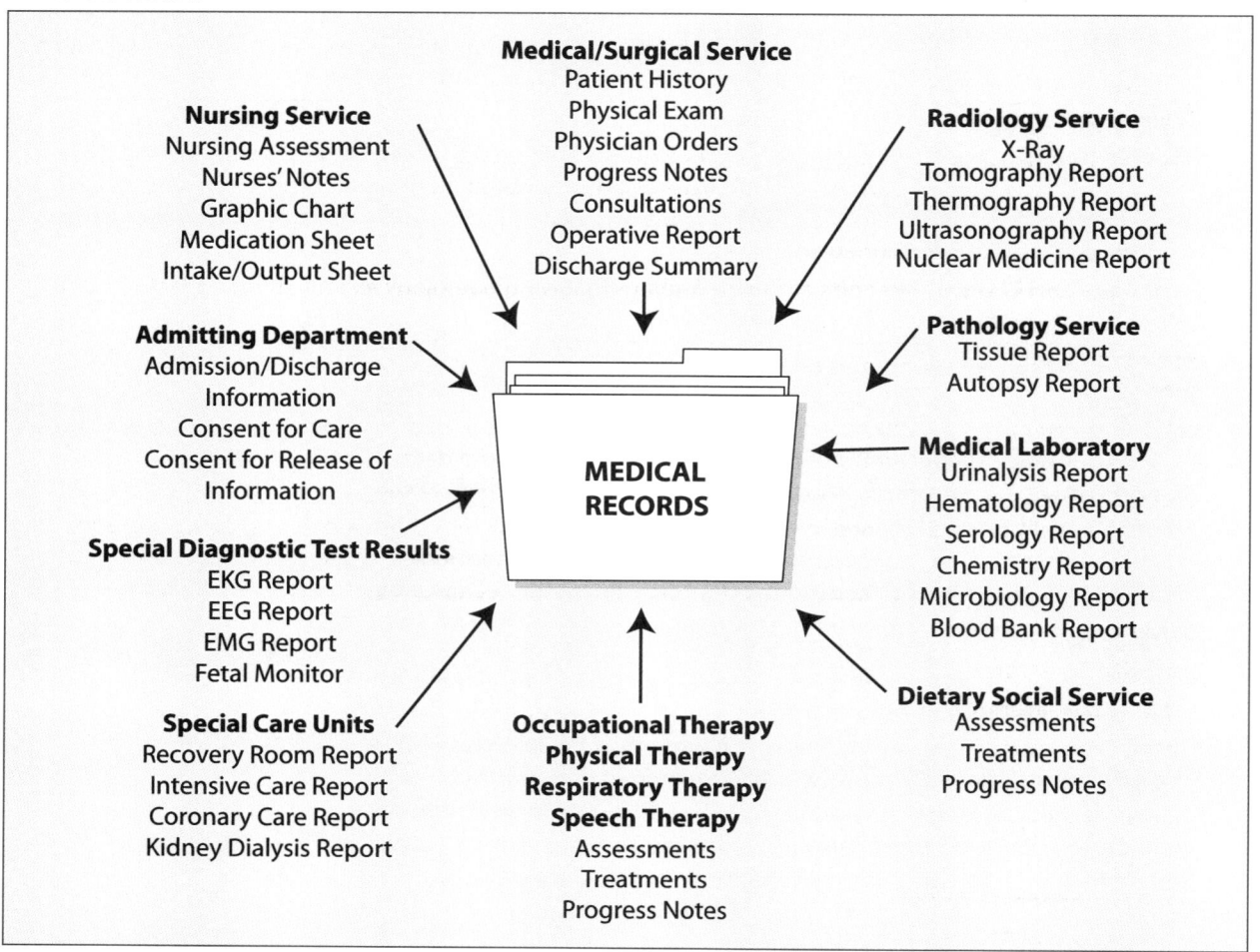

Exhibit 2-9
Medical Chart Records

Admission Record	Data required to accurately identify the patient; to include name, address, age, religious preference, marital status, next of kin, attending physician, payment source, admitting diagnosis, and type of admission.
Admission History & Physical Exam Report	Chief complaint, history of present illness, personal and familial history, body system review, physical examination, and admitting impressions/diagnosis.
Discharge Summary	Concise summary of the course of hospital stay including significant findings, procedures performed, condition of patient at discharge, and instructions given to patient and/or family.
Physicians' Orders	Diagnostic and therapeutic orders dated and signed by the attending physician and/or any other physician in attendance during the course of stay.
Physicians' Progress	Brief note written by any physician in attendance following an assessment of the patient or treatment of the patient to note findings and/or results.
Nursing Record	Record consisting of information on patient care assessment, planning, intervention, and evaluation.

Short Stay Record	A condensed record may be kept for patients who require fewer than 48 hours of hospitalization. Patient identification information, description of the condition, physician's findings, treatment given, and other data to justify diagnosis and treatment. No discharge summary is required.
Other Reports	
Consultation Reports	Attending physician requests an evaluation by another provider stating the purpose and the nature of the consultation desired. The report in return is a narrative description to the attending physician of findings and recommendations. Signed and dated.
Pathology and Clinical Laboratory Reports	Reports of clinical findings following pathology examinations and laboratory tests. Signed and dated.
Radiological and Other Diagnostic	
Laboratory Reports	Physician impressions following a review of the diagnostic procedure results per film video, scope, tracing, etc. Signed and dated.
Social Services	May contain intimate details of the patient's life. Some of the information obtained may also be considered hearsay. For this reason many hospitals require a summary of such records be made to include the information considered to be of value to the physician and other health-care personnel providing care.
Other Areas:	
Intensive Care Units	
Labor and Delivery	
Dietary	
Therapy	
Psychotherapy	
Speech Therapy	
Occupational Therapy	
Respiratory Therapy	
Physical Therapy	

Nevertheless, like in-hospital records, these records must meet JCAH and other legal standards. Therefore, the information in emergency room records should be concise and objective, documenting the need for services provided. The source of any information in emergency room records should always be identified.

Emergency room records include patient identification, time and means of arrival, pertinent history of illness or injury, physical findings, and vital signs. Also documented is emergency care given to the patient before arrival, such as that provided by the ambulance service, as well as the diagnosis and therapeutic orders given by the attending physician, and whether the patient declines any orders. Clinical observations, the disposition of the patient, and results of treatment are also reported. Any instructions given to the patient or family for follow-up care should be noted.

Ambulatory care records must meet JCAH standards for content and maintenance. Ambulatory care centers provide for outpatient surgical and diagnostic treatment requiring short-term care. Highly skilled medical providers can treat and monitor the patient on a same-day basis. Information for ambulatory records should include patient identification data; relevant history of illness or injury; physical findings; diagnostic and therapeutic orders; clinical observations, including results of treatment; reports of procedures and tests and their results; disposition of the patient; and the pertinent instructions to the patient and family for follow-up care. With changes in the health-care delivery system, more services are now being provided in these settings, and claim reviews will more frequently include services provided by these facilities.

All licensed medical facilities providing inpatient housing are required to maintain concurrent patient records. Rehabilitation centers, psychiatric facilities, and long-term care or nursing home facilities fall into this category. These facilities often maintain their records in a chronological diary system rather than by department, as is done with hospital records. The claim representative must often obtain the entire record to thoroughly review a case.

Emergency medical technicians and paramedics may provide emergency medical care under the supervision of a physician who monitors the case from a local trauma center. Any services must be recorded and maintained for legal purposes and for an attending physician to review in the emergency room. These records are important in establishing the facts of an accident and the nature of the trauma. The emergency service system that responds to the accident maintains a permanent file of these records.

Notes recorded by private duty nurses document the care and treatment provided to the patient and the patient's response. These records can establish whether the patient requires licensed nursing services or a nursing aid or an attendant. They can also establish the dates and times of nursing care and treatment. These details may be needed when the claim representative is considering reimbursement for hourly services billed by these medical professionals.

Chiropractor's SOAP Notes

Chiropractic records are often necessary for conducting an injury evaluation. A chiropractor's SOAP (subjective, objective, assessment, and plan) notes are useful in evaluating injuries. The SOAP notes detail the patient's complaints, the chiropractor's objective examination findings, the chiropractor's assessment (similar to a diagnosis) and the chiropractor's plan for treating the patient. The SOAP notes should be obtained as soon as possible to determine the injury and likely disability, and whether there is a need for medical case management.

Obtaining Medical Records

Obtaining medical records is usually a straightforward procedure. In any injury case, the claimant has made his or her medical condition an issue. Therefore, the claimant must produce evidence supporting the claim and will usually cooperate with a claim representative seeking medical records. The claim representative must obtain medical records with due regard for privacy rights and state law and must organize the records in a useful manner.

Privacy

Privacy is the degree of control that individuals have over the distribution of information about themselves; it is the right to a reasonable expectation of confidentiality.[7]

When under the care of a medical provider, patients share intimate details of their lives, hoping to give the provider the best foundation for making a diagnosis and prescribing treatment. The medical provider must record this information, which must be protected and released only when it is deemed relevant to do so.

A patient's *medical records* are owned by the patient himself or herself and the medical provider and/or the institution. The provider or institution owns the physical medical records. The patient owns and has a right to the information contained within the record. Patients have a right of access to their medical information at any time.

The Federal Privacy Act of 1974[8] was passed to protect individuals against invasions of privacy by federal agencies. It requires such agencies, except as otherwise provided by law, to do the following:

1. Permit individuals to determine what records pertaining to them are collected, maintained, used, or disseminated by such agencies
2. Permit individuals to prevent records pertaining to them, obtained by such agencies for a particular purpose, from being used or made available for another purpose without their consent
3. Permit individuals to gain access to information pertaining to them in federal agency records, to have a copy made of all of the records or any portion thereof, and to correct or amend those records
4. Collect, maintain, use, or disseminate any record of identifiable personal information in a manner that assures that the action is for a necessary and lawful purpose, that the information is current and accurate for its intended use, and that adequate safeguards are provided to prevent misuse of the information
5. Permit exemptions from the requirements with respect to records provided in the act only when there is an important public policy need for such an exemption, as has been determined by specific statutory authorities
6. Be subject to civil suit for any damages that occur as a result of willful or intentional action, which violates any "individual's rights" under the act[9]

This law affects the claim review process whenever information must be obtained through the Medicare or Medicaid system, military health records, federally owned and operated health-care institutions such as

Veterans Administration hospitals, or federal programs established and governed under the Federal Drug and Alcohol Abuse Act.

State Requirements

Each state's requirements for obtaining medical records vary. Claim representatives must know their own state or local requirements. For example, Alabama requires the express consent of a patient or representative in order to obtain records;[10] Tennessee requires that state hospital records may be obtained only with a *subpoena duces tecum* (a formal legal action to obtain records).[11]

Medical Authorization

The patient has the right to approve a release of information to any party. This approval is known as a medical authorization, authorization for release of medical information, or authorization for disclosure. A written release for disclosure of information gives the health-care provider authority to release the material contained in the medical record. The authorization for disclosure should clearly state the intent of the release.

An authorization should include the following information:

1. The name of the health-care provider or institution to which the authorization is addressed.
2. The names of the persons, firms, corporations, or public body to which the information is to be released.
3. An adequate description of the information to be disclosed.
4. The signature of the patient whose health record is requested or of the individual legally authorized to act on the patient's behalf.
5. The specific expiration date of the authorization. A patient may revoke an authorization at any time, although not retroactively.
6. Any prohibitions on the disclosure of specific information.
7. Any prohibition of proposed new use of information without the patient's additional consent.[12]

Organization of Medical Information

Once medical documentation has been received and the supporting claim file information (such as the loss report, statements, and bills) is in place, the information should be organized on the basis of *data* and *opinion*, then placed in chronological order.

Medical data is objective information that can be seen or measured by the health-care provider. **Opinions** are the provider's conclusions based on a review of the data, the patient's complaints, and often pure supposition. The claim reviewer can expect to find a mixture of data and opinion in the claim file. For instance, a file might include the following information: an X-ray showing a displaced shoulder (data), patient complaints of pain when rotating the shoulder (subjective information), and a physician's statement: "There was a displacement of the right shoulder sustained when the patient was thrown to the ground and landed on that shoulder" (opinion). In this case, it would be reasonable to accept the physician's opinion since it is supported by objective and subjective evidence.

Findings based on subjective evidence and supposition on the part of the medical provider require further investigation. For example, a patient may complain of headaches and nausea, but head X-rays may be negative. Because the patient states he did not have headaches before his recent accident, the medical provider might conclude that the headaches result from the accident. The claim representative should further review this situation to discover any pre-existing medical problems that might be contributing to the patient's discomfort. Additional information could also be provided by further diagnostic evaluation in the form of other tests or an independent medical exam.

When extensive medical services have been provided, or when multiple providers have been involved in the care and treatment of a patient, the bills and records must be organized chronologically. This arrangement recreates the course of treatment and enables the claim representative to understand the relevance of various services and to identify medical problems that may not be associated with the reported accident. The claim representative may also note gaps in the treatment plan that require additional investigation. A chronological review defines when, where, and how the initial diagnosis was made; it also illustrates the patient's progress during the course of care and treatment as well as any complications that arose during that process. Claim representatives should determine whether the various health-care providers appear to agree on the cause and treatment of the medical condition.

Expert Assistance

In certain cases, claim representatives need expert assistance. The two most commonly used expert services are retrospective reviews and independent medical examinations. Chapter 3 will discuss another type of expert service, utilization review.

Retrospective Reviews

As mentioned in Chapter 1, retrospective review is often used when there is a question about any of the following:

- The relationship between the injury and the known facts of the accident
- The relationship between the treatment and the injury claimed
- The necessity of ongoing medical treatment

A retrospective review is ordinarily performed by a medical provider who specializes in the same discipline as the treating physician, or in the area of medicine that most directly relates to the medical issue in the case. For example, if the treating physician indicates that the injured party has a thyroid imbalance that was traumatically induced by the accident, an endocrinologist (a specialist in the treatment of thyroid and other endocrine disorders) may be the physician of choice for the retrospective review.

The steps listed below should be followed in preparing for a retrospective review:

1. The claim representative should present the reviewing physician with the facts of the accident.
2. The claim representative should explain what issues should be addressed in the reviewing physician's report.
3. The claim representative must send to the reviewing physician all documentation, including clinical notes, hospital records, reports, and X-ray films, and any supporting materials from other attending health-care providers. Failure to provide the complete medical record may completely discredit the reviewing physician's report.
4. The claim representative should ask the reviewing physician whether any information seems to be missing from the records. A claim representative may not be aware that certain reports are available.
5. The claim representative must give the reviewing physician a deadline. In the claim review process, turnaround time is vital to an equitable decision. Various statutes require a decision on a claim within a specific period of time, typically thirty days.

Chiropractic Peer Reviews

As mentioned in Chapter 1, chiropractic reviews are often needed to confirm the appropriateness of chiropractic care. The guidelines below should be followed in the review of any case involving chiropractic care.

- There should be a clear diagnosis of the problem, documented by the clinical evaluation (neck or back pain is not an acceptable diagnosis).
- There should be a well-established plan of treatment with specific functional goals, descriptions of procedures, and estimates of frequency and duration of treatments.
- The usual chiropractic treatment consists of manipulation of the spine and one or two other "modalities." A modality is a specific form or type of treatment. The usual other modalities are hot packs; cold packs; diathermy; ultrasound; traction; massage; and electrotherapy (such as T.E.N.S. treatment). Other modalities may be acceptable but should be investigated because they may be unusual, unnecessary, or unrelated to the injury.
- There should be relevant diagnostic tests. This is a very difficult area for nonmedical experts to assess, but redundant tests and/or tests not directly related to the injured body parts should be rejected.

- Frequency of care should be decreasing. For a typical back injury claim, the reduction should occur *at least* every four weeks.
- There should be noted improvements as treatment progresses. Lack of improvement indicates that other problems may be making the claimant unresponsive to treatments.
- "Maintenance" care is beyond the stage of maximum improvement and should be minimal. Such care may not be the responsibility of the workers compensation or liability insurer.
- Chronic problems should be recognized because they cannot be cured by intense treatments, nor should they be treated as frequently as acute problems.

In addition to these guidelines, the following red flags should alert the claim representative to refer the case to an outside review firm:

- The patient receives more than three modalities per visit.
- Treatments begin long after the accident.
- The patient was treated before the accident.
- Thermographic charges (thermography is a controversial procedure that is generally not accepted) or charges for unknown and unusual modalities are included.
- Separate billings are made for diagnostic tests and treatments for different but related body parts, for example, the arm and the shoulder.
- Multiple diagnoses are included for the same condition.

Guidelines for the frequency of office visits are listed in Exhibit 2-10.

Exhibit 2-10
Office Visit Frequency Guidelines

> The following guidelines relate to the frequency of visits for chiropractic conditions; e.g., lumbosacral strain. Diagnosis may dictate a different treatment program. Supplemental information, such as the monthly status report, should be requested if:
> - Visits exceed one per day (for chronic conditions)
> - Visits exceed two per day (for more than two days for acute conditions)
> - One visit per day exceeding one week's duration
> - Three visits per week exceeding one month's duration
> - Visits exceed twelve to fifteen in the first month of care
> - Visits exceed twenty-four for two consecutive months of treatment
> - Visits exceed one per month for maintenance care unless justified by a special set of circumstances
> - Three modalities/procedures are used in addition to manipulation
>
> For purposes of these guidelines, start a new count of office visits if the patient has been free of treatment for sixty days or if there is a new diagnosis. If there is validation of a new diagnosis, cases of alleged exacerbation should quickly respond to the treatment program.

Reprinted with permission from *Medi-Call Moments, Chiropractic Guidelines for Claims Handling*, Aetna Commercial Insurance Divisions.

The guidelines listed in Exhibit 2-10 apply to ordinary lumbosacral strain and sprain. Complications such as intervertebral disk disease, facet joint syndrome, or degenerative joint disease can cause the treatment patterns to vary. Any questionable case should be referred to a UR firm specializing in chiropractic review for an informed evaluation.

Physical Therapy Peer Reviews

Like chiropractic care, physical therapy may be received frequently and continuously and is therefore subject to abuse. Unlike chiropractic care, however, physical therapy has a different origin, employs different techniques, and has always been accepted by the medical profession as legitimate treatment. Claim representatives must be familiar with the status of physical therapy as a treatment and with the guidelines against which the use of physical therapy is reviewed.

Status of Physical Therapy

Physical therapy is a form of health care that prevents, identifies, corrects, and alleviates acute or prolonged movement dysfunction of anatomic or physiologic origin. Physical therapists evaluate patients' functional limitations, select goals for improvement, and establish a treatment program to achieve those goals. Physical therapy programs include treatments that apply elements such as light, heat, water, electricity, and mechanical agents. Physical therapists also use hands-on techniques and training and education about patients.

All fifty states require physical therapists to be licensed. They must complete an education program accredited by the American Physical Therapy Association and pass a licensure exam. The license in each state prescribes the scope of physical therapy practice and the manner in which physical therapists can obtain patients.

Physical therapy is generally prescribed by a physician. Most states allow osteopaths to refer patients, but only a few allow chiropractors to do so. The prescription may or may not include specification of certain modalities or procedures. At the beginning of treatment, a physical therapist assesses the patient to determine the appropriate type of care, to set realistic goals and objectives, and to determine an appropriate length of time in which the treatment will produce the expected outcome.

Physical Therapy Reviews

In a physical therapy review, a claim representative should look for patient improvement relative to specific functional goals and for a reduction in treatment frequency over time. Many UR firms provide cost-containment services for physical therapy cases. Some of these firms specialize in physical therapy review.

Exhibit 2-11 lists the guidelines or red flags against which the use of physical therapy should be reviewed. If the case being reviewed shows evidence of the elements listed in the exhibit, the case may require further review. However, the red flags should not become the only criteria upon which the claim representative should base a decision to deny payment for treatment. A claim representative should obtain a professional UR before rejecting any bills for a course of treatment. Likewise, when in doubt about the validity of treatment, claim representatives should consult a physical therapy UR specialist.

Exhibit 2-11
Physical Therapy: Use of "Red Flags" for Utilization Review Activities

The listed items represent *"red flags"* or guidelines which enable the claim representative to identify those cases which may require utilization review/peer review. These red flags should not be confused with screens or practice standards. Evidence of red flags in a case *should not* result in outright denial of claims. Decisions regarding nonreimbursement should only result after a thorough UR/review process.
Red flags are divided into five categories as follows:
- The referral process
- Treatment records
- Physical therapy modalities/procedures/techniques
- Provider's credentials
- Billing statements

The Referral Process
- No evidence of patient referral for physical therapy
- Patient is treated concurrently by more than one provider (i.e., DC, DO)
- Extensive treatment (more than one month) without evidence of referral renewal/update
- Physical therapy treatment course not projected (i.e., 4-6 weeks)

Treatment Records
- Paucity of physical therapy documentation
- Tests performed without report submission
- Lack of established goal (short/long term)
- Physical therapy treatment log inconsistent with billing statement

Physical Therapy Modalities
- Local modalities (i.e., ultrasound, electrical stimulation) continued unmodified for more than two weeks without evidence of improvement of condition
- "Palliative" modalities extended beyond the normal tissue healing period (6-8 weeks)
- Daily use of more than three modalities
- Continued use of palliative modalities without exercises
- Lack of fading schedule of treatment

Provider's Credentials
- Services entitled "physical therapy" or "physiotherapy" without evidence of a licensed physical therapist's involvement
- Nonsupervision of "supportive personnel" (i.e., aides or assistants) by a licensed physical therapist or physician
- Absence of professional insignias/initials/titles
- Nonauthentication of clinical records (i.e., no signatures or treatment notes)

Billing Statements
- Fees appear to be high for geographic area
- Billing dates do not correspond to treatment notes
- Incomprehensible treatment codes, abbreviations and descriptions
- "Stacked modalities" (i.e., more than three local modalities per session)

This listing is not intended to be definitive of an all-inclusive red flag listing. However, involvement of two or more of these red flags may signal the need for further case review.

Reprinted with permission from Physical Therapy Review Services, Inc.

Independent Medical Examinations

As mentioned in Chapter 1, the purpose of an independent medical examination (IME) is to help the physician make a medical determination as to causation, current physical impairment, and the need for present or future treatment.

Independent Medical Examination Considerations

The timing of an IME and retrospective review can be important in liability claims, especially when court rules allow only one IME before trial. Under these rules, the IME should be scheduled only when the claimant has reached maximum recovery. If the IME is conducted while the claimant is still being treated, the medical examiner can only attest to the facts that an injury was sustained and that at the time of the examination recovery was in progress. The examiner will not be able to attest that a *full* recovery has been made. If partial or permanent disability is alleged at the time of trial, such a report would not provide a defense to that allegation. It is generally premature to request an IME before securing and reviewing the available medical records of the treating physician.

As with a retrospective review by a medical consultant, claim representatives must communicate with the independent medical examiner, must outline their medical questions, and must include all medical records and other pertinent file materials. The failure to forward complete medical records may discredit the exam.

The determination as to the type of medical professional to be used for an IME depends on the type of injury. If the injury involves a fracture, an orthopedic surgeon is generally chosen. If the condition involves scarring, the obvious choice would be a board-certified plastic surgeon. The selection process becomes more complex when the existence of the injury is based on subjective evidence only. If it is alleged that the head or neck was injured and that the injured party was unconscious for any period of time, a neurologist or neurosurgeon would probably be chosen. If the injury involves a strain, sprain, or disk herniation of the thoracic or lumbar spine, or if pain radiates to the legs, an orthopedist or orthopedic surgeon and possibly a neurosurgeon should be selected. Nerve involvement would normally indicate the need for a neurologist. General surgeons or internists might be chosen if numerous organs were extensively injured. A careful review of the treatment records along with some research by the claim representative should help to determine the type of medical professional best able to answer the claim representative's questions. In very complicated cases, the claim representative may want to consult with a local physician or defense attorney.

Obtaining Independent Medical Examinations

If wisely used, the IME remains one of the most effective strategies for managing workers compensation claims. Not every case is a candidate for an IME. The exam's cost must be weighed against the potential loss. It makes little sense to pay $700 for an IME if only a week's worth of temporary total disability is at stake. Claim representatives most frequently use IMEs in the specialties of orthopedics, neurosurgery, and neurology. With the increase in stress claims, psychiatric IMEs are becoming more common.

Claim representatives should ask the IME physician to address the following questions:

1. In all medical probability, are the claimant's ailments causally related to a specific on-the-job injury?
2. Are the frequency and type of medical treatment rendered reasonable and appropriate?
3. From an objective medical standpoint, can the claimant return to full duty?
4. Can the claimant perform light/limited/modified work, and what are the claimant's specific physical restrictions?
5. Does the claimant have any permanent disability, and, if so, what is the percentage?
6. Has the claimant reached maximum medical improvement?
7. Did pre-existing or unrelated medical problems contribute to the claimant's disability?
8. Is prospective medical treatment—surgery or hospitalization, for instance—medically necessary and appropriate?

The claim representative's cover letter to the IME physician should specify in detail what the claim representative needs. The letter should be accompanied by any medical records, including up-to-date copies of X-rays. A written job description from the employer may also be useful since the claimant's description of job requirements may not match the actual job duties. An example of a letter requesting an IME appears in Chapter 7.

The claim representative should give the claimant a reasonable amount of advance notice of an IME. Some jurisdictions allow termination of disability payments if the claimant refuses without good cause to attend an IME.

Many industry observers believe that the IME is an overrated tool. Compensation boards, mindful of the humanitarian aims behind compensation laws, tend to weigh more heavily the treating physician's opinion than the judgment of the IME physician. They reason that the treating physician is more familiar with the patient and is thus better qualified to speak about medical restrictions. The opposing argument is that the treating doctor may lack objectivity and may have become the claimant's advocate. Nevertheless, questions of fact—including medical fact—are frequently resolved in the claimant's favor.

Despite well-founded concerns, IMEs can be effective cost-cutting tools. However, IMEs are often misused. The following are some common problems undermining the effectiveness of IMEs:

- IME monotony. The insurer may choose the same doctor(s) all the time. Compensation boards give little credibility to doctors whose opinions are repeatedly paraded out by insurers. Ideally, doctors chosen for IMEs should derive only a fraction of their income from such consultations, having a substantial practice from ongoing treatment of their own patients.

- Choosing an "insurance company doctor" (physicians who do a great deal of work for insurers) may give claim representatives the opinion sought, but these practitioners generally have no more credibility in court than a known claimant-oriented physician.
- Using unqualified physicians. If the treating physician or the claimant's expert is board-certified, the IME doctor must have comparable credentials. Some doctors have subspecialties. A claim representative should not send a back injury claimant to an eminent hand specialist just because that doctor is an orthopedist.
- Failure to provide adequate background information to the IME physician. Copies of all medical records should be sent to the IME doctor well before the appointment. This will lend more credence to the doctor's opinion. Few tactics undermine an IME more than opposing counsel revealing that the consulting doctor did not have the benefit of the complete medical history. If credibility or causation issues exist in a claim, the background material need not be limited to medical records, but may also include statements from the claimant, supervisor, and witnesses.
- Poor communication with the IME physician. Form letters have the virtue of efficiency, but the cover letter to the consulting doctor must be adapted to the needs of a particular case. It should address questions such as the following: What is the purpose of the IME? What is the claim representative's prime concern? What major issues does the claim representative want the doctor to address in the medical report? Does the claim representative want to speak with the doctor before the doctor commits his or her impressions to paper? The claim representative must clearly explain his or her expectations to the IME physician in the cover letter.

The chances of an IME's success are directly proportional to the amount of intelligent forethought and groundwork given by the claim representative in the pre-IME stage. Used selectively and with appropriate timing, the IME remains perhaps the claim representative's strongest tool in managing injury claims.

Getting What Is Needed From Doctors

Claim representatives need information from physicians, but reports may not arrive when promised. When they do arrive, they may need to be clarified for the claim representative. Claim representatives must find effective ways to obtain the needed information from physicians. If the claim representative needs information or clarification from a doctor and cannot get a reply, he or she should phone the doctor's secretary. Physicians also have medical records clerks who can be helpful. If they cannot readily answer the claim representative's question, they can relay it to the doctor and call the claim representative later. Leaving messages with medical records clerks saves time for both the doctor and the claim representative.

Physicians are more accessible at certain times than at others. Claim representatives can rarely reach doctors between 9:30 A.M. and 4:30 P.M. They will have a better chance of reaching a doctor earlier in the morning or later in the afternoon. A claim representative should find out from the doctor's secretary what time the doctor will be able to speak by phone and should tell the secretary to have the doctor expect a call at that time. Questions should be written in advance. Claim representatives are often timid about talking to doctors or about pushing to get reasonable inquiries answered. But just as claim representatives overcome their initial fright of dealing with attorneys, they must learn to speak with physicians as one professional to another.

As is often the case with attorneys, sometimes the prospect of a face-to-face meeting will prompt a physician to relent and return a claim representative's calls. Nevertheless, in some cases, there will be little alternative to making an appointment to meet with the doctor.

Utilization Review

Case Study—How To Use UR for Management of Workers Compensation Claims

A claimant with a serious back injury did not respond well to two months of conservative chiropractic treatments. The claimant was re-examined by a physician who diagnosed a herniated disk and suggested back surgery.

The insurance company involved in the claim dealt with two cost-containment service firms. Firm A provided hospital bill audit services and medical rehabilitation services using only nurses. Firm B, which had higher fees, provided a full range of UR services and employed physicians with different specialties.

The claim representative referred the case to Firm B because of the need for an appropriate specialist who could talk to the treating doctor and hospital, and the likelihood that surgery and follow-up treatment would cost in excess of $15,000. The claim representative then wrote to Firm B summarizing the facts of the case and treatments to date.

After reviewing the case, a representative of Firm B suggested the following:

- Obtain a second opinion on the need for back surgery.
- If back surgery is necessary, have a medical specialist of Firm B work with the treating physician, the surgeon, and the hospital to monitor the claimant's condition, determine the length of hospital stay, and oversee all other services during this period.
- Monitor the treatment plan with the treating physician after the claimant is discharged from the hospital.

The claim representative suggested that a physician of Firm B should review the medical records to determine whether the physician could confirm the need for back surgery without a full examination of the claimant. The review confirmed the need for surgery, and the claimant was admitted to a hospital.

A medical specialist of Firm B consulted with the treating physician and the hospital and worked out a plan for discharge. Originally, the claimant was scheduled to be hospitalized for eight days.

Continued on next page.

> However, continuous monitoring showed that the claimant was ready to be discharged after five days. During this period, Firm B reviewed and suggested some changes in ancillary services and recommended the use of generic drugs, resulting in additional savings.
>
> Upon the claimant's discharge, the treating physician prescribed physical therapy. The claim representative agreed that a physical therapist employed by Firm B would review the initial evaluation of the claimant's physical therapist and would follow up if necessary.
>
> The claimant wanted to return to the chiropractor for more treatments. Upon review of the treatment plan, Firm B suggested to the claimant's treating physician and the chiropractor that the chiropractor's plan for treatments would essentially duplicate services provided by the physical therapist. The claimant's physician and the chiropractor agreed. Physical therapy was only authorized for one month, at the end of which the need for therapy was re-evaluated.

Problems With Expert Reviews and Examinations

Although expert reviews and examinations can provide valuable assistance to claim representatives, they do have drawbacks. They are expensive and difficult to arrange and may not affect the claimant's case at all.

Cost and Difficulty in Making Arrangements

The problems of cost and difficulty are related. Only a small minority of physicians are willing and able to perform these services: it has been estimated that there are forty to fifty patient-care physicians for every one performing independent medical exams.[13] The best IME physicians are scheduled long in advance because they are generally not available on short notice. As a result of their scarcity and the demand for their services, good IME physicians charge several hundred to a thousand dollars for their services.

Noneffect on Claimant's Case

Despite their cost, reviews and exams frequently fail to diminish the amount that the insurer must pay to settle the claim. In some cases, independent reviews and exams confirm the claimant's case. In those cases, the review or exam and its expense prove to be unnecessary. But it is valuable to learn that claimant's case is confirmed. Claim representatives should regard their responsibility to pay what is due on a case, not to pay the least possible.

More problematic are inconclusive independent reviews and exams. These cost as much as any other review or exam, but provide little or no useful information toward concluding the claim. Reviews or exams can be inconclusive for many reasons. The reviewing physician may not be the right kind of specialist. For example, an orthopedist may review a case in which the main issues are psychiatric. The reviewing physician may not wish to criticize a colleague, thus giving every benefit of the doubt to the treating physician. The case may involve issues that are on the frontier of medical knowledge, and the reviewing physician may not be fully acquainted with the scientific literature. Finally, like the treating physician, reviewing physicians must rely on the claimant for information about medical history and the accident in question. An IME may therefore fail to prove or disprove an injury.

Summary

In every claim for bodily injury, a claim representative must answer several questions related to a claimant's medical treatment. First, did the insured accident cause the injuries or conditions from which the claimant suffers? The answer may be "no" if the claimant has pre-existing problems, chronic problems, or intervening problems not related to the insured event. Second, was the treatment the claimant received necessary? Unusual and redundant treatment should not be reimbursed. Finally, what future treatment will be needed? The claim representative must answer these questions partly because patients and physicians have strong incentives to overtreat.

One of the claim representative's key responsibilities is to identify cases for which additional help is necessary from supervisors, managers, or outside experts. Serious cases can be identified by type of injury, dollar amount, length of disability, or medical complexity.

For the vast majority of cases handled by one claim representative alone, the claimant's medical records are the essential evidence. Claim representatives must understand what information is contained in different records, how these records are created and maintained, the type of institutions from which records may be obtained, and how records should be obtained.

For some cases, claim representatives use outside experts to evaluate medical issues. Consulting physicians might only review records in a retrospective review, they might examine the claimant in an independent medical examination, or they might do both. Reviews and exams can be expensive and difficult to arrange, and there is no guarantee that they will affect a claimant's case.

Chapter Notes

1. Kathleen A. Waters and Gretchen Frederick Murphy, *Medical References in Health Information* (Rockville, MD: Aspen Publishing, 1979), p. 257.
2. 66 Am Jur 2d, Records, § 46.5.
3. See, for example, Edna K. Huffman, *Medical Record Management*, 8th ed. (Berwyn, IL: Physicians' Record Co., 1985).
4. JoAnne C. Bruce, *Privacy and Confidentiality of Health Care Information* (Chicago: AHPI, 1984), p. 13.
5. *Accreditation Manual for Hospitals* (Chicago: Joint Commission on Accreditation of Hospitals, 1986), pp. 79-80.
6. *Accreditation Manual*, p. 80.

7. Arthur F. Southwick, *The Law of Hospital and Health Care Administration*, 2d ed. (Ann Arbor, MI: Health Administration Press, 1988), p. 322.
8. 5 U.S.C. § 552a.
9. Bruce, p. 57.
10. Ala. Code § 27-21A-25.
11. Tenn. Code § 10-7-504.
12. Adapted from Pennsylvania Bar Institute, *Analyzing Medical Records* (Harrisburg, PA, 1988), pp. 21-23.
13. Ronald E. Gots, M.D., "Medical Claims Flay Casualty Insurers," *National Underwriter*, September 18, 1989, p. 86.

Chapter 3
Impairment and Disability

Impairment and disability can both pose serious psychological, social, and economic problems that affect not only the injured individual but also his or her family and employer, the insurance industry, and the economy as a whole. Overcoming and improving the effects of impairment and disability can benefit all these parties. Claim representatives handling injury claims have enormous responsibilities toward the injured party and the insurer. No matter how well compensated, injury victims who have sustained a permanent impairment or disability have suffered and will continue to suffer greatly. Insurers help reduce this suffering when they compensate impaired and/or disabled individuals. This chapter describes the nature of both impairment and disability and explains how their deleterious effects may be lessened.

Definitions of Impairment and Disability

Certain key words related to the condition of disability appear often in medical, psychological, and vocational rehabilitation reports. A clear understanding of these definitions is essential to a claim representative's effectiveness in the claim evaluation process.

Impairment

Any deleterious alteration in health status can be termed **impairment**. Impairment refers to specific injuries, illnesses, losses, or deficits of function in the body, assessed by medical means.

The American Medical Association *Guide to the Evaluation of Permanent Impairment*, fourth edition, defines impairment "as a deviation from normal in a body part or organ system and its functioning." The Guide defines a "*permanent* impairment" as one that "has become static or stabilized during a period of time sufficient to allow optimal tissue repair, and one that is unlikely to change in spite of further medical or surgical therapy."[1]

Individuals injured in work accidents, motor vehicle accidents, or slip-and-fall accidents can sustain either a temporary impairment or a permanent impairment as a result of their accident-related injuries. Injuries and impairment (permanent or temporary) are established by using *medical* criteria. When an injured individual cannot meet his or her own personal, social, and occupational demands or other activities of daily living as the result of an impairment, that individual is considered disabled. Disability is normally assessed by *nonmedical* means because its causes and effects extend beyond medical problems.

Temporary Impairment

Impairment refers to damage to the body and/or general overall health, caused by an injury, condition, or disease. A **temporary impairment** is a transitory, as opposed to permanent, malfunction of the body or general overall health caused by disease, injury, or another condition. Upon healing of the disease, condition, or injury, the individual has no lasting residual effects.

For example, an injured worker may have mildly strained his wrist while lifting at work, which completely healed without any permanent impairment. During the time that the worker was medically evaluated and treated for his wrist, he would have been considered as having a temporary impairment. This injury would also be termed a **temporary partial impairment** because only part of the body's form and function (that is, the body itself and its physical abilities) was adversely affected. But consider the case of an individual who contracts a progressive and totally paralyzing condition known as Guillain-Barré Syndrome. In the most severe cases, the patient is totally paralyzed and dependent on a ventilator for months. In most cases, the condition completely heals with no residual ill effects. An individual having this condition, as described, would be considered as having a **temporary total impairment** because the individual's whole body form and function have been affected.

Permanent Impairment

As stated earlier, **permanent impairment** is a deviation from normal body form or function as the result of injury, disease, or condition that has become stabilized over a sufficient time period for optimal healing to have occurred. Any additional treatment or care given will not change or alter the outcome to any appreciable degree. Consider the case of a high school English teacher who suffers the loss of her little finger in a motor vehicle accident. She has sustained a **permanent partial impairment** to her hand. The impairment is partial in degree to both her body's form and function. But consider a middle-aged American actor who severs his spinal cord during a fall from his horse. He is permanently paralyzed from the neck and cannot breathe without a respirator. This person has suffered a **permanent total impairment** since it totally affects both his body's form and function. He will be unable to achieve his pre-injury level of health and functioning because his spinal cord was severed.

Physical Restrictions

Sometimes as the result of an injury, a disease, or a condition, an individual's physician might restrict the patient's functional abilities or physical activities as the result of an impairment. The restriction is a directive imposed on the patient by a third party (usually a doctor) to limit specific activities. The rationale for the placement of restrictions is to allow for healing to take place, to prevent the condition from worsening, and/or to prevent re-injury. Restrictions may be temporary or permanent. Whether restrictions will be permanent or temporary depends on the nature of the injury, condition, or disease; individual patient assessment; the patient's environment; and physician judgement. An electrical lineman who broke his leg while skiing might have **temporary physical restrictions** placed by his physician while he is in a long leg cast and non-weight bearing on that extremity. Following full recovery, the lineman could be returned to full physical activity with no permanent physical restrictions. But if the lineman did not achieve optimal healing of his fractured leg because of an underlying disease such as diabetes, for instance, he might be returned to work and other activities with some **permanent physical restrictions** limiting his activities. Claim representatives must ask the physician caring for persons injured in property casualty claims whether the patient will be left with any permanent restrictions as a result of an insured accident-related injury, disease, or condition. The medical placement of *restrictions* limiting any of the impaired individual's activities or level of functioning determines the patient's disability.

Disability

Disability is the inability, because of an impairment, of a person to meet his or her personal, social, or occupational demands, other activities of daily living, or statutory or other regulatory requirements. Disability is distinct from the related conditions of impairment and handicap. Whereas the determination of both impairment and physical restrictions can be made by medical means, the determination of disability is normally assessed nonmedically. A person can have an impairment that does not create a disability. For example, the impairment of an amputated leg may not disable a customer service representative from performing his or her job, though it may disable a field adjuster. An impairment that produces a social or personal disability but not a work disability will affect the value of a third-party liability claim much more than a workers compensation claim. The damages for social and personal disabilities are included in a claimant's "pain and suffering." These general damages are not included in workers compensation.

Workers Compensation Definitions of Work Disability

This section defines work disability as it applies to the state workers compensation system. In the same way that impairments can be temporary or permanent, and partial or total, workers compensation *disabilities* are categorized. The determination of disability in this context often depends on statutory definitions. The definition of work disability under workers compensation may not match the definition under other systems. Temporary-total and permanent-partial work disabilities account for most income benefits paid, as reported by the U.S. Chamber of Commerce.

Temporary-Partial

A temporary-partial condition means that an injured worker is temporarily unable to perform some job-related tasks but can go to work and perform other job tasks. For example, minor low back strains, superficial cuts, bruises, and burns are often regarded as temporary-partial disabilities. An injured worker can receive temporary-partial disability benefits if the disability meets statutory criteria.

Temporary-Total

Temporary-total means that the injured employee cannot to any extent perform any of his or her occupational duties, but the condition is not permanent. The overwhelming majority of injuries sustained in the course of employment and involving some work disability are in this category. For example, the lineman who broke his leg suffered a temporary-total disability.

Permanent-Partial

A permanent-partial disability is caused by an injury that involves the permanent loss of a member of the body, such as an eye, a foot, or a finger, or loss of some body function that interferes with the worker's ability to perform his or her tasks. Under most workers compensation laws, certain scheduled injuries are defined as partial disabilities even if the worker can perform his or her job duties. This disability is permanent in nature but partial in degree.

Permanent-Total

Permanent-total disability means that the injured worker is permanently and totally incapacitated from carrying on gainful work. Blindness in both eyes, double amputations, or a spinal cord injury would be considered a permanent-total disability. As with permanent-partial injuries, some workers compensation laws define certain injuries as a total disability regardless of whether the injured person is still working or can obtain employment.

Effect of Disability on the Value of Casualty Claims

The extent and duration of any disability are generally the key factors affecting the value of a claim. Disability usually affects the value of a claim even more than the injury itself. A serious injury from which a claimant is disabled for only a short time is likely to cost less than an ordinary injury from which a claimant experiences extended disability. The presence of a work or another disability is a key indication that a case is serious rather than routine, and the presence of a permanent work or another disability is a key indication that a serious case may be catastrophic. A claim representative must carefully investigate and verify any alleged disability, bringing serious and potentially serious cases to the attention of supervisors and managers.

Workers Compensation Claims

Claims involving medical payments represent only a small fraction of total workers compensation payments. Indeed, medical-only claims represent a minority of medical benefits. Most medical benefits are paid on cases involving some work disability.

In workers compensation, all indemnity payments are based only on claims involving work disability rather than disability related to the performance of personal activities. In 1998, indemnity payments represented approximately 50 percent of all compensation benefits. Furthermore, the amount of indemnity benefits paid on a given case is directly connected to the length of work disability. The longer the disability, the longer the benefits must continue. Determining when a claimant's work disability has ended and terminating disability benefits are among the most important tasks of a workers compensation claim representative. Compensation cases involving permanent work disability are serious and expensive enough to warrant the use of sophisticated claim-handling techniques such as vocational rehabilitation and retraining.

Liability Claims

As with workers compensation claims, the value of a liability claim is closely related to the extent and duration of work and other types of disability. However, in a liability claim, the presence of any disability related to the personal performance of activities can significantly increase the award of general damages. For example, the inability to hold and care for a child, as a result of an accident, would be considered in determining the award in a liability claim.

In a liability claim, the claimant can recover special and general damages. **Special damages** are compensation for out-of-pocket expenses such as medical bills and lost income. Thus, the extent of special damages that may be collected is directly linked to the amount of lost income as a result of the disability. **General damages** are compensation for the intangible effects of injury such as emotional pain and suffering, inconvenience, and disfigurement from scarring. One widely disparaged but just as widely practiced method for computing general damages is to equate general damages to several multiples of the special damages. Thus, general damages might be regarded as, for example, three times the amount of the special damages. Since lost earnings are already part of special damages, this approach increases the cost of disability well beyond its face value.

Besides formulas used to compute damages, the extent and duration of disability are widely accepted as indicators of general damages. For instance, if a person must be absent from work as a result of suffering caused by disability, the disability is clearly severe enough to interfere with normal activities. This kind of disability is adequate evidence for general damages.

Handicap

A handicap refers to the degree of functional limitation resulting from impairment. The existence of a handicap depends on the extent to which impairment impedes a person's functioning. Under federal law, a person may be considered to be handicapped "if he or she has an impairment that substantially limits one or more of life's activities, has a record of such impairment, or is regarded as having such an impairment."[2] Persons meeting any of the criteria in the above definition could be considered handicapped because the definition under federal law is so broad.

Consider the blue-and-white handicapped parking signs and spaces. Individuals with either temporary or permanent impairments or disabilities both qualify as handicapped under the federal definition of handicap. In order for individuals to receive a handicap sticker for parking, their licensed healing arts professional must fill out their respective states' disabled placard and/or license plate application. Exhibit 3-1 shows a disabled placard or plate application for Kansas.

The type of health-care professional who is permitted to sign these statements varies by state. Most states limit the types to physicians, podiatrists, and chiropractors. Kansas and a growing number of other states permit Christian Science practitioners and other alternative practitioners to sign the statement.

Behavior Effects of Impairments and Disabilities

How a person behaves *before* experiencing a serious impairment or disabling illness or injury usually indicates how that person will behave *after* the injury. Generally, if a person could overcome obstacles before an injury, he or she will be able to do the same after the injury, even though the obstacles may have changed. Personalities do not fundamentally change. Most disabled individuals learn to accept their limitations, although others find that adopting the role of a sick person suits their psychological needs. The nonimpaired or nondisabled cannot ever live the life of one who is impaired or disabled, but they can perform certain exercises, discussed later, to simulate the effects of impairment or disability.

Exhibit 3-1
Application for Disabled Placard or Plate (Kansas)

 KANSAS DEPARTMENT OF REVENUE
DIVISION OF VEHICLES

DISABLED PLACARD AND/OR PLATE APPLICATION

APPLICATION FOR DISABLED PLACARDS, PLATES AND ID CARDS MUST BE MADE AT YOUR LOCAL COUNTY TREASURER'S OFFICE

Name of Disabled Individual, Business or Agency _____

Address _____ City _____ KS ZIP _____

Applicant Signature _____ Phone No. ( ) _____ Date _____

PLEASE CHECK APPROPRIATE APPLICATION(S):

[ ] 1. **DISABLED IDENTIFICATION PLACARD APPLICATION** PERMANENT ($5.25 fee); TEMPORARY ($4.25 fee)
    [ ] Check here only if applying for (lost, stolen) replacement placard.* *No Licensed Professional's Statement needed for replacement placard.*
        *If Replacement Placard, Current Disabled ID Card Number _____

[ ] 2. **DISABLED LICENSE PLATE APPLICATION** (FEE: $3.25) plus 50¢ reflectorized plate fee
    Only applicants certified as PERMANENT disabled may apply for Disabled Plate.

BUSINESS OR AGENCY REPRESENTATIVE MUST CERTIFY AND SIGN THE FOLLOWING:
I, the undersigned, certify that the above named agency or business is responsible for the transportation of person(s) to be considered disabled as per K.S.A. 8-1,124, as outlined below, thus qualifying for accessible parking privileges.

Authorized Representative or Owner Signature (Rubber Stamp NOT Acceptable)   Title   Date

===== **HEALING ARTS LICENSED PROFESSIONAL'S STATEMENT** =====

Attending licensed professional *must* certify and sign the following:

I, the undersigned licensed professional, certify that (Disabled Individual's Name) _____
is considered to be disabled, as per Kansas Statute 8-1,124, due to at least one (1) or more of the following: (Must check at least one.)

[ ] 1. Has a severe visual impairment, or;

[ ] 2. Cannot walk two hundred (200) feet without stopping to rest, or;

[ ] 3. Cannot walk without the use of or assistance from, a brace, cane, crutch, another person, prosthetic device, wheelchair, or other assistive device, or;

[ ] 4. Is restricted by lung disease to such an extent that the person's forced (respiratory) expiratory volume for one second, when measured by spirometry, is less than one liter, or the arterial oxygen tension is less than sixty mm/hg on room air at rest, or;

[ ] 5. Uses portable oxygen, or;

[ ] 6. Has a cardiac condition to the extent that the person's functional limitations are classified in severity as Class III or Class IV according to standards set by the American Heart Association, or;

[ ] 7. Is severely limited in their ability to walk due to an arthritic, neurological, or orthopedic condition.

Licensed Professional's Signature *(Rubber stamp not acceptable)*   Date

MUST check one (1) of the below and provide requested information:
    [ ] PERMANENT   [ ] TEMPORARY**:➡ From (Date) _____ To (Date) _____
        ** Six (6) Months is the MAXIMUM Duration for a Temporary Placard.

Licensed Professional's Name Printed / Typed _____

Printed: Address   City   State   ZIP
TR-159 (3/93)

SEE REVERSE SIDE FOR INSTRUCTIONS

Adjusting to Impairment or Disability

When an individual is injured, especially if the injury is catastrophic and results in a permanent impairment, there may be the tendency to ask, "Why me?" Medical professionals who work with the disabled know it is not helpful to dwell on this question. It is more helpful to concentrate on the present, to plan for the future, and to avoid or prevent complications of the injury or disease. This positive approach (or response) develops gradually through a step-by-step process.

A well-known book provides a model that identifies the stages an individual may experience when one's own death is imminent or when a loved one is about to die or has already died. Professionals dealing with those who have suffered a sudden disability have observed disabled individuals experience very similar stages. These stages are denial, rage and anger, bargaining, depression, and acceptance.[3]

Not everyone who suffers a disability goes through each stage or does so in the same order. Understanding each stage makes it easier to understand what a person goes through after a serious injury or illness. As with the terminally ill, the fundamental and common experience of the disabled or seriously injured person is loss.

Denial

"No, not me." Denial is a typical reaction when someone learns that he or she is terminally ill. This response helps to cushion the effects of the patient's awareness of death. Denial is also a common reaction among the disabled.

Rage and Anger

"Why me?" The individual resents the fact that he or she has been affected. Likewise, newly disabled individuals are often enraged at what they perceive as the injustice of their disability.

Bargaining

"Yes me, but...." In this stage, people begin to recognize the fact of death, but because they have not totally accepted it, they remain on the edge of denial and feel as if they may still have some control over their circumstances. The state of mind of a disabled person in this stage would be, "I would do anything if my disability could be removed." The person is essentially trying to strike a bargain by offering to do anything in return for his or her health.

Depression

"Yes, me." The person mourns past losses, things not done, and wrongs committed. The disabled may face and feel sad about the reality of what they have lost and the limitations in their lives. When a person has suffered a serious accident, living through the anniversary of the accident is a significant milestone. The disabled person and his or her family often judge the recovery or lack of recovery at this date. Depression or other psychological setbacks are common around anniversary dates.

Acceptance

"My time is very close now, and it's all right." For those approaching death, this final stage is not a happy stage, but neither is it unhappy. It is devoid of feelings, but it is not resignation; it represents a victory.[4] The disabled at a similar stage accept their condition and look forward to dealing with the rest of their lives.

Adopting the Sick Role

Doctors have observed that some of their patients typically adopt a sick role that reflects popular attitudes towards sickness and treatment. This role includes being exempt from normal responsibilities and requiring help from others to get well, plus the duties to seek help and to regard the sickness as undesirable. In general, the sick role is a constructive relationship for purposes of treatment.[5] However, some patients adopt the sick role indefinitely. They claim to regard their sickness as undesirable, but they actually enjoy the experience. Such patients make the sick role their vocation unless they come to see the prospect of getting well as attractive as being sick. A person who has suffered a soft tissue injury of the back, such as lumbar strain and sprain, and has recovered is a common example. The temporarily impaired person may enjoy being disabled from household chores, grocery shopping, and child care. In fact, disability may become more desirable to the individual than resuming work and the other regular activities of daily living. Physicians and other health-care professionals refer to the advantages that an individual indirectly receives from their impairment or disability, such as attention, care, and release from responsibilities, as **secondary gain**.

Communications and Human Relations Involving People With Disabilities

The passage of the Americans with Disabilities Act (ADA) in 1990 addressed for the first time disability issues in public policy. (Although passed by Congress in 1990, the ADA did not go into effect until 1992.) The ADA uses the term "discrimination" to mean the segregation and exclusion of persons with disabilities, changing the focus from the limitations imposed by a disability toward the limitations posed by society through attitudinal and architectural barriers. This refocusing was an attempt to solve communication problems between people with disabilities and those without disabilities. People without disabilities sometimes have preconceptions about those with disabilities. These preconceptions can impose communication barriers and unintentionally convey disrespect for people with disabilities. Claim representatives need to counteract their preconceptions and develop skills for interacting with people with disabilities.

Although environmental adaptations can often compensate for physical disabilities, people with disabilities often find social relations much more formidable. Social barriers are much more difficult to detect and correct than physical barriers. The uncertainty that nondisabled people might feel about what to say and do when interacting with people with disabilities makes relations between the disabled and able-bodied challenging. Nondisabled people might feel self-conscious, uncomfortable, or constrained. Some might avoid interaction with people with disabilities. People sometimes receive conflicting advice about interacting with people with disabilities. Following is a list of suggestions for nondisabled people to consider when interacting with people with disabilities:

- Use a term like "people with disabilities" rather than "disabled people," "crippled," "victim," or "wheelchair bound." The goal is to stress the person, not the disability.
- Do not assume people with disabilities cannot speak for themselves or do things for themselves. Assume that they can do something for themselves unless they communicate otherwise.
- Do not force help on person with disabilities. They will indicate whether they want help. The goal is to involve the person with the disability as much as possible.
- Do not avoid interaction with people with disabilities simply to avoid discomfort.
- Remember that persons with disabilities have experienced others' discomfort and understand how others might be feeling.

People with disabilities might be sensitive to certain language and behavior that well-meaning people inadvertently express. For example, a claim representative who asks the question "What's wrong with you?" might trigger an adverse response from a person with a disability, who probably does not view the disability as "wrong." Similarly, a claim representative who asks "What happened to you?" is likely to encounter a hostile response because the questioner appears to be focusing only on the person's disability and ignoring other attributes of the person and other occurrences (both good and bad) in the person's life.

Person First, Disability Second

Rita, a claimant with paraplegia who drives a vehicle that has been adapted for her use, was involved in an auto accident. Rita's husband, who was a passenger in the car during the accident, attended the statement-taking interview with Rita. The claim representative, Jolene, asked Rita's husband, "Did she see the car at the intersection?" Rita answered, and the claim representative, continuing to look only at Rita's husband, asked, "Did she attempt to stop when she realized that the car was proceeding through the red light?" Later, before signing the statement, Rita reached around her wheelchair to retrieve her eyeglasses from her bag, which was strapped to the back of the wheelchair. Jolene jumped up to assist her although Rita did not ask for assistance and did not appear to be incapable of performing the task herself.

This example illustrates behavior that nondisabled people typically exhibit when interacting with people with disabilities. Jolene subconsciously assumed that the Rita could not speak for herself, probably to avoid direct interaction with her. Jolene also tried to assist Rita when nothing indicated that she needed assistance. Because Jolene's image of Rita was that of a helpless individual, Jolene assumed that Rita could not retrieve the glasses on her own. One of the primary complaints that people with disabilities have about interacting with nondisabled people is that nondisabled people see them first as disabled and second as a person. Claim representatives should reverse this view.

Determining the origin of a disability is sometimes necessary to properly handle a claim. Claim representatives should be aware that the origin might have been a traumatic event and that even a carefully worded question can elicit unfavorable responses. That does not relieve the claim representative of obtaining pertinent information. The claim representative could ask an open-ended question, such as "Did you have any disabilities before the accident that would have a bearing on this claim?" Because such a question should probably be asked of all claimants or insureds (since some disabilities, such as color-blindness and dyslexia, may not be apparent), it allows the person to talk about the disability at his or her own comfort level. The claimant or insured might provide the necessary information without need for specific questions. If the response is still insufficient, the claim representative could explain that "for legal reasons" or "because of the need to complete this form," "I need to ask some personal questions." This statement relays that the claim representative is trying to be sensitive but is obligated to obtain the information.

Discussing Disabilities in Claims

Following is a dialogue between Stan, a claim representative, and Joel, a claimant with a disability. The dialogue presents some subject matter about which people with disabilities might be sensitive and about which claim representatives might need to ask claimants.

Stan: Does your *crippled state impair* your ability to drive?

Joel: [*After a short pause*] No, I can drive perfectly well.

Stan: Is there anything *wrong* with you that might have *slowed* your reaction when our insured pulled out in front of you?

Joel: [*With increasing tension in his voice*] Like I just said, I'm a perfectly competent driver.

Stan: Did the accident further *damage your body* or in any way leave you *worse off* than you were before the accident?

Joel: [*Louder and with anger*] I am just as *well off* as before the accident except that my car is totaled because your insured cut me off.

Continued on next page.

Stan uses insensitive language in discussing Joel's disability, beginning by terming it a "crippled state." Joel shrugs off this first mistake, but is less tolerant when Stan asks if there's anything "wrong" with him. Stan then speaks of Joel's disability as one might speak of property damage. He also asks if Joel is "worse off" than before the accident, which indicates that Stan believes that Joel is not well off because of his disability. This improper language offends Joel.

Stan's last question, which is apparently redundant, also offends Joel. If it was necessary to rephrase the question to be thorough, Stan should have introduced the question by saying, "This might seem like a redundant question, but I'm obligated to be thorough in questioning claimants." An alternate approach would be to introduce this portion of the interview by disclosing the potentially sensitive nature of the questions. Introducing sensitive portions of the interview as such allows the person with the disability to prepare himself or herself. Disclosure might also decrease the damage done by the claim representative's using terms or phrases to which the person with the disability is sensitive. Compare the following revised dialogue between Joel and Stan.

> *Stan:* Some of the questions I'll ask next might concern sensitive subject matter. Because I'm professionally obligated to be thorough, some questions might seem redundant. Please bear with me as we complete the statement.
>
> *Joel:* Okay.
>
> *Stan:* Does your disability *affect* your ability to drive?
>
> *Joel:* My vehicle has been adapted to allow me to drive it without any problems, and I've been trained to drive it properly.
>
> *Stan:* This question might seem redundant. Could your disability have *affected* your reaction time when our insured pulled out in front of you?
>
> *Joel:* No, my reaction time is that of the average driver.
>
> *Stan:* Did you suffer any bodily injuries as a result of the accident?
>
> *Joel:* No. Just damage to my car.

In the revised dialogue, Stan begins with an introduction to prepare Joel for questions to which he might be sensitive. Stan uses the term "disability" rather than the various improper terms used in the first dialogue. Stan also uses the neutral verb "affect" instead of the verbs "impair" and "slowed," which created a negative impression. Stan asks Joel whether he suffered any bodily injuries rather than focusing the question on the disability as in the comparable question in the first dialogue.

Joel's replies are more informative than in the first dialogue. Stan learns more about Joel's driving abilities than in the first dialogue because Stan prepared Joel for the questions and uses inoffensive language.

Claim representatives should treat people with disabilities as people first. This means focusing on the person's overall characteristics rather than on the disability.

Simulated Disability

Students in nursing or rehabilitation counseling and social work, among others, commonly role-play scenarios involving the simulation of both impairment and resulting disability in order to study the effects that both conditions have on self-esteem and social interaction. Simulating impairment and disability in order to try to understand what an impairment and resulting disability feels like helps the student to empathize with a person who is impaired or disabled. The assumption is that empathy and experience will better prepare the student to respond and communicate more effectively with impaired and disabled persons.

Effects of Disability on the Employer of the Disabled

Although employers are encouraged to hire the handicapped, employers often do not have enough information to dispel myths about the disabled. Ideally, no group of people would be excluded from consideration for hire if the candidates for any position are suited for the job. However, some employers are not interested in any person for whom the job would have to be modified for that person to perform it well. Indeed, not many years ago, candidates were specifically asked on job applications if they had certain health problems because employers viewed problems such as diabetes or epilepsy as impediments to doing the job. Since then, the understanding of these two conditions has grown to the point that discrimination is relatively uncommon. It is hoped that discrimination against impaired and disabled candidates will similarly end. Nevertheless, legislation has been passed to ensure equal treatment for impaired and disabled candidates. In addition to legislation, disability affects the cost to employers through the loss of productivity of valuable employees.

The Americans With Disabilities Act

The passage of the Americans with Disabilities Act (ADA) was a clear statement by Congress that employers must *not* discriminate on the basis of disability. The ADA defines *impairment* in the following way: "Any physiological disorders or condition, cosmetic disfigurement, or anatomical loss affecting one or more of the following body systems: neurological, musculoskeletal, special sense organs, respiratory (including speech organs), cardiovascular, reproductive, digestive, genito-urinary, hemic and lymphatic, skin and endocrine. Do not include an individual who currently uses or is addicted to drugs." The definition of *disability* under the ADA is "A physical or mental impairment that substantially limits one or more major life activity, having a record of such an impairment or being regarded as having such an impairment."

The ADA prohibits discrimination on the basis of disability in regard to hiring, compensation, promotion, and other conditions of employment if the candidate is otherwise qualified. A qualified person is one who, with "reasonable accommodation," can perform the "essential functions" of a job. The failure to provide "reasonable accommodation" to a disability is specifically listed as an act of discrimination unless making accommodations would cause undue hardship. The ADA also provides guidelines on the accommodations that employers must make for disabled people.

The ADA defines "reasonable accommodation" as possibly including "making existing facilities used by employees readily accessible to and usable by individuals with disabilities; and...job restructuring, part-time or modified work schedules,...acquisition or modification of equipment or devices,...[and] the provision of qualified readers or interpreters...."[6]

Thus, federal law requires employers to adjust to the needs of the otherwise-qualified disabled. Protected by this law, the disabled who can perform the essential functions of a job can enter the workforce. In addition, prudent employers should review their hiring practices to be sure they are giving appropriate consideration to the disabled.

The Costs of Disability

The National Safety Council estimates that work-related accidents cause approximately 3.8 million disabling injuries and 125 million lost workdays in 1997, costing $127.7 billion in direct costs (an average of $980 for every person in the workforce) plus the value of lost productivity. Another estimated 60 million workdays will be lost in the future as a result of the permanent injuries that occurred in 1997.[7] Lost production time due to off-the-job accidents (mainly auto accidents) was almost twice as great.[8]

Determination of Disability

Making a determination of disability depends on two factors: (1) identifying a person's physical impairments and any corresponding medically placed restrictions and (2) describing the physical, psychological, intellectual, and social demands of that person's activities, including work. For instance, work disability cannot be based solely on impairment, unless such impairment would disable anyone from that particular job. Consider a truck driver who is blinded in an accident. This impairment, total blindness, would be permanently and totally disabling for driving a truck. Other impairments might not keep people from working. For example, an inside claim representative might still be able to do his or her job with a broken ankle because the impairment does not affect most of the job's tasks. The Appendix to this chapter discusses the determination of job demands in more detail.

Claim representatives have generally left the determination of disability to physicians. Although medical expertise is necessary to determine physical impairment and restrictions, many physicians know little or nothing about the demands of their patients' jobs when they make a disability determination. Such disability determinations should not be accepted at face value. When the physician does not know or fails to inquire about the demands of the patient's job, a statement about disability is made out of context and is therefore not wholly valid. The patient may in fact be able to work if the job is modified. Also a factor in a physician's determination of disability is that physicians tend not to be critical of what their patients say and are likely to accept a statement from a patient that he or she cannot work. When the physician fails to evaluate an injury in the context of occupation and is not critical of what the patient says, and when the claim representative is not critical of the physician's report, the patient/claimant essentially makes the determination of disability.

Claim representatives should be familiar with how physical impairments and restrictions are evaluated as they relate to job demands. This section describes the determination of physical impairment and the job demands of various occupations.

AMA Guide to the Evaluation of Permanent Impairment

Claim representatives regularly review medical reports that document a physician's determination of some percentage of impairment. To determine such percentages, a physician should use the American Medical Association (AMA) *Guide to the Evaluation of Permanent Impairment*, mentioned at the beginning of this chapter. This book was first published in a single volume in 1971 as a result of many years of ad hoc committee work on behalf of the AMA. The goal of the committee was to create a practical guide for rating physical impairments. The AMA has made a substantial effort to keep the book updated and has published three editions since 1971. In 1981, the AMA's Council on Scientific Affairs determined that twelve expert advisory panels were needed to update the clinical information supporting the impairment ratings. Editions of the guide published since 1981 have been improved as a result of the recommendations of such panels.

Purpose and Approach of the Guide

The guide espouses the philosophy that all physical and mental impairments affect the whole person, so all separate impairment ratings should be combined and expressed as impairment of the whole person.[9] The guide translates medical information and data into a form that can be used by nonmedical personnel in social, administrative, economic, or legal systems. Physicians are commonly asked about the functional capabilities of an individual who has an impairment. According to the guide, a physician cannot assess the ability of an individual to perform tasks or to meet functional demands because the physician is relying only on medical information, not on occupational requirements. The physician can, however, assess whether a particular medical condition has become stable. When a condition is stable, there is no medical reason to expect that an individual will gain or lose functional ability.[10] An individual should not be identified as being permanently impaired until he or she has been medically rehabilitated to the maximum level and the impairment is well established.

Impairment Criteria

The guide provides a set of medical criteria that form the basis for establishing well-formulated medical ratings of permanent impairment. Most criteria are quantitative, such as range of motion abilities in orthopedics. For instance, **goniometry**, the measurement of joint motion, would be used to establish quantitative criteria. The two arms of a goniometer have a pointer on one end and a protractor scale on the other. In addition to helping a physician diagnose a patient's functional loss, careful examination of joint motion can reveal the progression of a disease and can provide objective data for determining the effects of a treatment program. Exhibit 3-2 shows normal range of motion for different parts of the body. Other criteria are qualitative, providing the basis for assessing nonphysical impairments that are less easily quantified, such as psychiatric problems.[11] Although physical impairment is the usual cause of disability from work, intellectual and social impairments may be obstacles to retraining and obtaining new work. Evaluating intellectual and social impairments is *not* within the ability of most physicians. Such evaluations should be done by psychologists or psychiatrists.

Medical facilities have also been established to help physicians obtain information about patients' physical capability. This information is obtained through standardized evaluations, sophisticated equipment, and computers that accurately measure an individual's abilities. For example, a facility may use Cybex equipment to measure how much weight an individual can lift, pull, or push from floor to waist or waist to overhead. Information about functional capacity and complete medical data are essential to nonmedical agencies and people who make determinations of disability. The information gleaned from computerized functional testing such as Cybex helps physicians determine permanent physical restrictions after the patient has reached maximum medical improvement.

In determining impairment, the physician must include a physical examination, an analysis of the patient's medical history, and diagnostic and laboratory tests. The findings should be analyzed to determine the nature and extent of the loss and loss of use or derangement of the affected body parts, systems, or functions.[12] The physician must then compare the results of the analysis with medical impairment criteria. The guide states that this comparison need not be performed by the same physician who did the evaluation as long as the medical data is listed using standard notation. Thus, an independent medical examiner can review an impairment determination using records only. Finally, the physician must determine the impairment rating, taking into account that the final impairment value is applied to the "whole person."

Exhibit 3-2
Normal Range of Motion for Parts of the Body

		Range in Degrees
Neck	Flexion	45
	Extension	55
	Lateral flexion	40
	Rotation	70
Shoulder	Flexion	180
	Extension	50
	Abduction	180
	Adduction	50
	External rotation	90
	Internal rotation	90
Elbow	Flexion	160
	Extension	0
Wrist	Flexion	90
	Extension	70
	Ulnar deviation	55
	Radial deviation	20
	Pronation	90
	Supination	90
Hip	Flexion	120
	Extension	15
	Abduction	45
	Adduction	45
	External rotation	40
	Internal rotation	40
Knee	Flexion	130
	Extension	0
Ankle	Plantar flexion	45
	Dorsiflexion	20
	Inversion	30
	Eversion	20
Torso	Flexion	75-90
	Extension	30
	Lateral flexion	35
	Rotation	30

If a patient has several impairments, each must be evaluated separately. For instance, a physician would consider a soft tissue problem of the neck caused by an automobile accident and a low back strain and sprain from a work-related accident by evaluating each impairment separately, providing documentation for each area or body part. Additionally, if the patient has sustained injury to her low back in a prior work accident, for example, and received a rating of impairment to the low back and was subsequently injured in another work accident, the physician should be asked to apportion out the impairment rating for the current work injury. In order to do this, the physician would need the patient's prior records containing the previous impairment rating of the low back.

Reports of Impairment

Reports from examining physicians should contain clear, accurate, and objective information, with enough data that a knowledgeable reviewer can understand the rating and assess its validity for its intended use. The following is a comprehensive list of essential information:

- *Medical evaluation*
    1. Narrative history of the medical conditions with reference to onset and course, findings from previous examinations, previous treatment, and responses to that treatment.
    2. Results of the most recent clinical evaluation, including all of the following, when obtained: physical examination findings, laboratory test results, electrocardiogram, X-ray studies, rehabilitation evaluation, mental status examination and psychological tests, and any other special tests or diagnostic procedures.
    3. Assessment of current clinical status and statement of plans for future treatment, rehabilitation, and re-evaluation.
    4. Diagnosis and clinical impressions.
    5. Expected date of full or partial recovery.
- *Analysis of the findings*
    1. Explanation of the effects of the medical conditions on daily activities.
    2. Explanation of the medical basis for conclusions about the stability of the condition.
    3. Explanation of the medical basis for a conclusion that the individual is or is not likely to suffer incapacitation as a result of the medical condition.
    4. Explanation of the medical basis for any conclusion that the individual is or is not likely to suffer injury or risk of further medical impairment by engaging in activities of daily living or any other activity necessary to meet personal, social, and occupational demands.
    5. Explanation of any conclusion that restrictions or accommodations are or are not needed to perform the daily activities essential to meet personal, social, and occupational demands. If restrictions or accommodations are necessary, there should be an explanation of their therapeutic or risk-avoiding value.
- *Comparison of the data with impairment criteria*
    1. Description of specific clinical findings related to each impairment, with reference to how the findings relate to the criteria described in the guide. Reference to the absence of or to the examiner's inability to obtain pertinent data is essential.

2. Comparison of specific clinical findings with the criteria pertaining to the particular body system as listed in the guide.
3. Explanation of each percentage of the impairment rating, with reference to the applicable criteria.
4. Summary statement of all impairment ratings.
5. Combined or "whole person" rating when more than one impairment is present.[13]

Claim representatives reviewing a physician's report must remember that although permanent medical impairment is related to the health status of the individual, disability can be determined only with reference to the personal, social, or occupational demands or statutory or regulatory requirements that the individual cannot meet as a result of the impairment.[14]

Determining Temporary Work Disability

Ideally, temporary work disabilities would be determined by evaluating the worker's identified physical impairment and comparing it to the physical demands of the job. As the worker's condition improved, this comparison would be continually made to see what aspects of his or her job the worker could reassume. Unfortunately, temporary work disability is rarely determined so thoroughly. In a typical case of temporary work disability, after the claimant returns to work, the physician states a diagnosis and certifies that the claimant was disabled for exactly the period of time the claimant was actually away from work. The claim representative must evaluate the period of disability after it has ended.

The Claim Representative's Role

Despite the difficulty in analyzing a period of temporary work disability, claim representatives can complete this task. During the period of disability, the claim representative has a right to obtain an independent medical exam (IME). This right is usually available in workers compensation cases and liability claims in suit. In liability claims not yet in suit, the right may not exist, but the request for an IME is an effective and assertive claim-handling practice. The claimant may cooperate. If the claimant refuses to submit to an IME, the claim representative may infer that the claimant has something to hide.

Even after a period of work disability has ended, the claim representative can investigate the physical requirements of the claimant's job and insist on an explanation of specifically how the injury in question prevented the claimant from performing his or her job. With knowledge of the physical demands of the claimant's job, the claim representative may be in a better position to judge disability than a physician who only knows the claimant's medical impairments. This possibility is particularly important because the U.S. economy is increasingly dominated by sedentary and light-duty jobs. In such jobs, even a serious injury, such as a broken leg, may not be disabling if the claimant has transportation to and from work and if the job can be modified in minor ways.

It is pointless for claim representatives to contest every case of disability, because most cases are legitimate. A claim representative can best guard against disability claims that abuse the system by knowing the typical periods of disability for various injuries. These cases should receive special effort and attention.

Cooperative Physicians

Many physicians believe that a return to normal daily activities has a valuable therapeutic effect on patients. These physicians eagerly cooperate in an effort to return the patient to work. The vast majority of physicians cooperate in answering questions from a party with a legitimate interest in the patient's recovery, whether the party is the employer or the insurer paying the bills. In any case, the physician cannot be expected to provide information unless the patient has signed a medical authorization.

Assuming the physician is cooperative, the claim representative should obtain a predicted return-to-work date as soon as possible. If the return-to-work date seems unusual, the claim representative should seek an explanation. If job modifications are feasible, the physician should be encouraged to consider authorizing the claimant's return to work even before complete recovery. If the claimant is still disabled on the originally projected return-to-work date, the claim representative should ask the physician for an explanation and a new projected return-to-work date.

Overcoming Disability

The claim representative's goal in all cases of disability is to help and encourage the claimant to overcome his or her disability. In cases of temporary disability, the length of disability depends on the factors explained in this section. The claim representative's goal is to continually evaluate the length of disability in light of the claimant's medical needs. Permanent impairment, by definition, cannot be eradicated, but it need not always result in permanent disability. The ways in which a permanent impairment is prevented from becoming a permanent disability are also discussed in this section.

Factors Affecting the Length of Temporary Disability

Claim representatives must use the information in this exhibit with care. Numerous factors can affect the length of a given disability. The disability periods indicated in this exhibit are average periods. In addition, hospitalization periods have been declining in recent years as hospitals and doctors have more carefully reviewed hospital use.

The injuries that make up a great percentage of claims normally heal on their own in a short time. Eighty-five percent of patients with acute mechanical low back pain from soft tissue irritation recover within five days to two weeks.[15] Eighty to eighty-five percent of all patients with acute low back pain recover within three days to three weeks regardless of treatment.[16] Claim representatives should not accept a diagnosis of strain or sprain if the condition lasts for months. Simple strains and sprains will resolve much sooner. Strains and sprains outside of the claim context, such as those resulting from sports, housework, or yard work, always heal quickly. So should strains and sprains involving property casualty claims.

Aside from the nature of the injury itself, several factors play an important role in determining the length of temporary work disability. These factors include the claimant's age and occupation, preexisting or complicating conditions, and the claimant's motivation.

Age

In general, the older the person is who suffers an injury, the slower he or she heals. Older people are also more likely to have preexisting conditions or other frailties.

Injured workers in their late fifties or early sixties may view an accidental injury as justification for early retirement, especially workers in the construction business. Construction workers may have worked in carpentry, masonry, or electrical work, but as a result of injury may be restricted to light-duty work. Since most of construction is medium to heavy-duty work, a return to their previous occupation is impossible. In general, most workers are unaware of their transferable skills. As a result, when they are unable to perform their usual work duties, they see their future in other occupations as bleak. Therefore, regular disability payments may act as a disincentive to considering alternative employment, and older people may tend to view this money as the key to retirement.

Occupation

Temporary work disabilities are more common among blue-collar than white-collar workers. The incidence of injury is higher in jobs that require lifting or repetitive manual tasks, such as assembly-line work. In addition, an injured worker who must return to manual labor must be in better health and more completely recovered than an injured worker who can return to light or sedentary work.

Attitudes toward returning to work also differ among workers. People who work in factories at repetitive jobs tend to accept continuing workers compensation disability as relief from work that is boring and dull. Blue-collar workers commonly have an adversarial attitude toward their employers. This less-than-comfortable situation makes the return to work less attractive. In contrast, white-collar workers or general office workers usually minimize the seriousness of injuries and may try to return to work too soon. Of course, individual cases do not always correspond with these generalizations.

Preexisting Conditions

Preexisting conditions such as diabetes, heart disease, or psychiatric problems affect the recovery of an injured worker. Diabetes delays the healing of wounds; as a result, a longer course of antibiotics and a longer healing time may delay the return-to-work date. In addition, blood sugar is more difficult to control after the stress and damage to the body caused by a serious accident. In fact, the sugar level of diabetics is commonly uncontrolled for some time after a significant injury. A compensation insurer must often cover a hospital course followed by treatment at home, sometimes for many years, when a compensable accident has exacerbated preexisting diabetes.

Heart disease, another condition that often preexists an injury, directly affects an individual's recovery. Heart disease is commonly undiagnosed until stressful conditions bring on a heart attack.

Stroke, or cerebral vascular accident, is another body weakness that may exist before an accident and that may complicate injuries arising from an accident. It can also result from injuries. In any given case, the insurer must determine whether the accident caused the stroke or whether the stroke occurred first and the accident followed. A physician can review the following preexisting factors to determine the likelihood of a causal connection between a stroke and accidental injuries:

- Family history of stroke
- Smoking
- History of high blood pressure
- Symptoms of severe headache
- Obvious head injury or trauma

Psychiatric conditions can also precede or result from an injury. Both preexisting and resulting psychiatric conditions can complicate and delay recovery from physical injuries.

Complications

Complications are secondary diseases, illnesses, or conditions that develop after an initial injury and delay overall recovery. Osteomyelitis (bone infection), for instance, can complicate recovery from a fractured bone. This problem is usually treated with antibiotics and sometimes with surgery to remove dead bone. Recovery time is lengthened greatly when the physician fails to take early, aggressive action or delays referring the case to an appropriate physician with expertise in osteomyelitis. Other types of infections can also make a relatively simple problem much worse.

Sensitivity to medications can also complicate recovery. An individual who must take anti-inflammatory medication for low back sprain, but who has stomach-lining sensitivity, can suffer ulcers.

Motivation

The length of occupational disability can vary according to differences in motivation. Individuals who are motivated to work out of commitment or by a desire to return to their normal routine often return to work still in pain or not fully recovered. These individuals are also likely to be the most scrupulous in following doctors' orders and physical therapy routines that will hasten their recovery. In addition, someone who is not receiving any disability compensation may be highly motivated to return to work even before fully recovered.

On the other hand, a common but problematic reaction to physical disability is the desire to stay disabled. Claim representatives often see this condition when the case is in litigation or when the claimant stands to gain something from the injury. The gain might be financial or psychological if, for instance, the injured individual (no matter how slightly injured) receives, as part of complex family dynamics, the attention and love he or she may not have received before the accident. There may be very little motivation to recover from injury when the value of a case depends on the amount of medical bills generated in treatment. This situation is common in liability cases. In temporary work disability claims under workers compensation, the motivation to return to work may be low because of factors unrelated to the injury, such as impending layoffs, friction between the supervisor and the "injured" worker, or union rules that state that the worker must be 100 percent recovered before a return to work is permitted.

People with claims take longer to heal than people without claims, although true malingering is probably relatively rare. The most painful and difficult injuries naturally take the longest to heal and are most likely to generate a claim. So there is nothing unusual about the connection between delayed healing and the making of a claim. However, claim representatives and physicians have observed that the act of asserting a claim seems to delay recovery. This delay is not usually a result of malingering or the severity of the injury, but of unconscious motivations. To rationalize or to justify making a claim or suing another person, many claimants magnify their injuries and symptoms. A claimant who seems miraculously to stop ailing once a claim is settled has not necessarily been malingering, but may simply no longer need to justify the act of asserting a claim or maintaining a lawsuit.

Overcoming Permanent Impairment

Many who suffer injuries are left with permanent impairments. However, permanent impairments need not lead to permanent disability. Impaired people may be able to return to a former job if the work can be modified. Otherwise, they may be able to use their remaining abilities in other employment. Both a job analysis and an assessment of physical capabilities and transferable skills will help the injured person to overcome permanent impairment. A vocational rehabilitation counselor can assist the claim representative in assessing any case involving alleged permanent work or other disability due to impairment. In order to do so, the injured person must be deemed to be at maximum medical improvement (MMI) and also medically assessed for permanent restrictions as a result of the impairment. Once this information is obtained, the vocational counselor may begin to assess whether the individual is disabled from meeting any personal, social, or occupational demands. In the case of work disability, the vocational counselor will assist the injured person to obtain a job with pay commensurate with the pay he or she was receiving when injured, if he or she cannot return to his or her former job because of the nature of the impairment, imposed medical restrictions, or the employer's inability to provide reasonable accommodation. Nevertheless, some workers will suffer a permanent loss of earning capacity.

Job Analysis

An on-site job analysis performed by a vocational rehabilitation professional can help claim representatives determine the specific task requirements for a job. Everyone affected by a long-term work disability will benefit from a job analysis since the duties are clarified and quantified. The injured worker and his or her family, the employer, attorneys, and the insurance claim representative will better understand how to approach the case and what to expect about the worker's occupational future.

Job analysis is especially important in insurance claims in which a return to work is of utmost importance. A return to work is important in workers compensation because many states put the burden of proof on the employer/insurer to show that jobs are available and that the injured worker can physically do the job. Such burden of proof is easily met when an employee has returned to his or her former job.

After an accident that causes orthopedic or neurological injuries, the recovered individual must be able to perform all job duties safely. However, despite an injured worker's desire to return to work or an employer's desire to have an employee back on the job, reinstating the employee may be difficult unless everyone knows and understands the physical demands of the job.

The purpose of a job analysis is to determine what tasks and activities are required to perform a given job. It is preferable to perform a job analysis at the job site because the vocational rehabilitation professional can watch the job being performed. As a result, he or she will have a better idea of job requirements than would be provided by a written job description. Written descriptions may enumerate only the nonphysical aspects of the job, such as hours to be worked.

The vocational rehabilitation professional should observe the environment at the job site, noting any barriers such as stairs or narrow doorways. In watching the job being performed, the vocational rehabilitation specialist should observe the *activities* of the workers, not the characteristics of the individuals doing the job. This obligation will help the analyst include the important physical demands of the job in the analysis, such as standing, walking, sitting, lifting, carrying, pushing, pulling, climbing, balancing, stooping, bending, kneeling, crouching, crawling, reaching, handling, fingering, feeling, talking, hearing, tasting, smelling, and seeing. A job analysis should include the amount of weight the employee must lift, push, pull, or carry, as well as how frequently such work is done. Frequency of work may be expressed in number of times per hour or as a percentage of the workday.

It is also important to inspect any tools, machines, or assisting devices used on the job and to note the work hours and whether the job is performed indoors or out. Other environmental conditions such as temperature (hot, cold, or alternating), wetness, humidity, noise, vibration, and heights should also be addressed in the analysis. A sample form for a job analysis is shown in Exhibit 3-3.

Job analysis information is useful not only because it provides an overall picture of the job, but also as a means of identifying segments of the job that can be modified to allow a worker to return to work at an earlier date. Ultimately, the employer controls whether the job may be modified. Some changes are easy to accomplish, such as allowing a worker to use a stool to sit instead of standing 100 percent of the time or eliminating lifting by switching duties with another worker whose job tasks do not include lifting. However, employers should be encouraged to make substantial changes as well because an injured employee is usually most comfortable and most willing to try to return to work when he or she knows the job, the environment, and the employer.

Determining and Restoring Physical Capacities

The physical capacities form is another useful tool for claim professionals. It quantifies what an individual *can* do and is usually completed by a physician or work-hardening/work-tolerance specialist. Exhibit 3-4 shows a sample physical capacities form.

Work tolerance, or *work hardening*, operates on the premise that it is better to prepare a worker for strenuous work *before* he or she returns to work, thus reducing the possibility of injury on the job. The injured worker is most likely to be in a deteriorated physical condition because of the inactivity. Aerobic conditioning (bicycling, walking, and swimming) and strength conditioning are part of a work tolerance program.

A work-hardening specialist might use special equipment to evaluate an individual's ability to perform certain work-related tasks, such as lifting a pail of processed meat or pushing a dolly loaded with books. The actual activity is broken down into segments, which allows the examiner to test individual muscle groups with specific machines. For example, if an individual must pick up fifty-pound bags of potatoes and move them from a skid to a truck, the major muscle groups involved in the action would include the quadriceps (front of the thighs), biceps (arms), and abdominals. The injured worker would

Exhibit 3-3
Job Analysis Form

```
                                                    Claim # _____
    Claimant: _____
    Job Title: _____ D.O.T. #: _____
    Firm & Address: _____
    Person Contacted: _____ Phone No.: _____
    Job Summary/Description of Tasks: _____
    _____

    Work Schedule (hours, days per week):_____ Wage: _____
    Education/Training:
```

PHYSICAL DEMANDS:

- [ ] Standing _____ Hours/Day
- [ ] Sitting _____ Hours/Day
- [ ] Walking _____ Hours/Day
- [ ] Lifting _____ lbs.-how often/day
- [ ] Driving _____
- [ ] Carrying _____ lbs.-how often/day

- [ ] Pulling _____ lbs.-how often/day
- [ ] Climbing _____ Height _____ Frequency
- [ ] Balancing _____ Height _____ Frequency
- [ ] Bending/Squatting _____ Body part _____ Frequency
- [ ] Twisting _____ Body part _____ Degrees _____ Frequency _____
- [ ] Rotation _____ Body part _____ Degrees _____ Frequency _____
- [ ] Crawling _____ Distance _____ Frequency
- [ ] Kneeling on _____ Duration _____ Frequency
- [ ] Reaching _____ Distance _____ Frequency

ENVIRONMENTAL CONDITIONS:

Inside _____ % Outside _____ % Both _____ % Temp. extremes _____
Fumes _____ Dust _____ Gases _____ Odors _____ Mist
NOISE OR VIBRATION: _____
HAZARDS: _____
MACHINES, TOOLS, EQUIPMENT: _____
GENERAL COMMENTS: _____
_____
_____
_____

PHYSICIAN'S COMMENTS: _____

Analyzed by:_____ Job Approved: _____
                    SIGNATURE
Date: _____ Not Approved: _____

                          _____   / /
                           Physician's Signature   Date

Exhibit 3-4
Physical Capacities Form

Claimant Name:_____
Claim #:_____ Representative: _____
Insurance Co.:_____ Adjuster:_____

In an 8-hour workday, patient can: (Circle full capacity for each)

Sit	1	2	3	4	5	6	7	8	Hrs/Day
Stand	1	2	3	4	5	6	7	8	Hrs/Day
Walk	1	2	3	4	5	6	7	8	Hrs/Day

Patient can lift/carry: (Please check as appropriate)

	Never		Occasionally		Frequently		No Restriction
	Lift	Carry	Lift	Carry	Lift	Carry	
0-10 lb.	[ ]	[ ]	[ ]	[ ]	[ ]	[ ]	[ ]
11-25 lb.	[ ]	[ ]	[ ]	[ ]	[ ]	[ ]	[ ]
26-50 lb.	[ ]	[ ]	[ ]	[ ]	[ ]	[ ]	[ ]
51-100 lb.	[ ]	[ ]	[ ]	[ ]	[ ]	[ ]	[ ]
100+ lb.	[ ]	[ ]	[ ]	[ ]	[ ]	[ ]	[ ]

Patient can use hand for repetitive: (Please check as appropriate)

	Simple Grasping		Fine Manipulation		Pushing and Pulling	
Right	[N]	[Y]	[N]	[Y]	[N]	[Y]
Left	[N]	[Y]	[N]	[Y]	[N]	[Y]

Patient can use feet for repetitive movement such as foot controls: (Please check as appropriate)

Right	[N]	[Y]	Left	[N]	[Y]

Patient is able to: (Please check as appropriate)

	Not at all	Occasionally	Frequently	No Restriction
Bend	[ ]	[ ]	[ ]	[ ]
Climb	[ ]	[ ]	[ ]	[ ]
Crawl	[ ]	[ ]	[ ]	[ ]
Squat	[ ]	[ ]	[ ]	[ ]
Reach	[ ]	[ ]	[ ]	[ ]
Twist	[ ]	[ ]	[ ]	[ ]

Patient is able to drive: (Please check as appropriate)

	Not at all	Occasionally	Frequently	No Restriction
Car	[ ]	[ ]	[ ]	[ ]
Small Truck	[ ]	[ ]	[ ]	[ ]
Large Truck	[ ]	[ ]	[ ]	[ ]
Automatic Transmission	[ ]	[ ]	[ ]	[ ]
Standard Transmission	[ ]	[ ]	[ ]	[ ]
Heavy Equipment	[ ]	[ ]	[ ]	[ ]

RETURN TO WORK STATEMENT

As a result of this evaluation, patient could perform: (Please check as appropriate)

[ ] No Work
[ ] Part-time   Sedentary Work—10 lbs. maximum lifting or carrying articles.
[ ] Full-time   Walking/standing on occasion.
[ ] Part-time   Light Work—20 lbs. maximum lifting, carrying 10 lb. articles frequently.
[ ] Full-time   Most jobs involving sitting with a degree of pushing and pulling.
[ ] Part-time   Medium Work—50 lbs. maximum lifting with frequent lifting/carrying of up to
[ ] Full-time   25 lbs., frequent standing and walking.
[ ] Part-time   Heavy Work—100 lbs. maximum lifting with frequent lifting/carrying of up to
[ ] Full-time   50 lbs. frequent standing and walking.
[ ] Part-time   Very Heavy Work—lifting objects over 100 lbs. and frequent lifting/carrying of
[ ] Full time   50 lbs. or more, frequent standing and walking.

When will patient be released to return to work: [ ] Immediately   [ ] _____   (Please specify)
Date:_____   Physician's Signature _____

therefore be tested on equipment that isolates each of these muscle groups. A worker's performance on machines must be greater than, or at least equal to, what would be required on the job. Any inability on the behalf of the injured worker to meet the physical requirements of the job during the physical capacities evaluation would form the basis for physical restrictions placed by the physician who ordered the physical capacities test.

Both a job analysis and a physical capacities test are important in the recovery process and in resolving claims involving work disability because the results of both help to determine a disabled person's potential for all future work. Once the job requirements and the worker's physical capacities are known, there is little conjecture involved in deciding whether a recovered worker can return to work and what job he or she can perform.

Transferable Skills

Transferable skills are abilities that can be applied equally from one job to another. For example, making shipping arrangements over the telephone may be one job requirement of a mail room supervisor. The individual may not be able to perform the other duties of this job because of an inability to lift more than fifty pounds. However, telephone skills can be transferred to another job for which they are important and for which the physical tasks are not as strenuous. The worker might therefore be eligible for a job in telemarketing, for instance, which requires good telephone skills but no heavy lifting.

An understanding of transferable skills is important and useful knowledge when one must locate employment for an individual who does not know where to look. An injured worker ready to return to work should also be encouraged to identify transferable skills so that the job search will be less difficult.

Role of Vocational Rehabilitation and Counseling

Overcoming disability can be difficult for some people. A vocational rehabilitation counselor can assist an injured worker through recovery and help get him or her back to work. An important function of the vocational rehabilitation process is to build rapport with the injured worker and to develop and demonstrate trust, caring, and sensitivity to the worker's needs. However, the claimant must be aware that the vocational rehabilitation counselor will be communicating with the insurance company. Once this is clarified, the claimant should understand what the counselor is to do and to whom the counselor's reports are sent.

Most people have never had any vocational counseling. Family or friends usually influence where and for whom an individual works. Very little thought is often given to the job search process. A vocational rehabilitation counselor is experienced in assessing an individual's physical ability to work, level of motivation, job skills, educational preparation, and work experience. The vocational rehabilitation counselor can also identify the industries in which the claimant could return to work.

Job skills counseling, including résumé preparation and interviewing skills, is another way in which the vocational rehabilitation counselor can help. Intense preparation in job skills counseling may be necessary if, for example, the injured worker has worked for thirty years in construction as a carpenter and because of a back injury and subsequent surgery cannot return to carpentry.

Often an injured worker is fearful about returning to work because of the possibility of re-injury. A rehabilitation counselor fosters confidence that the injury will not recur when proper body mechanics are considered and safety measures are followed. Generally, in this role, the counselor is reinforcing information that the physician or physical therapist has already given to the claimant.

The vocational rehabilitation counselor may also search for a job on behalf of the claimant. The counselor will search for job openings that fit the physical capabilities, work experience, and education of the injured worker and then pass on to the injured worker any useful information.

Determination of Loss of Earning Capacity

Determination of loss of earning capacity is important in claims. If an individual is injured and unable to return to his or her job, the claim representative must determine the difference between the salary at the time of the injury and the salary that the individual is now *capable* of earning upon return to work. The worker need not have actually returned to work for the latter to be determined. A claim representative will rely heavily on a vocational rehabilitation professional for information about available jobs and for job analyses.

The problem of reduced earnings is particularly common among injured construction workers. For example, workers in construction typically earn more than $20 per hour for their work. Should an injury prevent a worker from returning to this work, the worker's earning capacity outside of construction may be only $8 to $10 per hour if he or she has only an elementary or high school education.

Summary

Work disability, which is different from impairment and handicap, is a major concern of claim representatives who handle injury claims. The extent and duration of any disability are probably the key factors affecting the value of any type of property casualty injury claim. In addition to its effect on claims, any permanent disability has a profound effect on society, the employer, the economy, and, of course, on the disabled themselves.

Disability can only be determined by analyzing an individual's physical impairment and the medical placement of any permanent restrictions, and comparing these restrictions to the demands of that individual's personal activities or job. The AMA has standardized the evaluation of physical impairment in its *Guide to the Evaluation of Permanent Impairment.* Temporary disabilities generally cannot be analyzed as thoroughly as permanent disabilities. Nevertheless, claim representatives should know typical lengths of disability for various injuries so that they can concentrate their effort and attention on cases that may be abusive to the system.

Other than the nature of the injury, the length of temporary disabilities depends on the age and occupation of the individual, the presence of preexisting or complicating conditions, and the individual's level of motivation. Overcoming permanent impairment may require job analysis, assessment of the individual's physical capabilities, services from a vocational rehabilitation counselor, and assessment of transferable skills.

Chapter Notes

1. American Medical Association, *Guide to the Evaluation of Permanent Impairment* (Chicago: AMA, 1993), p. 1.1.
2. *Guide to the Evaluation of Permanent Impairment,* p. 1-2.
3. Elizabeth Kubler-Ross, *Death: The Final Stage of Growth* (New York: Simon and Schuster, 1986), p. 10.
4. Kubler-Ross, p. 10.
5. Hoyle Leigh, M.D., and Morton F. Reiser, M.D., *The Patient: Biological, Psychological, and Social Dimensions of Medical Practice,* 2d ed. (New York: Plenum Medical Book Co., 1985), pp. 18-23.
6. All quoted language is based on Senate bill S.933. The final law was enacted July 26, 1990.
7. *Accident Facts 1998 Edition* (Chicago: National Safety Council), p. 51.
8. *Accident Facts,* p. 53.
9. *Guide to the Evaluation of Permanent Impairment,* p. iii.
10. *Guide to the Evaluation of Permanent Impairment,* p. x.
11. *Guide to the Evaluation of Permanent Impairment,* p. vii.
12. *Guide to the Evaluation of Permanent Impairment,* p. viii.
13. *Guide to the Evaluation of Permanent Impairment,* p. 223.
14. *Guide to the Evaluation of Permanent Impairment,* p. x.
15. Rene Calliet, *Soft Tissue Pain and Disability* (Philadelphia: F.A. Davis Co., 1988), p. 95.
16. Ralph E. Matkin, *Insurance Rehabilitation: Service Applications in Disability Compensation Systems* (Austin, TX: Pro-Ed, 1985), p. 117.

Appendix

Determining Job Demands

The most thorough and reliable way to determine the demands of a job is through a job analysis, described in the final section of this chapter. However, for cases in which a job analysis is not possible or practical, standard references provide information about thousands of occupations. These references are the *Dictionary of Occupational Titles* and the *Selected Characteristics Companion Volume*.

Dictionary of Occupational Titles

Since the first edition was published in 1939, the *Dictionary of Occupational Titles* (DOT) has provided the U.S. Employment Service and others with detailed standard occupational information essential to the effective classification and placement of job seekers. It describes the job duties and requirements for virtually all jobs in the U.S. The fourth edition, published in 1977, describes approximately 20,000 jobs.

In addition to job placement, the DOT is useful for employment counseling, occupational and career guidance, and labor market information services. Originally, the primary use of the DOT was to match job openings with the qualifications of job applicants at the U.S. Employment Service. The Employment Service needed to standardize all job information and to provide a uniform occupational language for use in all of its offices. Although the book was originally created to meet a need of the Employment Service system, it is used today by vocational rehabilitation counselors, rehabilitation nurses, job placement specialists, and others in the private sector of rehabilitation service delivery to help determine job tasks.

As used in the DOT, "occupation" refers to a collective description of numerous individual job duties performed, possibly with many variations, in many establishments.[1] The DOT organizes occupations in a variety of ways. First, the DOT looks at occupations based on similarities of jobs. Every occupation has a nine-digit *occupation code*. For example, 241.217-010 is the code for "CLAIM ADJUSTER (bus. service.; insurance) insurance adjuster; insurance-claim representative; or insurance investigator." This occupation is described as follows:

> Investigates claims against insurance or other companies for personal, casualty, or property loss or damages and attempts to effect out-of-court settlement with claimant: Examines claim form and other records to determine insurance coverage. Interviews, telephones, or corresponds with claimant and witnesses; consults police and hospital records; and inspects property damage to determine extent of company's liability, varying method of investigation according to type of insurance. Prepares report of findings and negotiates settlement with claimant. Recommends litigation by legal department when settlement cannot be negotiated. May attend litigation hearings. May be designated according to type of claim adjusted as AUTOMOBILE-INSURANCE-CLAIM ADJUSTER (bus. ser.; insurance); CASUALTY-INSURANCE-CLAIM ADJUSTER (clerical); FIDELITY-AND-SURETY-BONDS-CLAIM ADJUSTER (bus. ser.; insurance); FIRE-INSURANCE-CLAIM ADJUSTER (bus. ser.; insurance); MARINE-INSURANCE-CLAIM ADJUSTER (bus. ser.; insurance); PROPERTY-LOSS-INSURANCE-CLAIM ADJUSTER (clerical).[2]

The first three numbers in an occupation code identify the occupational group. All occupations are grouped into nine broad "categories," identified by the first digit, such as professional, technical, or, in the case of "claim adjuster," *clerical and sales occupations* (2). The second digit refers to a "division" within a category, in this example (4), *miscellaneous clerical occupations*. The third digit specifies the particular occupational group within the division, in this case (1), *investigators, adjusters, and related occupations*.

The *middle three digits* of the code are the worker functions ratings of the tasks performed in the occupation. Every job requires a worker to perform (or to function) in relation to data, people, and things. The worker function rating identifies the difficulty or complexity of the functions of a given job as they relate to data, people, and things. Worker functions that involve more complex responsibility and judgment are assigned lower numbers. Less complicated functions are assigned higher numbers. For example, synthesizing data (0) is a higher-level skill than comparing data (6). The listing of all codes is shown in Exhibit A3-1. The coding for claim adjusters (217) indicates the need for a fairly high level of skill handling data (2), an even higher level skill in handling people (1), but little skill in handling things (7).

The *last three digits* in the occupational code indicate the alphabetical order of occupation titles within six-digit code groups if more than one occupation is included within a given six-digit code. These last three digits differentiate a specific occupation from all others. All jobs listed in the DOT have a unique nine-digit code.

Exhibit 3A-1
List of Codes in the Dictionary of Occupational Titles

DATA (4th Digit)	PEOPLE (5th Digit)	THINGS (6th Digit)
0 Synthesizing	0 Mentoring	0 Setting up
1 Coordinating	1 Negotiating	1 Precision working
2 Analyzing	2 Instructing	2 Operating-controlling
3 Compiling	3 Supervising	3 Driving-operating
4 Computing	4 Diverting	4 Manipulating
5 Copying	5 Persuading	5 Tending
6 Comparing	6 Speaking-signaling	6 Feeding-offbearing
	7 Serving	7 Handling
	8 Taking instructions-helping	

The DOT also lists occupational title, industry designation, and alternate titles as part of occupational information and includes a brief description of the tasks performed.

Selected Characteristics Companion Volume

The *Selected Characteristics of Occupations Defined in the DOT* is a companion volume that was developed in response to a need for more detailed information about the occupational characteristics listed in the DOT. The *Selected Characteristics* volume includes information about environmental conditions, mathematical and language development, specific vocational preparation, and physical demands.

Environmental conditions are the physical surroundings for a job. Designations include "I" for inside, "O" for outside, and "B" for both, and exposure to extremes of cold, heat, wetness, or humidity.

Mathematical and language development codes and requirements range from Level 6 to Level 1. Level 6 mathematical development means that advanced calculus, algebra, and statistics are required on a job. Level 6 language development means that the job includes reading and writing novels, technical journals, and manuals, and persuasive speaking. Level 1 math skill requires adding and subtracting two-digit numbers. Level 1 language skill requires reading and writing compound and complex sentences.

Specific vocational preparation training time codes and requirements range from Level 1, short demonstration, to Level 9, over ten years. This information, plus the extent of language and mathematical skill required for a job, is crucial in determining the feasibility of a new career for someone disabled from his or her former job. A job requiring much higher skills than a worker currently possesses is not a likely choice.

The physical demands of a job are expressed in terms of the following factors:

1. Strength
2. Climbing and/or balancing
3. Stooping, kneeling, crouching, and/or crawling
4. Reaching, handling, fingering, and/or feeling
5. Talking and/or hearing
6. Seeing

Strength, the first physical demands factor, is expressed in terms of the kind of work required—sedentary, light, medium, heavy, and very heavy. These degrees of strength are stated as follows:

- S—Sedentary work. Lifting ten pounds maximum and occasionally lifting and/or carrying such articles as dockets, ledgers, and small tools. Although a sedentary job is defined as involving sitting, some walking and standing are often necessary in carrying out job duties. Jobs are sedentary if walking and standing are required only occasionally and other sedentary criteria are met.
- L—Light work. Lifting twenty pounds maximum with frequent lifting and/or carrying of objects weighing up to ten pounds. Even though lifting of weights may be negligible, a job is in this category when it requires walking or standing to a significant degree, or when it involves sitting most of the time with a degree of pushing and pulling of arm and/or leg controls.
- M—Medium work. Lifting fifty pounds maximum with frequent lifting and/or carrying of objects weighing up to twenty-five pounds.
- H—Heavy work. Lifting 100 pounds maximum with frequent lifting and/or carrying of objects weighing up to 50 pounds.
- V—Very heavy work. Lifting objects in excess of 100 pounds with frequent lifting and/or carrying of objects weighing 50 pounds or more.[3]

The physical demands are described with reference to the worker's position and movements as defined below:

- Worker position(s)

    Standing: remaining on one's feet in an upright position at a workstation without moving about

    Walking: moving about on foot

    Sitting: remaining in the normal seated position

- Worker movement of objects (including extremities used)

    Lifting: raising or lowering an object from one level to another (includes upward pulling)

    Carrying: transporting an object, usually holding it in the hands or arms or on the shoulder

Pushing: exerting force upon an object so that the object moves away from the force (includes slapping, striking, kicking, and treadle actions)

Pulling: exerting force upon an object so that the object moves toward the force (includes jerking)

The following example represents a typical listing for an occupation. The listing for "Claim Adjuster, DOT #241.217-010," would be shown as follows:

- Environment = B (both inside and outside)
- Mathematical = 3 Compute discount, interest, profit, and loss; commission, markups, and selling price; ratio and proportion; and percentages. Calculate surfaces, volumes, weights, and measures.

  Algebra: Calculate variables and formulas, monomials, and polynomials; ratio and proportion variables; and square roots and radicals.

  Geometry: Calculate plane and solid figures, circumference, area, and volume. Understand kinds of angles and properties of pairs and angles.
- Language = 5

  Reading: Read literature, book and play reviews, scientific and technical journals, abstracts, financial reports, and legal documents.

  Writing: Write novels, plays, editorials, journals, speeches, manuals, critiques, poetry, and songs.

  Speaking: Conversant in the theory, principles, and methods of effective and persuasive speaking, voice and diction, phonetics, and discussion and debate.
- SVP (specific vocational preparation) = 6 (over one year up to and including two years)
- Physical Demands = 1 = L (Light) and 5 (Talking and Hearing)

Appendix Notes

1. U.S. Department of Labor, *Dictionary of Occupational Titles*, Employment and Training Administration, 4th ed. (1977), p. xv.
2. *Dictionary of Occupational Titles*, p. 196.
3. U. S. Department of Labor, *Selected Characteristics of Occupations Defined in the Dictionary of Occupational Titles*, Employment and Training Administration (1981), p. 465.

Chapter 4
Rehabilitation

Broadly defined, rehabilitation is a dynamic process whereby an individual achieves maximum physical, cognitive, emotional, social, and economic capability. Rehabilitation includes two disciplines—physical/psychosocial rehabilitation and insurance rehabilitation. This chapter will examine the similarities, differences, and scope of practice of both types of rehabilitation and the professionals who work in each field. Finally, the chapter will discuss the effects of both types of rehabilitation on the injured and all other key parties involved in the rehabilitation process.

Overview of Rehabilitation

During both physical/psychosocial rehabilitation and insurance rehabilitation, injured individuals can maximize their functional abilities and regain their independence. **Physical/psychosocial rehabilitation** refers to the application of the paramedical and social sciences that optimize an individual's level of functioning after an impairment for the purposes of limiting and/or preventing disability. The services provided the individual may consist of treatment modalities such as hot packs and other profession-specific methods such as education, counseling, and exercise designed to retrain and reeducate an impaired individual's mind and body. Physical/psychosocial rehabilitation generally takes place in medical centers, clinics, or other outpatient facilities.

Insurance rehabilitation is defined by the Commission of Disability Management Specialists (formerly known as the Commission of Insurance Rehabilitation Specialists) as "the integration of medical, vocational and employer information to facilitate communication, return to work, and restoration of the individual to be able to function in society."[1] Insurance rehabilitation is typically provided over the telephone or face to face in the person's home, in the workplace, or in a testing center. Insurance rehabilitation professionals offer only consultation management services. The name "insurance rehabilitation" indicates that the field is allied closely to the insurance industry, which generally contracts for these services. As hired contractors, insurance rehabilitation professionals are termed rehabilitation vendors.

The Need for Rehabilitation

Bodily injuries represent a multi-billion dollar annual cost to the casualty insurance business. Workers compensation, auto liability, general liability, and medical malpractice claims, as well as the other coverages protecting against bodily injury, represent a substantial exposure for casualty insurance carriers providing these services. Although the issues of liability and coverage make some injury claims questionable, perhaps even mitigating the effects of these exposures, most injury claims are legitimate liabilities that are fully covered by the insurer. Claim representatives must manage the financial consequences and be aware of the social consequences that bodily injury claims produce. This challenge to and the accountability of claim representatives handling injury claims arise out of pressures from outside and support from within the insurance industry.

Pressures From Outside the Insurance Industry

The following case illustrates society's and the insurance industry's interest in providing more than just financial reimbursement for an injury.

Without Rehabilitation...

A machinist who worked for his employer for fifteen years took great pride in his work and was considered a valuable employee. One day, he caught his hand in a press, resulting in the amputation of his hand just above the wrist. The workers compensation insurer provided prompt payment of indemnity (lost wages) benefits and paid for the expense of the hospital and follow-up medical care. No insurance rehabilitation vendor was assigned to the case. Thus, his follow-up care after the amputation was not monitored, nor was a rehabilitation nurse or other case manager provided to attend to the psychological effects of the injury, which were substantial. Without an insurance rehabilitation professional assigned to his claim to coordinate vocational rehabilitation and ensure his prompt return to employment, the machinist was devastated by the loss of his hand. Although fitted with a prosthesis, he considered himself a "cripple" and refused to wear it. His employer hired a replacement because it appeared that the machinist would not return to work. Once the machinist was informed that he had no job to return to, he began to drink heavily. The man's life began to spiral out of his control, and he became estranged from his family.

This case demonstrates that financial reimbursement alone does not always "compensate" an injury. The injured worker lost not only his hand but his family as well. The employer lost a valuable employee and would have been better off not having to hire and train another worker. Society lost a productive member, who now presents a burden. The social consequences create pressures for insurers to intervene with a rehabilitation vendor. A better way to handle the case would have been through rehabilitation. Arthur Larson, a leading authority on workers compensation, has stated:

> It is probably no exaggeration to say that in this field [rehabilitation] lies the greatest single opportunity for significant improvement in the benefits afforded by the workers compensation system.[2]

The case involved workers compensation coverage, but rehabilitation offers similar opportunities in other lines of casualty insurance, such as auto and general liability.

Among the outside pressures to manage the bodily injury exposure is the erosion of common law defenses, such as assumption of risk, which results in insurance benefits for a greater number of persons and fewer legal strategies for mitigating the bodily injury exposure. The loss of legal remedies creates pressure to have a "safety net" that provides rehabilitation services.

Another major pressure is the growth of no-fault insurance. Workers compensation is a form of no-fault insurance that has existed since the early 1900s, but benefit levels and the numbers of employees covered have broadened the extent of this no-fault coverage, resulting in additional pressure to control costs under this type of system. Several states also mandate no-fault or first-party medical auto coverage, which increases the reach and the resultant exposure of no-fault coverage.

Support From Within the Insurance Industry

The insurance business itself has set out to meet society's expectations for providing rehabilitation services. The Insurance Rehabilitation Study Group is composed of representatives from among the largest casualty insurers in the United States and is influential in the casualty insurance industry generally. In a 1975 report, the Study Group stated the following:

> While insurance losses and benefits are usually stated in monetary terms, the full consequences of human disability cannot be measured by money alone. Earnings lost due to accident or sickness can be replaced and medical expenses can be reimbursed, but there is no meaningful way to financially translate the value of an arm or a leg, or the personal dignity of being able to contribute to society as a useful member rather than merely existing disabled and dependent. If insurance is to protect against these human losses, it must do more than provide financial compensation alone. It must also strive to restore such losses. Insurance should provide the means for disabled workers to return to gainful employment whenever possible, and to regain as much functional independence as they can, even if they cannot return to work. Compensation cannot accomplish these goals without rehabilitation.[3]

The National Commission on State Workers Compensation Laws, a group of representatives from major workers compensation insurers, the government, and other experts, made several recommendations in the early 1970s to improve the workers compensation system in the U.S., including the following:

- Reduce litigation in all workers compensation claims
- Increase benefits to equitable levels in all states
- Provide quality services (including rehabilitation) in a uniform manner in all states

There is clearly support within the insurance industry itself for the use of insurance rehabilitation in bodily injury claims.

Costs and Benefits of Insurance Rehabilitation

Although insurance rehabilitation services may produce great benefit, inappropriate use of provided service can be a significant claim expense. Costs can range from hundreds to thousands of dollars per case. Claim departments are reluctant to authorize such expenses unless they can foresee substantial savings on the cost of the underlying claim. Studies on the use of insurance rehabilitation provide some insight into whether the benefits justify the cost. There is no consensus on what constitutes an acceptable return-to-work rate, and there is no consensus on an average cost per case that defines cost-effective insurance rehabilitation services. Insurance rehabilitation services will likely continue as benefits of workers compensation insurance. The studies to date reaffirm that insurance rehabilitation is working, but not without problems. It can be improved by making it more cost-effective and by emphasizing the need to manage the insurance rehabilitation process to ensure that the costs do not outweigh the benefits.

The Practice of Physical/Psychosocial Rehabilitation

The many different professionals who deliver "hands-on" physical/psychosocial rehabilitation care or treatment are termed **rehabilitation providers**. The professions making up the field of physical/psychosocial rehabilitation are closely related to the medical profession, from which they all developed.

Many types of medical professionals practice physical/psychosocial rehabilitation. One of the primary professions within this area of physical rehabilitation is physiatry. **Physiatrists** are physicians of **physical medicine and rehabilitation (PM&R)**, or simply rehabilitation physicians. Only medical physicians, either doctors of medicine (M.D.s) or doctors of osteopathy (D.O.s), have the required qualifications to become a physiatrist or a physician of any other medical specialty. The American Board of Physical Medicine and Rehabilitation defines **physiatry** as "The medical specialty concerned with diagnosing, evaluating and treating patients with impairments and/or disabilities which involve musculoskeletal, neurologic, cardiovascular or other body systems. The primary focus is on maximum restoration of physical, psychological, social and vocational function and alleviation of pain...."[4]

A **physical therapist** is a licensed medical professional who by means of examination, treatment, or instruction detects, assesses, prevents, corrects, or limits physical disability, bodily malfunction, or pain. A physical therapist also administers and evaluates tests of bodily function and structures, most often involving the neck, the low back, and the upper arm and lower extremities.

A physical therapist evaluates the neuro-muscular-skeletal systems of the patient and sets short- and long-term goals as appropriate. The therapist then develops and implements a treatment program that emphasizes exercises and activities that will lead to the highest level of independence. This treatment program may include the use of adaptive equipment. As appropriate, the therapist will also participate in the discharge plans, including home modifications, and setting up a follow-up procedure. Physical therapists must complete a minimum of a bachelor's degree, and most states require licensure to practice.

Occupational medicine is a medical specialty involved in physical rehabilitation. **Occupational medicine** was first defined by the American Medical Association (AMA) over a quarter-century ago so accurately that the definition continues to be the official definition recognized by the American College of Occupational Medicine:

> A specialty field of medicine concerned with: 1. the appraisal, maintenance, restoration and improvement of the health of the worker through the application of the principles, of preventive medicine, emergency medical care, rehabilitation, and environmental medicine; 2. the promotion of a productive and fulfilling interaction of the worker with his work through the application of the principles of human behavior; and 3. the active application of the social, economic, and administrative needs and responsibilities of both the worker and the work community.

The discipline known as **occupational therapy** was introduced in the United States during World War I. Physicians and nurses caring for injured soldiers after their acute period of recovery noticed that they were bored and depressed because they had nothing to focus on except their impairment and disability. In addition, the prevailing attitude of the time conveyed that people who were less than mentally and physically whole and perfect were valueless to society. Therefore, physicians urged the nurses to keep the soldiers occupied with some type of activity that would engage both their minds and bodies. The ward nurses caring for the recovering soldiers gave them "occupations" like pottery making, basket weaving, and other crafts. These activities helped the injured soldiers' state of mind and improved their manual dexterity. In time, this treatment of the injured and disabled became known as occupational therapy, keeping the recovering impaired and disabled busy with an occupation.

Today, the focus of occupational therapy is similar in many ways to physical therapy. An occupational therapist provides group and individual services to maximize the independence of individuals with physical, behavioral, and cognitive impairments, through education and treatment. The services that occupational therapists provide include teaching daily living skills; developing the motor skills and sensory functioning needed for avocational, pre-vocational, and vocational abilities; designing, fabricating, and applying selected orthotic devices or adaptive equipment; administering and interpreting tests, such as manual muscle and range of motion of the upper extremities; modifying environments; and driver training for the impaired. Occupational therapists must complete a bachelor's degree at a minimum, and most states require licensure to practice.

Specialists interact with providers in the rehabilitation process. Both **neurology** and **neurosurgery** are specialties focused on treatment of the nervous system, and both play an important role in the treatment of neurological injuries and subsequent rehabilitation. The physicians in these fields are experts in the diagnosis and treatment of disorders of the brain and spinal cord (central nervous system) and the peripheral nervous system (sensory and motor nerves throughout the body). Whereas **neurologists** perform neurodiagnostic testing and treat their patients medically, **neurosurgeons** perform surgery on the brain, spinal cord, and other nerve-related structures.

Orthopedic physicians are another group of providers involved in treatment and rehabilitation. **Orthopedic medicine** involves the treatment, prevention, or correction of disorders involving the skeletal system (bones), its articulations or joints, and related supporting structures such as muscles, tendons, fascia, disks and ligaments. **Orthopedic surgeons** practice surgery as well as orthopedic medicine; neurosurgeons' practice is generally limited to surgery only. Both neurosurgeons and orthopedic surgeons can perform the same types of surgeries, such as the removal of part of the bony spinal column (laminectomy) and removal of the disks between the vertebrae, which is called a discectomy.

Individuals who have sustained an impairment as the result of an injury, a disease, or a condition are often cared for, after any emergency treatment, by their family physician, also known as that individual's **attending physician**. This physician has the primary responsibility for the patient and the patient's medical disposition. Often, the attending physician is a specialist in family practice medicine or internal medicine.

In contrast, a **consulting physician** has a different specialty than the attending physician and is asked by the attending physician to advise or to treat the patient on a limited basis. Occasionally, depending on the nature and extent of the patient's condition, the consulting physician may assume the full responsibility for the patient until the patient can be medically dismissed from the consulting physician's service and be remanded back to the attending physician.

Patients with any condition requiring hospitalization are cared for by a **registered nurse (RN)** or **licensed practical nurse (LPN)** specializing in hospital-based patient care. The **hospital-based nurse** is responsible for developing the patient's nursing care plan, which includes an assessment of basic needs including but not limited to nursing care relative to the medical diagnosis, fluid and nutritional intake, elimination needs, skin care, and the delivery of medications. Often, nurses motivate patients to progress beyond their initial response to both impairment and disability. Nurses are either diploma- or degree-prepared, in addition to being licensed by the state in which they practice.

Interaction of Treatment and Rehabilitation Providers

A worker sustains a back injury in a work-related motor vehicle accident and is taken by ambulance to the emergency room (ER) of the local hospital. The ER physician will initially evaluate the patient and then notify the patient's attending physician. Depending on the nature and severity of the case, the attending physician may come in to see and evaluate the patient in the ER, or the attending physician and ER physician may together decide to call in an orthopaedic surgeon on consult. The orthopedic surgeon arrives at the ER, examines the patient, and determines that the patient has sustained nerve damage to the back that requires emergency surgical intervention. The ER physician and attending physician agree, and the patient is admitted to the hospital through the ER for removal of part of the backbone and disk. Following the back surgery and the patient's dismissal from the hospital, the orthopedic surgeon prescribes the patient to be evaluated and treated by a physical therapist three times a week for four to eight weeks. All of the providers share in the ultimate goal of returning the patient to a productive status.

Some of the other professionals involved in the physical and psychosocial rehabilitation of the impaired and disabled are as follows:

- Speech pathologists
- Audiologists
- Prosthetists
- Certified orthotists
- Recreational therapists
- Medical social workers
- Social workers
- Psychologists
- Psychiatrists

A **speech pathologist** typically evaluates a patient through observation and formal testing to diagnose speech, language, and cognitive/communication deficits. Areas of treatment based on the evaluation and diagnoses may include swallowing therapy to re-establish eating by mouth; oral and language exercises to improve swallowing or voice or speech intelligibility; and cognitive/communication treatment to improve attention, orientation, memory, speed of processing information, thought organization, and higher-level reasoning and problem-solving skills. A speech pathologist may also teach sign language to a hearing-impaired individual. Speech therapists must complete a master's degree and pass a national examination in order to practice.

An **audiologist** provides diagnosis and treatment for hearing loss. This treatment may involve the testing and fitting for a hearing aid or training in lip reading and maintaining speech quality. An audiologist must complete a master's degree, have one year of work experience, and pass a national examination for registration to practice.

A **prosthetist** designs and fits artificial limbs for individuals who have suffered an amputation. Prosthetists complete at least two years of prosthetic school, although some colleges offer a bachelor's degree in prosthetics/orthotics. No registration or licensure is required to practice in most states.

A **certified orthotist** provides care for patients with disabling conditions of the limbs and spine through the use of devices known as orthoses. The certified orthotist is responsible for evaluating the patient's orthotic needs, formulating the design of the orthosis, and selecting materials and components; making all casts, measurements, model modifications, and layouts; performing fittings, including static and dynamic alignments; evaluating the orthosis on the patient; instructing the patient in its use; and maintaining patient records. Like prosthetists, orthotists complete a two-year orthotic school, and some colleges offer a bachelor's degree in orthotics. Some states require licensing in order to practice.

A **recreational therapist** assists the injured person in selecting activities, hobbies, sports, and exercises that maximize the injured person's recreational opportunities. A recreational therapist must complete a bachelor's degree. No license or registration is required in most states.

In the hospital setting, the **medical social worker** does a complete assessment of the injured person and family. In many rehabilitation hospitals, this social worker acts as the case manager, interacting with the insurance carrier and outside rehabilitation professionals.

Social workers interview the claimant and family to identify nonmedical psychosocial, financial, and discharge needs. Social workers also provide individual, group, and family counseling, and serve as an advocate and referral agent for continuing care needs. A social worker must complete a bachelor's degree at a minimum to practice. In jurisdictions that require licensing, a master's degree is generally required.

A **psychologist** treats an individual through counseling in an attempt to help overcome emotional or psychological reactions to an injury or a disease. A psychologist may also administer psychometric tests (paper-and-pencil tests that assess personality characteristics) to diagnose an emotional or psychological problem, or to define vocational potential. Generally, psychologists must complete a doctorate (Ph.D.) and be licensed in the state in which they practice; however, some states allow master's level preparation with licensure restriction.

The role of a **psychiatrist** is very similar to a psychologist's role in regard to treating and evaluating injured persons. A psychiatrist is also a medical physician (M.D. or D.O.) and is thus qualified to prescribe medication and admit patients to a hospital for psychiatric evaluation and treatment.

Example—The Potential Benefits of Rehabilitation

The following case study illustrates how intensive physical/psychosocial rehabilitation effectively reduced the potential disability consequences of a serious impairment to a child. This illustration demonstrates how timely, appropriate care can help to control costs.

Joey was five years old when he had open-heart surgery. Because of an anesthesiology accident, he suffered severe brain damage. It appeared that he would be institutionalized for life. His family was devastated. The insurer was facing a malpractice lawsuit with a $1 million policy limit. Intensive physical and psychosocial rehabilitation was begun immediately after surgery. While still unconscious, Joey had physical therapy to help him regain his gross motor movement. He also had occupational therapy to assist with strengthening his fine motor skills. The hospital social worker and the occupational therapist visited Joey's home while Joey was still hospitalized to determine whether any modifications needed to be made there. When Joey came out of the coma, recreational therapy and speech therapy were begun. In addition, Joey underwent audiological testing to make certain that he had not suffered deafness as a result of the brain damage. Speech therapy, occupational therapy, and physical therapy continued after Joey was sent home. All of these efforts helped Joey make a spectacular medical recovery. As a result, he mainstreamed in public school and lived at home with his parents. By age eight, Joey walked with a limp and needed continuous tutoring to stay competitive in school, but he was functioning at the level of his peers and leading a fulfilling life. The case was resolved through an annuity settlement at well under half of the policy limit. Joey's successful physical and psychosocial rehabilitation eliminated the original projected outcome of "severe brain damage," dramatically reducing the expected disability caused by the original impairment and substantially reducing the insurance company's exposure in the claim.

The Practice of Insurance Rehabilitation

As mentioned earlier, the purpose of insurance rehabilitation is to integrate medical and nonmedical disciplines to help return injured parties to a productive status and minimize the disability that results from an injury. The focus is on the financial and the medical aspects of an injury. Insurance rehabilitation can help injured parties overcome their problems while helping insurers to control claim costs through the use of medical case management, vocational rehabilitation, and psychosocial adjustment, or forensic rehabilitation (in contested cases). Insurance rehabilitation as applied to all lines of casualty insurance diminishes the effects of an accident or illness for the person and his or her family. Successful insurance rehabilitation efforts restore the individual to the highest level of functioning. This section discusses the practice of and professionals involved in insurance rehabilitation. The two main disciplines within insurance rehabilitation are medical case management and vocational rehabilitation counseling. Other areas of insurance rehabilitation include forensic rehabilitation and psychosocial adjustment.

Medical Case Management

The Commission for Case Manager Certification defines **medical case management** (sometimes simply referred to as "case management") as "a collaborative process which assesses, plans, implements, monitors, and evaluates options and services to meet an individual's health needs through communication and available resources to promote quality, cost effective outcomes."[5] The commission also asserts that "case management is not a profession in itself but rather an area of practice within one's profession." **Case managers** have nursing, social work, physical therapy, and occupational therapy backgrounds. Medical case management—expediting maximum medical improvement or recovery—is accomplished through but not limited to services such as the following:

- Selection and use of qualified physicians and medical practitioners
- Selection and use of qualified health-care facilities
- Use of additional medical specialists and consultants
- Use and control of ancillary health-care providers (such as physical therapists and occupational therapists)
- Control of medication use
- Procurement of durable medical equipment (such as prosthetic devices, orthopedic braces, and wheelchairs)
- Pursuit of all medical management activities while trying to secure quality care at the lowest cost.

Vocational Rehabilitation

Vocational rehabilitation is a profession whose members hold either a master's degree or doctorate in vocational counseling. A vocational rehabilitation professional may also be a certified rehabilitation counselor (CRC). Vocational rehabilitation involves the restoration of an impaired or disabled individual to a meaningful occupation. The scope of practice of vocational counselors has broadened to include other activities such as life-care planning. The case managers (including medical case managers) and vocational counselors who render insurance rehabilitation services either are self-employed consultants or work in-house for an independent or national rehabilitation company. These consultants educate and advise their client companies about the case management vocational needs of individuals injured in property casualty insurance claims. Because they do not render hands-on care, they are called rehabilitation vendors to distinguish them from their colleagues in physical/psychosocial rehabilitation who do provide hands-on care. Vocational rehabilitation—expediting a return to employment—is accomplished through but not limited to services such as the following:

- Return to work in the prior job without medical restrictions
- Return to work in the previous occupation through job modification and/or work hardening

- Return to work in an alternative new job with the prior employer
- Transferable skill analysis to identify alternative career options
- Formal vocational evaluation to identify alternative career options in the absence of obvious transferable skills
- Job-seeking skills training to prepare for a job search
- Job placement with a new employer
- On-the-job training with a new employer
- Short-term training or formal retraining

> **Workers Compensation Example of Insurance Rehabilitation**
>
> After raising her family, Mary worked at a nursing home for five years as a nurse's aide. She was a dedicated employee who was very fond of the patients. One day, she injured her back lifting a patient; her condition required surgery. Her post-surgical progress was slow, and her treating physician placed permanent restrictions on Mary's physical activities that were incompatible with the functional demands of the nurse's aide position. Anticipating a case of total work disability, the claim representative initially thought that the case should be reserved for several years of wage loss and continued care. The claim supervisor then suggested that the claim representative refer Mary's case to an insurance rehabilitation vendor for a vocational evaluation. Her employer would not allow her to return to work unless she could perform her prior job without restriction. The evaluation revealed that Mary had a strong aptitude for office work. Job placement efforts began, and within weeks Mary was placed as a medical receptionist. The vocational rehabilitation services provided to Mary radically changed her future and saved the workers compensation insurer thousands of dollars in wage loss benefits.

Psychosocial Adjustment

Psychosocial adjustment—maximizing psychosocial and social adjustment to the disability—is a broad term for activities that address the psychosocial challenges in returning injured parties to a productive status. Psychosocial adjustment is accomplished through but not limited to services such as the following:

- Informal assessment of the disabled person's attitude and understanding, spouse and family support, and financial resources
- Formal counseling on adjustment to disability, pain, chemical dependency, or vocational change
- Formal psychosocial assessment with individual or group therapy

Case studies have frequently been offered as evidence of the cost-effectiveness of insurance rehabilitation. Such studies provide anecdotal evidence of the costs and benefits of insurance rehabilitation. Two cases are included here (one workers compensation and one auto liability) to demonstrate that the successful application of insurance rehabilitation services significantly mitigated the exposure for the casualty insurer.

Auto Liability Example of Insurance Rehabilitation

Fred had just turned twenty-one years old when he fractured his left ankle in an automobile accident. He lived in a small rural community and was cared for at the local hospital emergency room by a general surgeon who was used to handling orthopedic cases. Fred was medically restricted from all work activity. As the days and weeks turned into months, Fred seemed to be getting no better. Five months passed, but the general surgeon did not answer any of the letters requesting medical information that the claim representative sent to him. The claim representative decided to refer the case to an insurance rehabilitation vendor for medical case management. The registered nurse assigned to the case traveled to meet with Fred and his wife at their home. The nurse's assessment revealed that Fred's ankle was not healing properly. She immediately contacted the claim representative and received authorization to transfer Fred's medical care to a large urban medical center 150 miles away. In the days that followed, the professor of orthopedic surgery assigned to Fred's case determined that Fred was going to need more ankle surgery as well as intensive physical therapy (PT), post-operatively, with the additional possibility of work hardening following PT. The rehabilitation nurse case manager arranged for Fred and his wife to stay in a motel next to the university hospital while he was receiving care. The subsequent ankle surgery was successful with Fred achieving full recovery. After intensive outpatient PT and work hardening at the university hospital following his surgical recovery, Fred returned to work full duty. The medical case manager assisted Fred in obtaining efficient medical care for his broken ankle, including needed outpatient physical rehabilitation services and a rapid return to work for him just three months after the claim representative had made the referral. Contrast Fred's improvement after the intervention of the nurse case manager to the five months after the accident without Fred's experiencing any improvement of his injury, much less return to work. The auto insurer had been anticipating a long, expensive claim. Through the insurance rehabilitation service of medical case management, Fred recovered and returned to full duty work in only three months after appropriate intervention was provided.

Forensic Rehabilitation

Insurance rehabilitation includes an alternative fourth component known as **forensic rehabilitation** when the underlying insurance presents questions of liability or coverage. Forensic rehabilitation may also become the primary focus when an injured person refuses to cooperate with voluntarily offered rehabilitation services and the insurance carrier plans to contest this lack of cooperation in court. Forensic rehabilitation involves objective medical, psychological, or vocational evidence that is used as expert testimony or evidence in the litigation of an insurance claim. Forensic rehabilitation is accomplished through but not limited to use of independent medical examiners, creation of a life-care plan detailing future medical costs, and completion of a labor market survey to prove job availability.

Some of the services included in the insurance rehabilitation process may overlap with claim-handling techniques. For example, qualified physicians and medical practitioners should be selected even if the claim is not set up for insurance rehabilitation services. Also, claim representatives may expedite an injured person's return to employment without assigning a rehabilitation professional to do this important task.

Parties to the Insurance Rehabilitation Process

This section describes the roles of key participants in the insurance rehabilitation process:

- The claim representative
- Rehabilitation professionals
- The injured person
- The injured person's family and friends
- The injured person's employer

This section also provides an overview of the different types of rehabilitation professionals involved in insurance and explains their scope of practice.

The Claim Representative

The claim representative must decide which cases should receive insurance rehabilitation services and what kind of services should be provided. Not every case will benefit from rehabilitation services. If the medical management of a case is already appropriate, if the injured person's vocational future is secure, and if that person's psychosocial adjustment is satisfactory, insurance rehabilitation services would be a waste of money.

The auto lability and workers compensation cases mentioned earlier demonstrate that some injury claims clearly benefit from insurance rehabilitation services and can provide enormous savings on the claim and an important humanitarian service. With an adequate understanding of the insurance rehabilitation process, claim representatives can ensure that money allocated for these services is well spent.

The claim representative's role usually includes identifying the injury claims that could benefit from insurance rehabilitation services and obtaining approval for these services from claim management and any other appropriate key party. In addition, the claim representative communicates regularly with both the insurance rehabilitation vendor and the insurance rehabilitation professional assigned to the case. The claim representative and the insurance rehabilitation professional should initially establish objectives and guidelines for each rehabilitation case and regularly monitor the progress. The claim representative must determine the extent of the insurer's financial commitment to the rehabilitation plan (although in several states, like California, rehabilitation is a *required* part of workers compensation and details for the use of rehabilitation are dictated by statute). The claim representative must also maintain communications with the medical practitioners and the employer. Perhaps most important is communication with the injured person in order to clarify the benefits and the goals of insurance rehabilitation.

The claim representative and the insurance rehabilitation professional should clearly define one another's role throughout the process to make sure there are no overlapping activities. A claim representative is the person clearly responsible for investigating the claim for coverage and liability, setting reserves to cover anticipated benefits, making all benefit payments, and handling all legal issues. An insurance rehabilitation professional's role should not overlap with these activities. The insurance rehabilitation professional needs to focus on medical case management, vocational rehabilitation, and/or the psychosocial components of rehabilitation and not become an investigator and benefit administrator. An insurance rehabilitation professional may assist a claim representative in setting reserves, by projecting anticipated medical costs or the length of anticipated time off from work, but the claim representative must still exercise final judgment on reserving.

Quality assurance is another important goal for rehabilitation that claim representatives can help achieve. Claim representatives, though not licensed to evaluate insurance rehabilitation outcomes, must still make some judgments on the quality of service being provided by the rehabilitation vendor. The value of rehabilitation vendors will be assessed not only by casualty insurers but also by state legislators and regulators. Several states, including California, Minnesota, and Georgia, have established extensive rules regarding a rehabilitation vendor's conduct in handling workers compensation claims. Yet even those states have no comprehensive service standards against which to measure the service of a insurance rehabilitation vendor.

In the absence of clear service standards, a casualty insurer is encouraged to develop its own checklist of expectations by which to monitor a rehabilitation vendor. Following are examples of activities that can be included in such a checklist:

- The case manager or vocational counselor must contact the injured person within a few days of referral to minimize any delay in the insurance rehabilitation process.
- The rehabilitation vendor must contact the claim representative within a week after the assignment to the insurance rehabilitation vendor to discuss the preliminary rehabilitation plan and to minimize any rehabilitation activity that the claim representative has not authorized.
- A written report must be submitted to the claim representative within thirty days of referral, outlining the insurance rehabilitation plan.
- The insurance rehabilitation plan must include ultimate goals, steps to reach those goals, and time and cost estimates.
- The insurance rehabilitation case manager or vocational counselor should communicate with the claim representative at least every thirty days.
- The rehabilitation vendor must contact the claim representative immediately by phone when any significant change or deterioration in the progress in the insurance rehabilitation plan develops.

- A formal case conference must be held for any case that continues to require insurance rehabilitation services beyond six months or $2,000 in rehabilitation costs. The case conference should include the claim representative, the insurance rehabilitation case manager or vocational counselor, and the injured person. Progress and problems should be reviewed and discussed. Both the claim representative and the insurance rehabilitation professional should be aware of both (1) the steps needed to conclude the insurance rehabilitation plan and terminate further vendor services and (2) the situations in which such action is required. One example of (2) would be if the injured person proves to be completely noncompliant with any insurance rehabilitation efforts.

This is certainly not an exhaustive list, but without other standards for quality assurance, it provides claim representatives with an initial basis for monitoring the insurance rehabilitation process.

The Professional Rehabilitation Vendor

Insurance rehabilitation has traditionally taken place through public, nonprofit service providers. For example, the earliest providers were veterans' hospitals since the early federal rehabilitation laws focused primarily on veterans injured in World War I.

Over the years, however, the number of insurance rehabilitation companies providing services for profit has grown enormously. The term insurance rehabilitation vendor refers to companies or organizations that employ rehabilitation professionals in these private companies as opposed to traditional public services.

Private For-Profit Rehabilitation Services

The oldest and one of the largest private for-profit rehabilitation providers (currently employing over 2,500 nurses and counselors) is Intracorp. Intracorp was established by CIGNA (previously the Insurance Company of North America, INA), one of the largest casualty insurance corporations in the United States. The hundreds of other private rehabilitation firms range from national groups such as CRA Managed Care, Crawford Health and Rehabilitation Services, and Corvel to individual sole practitioners.

In-House Rehabilitation Professionals

Many casualty companies employ their own in-house insurance rehabilitation staff. These professionals perform many of the same functions that outside rehabilitation vendors do. The in-house staff has the advantage of sole dedication to their employer, as opposed to the outside vendor companies that serve many insurers.

In-house professionals may face a unique challenge in staying focused on the rehabilitation process and not becoming involved in claim handling activities. They have to work closely with claim representatives who may not understand the rehabilitation process and thus request services that are outside the scope of rehabilitation.

Despite this challenge, companies that employ their own professionals have demonstrated outstanding results.

Qualifications of Rehabilitation Professionals

Rehabilitation vendors employ medical case managers and/or vocational rehabilitation specialists who are directly responsible for the overall development and management of the rehabilitation process for a case referred by a casualty insurance company. These case managers coordinate all rehabilitation efforts and counsel the injured person in moving toward maximum medical improvement and/or a return to employment. Their experience in insurance rehabilitation and in their own professions qualifies these professionals. Many are registered nurses, physical or occupational therapists, or vocational counselors with either a master's degree or Ph.D. in rehabilitation counseling. These professionals neither provide hands-on therapy nor practice medicine. In-house rehabilitation professionals need these same credentials and expertise.

There is some controversy about the qualifications required of a rehabilitation professional case manager and vocational counselor. Some states have passed licensure laws that require a rehabilitation case manager or vocational counselor to hold a master's degree and pass a national examination in order to practice. Georgia, for example, requires rehabilitation case managers and vocational counselors handling workers compensation cases to hold a master's degree and pass the national certification examination that gives the provider the designation of certified rehabilitation counselor (CRC).

Most states do not regulate case managers and vocational counselors, however. Thus, persons with or without a bachelor's degree or experience in working with disabled persons may be considered qualified. In response to this absence of regulation, many persons and a growing number of registered nurses have taken the national examination for the designation of Certified Disability Management Specialist (CDMS), Certified Case Manager (CCM), or Certified Rehabilitation Registered Nurse (CRRN). Claim handlers often see rehabilitation case managers and vocational counselors with the CRC, CCM, CRRN, or CDMS designation. A claim representative may also see the credentials M.A. (Master of Arts degree), M.S. (Master of Science degree), RN (registered nurse), or B.S.N. (an RN with a Bachelor of Science degree). Any of these designations reflects valid and important qualifications for the professional case manager. A claim representative should also contact the state licensure board and the state's industrial commission to determine whether specific qualifications are required for a rehabilitation professional case manager or vocational counselor to practice in that state.

Several professionals are involved in vocational rehabilitation, including work evaluators and job placement specialists.

A **work evaluator** administers tests and work assignments to an injured person to formulate a vocational rehabilitation plan. These professionals may carry the title of vocational counselor or vocational specialist.

The work evaluator should hold a bachelor's degree; some hold master's degrees. No licensure or certification is required to practice in most states, but Georgia requires a certification as a CRC, as mentioned earlier. A national certification examination is available, however, that gives the title of Certified Vocational Evaluator (CVE).

A **job placement specialist** helps the injured person to find appropriate employment. The job placement process includes training the person in the proper completion of a job application, preparation of a résumé if appropriate, strengthening interview techniques, and contacting prospective employers. A job placement specialist should hold a bachelor's degree or have at least two years experience in a private employment agency. No licensure or certificate is required to practice in most states.

In addition to the medical case manager or vocational counselor and other rehabilitation professionals, several other key parties participate in the insurance rehabilitation process, not the least of whom is the injured person. The family, the employer (when relevant—rehabilitation is not limited to employed persons), the claim representative, and an attorney (when involved, who can take a supportive role but often takes an adversarial role) all play important roles in the success. There may be other parties not listed here as well.

The Injured Person

The ongoing assessment of the injured person's reaction to the treatment program is essential for effective medical case management, as is communication with the claim representative about the patient's rehabilitation progress. These two activities continue through the life of the case, until resolution is achieved by the patient's attaining maximum medical improvement with or without the medical placement of permanent restrictions. If the patient is left with permanent restrictions that in any way impede his or her activities of daily living and/or return to work, the claim representative may decide to refer the case to a vocational counselor upon medical case management closure.

People who suffer serious injuries react in similar ways. The injured person often initially reacts with denial or anger, then gradually moves through a period of depression to acceptance. Very few individuals can accept a disability immediately after an injury or illness. Rehabilitation should not be delayed until the individual accepts a disability. Rehabilitation can help the injured person to accept the disability.

The medical case manager should continually assess the injured person's reaction to the treatment program. This assessment is accomplished through personal contact with the person, spouse, family, and health-care providers. The assessment should include continued support of the injured person through the various stages of recovery, motivating and encouraging the person toward acceptance. This activity may also include initiating plans for a return to work or making preliminary arrangements for vocational counseling, if relevant.

The Family

The injured person's family may react to the condition in the same way as the affected person. The spouse and other family members may deny the disability; may become angry, depressed, or fearful; or may accept the disability. Sometimes the injured person accepts the disability, but the spouse or family does not. The family may see the injured individual as a different person, a stranger, difficult to accept and love. This reaction would obviously have a negative effect on the injured person. Few injured persons can begin to accept their injuries without the support of a spouse or family.

The Employer

The employer can play an important role by providing an opportunity for the employed injured person to return to return to work by modifying the job, transferring the person to a new job that can be performed despite the disability, or developing new position. This kind of concern and involvement can contribute to the emotional and psychosocial well-being of the person. Lack of concern and communication from the employer can prolong disability and, in some cases, set the stage for a potential total disability attitude in the mind of the worker.

The Insurance Rehabilitation Process

Rehabilitation has been defined as a "process" that mitigates the effects of an accident or disease upon the affected person and family. This section further describes this process. Exhibit 4-1 is a flowchart of the rehabilitation process. The three major components of the process—medical management, vocational rehabilitation, and psychosocial rehabilitation—occur simultaneously. This does not, however, mean that progress will be equal in all areas.

Forensic rehabilitation is not included in this flowchart; it runs its own course, very different from rehabilitation that is provided for the benefit of the injured person. Forensic rehabilitation does not follow any one specific course and is limited to one activity, such as the arrangement of an independent medical examination (IME) or completion of a labor market survey.

Both physical/psychosocial rehabilitation and insurance rehabilitation begin with an injury or illness. Once the claim representative receives a notice of loss, he or she must make decisions regarding the initiation of insurance rehabilitation services. If the injury is identified as severe, the decision is heavily weighted in favor of initiating insurance rehabilitation services. If the injury or illness is less severe, the claim representative may use certain formal evaluation tools (described later) and exercise good judgment in deciding whether and when to begin insurance rehabilitation. A good basic guideline to follow in the

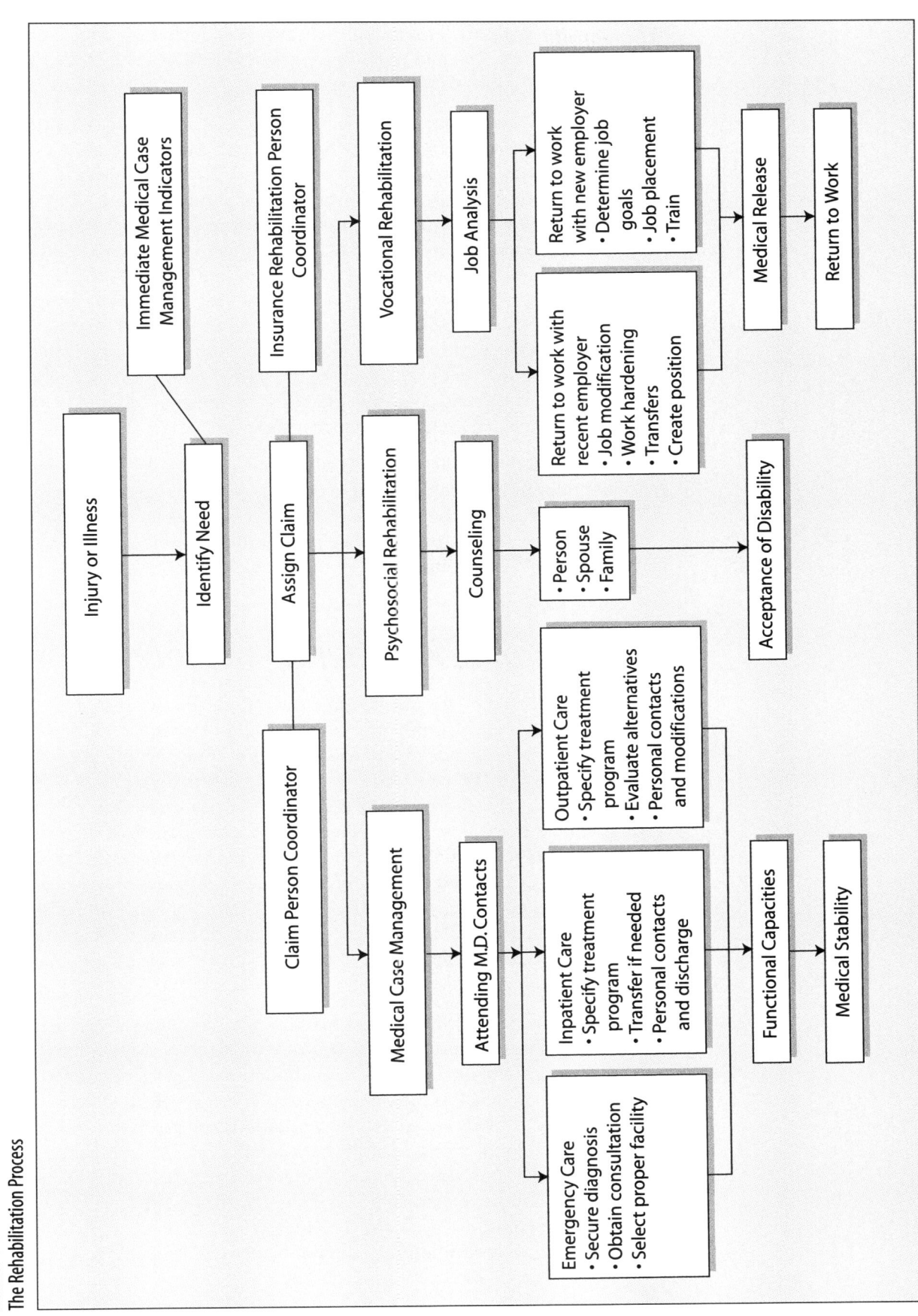

Exhibit 4-1
The Rehabilitation Process

absence of formal evaluation tools, however, is that insurance rehabilitation services should be considered whenever normal recovery and/or a prompt return to work is in question.

Once the claim representative has identified the need for medical case management, vocational rehabilitation, or some other type of insurance rehabilitation service, he or she must determine who will provide the rehabilitation services. The claim representative may select an in-house insurance rehabilitation staff member or an outside rehabilitation vendor to either provide or coordinate insurance rehabilitation services. An in-house insurance rehabilitation staff member, if available, is typically the first choice because of the obvious advantages of quality control, ease of communication, and reduced expense. However, some insurance companies that employ in-house insurance rehabilitation staff may not allow them to provide insurance rehabilitation services themselves, but will allow them to coordinate the services of insurance rehabilitation vendors that will.

If in-house insurance rehabilitation staff is not available, the claim representative would contact an outside insurance rehabilitation vendor. In this case, the claim representative must assess the qualifications of the vendor company and the prospective medical case manager or vocational counselor.

The basic qualifications for licensure of rehabilitation providers were discussed earlier in this chapter. Beyond these credentials, the claim representative should question the owner or manager of the firm about the education and experience of all staff, the firm's philosophy, the methods used by the firm to serve the injured person, the vendor's fee structure, and the firm's professional liability insurance coverage. The rehabilitation vendor should be questioned about experience with the specific injury in question. A list of other insurers who have used the firm should be obtained, and several of these insurers should be called for a reference. The claim representative can also contact the state industrial commission to determine whether the firm or individual provider is required to be registered and whether any complaints have been filed (if a registration and complaint process exists in the particular jurisdiction). The likely personality match between the insurance rehabilitation professional and the injured person is also an important factor to be considered.

Once the need for insurance rehabilitation services has been identified and the professional who will coordinate those services has been selected, the formal insurance rehabilitation process begins. The services included in the three major components of the process (medical management, vocational rehabilitation, and psychosocial rehabilitation) are performed. Ideally, the services in these components will be pursued simultaneously since progress in each area contributes to progress in the remaining areas. However, there are exceptions. For example, return to work may be unfeasible or irrelevant. In that case, vocational rehabilitation would not be pursued. If return to work is feasible, progress in vocational rehabilitation (such as a specific job offer from an employer) may encourage the injured person to return to work on a trial basis rather than to stay away from the workplace, which in turn may speed medical recovery as well.

The steps in the insurance rehabilitation process, including the four major components, include identification of rehabilitation candidate and then applying medical case management, psychosocial rehabilitation, and vocational rehabilitation.

Identification of the Insurance Rehabilitation Candidate

Studies of insurance rehabilitation have concluded that the shorter the gap between an injury or onset of disease and the beginning of the formal insurance rehabilitation process, the better the outcome. Candidates for insurance rehabilitation should therefore be identified as soon as possible. With this in mind, the claim representative may apply the following insurance rehabilitation referral guidelines to most casualty claims.

Identification by Type of Injury

Rehabilitation should be considered *upon first notice of loss* in the following types of severe injury, assuming coverage and liability exist:

- Spinal cord injury or suspected paralysis. With this type of injury, the individual depends on a wheelchair and may require home modifications, attendant care, and extensive medical follow-up.
- Head injury or suspected brain damage, including CVA (cerebral vascular accident, or stroke) and post-concussion syndrome. With this type of injury, the individual depends on others for activities of daily living and may require long-term residential care.
- Myocardial infarction. Although many persons survive heart attacks, the psychological effects can easily lead to total disability.
- Moderate or major burns. Burns are considered moderate to major when they involve second-degree and third-degree burns over 15 percent of the total body surface (not including eyes, ears, face, or genitalia) or any second-degree or third-degree burn of the eyes, ears, face, or genitalia.
- Amputations other than fingers and toes. Although many types of prostheses are available, the psychological effects of the loss of a hand or leg may easily lead to total disability.
- Multiple fractures or any type of crushing injury. These injuries may lead to partial or full amputation of an extremity or require repeated surgeries, resulting in less than full function.
- Injury to the brachial plexus (the major nerve root in the shoulder). This injury is extremely painful and can easily lead to the complete loss of arm function.
- Oscalsis (heel bone) fracture. These injuries often require multiple surgeries and a year or more of recovery. These fractures often occur bilaterally (both heels are fractured).

- Vision loss. In addition to its enormous practical effect, blindness, whether partial or complete, can be psychologically devastating.
- Hearing loss (over fifty decibels bilaterally). Although many types of hearing aids are available, the psychological effects of hearing loss can lead to total disability.
- Post-traumatic stress disorder. This is a legitimate disorder when it is provoked through experiencing a highly traumatic event (such as witnessing the death or severe injury to a coworker) or severe injury to one's self.

Identification by Formal Evaluation Tools

Some casualty insurers use evaluation tools rather than specific types of injury criteria to determine the need for insurance rehabilitation services. Two examples, shown in Exhibits 4-2 and 4-3, are for workers compensation and liability, respectively. Even when the actual form is not used, claim representatives who are experienced in selecting cases for insurance rehabilitation are probably mentally reviewing the factors included in the form. The claim representative should consider insurance rehabilitation services for any claim for which medical recovery and/or a prompt return to employment is questionable.

Perhaps the best tool for identifying injury claims that would benefit from insurance rehabilitation services is good judgment. A list of severe injuries and illnesses or a formal evaluation tool to identify the need for medical case management or vocational counseling cannot substitute for the claim person's judgment. For example, a relatively minor physical injury may lead to total work disability because of the injured person's emotional response to the injury. A condition known as reflex sympathetic dystrophy is a good example of this phenomenon. The syndrome can start with a simple strain of extremity (hand, arm, or leg) and progress to the point at which the limb becomes useless as a result of self-inflicted immobility. Although a list of severe injuries and a formal evaluation system will ensure that most persons needing insurance rehabilitation services are identified, reflex sympathetic dystrophy is not included in the list of severe injuries, nor does it meet the criteria of the formal evaluation tool, yet medical case management would be advisable for a case like this. Therefore, good judgment is required to identify candidates for rehabilitation who do not otherwise meet the selection criteria.

Workers Compensation Cases

The factors listed in Exhibit 4-2 apply to workers compensation claims. Several studies have investigated socio-demographic variables that can be used to predict the chances of an injured person's becoming totally disabled or returning to a productive life. For example, advanced age and lack of medical progress appear to predict total disability.[6] Researchers have found that education,[7] wages compared to the compensation rate,[8] and the physical demands of the work[9] may also predict total disability. Perhaps the strongest predictors identified are a history of prior injury and job dissatisfaction.[10]

Exhibit 4-2
Evaluation Tool To Identify the Need for Rehabilitation in Workers Compensation Case

FACTORS	POINTS			
	1	2	3	4
AGE	Under 20	20-40	41-55	Over 55
TIME ON JOB	Over 10 yrs	5-10 yrs	1-4 yrs	Less than 1
TYPE OF WORK	Light	Moderate	Heavy	Extra Heavy
NET WAGES	More than 2X comp	2X Comp	Equal to Comp	Less than Comp
JOB MARKET	Many	Some	Few	None
EDUCATION	H.S. Grad	Some H.S.	Grade School	Some Grade School
MEDICAL PROGRESS	Improvement Noted	Some Improvement	No Improvement	Condition Worsened
OTHER FACTORS*				

TOTAL SCORE [ ]

*To include current and/or pre-existing problems that may negatively affect the period of time until maximum medical recovery and/or return to work will occur (that is, current and/or pre-existing medical problems, level of claimant's/insured's cooperation, and so forth).

SCORING KEY

- 25 = Refer to rehabilitation immediately.
- 20-24 = Strong rehabilitation potential. Monitor closely and refer to rehabilitation if no RTW by 30 days post injury.
- 15-19 = Claim has rehabilitation potential. Monitor closely and refer if no RTW during next 60 days or 90 days post-injury.
- 0-14 = Claim may have rehabilitation potential. Monitor closely and consider referral to rehabilitation if no RTW during next 60 days or 150 days post-injury.

The factors included in the sample evaluation tool have been taken from such studies and weighted. Age, for example, is weighted so that a young person (under twenty) would be considered a low risk of total disability compared to an older person (over fifty-five). A person whose time on the job is longer (over ten years) is considered a lower risk than a relatively new employee is (less than one year). A person with prior injuries is weighted more heavily, as is a person who expresses job dissatisfaction. The significance of some of these factors may appear to be obvious. A person with good medical progress is obviously a better risk than a person whose condition has worsened. However, in any given case, a person who receives wages that are two times greater than his or her compensation rate may or may not be a better risk than one who receives wages equal to or less than compensation. Motivation compared to wages is a complex relationship and is not always a good predictor. The sample evaluation tool is not infallible. It is a guide to the claim representative in determining the risk of extended disability and identifying the need for insurance rehabilitation services in a workers compensation claim.

An "other factors" category is included to leave room for the claim representative's judgment. An example of one "other factor" may be attorney representation, which has been found to delay a return to work for people with low back injuries.

Liability Cases

The factors in Exhibit 4-3 apply to liability claims. Some are similar to the workers compensation factors (age and the claimant's general health after accident), but three key factors that are relevant to liability cases are not as important in workers compensation cases:

- Determination of legal liability
- Policy limits
- Claimant's and his or her family's attitude

Exhibit 4-3
Evaluation Tool To Identify the Need for Rehabilitation in Liability Cases

FACTORS	POINTS				
	0	1	2	3	4
DETERMINATION OF LEGAL LIABILITY	Less than 50	50/50	60/40	70/30	80/20
POLICY LIMITS	0-$250,000	$250,000	$300,000	$500,000	More than $500,000
CLAIMANT'S/ FAMILY'S ATTITUDE	–	Negative	Neutral	Positive	Requests Rehabilitation
CLAIMANT'S AGE	–	More than 55	41-55	30-40	Less than 30
CLAIMANT'S GENERAL HEALTH AFTER ACCIDENT	–	Good	Fair	Poor	Very Poor
DEGREE TO WHICH IMPAIRMENT BLOCKS EMPLOYMENT	–	No Effect	Mild Effect	Moderate Effect	No Return Possible
ESTIMATED LENGTH OF DISABILITY	Less than 90 Days	3-4 Months	5-8 Months	9-12 Months	More than 12 Months
				TOTAL SCORE	

SCORING KEY
20+ = Refer to rehabilitation immediately.
10-20 = Consider referral to rehabilitation for evaluation.
0-10 = Low potential for rehabilitation.

Liability claims by definition require a determination of legal liability. For instance, cases in which the defendant has a greater than 50 percent chance of a successful defense would likely not be rehabilitation candidates since the primary liability of the defendant is doubtful. On the other hand, if the defendant has an 80 percent or more chance of an unsuccessful defense, negligence is probable, which encourages a strategy like rehabilitation to mitigate damages.

Policy limits also affect the decision to support rehabilitation. A severe injury involving low policy limits (less than $250,000) would likely exhaust policy limits, so insurance rehabilitation services would only represent a cost beyond the insured's policy limits. On the other hand, with high limits, even severe injuries might be controlled through medical case management and/or vocational counseling, resulting in savings to the insured. In this case, insurance rehabilitation services are more likely to be supported.

Finally, the claimant's and his or her family's attitude in a liability claim is very important since insurance rehabilitation is not required in this line of casualty insurance. Workers compensation statutes (in all states but Indiana) mandate some provision for rehabilitation (although the actual provision is only enforced in a small number of states, including California, Minnesota, Florida, Oregon, and Georgia). No statute mandates medical case management or vocational counseling in general liability or in professional liability cases, and only a handful mandate vocational counseling in auto no-fault cases. Thus, the voluntary acceptance of rehabilitation services is crucial in a liability claim. An insurer would probably have to agree to make advance payments before a liability claimant would be cooperative. Advance payments are payments for medical or other expenses as they are incurred rather than payments made after the final settlement or judgment. An insurer receives credit for the amount of any advance payments in a final settlement or judgment.

Example—Good Judgment in Action

C.R. Smith was an experienced claim representative who worked for an insurance carrier that employed in-house rehabilitation nurses. C.R. noticed an increasing number of carpal tunnel syndrome claims that all seemed to follow the same pattern—a quick determination that surgery was warranted, surgery being scheduled weeks later, and a recovery period of four to eight weeks before any return to work was considered. C.R. used a formal tool to evaluate the need for rehabilitation in these claims, but typically the score after applying the tool suggested that rehabilitation could be delayed.

One day, C.R. was complaining about how carpal tunnel claims all involved surgery and a substantial amount of lost time. He decided that the next time he saw a recommendation for surgery he would try another approach, irrespective of what the formal evaluation tool would tell him about the need for rehabilitation. He received a first notice of loss that same day in which the injury was described as possible carpal tunnel syndrome. He called the attending physician's office and asked the office assistant to pull the medical file and read the diagnosis. Sure enough, the diagnosis was carpal tunnel syndrome. He asked about the treatment plan, and the office assistant told him that surgery was scheduled.

C.R. referred the claim to the in-house rehabilitation nurse that same day. His good judgment paid off. The in-house nurse immediately scheduled an appointment with an orthopedic hand specialist who concurred with the diagnosis but who did not agree that surgery was warranted. After two weeks of splinting and occupational therapy, the injured worker was back at work through a few minor job modifications that the rehabilitation nurse coordinated. The injured worker lost a total of four weeks of work as opposed to the typical ten-plus weeks. Surgery was avoided, saving medical costs and the potential permanent partial disability award typically given after surgery.

Medical Case Management

Medical case management, the first of the three major components of insurance rehabilitation, occurs over several stages of treatment. Its purpose is to help optimize and expedite the healing of an injured person. Medical case management begins as soon as possible after the onset of an injury or disease and continues until maximum medical improvement is achieved. Medical case management can be valuable during emergency care, inpatient care, and outpatient care. Exhibit 4-4 gives a list of claim types requiring immediate medical management. Many of these are the same as the injuries and claims requiring immediate rehabilitation mentioned earlier. Some on this list are factors unrelated to the injury.

Exhibit 4-4
Summary of Factors Indicating the Need for Immediate Medical Case Management

- Spinal cord injuries
- Head injury or suspected brain damage
- Myocardial infarction (heart attack)
- Psychiatric/stress diagnosis
- Moderate to severe burns
- Multiple fractures and/or crushing injuries
- Injury to brachial plexus
- Vision or hearing loss
- Amputations (other than finger or toe)
- Heel bone fracture
- Post-traumatic stress disorder
- Loss of consciousness (could indicate head or cardiac trauma)
- Neonatal injury
- Injury of pregnant employee
- Possible chemical or substance abuse
- Previous injuries/disabilities
- Questionable injury causation
- Injuries related to serious personnel problems (pending layoff, pending strike)

Emergency Care

The injured person has his or her first contact with an attending physician in an office or emergency room. This contact is significant and should be positive. The injured person should receive concrete information: a definitive or presumptive diagnosis regarding his or her condition. A **definitive diagnosis** describes the condition and what caused it; the **presumptive diagnosis** denotes a condition that may have other causes and is sometimes referred to as a **"rule-out" diagnosis** or a **working diagnosis**. Consider the case of an injury victim who comes to the ER after a motor vehicle accident (MVA), complaining of a headache. An expected and relevant presumptive diagnosis might be "closed head injury" because of the circumstances causing the patient's symptoms. However, depending on other patient findings, a presumptive diagnosis of "rule out brain tumor" might also be appropriate. The former diagnosis would be related to the MVA, but the latter would not. Diagnostic relatedness to the insured event is just one circumstance facing claim representatives as they review medical records. Claim representatives should expect diagnoses that accurately reflect the patient's condition rather than reflecting the cause of their symptoms or just listing the symptoms themselves. For example, bills for ER treatment that describe the cause of the patient condition as a chemical burn or a motor vehicle accident or bills or clinical notes that denote neck pain or dizziness should be questioned because a true medical condition is not being described. Circumstances such as these may require the implementation of some sort of medical management service, such as review of the medical records or bills. These services were discussed at length in Chapter 1. As a rule of thumb, medical management is the umbrella under which fall other services such as utilization review and medical records review. Technically, medical case management also falls under this umbrella.

There can be delays to initiating medical case management. The insurance company is not always aware of the initial office or ER visit until days or even weeks after it occurs. However, ideally, medical case management should begin at the time of the emergency care. Medical case management at this stage includes the following:

- *Diagnosis*

  A definitive diagnosis based on a complete medical history, thorough examination, and appropriate diagnostic testing should be secured from the patient's attending physician. If the patient does not have a definitive medical diagnosis, but rather a presumptive one or a collection of symptoms, the medical case manager would begin by securing a definitive medical diagnosis related to and/or caused by the insured event.

- *Consulting physician*

  If a diagnosis is not available, the services of a consulting physician should be secured to determine a definitive diagnosis. This is done by referring the injured person to a specialist recommended by the attending physician or by the medical case manager.

- *Selection of proper facility*

  If the injury is severe, a proper medical facility for initial inpatient care should be selected. For example, a person who sustains third-degree burns may not be properly treated in a hospital that does not have a formal burn unit. In workers compensation claims, for example, the patient may be transferred to a burn treatment center at the request of the attending physician or medical case manager.

Inpatient Care

Medical case management is especially important when the injured person is hospitalized. The length of hospitalization can vary from a day to several months depending on a variety of factors. The medical case management of a hospitalized individual usually includes performing the following activities and/or monitoring the following issues:

- Clarification of treatment program
- Transfer
- Discharge from hospital

Clarification of Inpatient Treatment Program

Upon the patient's admission to the hospital, the medical case manager should determine whether any surgery or other invasive procedures are planned, or whether conservative care will suffice. If conservative care is the course of treatment, what specific therapies will be involved? The most ideal information would be forthcoming from the treating physician. The medical case manager may also visit with the hospital's quality assurance department after first providing the staff with a medical authorization signed by the patient. Without this authorization from the patient and clearance through the hospital's quality assurance department, acquisition of any information would be difficult.

Transfer

If the treatment plan does not seem to be resulting in progress within reasonable time limits, the medical case manager might consider a transfer of the patient to another medical facility. Transfer can be accomplished by the medical case manager negotiating arrangements with the patient's physician. An example of a case that is a candidate for transfer is a spinal cord injury treated in a local community hospital whose staff may not have the expertise to treat this challenging type of injury. The nationwide network of designated regional spinal cord rehabilitation centers is better equipped to treat spinal cord patients. Transfer to this type of facility would provide more appropriate, higher quality treatment. There are similar networks for brain injuries, burns, and cardiac care. Reinsurance claim departments are usually a good source of referrals for locating these resources since the expense of these cases often involves reinsurance. Medical case managers would also be an excellent resource for local or regional medical facilities.

Discharge From Hospital

The need for the patient's continued treatment upon discharge from the hospital should be identified by the medical case manager and confirmed with the treating physician. At discharge, the medical case manager can review treatment center options for the most efficacious outpatient care with the patient, physician, and claim representative.

Outpatient Care

During outpatient care, the person usually still needs medical treatment while adjusting to the activities of daily living; while adjusting to the attitudes and reaction of spouse, family, and society; and while planning for a return to work. Medical case management activities usually consist of clarification of the outpatient treatment program, discussions of alternative treatment plans, and preparations for return to work.

Clarification of Outpatient Treatment Program

The medical case manager monitors the person's rehabilitation process and investigates whether re-hospitalization or future surgery is anticipated. Additionally, if the patient is receiving any physical therapy or occupational therapy, the patient's progress will be monitored. If the therapy does not result in progress, the medical case manager will alert both the claim representative and the patient's physician. Depending on the patient's progress, the medical case manager might suggest a change of outpatient facilities or a second opinion exam to clarify any patient impediments to the rehabilitation process. The medical case manager would also oversee any needed home modifications, equipment purchases, arrangements for attendants, or nursing care for cases involving severe impairments and disability, such as spinal cord injuries or brain damage.

Alternative Treatment Plan

If the treatment plan does not produce results, an alternative treatment plan should be developed. This is accomplished by discussing alternative treatment options with the patient's treating physician, the claim representative, the injured person, and his or her family. The injured person and his or her family must agree with the decision to begin alternative treatment.

An example of the need for alternative treatment might be a low back injury treated by a family physician. The treatment plan will typically involve weeks of bed rest. Studies have shown that bed rest beyond two to three days after the injury produces no therapeutic value and in fact can complicate recovery by deconditioning the patient.[11] The treatment may also involve the use of medications for pain relief. However, medications can be narcotic, creating the potential for dependence. Such a treatment plan would be more disabling than helpful. In such a case, the medical case manager should first identify alternatives designed to treat low back injuries, perhaps including physical therapy modalities designed to initially decrease pain and swelling of the soft tissues in the low back. Treatment should then be centered on active exercise and conditioning to increase endurance, stamina, and strengthening of the musculature.

Physical therapy programs, which emphasize exercise rather than bed rest and focus on an active rather than passive regimen, engage the injured person's mind and body. The longer an able-bodied person stays idle, the more difficult it is for him or her to want to return to full activity, including work. A person engaged in an active physical therapy program has an easier time moving towards a return to work than does someone who lies bedridden. Medical case managers understand this fact; as they are monitoring the patient's rehabilitation progress in physical therapy, they will work with the patient's treating physician, physical therapist, and employer to secure a medical release allowing the person to return to modified work in the shortest time possible. Work is "good medicine" in its own right, and a prompt return to modified work often speeds the healing process as the person focuses on his or her abilities rather than on any disability.

The medical case manager should be continually reviewing the patient's prescribed treatment plan and the patient's response to it with the treating physician. If the patient fails to progress in rehabilitation and the treating physician is not amenable to alternative suggestions by the medical case manager, the claim representative should be contacted. Together, the medical case manager and the claim representative might want to secure a second opinion examination of the patient from a consulting physician to recommend treatment options.

Medical case management at this stage also includes monitoring how the patient is using medication, regardless of the specific injury or illness involved. This can be accomplished by the medical case manager's formulating a medication profile. The profile documents all of the medications that the patient is currently consuming. This document helps to avoid improper medication use, since medication overuse and abuse are common.

Return to Work

In order for the injured person to return to work, the patient's functional capacities must be determined and a release to work must be secured. **Functional capacities** are the residual physical abilities of the injured person. A **release to work** is a physician's approval for the person to return to some level of work. The medical placement of permanent physical restrictions, the patient's assessment of functional capacities, and the release to work are all used to define the for re-employment. This is a fundamental aspect of vocational rehabilitation. A release to work is needed before the person is ready to resume employment, although vocational rehabilitation can begin sooner. As already noted, a person may be able to return to a modified work position before the completion of medical treatment. In that case, an initial release to return to modified work will be secured with a later final release to the person's pre-injury employment upon termination of medical care. An assessment of functional capacities can also serve as a foundation for evaluating the patient's ability to handle the activities of daily living.

Vocational Rehabilitation

Vocational rehabilitation helps the injured person engage in suitable work as soon as possible after a disabling injury. The vocational rehabilitation process usually begins when the vocational rehabilitation counselor contacts the most recent employer and conducts a **job analysis**. As described in Chapter 3, a job analysis is a formal assessment of the physical demands of a job determined through an on-site visit and guided by a comprehensive checklist of physical demands, including lifting, standing, walking, sitting, reaching, climbing, and environmental demands. The job analysis is a fundamental means for determining the patient's potential to return to his or her former job, for determining the feasibility of modifying that job, and for obtaining a release to work from the attending physician.

The rehabilitation professional should always start the vocational rehabilitation process by exploring existing return to work opportunities with the former employer. The employer is already aware of the employee's value and skills, and the injured person should have less fear about a return to work in a familiar environment. The Americans with Disabilities Act (ADA) strongly encourages employers to make *reasonable accommodations* for their injured workers.[12] The rehabilitation professional can help educate employers about their obligations to their injured workers under this federal law. The ADA applies not just to workers collecting workers compensation, but to all workers who cannot return to their prior job because of the effects of an injury or illness that is expected to result in some limitation to a major life function.

Return to Former Employer

If the injured person cannot perform his or her existing job, the first alternative would be a *job modification*, that is, a change in the physical demands, number of duties, emotional demands, and/or hours required in that job. In most cases these changes will be temporary. When the changes are temporary and the goal is to resume full duty gradually, job modifications are called **work hardening** or **transitional work**. Work hardening/transitional work is a technique that helps the injured party to gradually readjust to the physical demands of a job. The person practices job-related tasks using less weight, or for shorter periods of time, or at a slower pace than is required in the actual job. This process is similar to an athlete who gradually returns to the playing field. The rehabilitation professional assists the employer in identifying opportunities for job modification and coaches the worker during work hardening exercises.

The following case illustrates the use of a job analysis, followed by work hardening and a permanent but simple **job modification**, which can be permanent but is typically temporary and involves very little cost to the employer.

Appropriate Job Modifications

A records clerk who worked in an insurance company slipped on a tile floor (where a coworker had spilled coffee) and injured her lower back. She was treated by her family physician who had treated her high blood pressure for years. After four weeks of bed rest and medication, she still did not feel capable of returning to her job. Her supervisor described her job as "very easy" and could not understand why she did not return. The claim representative handling the case brought in rehabilitation services.

The provider's first step was to meet with the supervisor and conduct a job analysis. She found that the supervisor was correct in that most of the records clerk's job was "easy" in terms of physical

Continued on next page.

demands. The clerk sat 75 percent of the time, setting up new files, typing forms, and providing back-up at the switchboard. However, she stood for 25 percent of the time while sorting mail, pulling claim files, and delivering stacks of files to managers. The clerk also lifted plastic buckets of mail, which at times weighed over 40 pounds.

With the job analysis in hand, the provider asked whether the supervisor would allow the clerk to return to work only part time at first and to perform only the sit-down portion of her job. The supervisor agreed to this job modification. A schedule of increasing hours was then worked out so that after six weeks the clerk would be performing her regular duties. The work hardening plan was set. The rehabilitation provider then met with the clerk and her family physician to discuss the job analysis, temporary job modification, and work-hardening plan. All parties agreed to the plan.

After only three weeks in the plan, the clerk began to resume her duties of lifting the plastic tubs of mail and delivering stacks of files. These duties resulted in a setback in her medical progress. A permanent job modification was negotiated whereby the mailroom brought smaller tubs weighing no more than 20 pounds when filled, and a cart was purchased to use in delivering the files. After six weeks, the clerk was back to her regular duties with the modifications noted.

A job analysis does not need to be performed for every job, nor does it always need to be performed by an insurance rehabilitation vendor. Some employers list physical demands in their job descriptions to comply with the ADA, which requires employers to identify the *essential functions* of jobs.[13] The essential functions focus on the job's physical demands. A claim representative can simply request a job description and review these essential functions. In addition, some jobs may have been previously analyzed by a rehabilitation professional, so the claim representative may obtain a copy of the job analysis from the employer or a claim file.

If job modification is impossible, then a transfer to another position within the company should be explored as the next step in the vocational rehabilitation process. If a transfer is not feasible, the vocational rehabilitation professional should explore the possibility of creating a new position with the employer.

Placement With a New Employer

If a return to work with the former employer is not feasible, then *job placement in a new employer* would be the next step in vocational rehabilitation. Job placement can only be successful if the rehabilitation professional identifies specific *job goals*. An unfocused "take what you can get" effort is rarely, if ever, successful. In fact, the latter approach is likely to lead only to a less than suitable and/or a temporary position, thus frustrating the injured person, leading to adversity and potential litigation, which significantly impede the rehabilitation process.

Job goals are usually identified through one of two methods. First, transferable skills can be identified by analyzing the skills a person has developed through his or her prior work experience. For example, a warehouse supervisor would be expected to have management skills that could be considered transferable to a management trainee position. The second method is to conduct a formal vocational evaluation (described under the next heading) when transferable skills are not obvious upon review of the work history.

Once job goals are identified, the disabled person must be trained in **job-seeking skills**, that is, instruction and practice in completing job applications and résumés, approaching a prospective employer, and interviewing. Next, a **labor market survey** must be completed. This is a formal exploration of job openings in the local community based on local employment service listings, newspaper ads, and direct employer contacts. Finally, the rehabilitation professional would assist the injured person with actual work of contacting prospective employers, called **job development**, and following up to secure a position.

Vocational Evaluation

If transferable skills are neither evident nor extensive enough for suitable job placement, formal **vocational evaluation** or testing should be pursued. This testing should consist of an assessment of the person's intelligence, academic achievement levels, aptitude, vocational interests, and personality. The assessment is usually made through psychometric tests administered by a work evaluator or psychologist under the supervision of the rehabilitation professional.

Psychometric Tests

The following psychometric tests are frequently used in a vocational evaluation.

Tests of Intelligence   Two common intelligence tests are used.

- The Wechsler Adult Intelligence Scale (WAIS) measures intelligence comprehensively, differentiating between verbal intelligence (the ability to learn by written or verbal expression or instruction) and performance intelligence (the ability to learn by demonstration, visual perceptual skill). For example, the picture completion test requires the testee to fill in missing features. The picture arrangement test requires the subject to put pictures in proper sequence. The object assembly test measures the ability to visually synthesize parts into a whole.
- Beta measures intelligence on performance-oriented items. This examination was developed to test illiterate and foreign-speaking Army recruits.

Tests of Educational Achievement   Two tests of educational achievement are as follows:

- The Wide Range Achievement Test (WRAT) was designed to measure reading (word recognition only), spelling, and mathematical performance levels.
- The Adult Basic Learning Examination (ABLE) measures reading (vocabulary and comprehension), spelling, and mathematics performance levels.

Tests of Aptitude Commonly used aptitude tests include the following:

- The General Aptitude Test Battery (GATB) measures six verbal-perceptual aptitudes (general learning ability, verbal aptitude, numerical aptitude, spatial aptitude, form perception, and clerical perception) and three physical aptitudes (finger dexterity, hand dexterity, and motor coordination).
- The Bennett Mechanical Comprehension Test measures understanding of mechanical principles or the ability to learn skills such as complex machine operation and repair.

Tests of Interest Patterns Tests of interest patterns include the following:

- The Strong-Campbell Interest Inventory (SCII) measures occupational interests in jobs requiring technical or college training.
- A career assessment inventory (CAI) measures occupational interest in jobs requiring less formal training.

Tests of Personality Finally, vocational rehabilitation professionals may use the following personality tests:

- The Minnesota Multiphasic Personality Inventory (MMPI) measures over ten personality variables (such as introversion and extroversion) and is used primarily for differential diagnosis of psychological/emotional disorders. The MMPI has been used in the vocational evaluation process to assess the emotional stability of the injured person for occupations such as police officer and business manager, jobs for which emotional stability is particularly important.
- The Edwards Personal Preference Schedule (EPPS) measures sixteen needs or motives (such as autonomy versus dependence) that may influence suitability for an occupation.

Work Samples

A vocational evaluation may include the administration of **work samples**. This aspect of vocational evaluation was developed and first performed in rehabilitation workshops. A work sample is a defined work activity that uses tasks, materials, tools, and equipment that are similar to those used in an actual job. For example, a soldering work sample may assess the injured person's ability to do electronics assembly without putting the person on the assembly line. A work sample is normed; that is, the time required by a normal industrial employee to perform a task and the accuracy with which that task is performed are known, and the injured person's performance is compared to that performance standard. The purpose of a work sample is to define skills, the person's interest in the job, physical capabilities, and work behaviors. Work samples are most commonly used in cases involved severe disability (brain damage) for which psychometric tests may not be feasibly administered.

Work samples more accurately reflect the individual's true skills and abilities than psychometric tests because the person actually performs the task. Work samples are often better than a medical report for evaluating physical capacities because the person is concentrating on the tasks and pushing his or her limits, rather than concentrating on physical limitations. Work samples can assess whole-body physical capacities such as lifting, standing, and bending. Finally, work samples can assess work behaviors such as the ability to complete a task once it is begun, to work around others, and to comply with work schedules.

Work samples typically take longer to administer and the results take longer to assess than a one-hour analysis of transferable skills or a two- to six-hour psychometric test session. Work samples are usually administered over a period ranging from a minimum of one day to several weeks, depending on the variety of samples. Some evaluations require one to two days to allow the person to work through a battery of work samples. An example is the Val Par System, which consists of thirteen work samples ranging from tasks that test whole-body range of motion to money handling. Some evaluations involving a large battery require weeks. Some providers have developed unique work samples to assess specific types of jobs such as auto parts counter work or wood lathe operation.

Special Training

If the preceding steps fail, the rehabilitation professional should consider some level of training that may involve remedial education, obtaining a high school diploma, vocational-technical institute courses (such as electronics), business school courses (such as accounting), a two-year program at a community college (associate's degree), or four years of college (bachelor's degree), though the last is very rare. Apprenticeship program opportunities may be explored outside of the most common building trade apprenticeships that would likely be beyond the function capacities of the injured person. An example of an apprenticeship program that might be appropriate for some physically disabled persons is the trade of a locksmith. An on-the-job training (OJT) contract between a new employer and a funding source (such as a casualty insurance company) can provide the injured person with concurrent training and employment. The incentive for the new employer may be an arrangement such as a 50-50 agreement for wages paid during the training period. In unique situations involving severe disability (such as brain damage), sheltered employment in a rehabilitation workshop may be the best interim step to employment in the larger community.

Psychosocial Adjustment

The insurance rehabilitation professional should meet with or telephone the injured person. Regular contact between the insurance rehabilitation professional and the injured person is vital to assess the person's initial reaction to the injury, his or her available support systems, any barriers to recovery and/or return to work, and the need for psychosocial adjustment/rehabilitation.

Psychosocial adjustment/rehabilitation is achieved primarily through counseling. Counseling focuses on the injured person's adjustment to his or her disability, pain, vocational change, and family support. For a complete approach to psychosocial and social adjustment to a disability, counseling should consider both the person and the family.

The success of counseling is often a prerequisite to the success of any rehabilitation process. Some injured people continue to feel totally disabled by their injury or disease despite the finest medical case management and vocational rehabilitation.

The rehabilitation professional is heavily involved in this counseling process. He or she must continually encourage the injured person to focus on ability rather than disability. A "carrot and stick" approach is used, with praise and support given for all positive efforts by the injured person to reach a goal (such as attendance at appointments, participation in therapy, and active job seeking). Nevertheless, the person is firmly confronted when he or she has been irresponsible (missed appointments, responded passively to therapy, or failed to seek work).

The counseling needs of the injured person may be beyond the capability of the rehabilitation vendor. For example, the injured person may continually demonstrate inappropriate or uncontrolled crying, irrational conversation, or extreme verbal hostility. In such complicated cases, a psychological evaluation and/or treatment by a psychologist or psychiatrist may be included as a part of the rehabilitation process. The financial liability for such an evaluation must be carefully considered before implementing the evaluation, weighing such factors as history of psychiatric disorders. This treatment is often funded through health insurance rather than through the casualty insurer. An insurer will be reluctant to finance such treatment unless the accident in question clearly caused the psychological problem.

Counseling also presents the possibility of professional malpractice. Most rehabilitation vendors are neither qualified nor licensed to perform psychotherapy. Insurance rehabilitation vendors can be legally liable if their medical case managers and vocational counselors fail to refer the injured person to a licensed and qualified psychologist or psychiatrist. Providers of psychotherapy differ in their philosophies regarding the therapeutic value of work in the recovery process. Some believe it is therapeutic to return to productive work in the shortest possible time. Others believe it is harmful to subject the patient to the stress of the work environment. The insurance rehabilitation professional or the claim representative should know the philosophy of any psychologist or psychiatrist who becomes involved in the care of an injured person.

Cases with a primary diagnosis of post-traumatic stress syndrome are particularly challenging to control because psychological and psychiatric care can be costly. The claim representative must work closely with the insurance rehabilitation professional and the attending medical practitioners to develop reasonable time limits for treatment and realistic anticipated outcomes. Otherwise, treatment can continue unchecked, and a return to employment (if relevant) becomes more unlikely with each month away from work.

Forensic Rehabilitation

Forensic rehabilitation was mentioned earlier as a component of the insurance rehabilitation process that is only used in cases in which liability or coverage is questioned or the person will not cooperate with voluntarily offered rehabilitation services. As illustrated in the case, forensic rehabilitation is the use of rehabilitation expertise in a court or claim system. This chapter has defined and discussed rehabilitation from a cooperative, perhaps even paternalistic, perspective. That is, it has been assumed that the injured person is basically cooperative and has voluntarily accepted insurance rehabilitation services. The process itself is based on the same assumption. In fact, experience and several studies of rehabilitation reveal that over 70 percent of the persons offered insurance rehabilitation voluntarily accept and cooperate with the service. Nevertheless, the remaining 30 percent who do not accept rehabilitation[14] need to be addressed. Forensic rehabilitation has grown to some extent in response to this need, but forensic rehabilitation has grown primarily as a strategy in the defense of contested cases.

The Use of Forensic Rehabilitation

A woman slipped on a wet floor at a major department store, fracturing her ankle. Her medical recovery progressed well, but she alleged total disability because of continued pain in her ankle. She terminated her usual employment at a local assembly plant because she could not tolerate the standing her job required. She changed doctors, deciding to consult a practitioner who ordered the use of a wheelchair and home health care. A general liability suit was filed against the department store for $1 million in damages based on extensive continued medical care, loss of future wage-earning capacity, and pain and suffering.

The insurer offered rehabilitation services under a reservation of rights agreement, which were refused. A rehabilitation provider was asked to review the medical record and to conduct a job analysis at the prior employment site. The rehabilitation provider was a registered nurse who had also completed a master's degree in rehabilitation counseling, qualifying her as an expert witness in both medical and vocational matters. During discovery, the rehabilitation provider was deposed. She testified that the medical care of the original treating physician was appropriate and produced a statement that the job analysis revealed that the woman's job could be performed from a sitting position. She also produced a statement from the prior employer that an appropriate job opportunity existed. This woman's claim settled before trial for a very reasonable amount largely as a result of the rehabilitation provider's expert testimony.

The foundation for forensic rehabilitation was set in a landmark 1960 court of appeals case *Kramer v. Flemming*.[15] The court ordered the use of a rehabilitation professional for expert testimony in a Social Security case. Since this case, the use of vocational rehabilitation counselors as expert witnesses has spread to hearings on workers compensation, general liability, auto liability, professional liability, and even ocean marine bodily injury claims.

To qualify as an expert witness, an insurance rehabilitation professional must be shown to have qualifications relevant to the subject matter of his or her testimony. An insurance rehabilitation professional testifying about treatment matters should be a registered nurse or an occupational or physical therapist. An insurance rehabilitation professional testifying about vocational matters should be a CRC or otherwise qualified in vocational matters.

Expert testimony in rehabilitation is generally given in answer to a hypothetical question concerning the injured person's rehabilitation potential. The freedom to give an opinion is extremely important because the provider may not have even met the injured person and may have to rely solely on employment and medical records as the basis of his or her testimony.

Summary

Both physical/psychosocial rehabilitation and insurance rehabilitation help to reduce the effect of injuries on the injured person, the family, the employer, the economy, and the insurance business. Both types of rehabilitation can be of great value in assisting the injured person to regain optimal healing and function, and to restore an individual's self-esteem.

Physical/psychosocial rehabilitation denotes services ordered by a patient's treating physician as a part of the medical regimen that are carried out by various rehabilitation providers who render the care or service. In contrast, insurance rehabilitation services refer to consultative services that are generally instituted at the request of the insurance company and can be of great value in certain types of injury claims.

Since physical/psychosocial services are ordered by the patient's treating physician, they are generally not regarded as optional. However, the services that are offered by insurance rehabilitation specialists at the request and direction of the casualty insurer are considered to be optional except when specified by law. Since insurance rehabilitation services can be expensive, claim representatives must be able to identify cases that are likely to benefit and recognize which services are suitable for a given case.

In both rehabilitation systems, the key person throughout the entire process is the injured person. This person may have a variety of reactions to the impairment and resultant disability that may help or hinder the rehabilitation process. The family, employer, plaintiff attorney, and claim representative can all play vital roles in rehabilitation of an injured person.

The claim representative must realize that both rehabilitation processes consist of often simultaneously performed services in the areas of medical case management, vocational counseling, and psychological rehabilitation. Rehabilitation professionals also provide expert testimony in what is known as forensic rehabilitation.

Chapter Notes

1. The Foundation for Rehabilitation Certification, Education and Research, *CIRS Study Guide* (The Foundation for Rehabilitation Certification, Education and Research, 1993), p. 26.
2. Arthur Larson, *Workers Compensation*, desk ed. (Albany, NY: Matthew Bender, 1994), § 61.20.
3. As cited in Chancy Croft, "Something More Important Than Money—Vocational Rehabilitation in Workers Compensation Cases," *Alaska Law Review*, vol. 3, 1986, p. 54.
4. Definition of Physical Medicine and Rehabilitation by the American Board of Physical Medicine and Rehabilitation.
5. The Commission for Case Manager Certification, "CCM Certification Guide" (Rolling Meadows, IL: Commission for Case Manager Certification, November 1992).
6. John Gice, "Return to Work Versus On-Going Disability," *Legal Insight*, 1988, pp. 13-16.
7. L. Nowak, *American Economist*, vol. 27, 1983, pp. 23-29.
8. D. Lengham, "Vocational Rehabilitation Cost Effectiveness Study," *Journal of Private Sector Rehabilitation*, vol. 3, 1988, pp. 15-25.
9. R. Treitel, *Social Security Bulletin*, vol. 3-23, no. 4, 1979.

    H. Hester et al., *Menninger RTW Scale* (Topeka, KS: Menninger Foundation, 1986).
10. Stanley Bigos, et al., "A Prospective Study of Work Perceptions and Psychological Factors Affecting the Report of a Back Injury," *Spine*, vol. 16, no. 1, 1995.
11. "Is Normal Activity the Best Treatment for Back Pain?", *The Backletter*, vol. 12, no. 2, 1997.
12. Americans with Disabilities Act, *Technical Assistance Manual on Employment Provisions* (Indianapolis: JIST Works, Inc., 1993).
13. Americans with Disabilities Act, *Technical Assistance Manual on Employment Provisions*.
14. J. Gardner, *Vocational Rehabilitation in Florida* (Cambridge, MA: Workers Compensation Research Institute, 1987).
15. 283 F.2d 916 (1960).

Chapter 5

Low Back Injury Claims

Claim representatives who handle injury claims inevitably encounter low back injury claims. The lower back is the part of the body most frequently cited in injury claims, and disability due to low back pain is growing at a higher rate than any other disability category.[1] Low back pain is responsible for tens of billions of dollars each year in medical, lost work time, and employee retraining costs.[2] As much as 85 percent of Americans experience low back pain at some time in their lives.[3] The significance of low back injury claims justifies the extensive coverage given in this text.

Back injury claims are prevalent in workers compensation, automobile liability, medical payments, uninsured motorist, and premises liability claims. Claim representatives who handle these types of claims must understand the issues related to low back injuries. Almost one third of all workers compensation, lost-time claims are due to back injury claims and more than 90 percent of these are *low* back injury claims. In 1997, the average cost of one lost-time, low back injury workers compensation claim was $11,645.[4] A study by the Insurance Research Council found that 45 percent of automobile accident claimants reported back sprains and strains,[5] and the average automobile bodily injury payment for a back sprain was $7,240.[6] For those back sprain injury cases that went to trial in 1997, the median jury award was $7,800 for automobile accident cases[7] and $25,000 for slip-and-fall cases.[8]

For claim representatives to properly evaluate and manage a low back injury claim, they must understand the anatomy of the back, be able to analyze medical records, recognize the limitations of diagnosing and treating back injuries, and identify claims requiring outside experts who can help control the costs of back injury claims.

Challenges of Handling Back Injury Claims

Back injury claims pose more potential challenges to claim representatives than any other type of claim. Brain injuries and spinal cord injuries are more severe and often more complicated, but with brain and spinal cord injuries, claim representatives will usually have several outside medical experts assisting them from an early stage. With back injuries, claim representatives usually do not have that same degree of outside support, and, in about 80 percent of the cases, outside assistance is not required. However, about 20 percent of back injury claims can be as complicated as a brain injury claim. The following factors influence the length of disability for back injury claims and relate to the complexity of evaluating back injury claims:

- The anatomical cause of the pain
- Whether the pain is acute or chronic
- The claimant's job activity level
- The claimant's job satisfaction
- The claimant's wages
- The claimant's family status (divorced, widowed, etc.)[9]
- The claimant's individual personality traits, measured by Minnesota Multiphasic Personality Inventory (MMPI) test
- The claimant's general level of stress
- Litigation/attorney involvement
- The method of treatment

Several of the factors listed, such as job satisfaction, wages, family status, and individual personality traits, might seem insignificant because they are not physical conditions, but these psychological factors have a strong correlation to the length of disability. Other factors unrelated to injury type or severity such as litigation and attorney involvement also affect the length of disability. Lawyers represent two-thirds of automobile bodily injury claimants with back injuries.[10] Lawyer involvement adds an additional challenge to handling back injury claims. Another difficulty is that a high percentage of back sprains, like sprains in general, involve some element of insurance abuse. This percentage, about 40 percent in 1994, appears to be increasing.[11]

Problems in Diagnosing Back Problems

Medical providers often have difficulty correctly diagnosing most low back injuries. Diagnostic terms for back pain are continually changing. Current diagnostic terms rely on archaic, inaccurate, or vague words, such as arthritis, fibrosis, degeneration, tension state, disk disease, and subluxations. Broad terms like these make it difficult for the legal profession, insurers, and patients to understand the cause of the pain. Even the term diagnosis has different meanings to different health-care providers. The medical definition of diagnosis addresses the cause of a person's condition, while the chiropractic definition does not.

> **Comparing the Definitions of Diagnosis**
>
> *Medical Definition (from* Taber's Medical Dictionary*)*
>
> **diagnosis** (pl. diagnoses): 1. The term denoting the name of the disease or syndrome a person has or is believed to have. 2. The use of scientific and skillful methods to establish the cause and nature of a person's illness. This is done by evaluating the history of the disease process; the signs and symptoms present; laboratory data; special tests such as x-ray pictures and electrocardiograms. The value of establishing a diagnosis is to provide a logical basis for treatment and prognosis.
>
> *Chiropractic Definitions*[12]
>
> **diagnosis**: A specific decision regarding the nature of the patient's complaints. A nominative decision is based on subjective or "soft" information. A substantive decision is based mainly on objective or "hard" information (such as X-rays).
>
> **assessment**: An examination performed for the purpose of obtaining information regarding the patient's state with the intent of arriving at a qualitative or quantitative description of a patient's condition.

Most low back injuries have no identifiable injury cause. When the origin of the injury is not traceable to a specific event, policy coverage is questionable. Some low back pain is not caused by back trauma. Low back pain is sometimes caused by metabolic diseases, circulatory problems, kidney infections, stomach ulcers, viral pneumonia, tipped uterus, ovarian infections, and cancer.[13] Because back pain can have many causes, claim representatives must not allow a description of symptoms to substitute for a diagnosis. Claim representatives should insist that providers describe the injury diagnosis in causation terms. For example, "low back pain" is not a proper diagnosis because it does not indicate the cause or suspected cause.

Health-care professionals distinguish between chronic and acute low back pain. **Chronic** refers to a condition that has a long duration, recurs frequently, and changes little. Chronic back problems are not usually caused by a specific accident, but they might be aggravated by an accident. Acute is the opposite of chronic. **Acute** refers to a condition with a sudden and severe onset that is often traceable to a specific event. Acute low back pain usually has a short duration. Back muscles strained by overexertion that quickly heal would be an example of an acute low back problem. An episode that lasts for more than three months is considered chronic.

Claims involving chronic back pain are more problematic for claim representatives than claims involving acute back pain because chronic back pain is often categorized as nonspecific low back pain (NSLBP), that is, the pain has unidentifiable causes.

The known, specific physical causes of low back pain, identifiable by modern technology, are:

- Disk herniation
- Spondylolisthesis and spondylosis (usually in young individuals)
- Spinal stenosis (usually in the elderly)
- Vertebral fractures, tumors, infections, and inflammatory diseases

The challenge for health-care providers and claim representatives is that 85 percent of low back pain claims cannot be traced to one of these specific known causes.[14]

NSLBP is commonly attributed to muscles sprains, worn joints, and pinched nerves, but diagnostic tests often do not accurately identify the source of the problem and many individuals who have these problems show no symptoms. In the industrial setting, most workers reporting back injuries are unable to clearly relate it to a specific incident.[15] One reason that a low back injury is not always traceable to a specific incident is because of degenerative back conditions caused by "wear and tear" over an extended period of time.

Another problem for health-care providers, and consequently for claim representatives, is that the pain and suffering of a claimant does not clearly correlate to the amount of observable "damage" to the back. Patients who have the same observable physical condition express varying levels of pain. Since a doctor cannot verify the level of pain, a patient's complaint must be considered in the diagnosis. Consequently, a physician's diagnosis for a back injury claim may in some cases differ solely because of the level of pain expressed by the patient.

Preexisting Conditions in Backs

A study appearing in the 1994 *New England Journal of Medicine* found that nearly 28 percent of individuals with *no* symptoms of back problems who were tested by magnetic resonance imaging (MRI) were diagnosed with herniated disks. Were these individuals potential back injury claimants or are herniated disks not necessarily a cause of low back problems? Research is still being conducted on this issue.

A prior back injury claim is a good predictor that someone will make a back injury claim in the future. Studies show that 39 percent of workers with prior back injury claims ended up making subsequent back injury claims.[16] This would be expected if back injuries are caused by degenerative diseases ("wear and tear") of the back, congenital problems, muscle weakness, and other factors that are peculiar to an individual claimant.

A well-established rule of law is "a claimant must be accepted the way he or she is found." Normally this means that a claimant cannot be denied compensation because of his or her preexisting conditions. For example, a claimant with a preexisting back condition, who is injured in a subsequent accident, must still be compensated for injury caused by the accident. The responsible party cannot argue that, if the person had a perfectly healthy back, the injury would not have occurred (even if that were true). If an accident aggravates a preexisting condition, then the claimant must be compensated to the extent of this aggravation. However, this determination is complicated because a recurrence of an old injury, unrelated to a subsequent incident, is not compensable. Distinguishing between recurrence and aggravation can be time-consuming and challenging for the claim representative, especially when the flare-up occurs near the time of the accident. Because health-care providers sometimes do not distinguish between the two in their initial, presumptive diagnosis, claim representatives may need to press the providers for their opinion on causation.

Nonphysical Factors in Back Injury Claims

Back pain and disability related to back pain are strongly influenced by nonphysical factors. Nonphysical factors can be monetary (such as a settlement), emotional (such as concern and support from friends and family), or psychological (such as job satisfaction). As mentioned earlier, these create challenges for claim representatives and health-care providers. Back injury claims often involve more nonphysical issues than other types of injury claims. Nonphysical factors affect whether injured parties will make a claim and whether treatment will be effective.

Claimants with the same physical back condition and the same objective diagnosis respond differently depending on psychological factors. For example, individuals who are dissatisfied with their jobs are more likely to make back injury claims and not return to work than individuals with the same injury who are satisfied with their jobs. Individual personality traits also affect whether a person is likely to report back injuries.[17] The type and amount of compensation received by a claimant can influence the effectiveness of treatment.[18] Many individuals with chronic back problems are people who have a high level of stress. These individuals seek health care as a way to reduce stress. These individuals are not looking for more money, except to the extent that it buys them more health care and stress relief.[19] This variance from one claimant to the next makes it difficult for the claim representative to set reserves, evaluate damages, and manage back injury claims.

In addition to claimant variability for the same injury, the psychological factors related to back injury claims make it difficult for claim

> "Symptom magnification" is replacing the older term "malingering" in most modern medical texts. Malingering has a more specifically defined meaning based on medico-legal criteria.

representatives to determine the motivation of the claimant. For example, it may be difficult to distinguish claimants who intentionally *magnify symptoms* to try to increase their settlements from claimants who honestly believe they can not return to work. What does this difference matter if the objective findings are the same?

This difference affects the approach needed to manage and conclude the claim. For example, a claimant's motivation may affect the claim representative's decision to obtain independent medical exams, consult with lawyers, and engage other medical specialists to evaluate the claimant.

Consider the following examples of motivational differences among three different claimants who have nonspecific low back pain and have not returned to work after three months. Each of these individuals has different motivations and requires claim representatives to apply different approaches to conclude the claims.

Bob, who has had a history of back problems, is motivated by a desire to avoid working and wants to obtain as large an injury settlement as possible. Bob has conscious control over his own treatment and his own emotions about the injury. His purpose is to maximize the amount of compensation. Bob will respond to a direct approach and will negotiate on financial terms.

Tom, on the other hand, is preoccupied with making sure his back heals, and for that reason is not willing to return to a job because he doesn't consider the job worth the risk of re-injury. Talking to Tom in financial terms will not be effective. Tom will more likely respond to having a doctor that Tom trusts explain to him that normal activity can prevent an acute problem from becoming a chronic one.

Laura is lonely and divorced. She sometimes feels like her life is out of control. She likes her job but enjoys the stress relief and the attention she gets from her chiropractor. Laura is afraid that if she returns to work, the treatments will stop. Instead of talking to Laura about her pain and suffering damages, negotiations with Laura may be more effectively framed in terms of how many treatments a settlement will provide her. The claim representative may even be able to arrange with the provider for discounted fees that would enable Laura to have more treatments.

Anatomy of the Spine

Claim representatives must have a working knowledge of the anatomy of the back in order to evaluate low back injury claims. As mentioned previously, some back problems do have specifically identifiable causes, but most low back injury claims do not. For this reason, the diagnosis for low back pain by health-care providers can be somewhat speculative. Regardless of this problem, an understanding of the diagnosis, the anatomy of the back, and pain causation can help the claim representative evaluate the likelihood of disability, the return-to-work potential, and the need for independent medical examinations or other outside expert consultation.

Exhibit 5-1 shows the **vertebral column** (sometimes called the backbone, spine, or spinal column). The vertebral column is made up of seven **cervical vertebrae** in the neck area, twelve **thoracic vertebrae** in the middle of the back, five **lumbar vertebrae** in the small of the back, the **sacrum** formed by the fusion of five small sacral vertebrae, and the **coccyx** (or tailbone) formed by the fusion of four or five small vertebrae. The first (top) cervical vertebra is called the atlas. It articulates with the head.

Exhibit 5-1
Vertebral Column

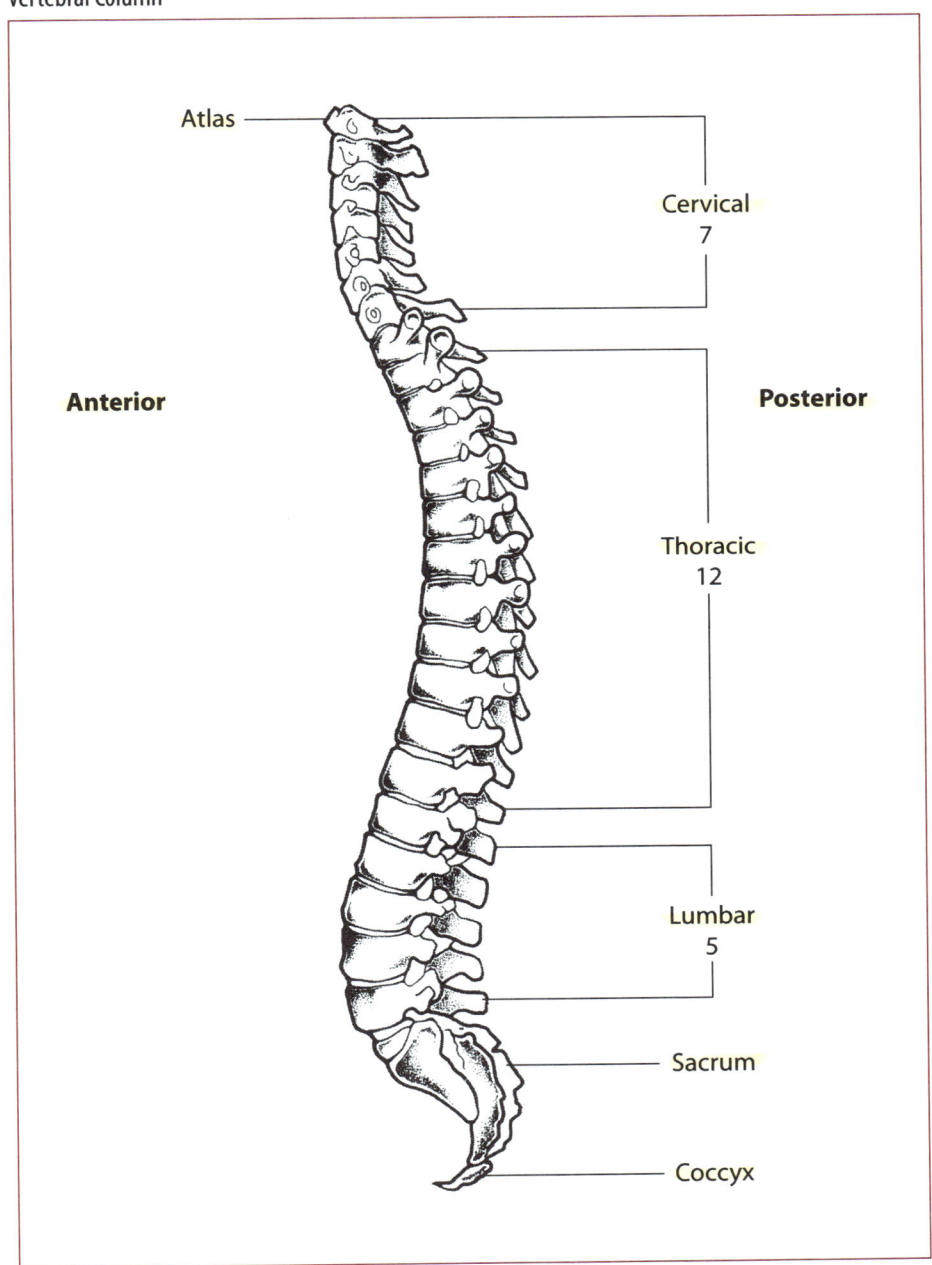

Individual vertebras are identified by location and number. For example, T8 is the eighth thoracic vertebra (counting from the top), and L4 is the fourth lumbar vertebra. Ligaments link the vertebrae, and intervertebral disks separate them. An **intervertebral disk** is made of compressible cartilage and acts as a shock absorber between the vertebrae.

In addition to protecting the spinal cord, the vertebral column also provides protection for thirty-one pairs of spinal nerves. The spinal nerves exit the vertebral column through spaces between the bones, called the intervertebral foramen. Exhibit 5-2 shows the spinal cord, intervertebral disks, and spinal nerves.

Exhibit 5-2
Spinal Cord, Intervertebral Disks, and Spinal Nerves

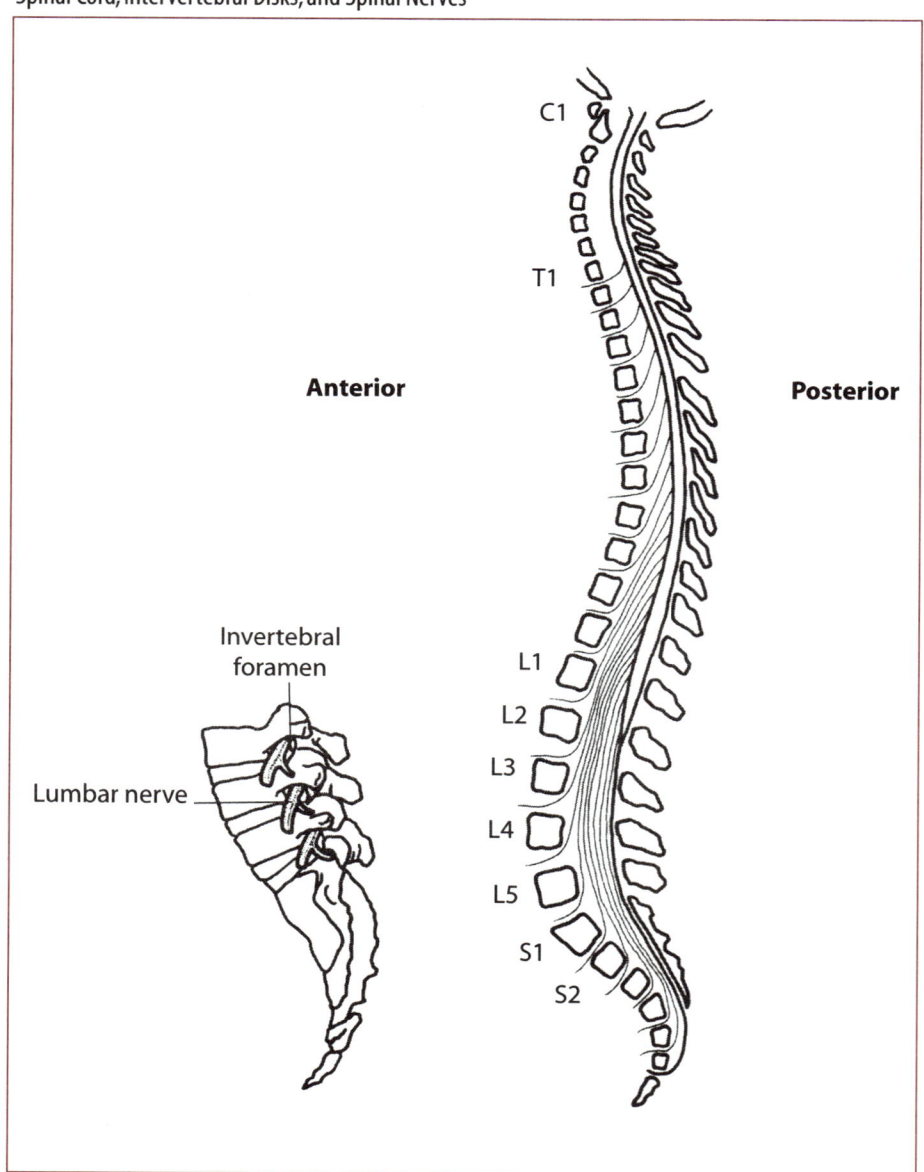

The cervical vertebrae are very flexible, allowing for a wide range of motion in the neck. The thoracic vertebrae become progressively larger from the upper to the lower portion of the vertebral column. They have distinctive smooth areas for articulation with the ribs. These smooth areas are called **facets**. The sacrum is concave, curving toward the front of the body, and fills the back portion of the pelvis.

Most low back injury claims are related to the five lumbar vertebrae in the small of the back. The lumbar vertebrae are large because they support most of the weight of the back. Most low back pain involves the L4 and L5 vertebras. Exhibit 5-3 shows a cross-section of one lumbar vertebra. Extending *posteriorly* from the body of the vertebra are two short projections called **pedicles**. (Refer to Appendix 5-B at the end of this chapter for the definitions of common positional terms, such as posterior.) Arising from the pedicles is a pair of bony plates that meet and fuse in the midline posteriorly. These plates are known as the **laminae**. The two laminae meet and project downward and backward creating the **spinous processes**, which can be felt under the surface of the skin of the back. On either side of the vertebra, **transverse processes** extend laterally from the junction of the pedicle and the lamina. Transverse processes serve as bony attachments for the muscles and ligaments.

Exhibit 5-3
Lumbar Vertebra

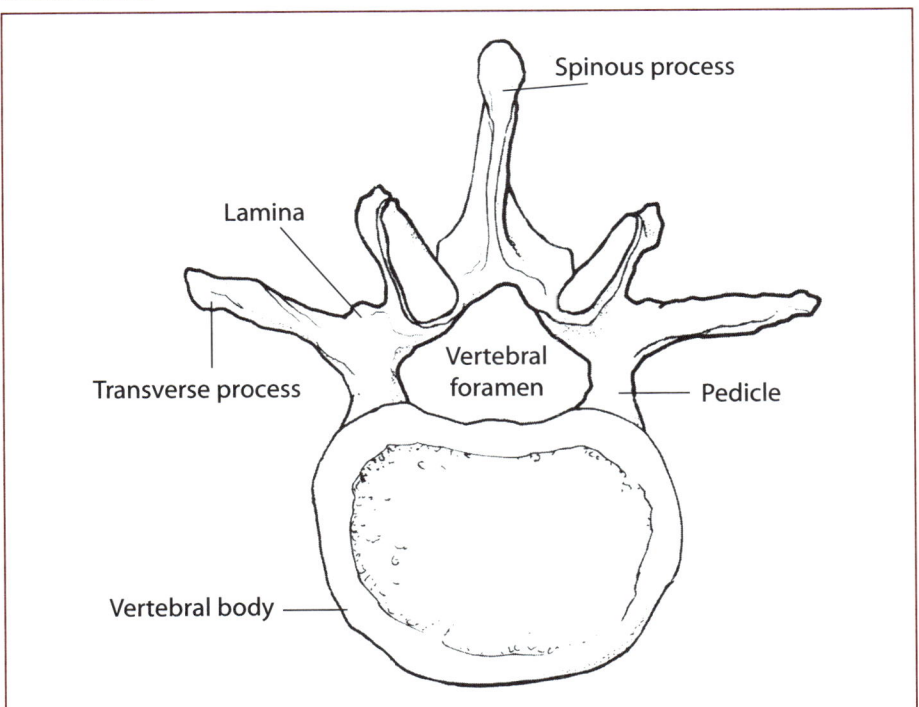

The inferior processes of one vertebra articulate with the superior processes of the vertebra below it. Thus, each vertebra has three joints with both the vertebra above and the vertebra below. The three joints are where the vertebra come together and where the two processes articulate.

A newborn's spine is concave forward. When the child begins to walk, secondary curves begin to develop in the spine. Some exaggerated curves may result from disease, injury, or posture problems. An increase in the thoracic curve is known as "humpback," or **kyphosis**. An increase in the lumbar curve is referred to as "swayback," or **lordosis**. A lateral curvature is referred to as **scoliosis**, and is present to some degree in almost all people.

Back Injuries and Conditions

Injuries and disorders of the spinal joints are likely to be painful and disabling because of the close physical and functional relationship between these joints and the nervous system. In normal body mechanics, the spinal nerves and skeletal system are aligned. Injuries to the spine or elsewhere can alter normal body mechanics. Scar tissue can also develop, hindering joint movement, irritating nerve roots, and causing pain and dysfunction of muscles.

In the casualty claims environment, low back injury claims are often attributed to one or more of the following:

- Spinal fractures
- Spondylolysis/spondylolisthesis
- Herniated or bulging disks
- Back strains and sprains
- Dislocations

Some of the chronic causes of back pain are:

- Congenital conditions
- Degenerative problems

Each of these will be discussed in detail.

When a patient comes to a health-care provider with low back pain, the provider makes a presumptive diagnosis based on the symptoms reported. As the patient's medical history is reviewed and as tests are conducted, the presumptive diagnosis will change to a definitive diagnosis. One of the purposes of reviewing a patient's history and performing an examination is to rule out the serious injuries. The order presented in this text, from the most serious back injury to least serious one, is the order that a provider would follow in ruling out injuries and conditions.

Spinal Fractures

A fracture of the vertebral bones, commonly called a broken back, can initially require significant care but usually heals without residual problems. In this respect, fractures are less of a problem than many chronic back conditions. Fractures of the thoracic and lumbar vertebrae usually result from a fall on the buttocks or feet. These fractures are usually wedge compression or bursting compression fractures.

Major injuries of the vertebral column are generally assessed in terms of their stability, the likelihood that the injury could become worse. Stable injuries, such as compression fractures, are protected from displacement by the rear spinal ligaments. Unstable injuries, such as dislocations, are displaced and may become further so if the ligaments have been torn. More serious fractures and dislocations of the spine can occur in automobile and industrial accidents. These can be unstable, and the spinal cord may be damaged as well. X-rays of the spine in various degrees of flexion and extension may be necessary to determine stability.

When the spine is flexed (bending forward), a force from below or from above can cause the spine to suddenly flex beyond its normal range. In this position, the force is greater on the forward portions of the vertebra. The rear ligaments remain intact causing the vertebra to be crushed in the forward portion, resulting in a wedge compression fracture.

The symptoms of a wedge compression fracture may be mild with only localized tenderness, since such fractures are stable and the spinal cord is not involved. Conservative treatment is usually used. Conservative treatment involves a short period of bed rest followed by physical therapy. In more severe cases or when patients complain of increased pain, a body cast is sometimes applied. With elderly patients, a brace or corset is often recommended.

If the spine is straight when compression force is applied, a bursting compression fracture results. The intervertebral disk is driven into the porous bone of the vertebra, and fracture fragments burst outward in all directions. Because the rear spinal ligaments usually remain intact, the spinal column remains stable. Also, it is rare for a fragment to be driven backward far enough to cause spinal cord injury. The symptoms of a bursting compression fracture will be more severe than those of a wedge compression fracture. However, several weeks of bed rest or a fitted body cast for six to eight weeks will usually result in healing with few or no further problems.

Spondylolysis and Spondylolisthesis

Spondylolysis and spondylolisthesis are often confused. **Spondylolysis** is a defect in a specific facet of a L4 or L5 vertebra at the point it meets another vertebra. This condition is sometimes described as a fracture or nonunion of the bones. A simple definition of **spondylolisthesis** is the forward slippage of one vertebra on another. Spondylolisthesis usually occurs at the L4 or L5 location as well. Spondylolysis may or may not be associated with spondylolisthesis.

Spondylolysis is believed to occur during childhood when the cartilage fails to harden. This is often an inherited characteristic but it can also be brought on by an injury to the spine or by degenerative changes. This condition can cause nerve root compression and have the same symptoms as spondylolisthesis. Spondylolysis may be a defect leading to spondylolisthesis.

Symptoms of spondylolisthesis include hamstring tightness or spasms. Patients with low grade slippage (Grades I or II) rarely have symptoms other than hamstring tightness, whereas patients with Grades III and IV may have forward spinal curvature, noticeable by an abdomen that appears to thrust forward. Scoliosis (a sideways curvature of the spine) may also be present in some patients. Exhibit 5-4 shows that displacement is less significant with spondylolysis than with spondylolisthesis.

Exhibit 5-4
Spondylolysis Versus Spondylolisthesis

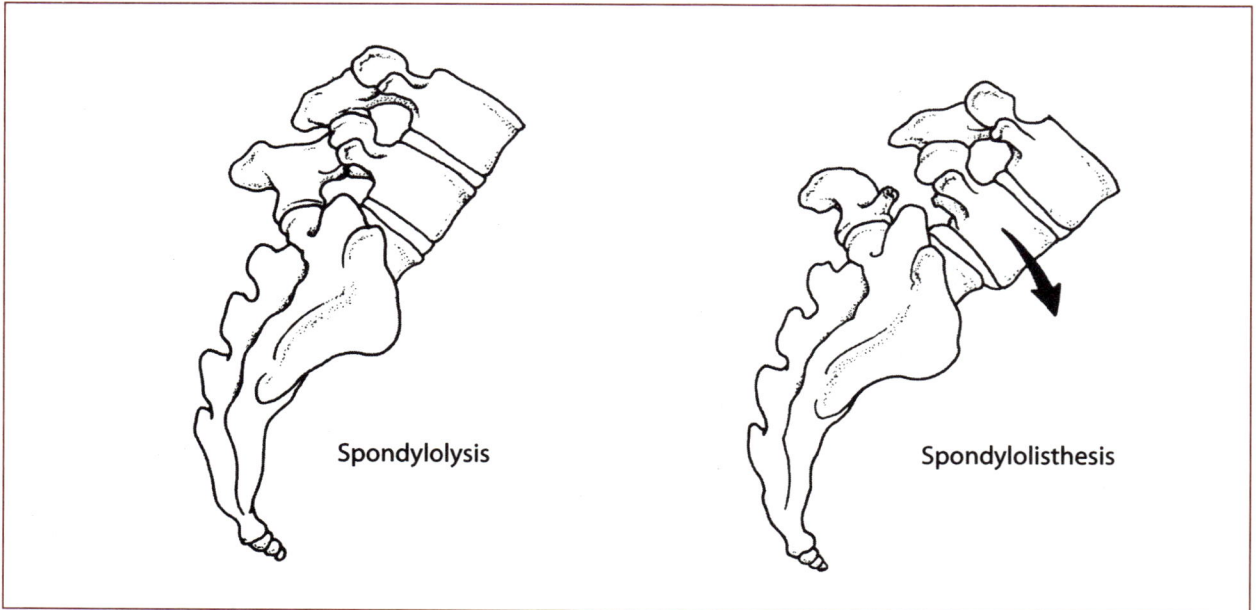

Advisory

One important fact that claim representatives should be aware of is that the displacement shown in Exhibit 5-4 is not visible with AP or lateral ("straight on") X-ray views of the spine, as shown above. They are only visible from oblique (slanted, diagonal) views. Often oblique views are not taken initially and therefore the diagnosis for spondylolisthesis may not be given. Without the oblique views, spondylolisthesis should not be ruled out as a possible cause of low back pain.

There are five classes of spondylolisthesis: congenital, isthmic, traumatic, pathologic, and degenerative. Congenital spondylolisthesis, a condition people are born with, may have no symptoms. Isthmic spondylolisthesis often coincides with growth spurts in children and may be related to stress or fatigue fractures occurring from increases in certain activities such as back walkovers in gymnastics, students carrying heavy backpacks (also seen with military recruits), and weight lifting. Traumatic spondylolisthesis (the type most commonly claimed in casualty losses) results from an acute fracture in the area of the pedicle, lamina, or facets of the bone. Degenerative spondylolisthesis, the most common class of spondylolisthesis, results from long-lasting ligament instability caused by facet and intervertebral disk deterioration. Symptoms include weakness, numbness, and burning in the lower back, buttocks, or thighs. Degenerative spondylolisthesis affects between 4 percent and 10 percent of the population. Women are five times as likely to be affected.[20]

In the majority of traumatic spondylolisthesis, symptoms will resolve with conservative treatment within a few weeks. Spinal manipulation may be effective in relieving pain but should not be performed if the patient's condition is already stable. Patients with high-grade cases may be counseled to avoid occupations requiring heavy lifting. Surgery may be required for individuals who do not heal with conservative treatment. About 15 percent of patients require surgical intervention.[21]

In an oblique X-ray of the spine, a spondylolisthetic defect looks like a collar on a Scottie dog's neck (see Exhibit 5-5). The "Scottie dog" describes the appearance of the facet joints and pars interarticularis (the dog's neck) in the X-ray.

Exhibit 5-5
"Scottie Dog"

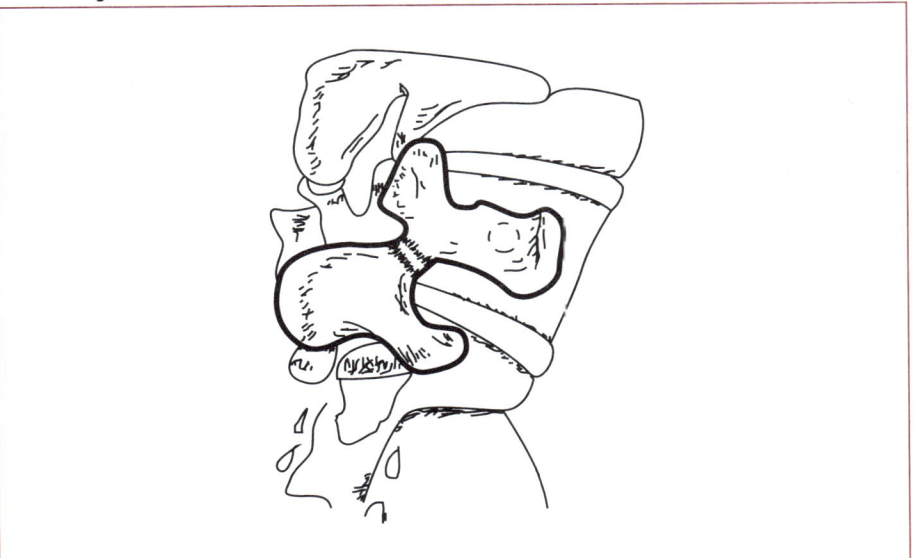

Disk Bulging and Herniation

Disk problems, such as disk bulging, disk herniation, and disk degeneration, are extremely common in adults. In the low back, the L4-L5 and L5-S1 disks are most frequently affected. About 90 percent of all low back injuries caused by nerve compression from a disk herniation occur in this area of the back. Degenerative disk disease, common in people over thirty, will be discussed in detail later in this chapter.

Bulging or herniated disks can cause severe pain and disability. The spinal nerves and spinal cord are vulnerable to bulging and herniated disks because of their proximity to the vertebrae and intervertebral disks. Exhibit 5-2 shows a section of the spine with nerve roots passing through the intervertebral foramen. The semisolid center of a disk may shift or bulge and press the nerves. In more severe cases, a disk may rupture (or herniate) through its capsule and press against the spinal nerves. On the other hand, disks may bulge or herniate in such a way as to produce minimal symptoms.

Technical Note

Although the definitions for bulging and herniated disks are not codified in the medical community, in this text, *bulging* refers to a protrusion of a disk, while *herniation* refers to a protrusion with a rupture of the disk lining.

There are four types of disk protrusions:

1. A posterior protrusion
2. A posterolateral protrusion
3. A posterolateral protrusion with a rupture of the annulus fibrosus
4. A posterolateral protrusion with a rupture of the annulus fibrosus and fragmentation

A posterior protrusion bulges in the direction of the rear of the disk, pressing directly on the vertebral column. A posterolateral protrusion bulges to the left or right side of the spinal cord. A posterolateral protrusion with a rupture of the annulus fibrosus involves a tear of the tough membrane containing the gelatin-like material in the center of the disk. This injury allows the semisolid disk center to escape the tough capsular disk. In a posterolateral protrusion with rupture of the annulus fibrosus and fragmentation of the disk substance, the disk material fragments and may escape into the spinal canal. Exhibit 5-6 shows top views of disk protrusions and a normal disk. In many instances, protrusions falling into the first two categories will respond to conservative treatment. The disk does not reabsorb itself and tends to atrophy slightly. The patient is given a series of spinal exercises to strengthen the back muscles and protect against future episodes.

Exhibit 5-6
Healthy Versus Protruding Disks

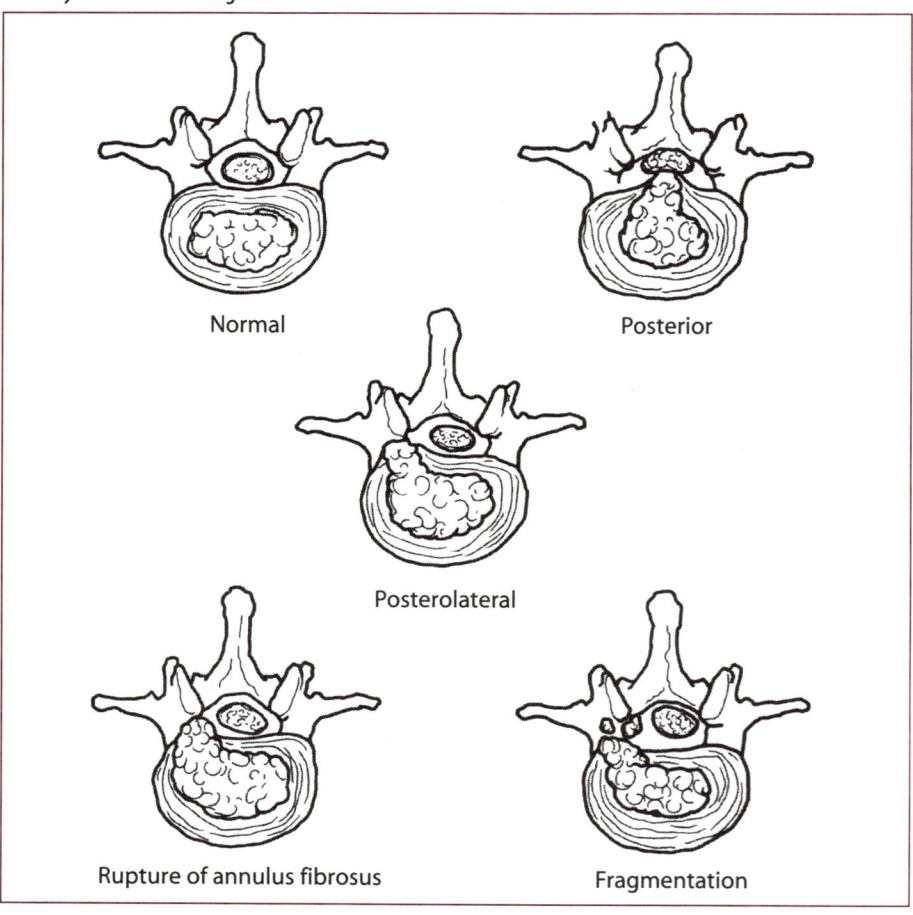

Disk herniation frequently occurs at the level of the sciatic nerve located near the L4 through S2 disks. Pain in the back of the thigh and leg along the sciatic nerve is called **sciatica**. Sciatica is a vague diagnosis that means pain along the sciatic nerve. This diagnosis does not address the cause of the pain although it is often assumed to be caused by a bulging or herniated disk. The sciatic nerve is responsible for movement and sensation in the lower extremities. It exits the spine between disks L4, L5, S1, and S2 disks (see Exhibit 5-2). Sciatica is an extremely uncomfortable condition. Usually described as a dull ache, it can become very sharp and piercing. Pain is usually noticed on one side of the buttocks or the other. The pain can extend from the buttocks to the thigh, knee, and toes. The pain is usually centralized at the back of the thigh and leg. Pain can occasionally be felt in the front or side of the leg. The pain can be an annoyance, or it can become completely disabling. If pressure or pinching on the spinal nerve continues, actual nerve damage can result, causing either numbness or muscle weakness in the leg.

Back Sprains and Strains

There are numerous causes of back sprains and strains. Poor posture, lack of exercise, emotional stress, and obesity increase a person's chances of back sprains and strains. Poor posture strains the lower back and makes it more vulnerable to injury. Weak and flabby abdominal muscles deprive the back of its greatest support. Being overweight adds to the strain.

Sprains occur when back muscles or ligaments are stretched or torn. Sprains usually result from improper performance of ordinary activities such as bending, lifting, standing, or sitting. Sprains may also result from the wrenching caused by an accident or injury.

Strains can have a more subtle history of aggravation from a repetitive activity. Strains result from working a muscle beyond its normal capacity. An example would be lifting too much weight. The range of motion may be normal and the ligaments and tendons are not torn but the muscle is overexerted. One of the most common findings associated with muscle strains is pain upon palpation of the muscle, but no pain upon palpation of the joint.

Exhibit 5-7 shows the relationship between the causes of soft tissue injury pain, such as back pain, and the resulting impairment. Emotional tension (such as work stress), physical trauma (such as lifting), infections, and immobilization (leading to muscle weakness) can all cause irritations in the back. Enough irritation can cause pain and muscle tension. Muscle tension can cause inflammation that can lead to muscle shortening from its normal range, restrictions in joint movement, and limitations in tendon function. These combined effects can cause an impairment. This same chain of events leading to impairments in the back apply to soft tissue injuries in other parts of the body (for example, the neck). Conservative back injury treatment attempts to break this chain and eliminate or reduce the impairment.

Exhibit 5-7
The Cause and Effect Chain for Soft Tissue Injuries

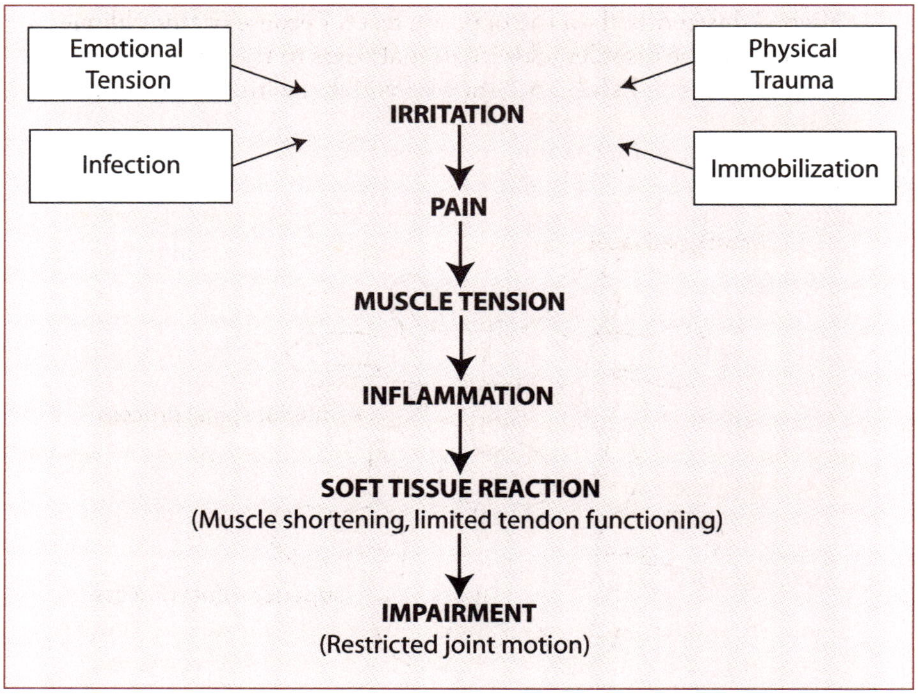

```
Emotional Tension ──┐              ┌── Physical Trauma
                    ↓              ↓
                     IRRITATION
Infection ──────────→   ↓   ←────── Immobilization
                       PAIN
                        ↓
                   MUSCLE TENSION
                        ↓
                   INFLAMMATION
                        ↓
               SOFT TISSUE REACTION
        (Muscle shortening, limited tendon functioning)
                        ↓
                    IMPAIRMENT
               (Restricted joint motion)
```

Dislocations

A **dislocation** is the complete displacement of one or both bones of a joint. A **subluxation** is a partial displacement of bones away from their customary alignment in the joint. Subluxation of joints in the lumbar spine is common. While dislocations are almost always caused by external trauma, subluxation may be a recurring problem. Although the dislocated and subluxated bones may return to their normal alignment in time, complications can occur. Surrounding structures may be damaged, chip fractures of the bones may occur, and traumatic arthritis may result. Generally, resting the affected joints is sufficient to allow surrounding tissues to heal.

> The chiropractic use of the term *subluxation* refers to an aberration of normal spinal biomechanics, usually involving a restriction or loss of normal movement of a motion segment.

Congenital Problems

Patients who cannot trace their back pain to a specific incident or whose pain does not subside in the normal healing period may have other under-lying congenital or degenerative problems. Congenital problems exist at birth. With trauma superimposed on a preexisting condition, it is often difficult, if not impossible, to distinguish between the causes of the patient's pain. Minor congenital back problems are so common that a variation from normal is detectable in more than half of the population.

Facet Tropism

Facet tropism is a common congenital problem. The facet joints on the spine are where the superior spinal process of one vertebra joins the inferior spinal process of the vertebra above it. Facet tropism is characterized by misalignment of facets in a specific vertebra. Facet tropism typically occurs in the lumbar spine. A facet on one side is aligned differently than the opposite facet. Because of this oblique alignment, the disorder adds rotational stress to the already strained lumbar vertebra. Exhibit 5-8 shows a vertebra with facet tropism.

Exhibit 5-8
Facet Tropism

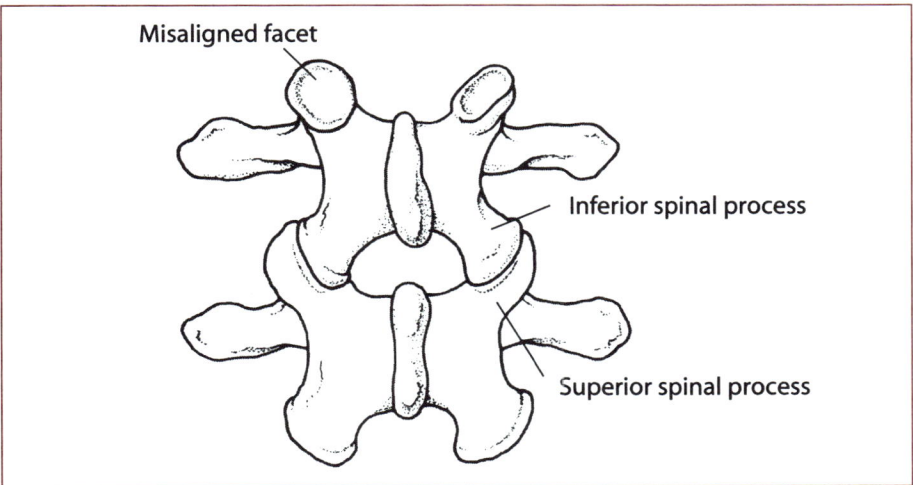

Sacralization and Lumbarization

Sacralization of a lumbar vertebra is one of the most significant congenital abnormalities causing low back pain. This condition is also known as Bertolotti's syndrome. Sacralization occurs when the fifth lumbar vertebra is fused into the sacrum. When this happens on just one side of the vertebra, it places unusual stress on the disk above and frequently causes herniation.

Similarly, lumbarization of a sacral vertebra, which occurs in sixth rather than fifth lumbar vertebra, also causes great stress on the joint of the L5 and S1 disks. If herniation or nerve root entrapment occurs, surgery to decompress the disk should include fusion to weld the affected vertebra.

Spina Bifida

The most common congenital abnormality of the spine is spina bifida. Spina bifida is the incomplete bony closure of one or more spinal processes leaving the neural arch open. This defect may occur at any level of the spine but most often occurs in the lumbosacral region. This condition is usually accompanied by a neurological deficit and may range from mild muscle weakness to complete paralysis of the lower limbs. The mildest degree of spina bifida, known as spina bifida occulta, occurs without any external manifestation. It is detectable only through X-rays. This common form occurs in about 10 percent of the population.

Scoliosis

The spine can develop abnormal curvature in three directions: to the front (kyphosis), to the back (londosis), and to the side (scoliosis). Scoliosis, or lateral (sideward) curvature of the spine, is a common congenital abnormality. Approximately 80 percent of the cases of scoliosis are without a known cause. Noncongenital scoliosis can result from muscular contractions due to disk herniation. Non-congenital scoliosis is usually not noticeable, and discovery of the condition is usually made only when X-rays are taken for some other purpose. Severe scoliosis is usually associated with multiple congenital abnormalities of the ribs as well. Severe, progressive scoliosis requires early surgical intervention, including spinal fusion, to prevent extreme deformity.

Degenerative Disorders

There are four major degenerative back disorders: (1) spondylolysis (discussed earlier), (2) osteoarthritis, (3) degenerative disk disease, and (4) spinal stenosis. Although degenerative back disorders often occur in combination, each condition alone can lead to spinal nerve root entrapment. Irritation, pinching, and pressing of the spinal nerves can cause severe pain and disability. Traumatic injuries frequently occur in people already affected by a degenerative disorder. The resulting problems will almost certainly be worse than with a traumatic injury alone, making the claim more difficult to resolve and more expensive.

Osteoarthritis

Osteoarthritis involves metabolic and cellular activity within joint cartilage. In the spine, the facet joints are involved. Blood vessels from the resident bone invade the cartilage, exposing the normally bloodless cartilage to the circulatory system and wearing the softened cartilage, resulting in complete loss of the cartilage space. The cartilage responds to the blood vessel invasion by forming a thickened growth known as chondrophyte. This growth subsequently undergoes ossification and becomes what is known as an osteophyte, or bony spur. This defect alters the distribution of stresses on the affected joints and can press on the spinal nerves.

Metabolic problems and infection can also cause osteoarthritis (as well as other types of arthritis). As mentioned, trauma may be but is usually not the cause of osteoarthritis, although it may aggravate preexisting conditions of osteoarthritis. In cases of alleged traumatically induced osteoarthritis, the claim representative should determine whether the osteoarthritis existed before the injury or whether it would have become just as bad regardless of the injury. Such a defense requires careful analysis of a claimant's medical records and involves complex medical issues.

Degenerative Disk Disease

Degenerative disk disease is an acceleration of the normal aging process and may be aggravated by trauma. Degeneration of the disk begins in the nucleus pulposus. Degenerative disk disease is characterized by a loss of thickness in the disk space. Initially the disk contains 85 to 90 percent water, but the amount decreases to 65 percent with age[22] (a major reason why people shrink as they get older). As the nucleus pulposus reabsorbs water, its gelatinous texture becomes somewhat lumpy. The annulus fibrosus, the tough capsule surrounding the nucleus, loses elasticity, making it more susceptible to separation or tearing. Smooth motion in the spine is replaced by uneven and excessive motion. Because of this instability, the joints may react by forming small osteophytes.

Herniation of a disk is not the same as disk degeneration. Herniation may result from a specific incident, but may also occur as a complication of degeneration.

Spinal Stenosis

Spinal stenosis, shown in Exhibit 5-9, is a disorder characterized by bony narrowing of the central spinal canal or the lateral nerve root exits. Spinal stenosis can be congenital or secondary to advanced stages of degenerative disk disease. It can also result from spinal fusion. The pain from spinal stenosis may be diffused or radicular (like sciatica) depending on whether the location of the disorder is centralized or lateral, respectively. This pain is caused by the narrowing of the space where the nerve root exits the vertebral column.

Exhibit 5-9
Spinal Stenosis

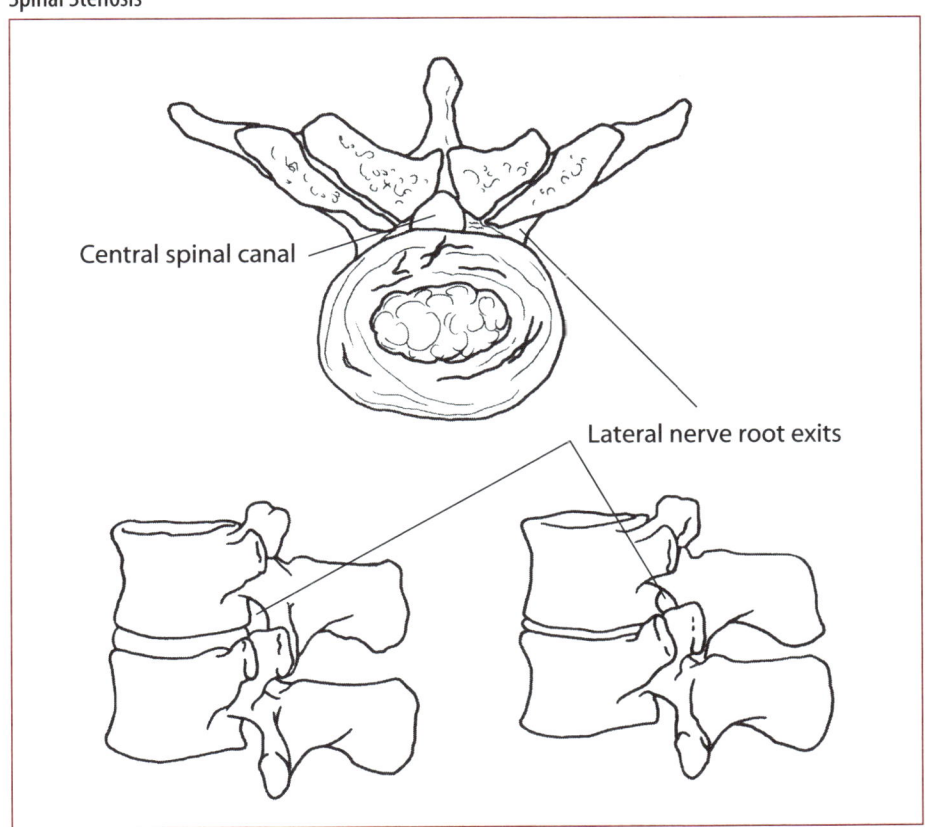

A condition related to spinal stenosis is facet joint impingement. This is a chronic degenerative problem in which the nerve root exits become narrowed by osteophytes and subluxation. The nerves, like the central spinal canal in spinal stenosis, become pinched and pressured as a result of this bony narrowing. Facet joint impingement is treated with mobilization. A condition known as facet joint sprain can likewise involve subluxation of facet joints, but like any sprain, it is better treated with rest than with mobilization.

Diagnostic Testing for Back Injuries

Most cases of low back pain do not require diagnostic tests because they are acute cases that are resolved in a matter of days. However, for that minority of more serious cases, early proper diagnostic testing can mean the difference between recovery and permanent disability. A diagnosis is formed from information gathered from three broad categories:

1. Medical history
2. Physical examinations (and clinical tests)
3. Diagnostic imaging tests

As mentioned earlier, the health-care provider makes a presumptive diagnosis based on the patient's symptoms when the patient comes to the provider. As the doctor reviews the medical history, conducts the examinations, and interprets the diagnostic tests, the diagnosis becomes more definitive. Often the most serious injuries and conditions are ruled out by simple observation or by reviewing the patient's history.

Medical History

A patient's medical history is one of the most accurate methods for diagnosing the cause of low back problems. Information obtained about the patient forms the foundation of the investigation leading to a diagnosis. The patient's age helps to direct the focus of the provider's search for a diagnosis. For example, disk problems are more likely to occur between the ages of fifteen and forty, while spondlylosis and osteoarthritis are more common in people older than forty-five. The patient's occupation and gender can also help in the diagnosis. Does the person's job require strenuous lifting? The time of day of the pain and activities associated with the pain are also helpful in forming a diagnosis. Morning stiffness is often associated with osteoarthritis of the facet joints.

The way pain radiates through the body can be helpful in locating a cause. For example, a patient who describes a history of pain radiating below the knee as opposed to pain radiating just to the posterior thigh indicates the likelihood of a spinal nerve root disease. A history of numbness or weakness in the leg further increases the likelihood of some neurological condition.

The doctor should determine when the pain first began, the exact location of the pain, what activities worsen it, and what activities improve it. The patient's hobbies, work, and daily routine should be identified. Some providers believe that a good medical history is 90 percent of a diagnosis. The problem with medical histories is that they can be "contaminated" by misinformation given by the patient. For example, a patient may indicate that he has to lift 200-pound sacks at work and does not explain that this is an infrequent task that he receives assistance with when asked to perform it. Another example would be when a patient tells the doctor that his car was "totaled." The doctor might assume that this indicated a serious impact. In reality, the car might be an older car worth only $1,500 that was involved in a minor impact accident where the repairs only slightly exceeded the vehicle's value. The contamination of the medical history with misinformation may affect the diagnosis and the doctor's recommendations for treatment.

Physical Examinations and Clinical Tests

After reviewing the medical history, physical examinations and clinical tests are the next step in diagnosing and eventually treating low back pain. Clinical tests are performed on (and with) the patient and involve testing reflexes and specific neurological functioning.

During physical exams, the physician notes areas of tenderness and muscle spasm, muscular weakness or atrophy, and changes in sensation in the lower extremities. The doctor notes posture and general physical condition and should have the patient flex, extend, and rotate the body to determine the degree of motion the patient is capable of and to identify movements that produce pain. The doctor may also make pin pricks along the extremities and tap various muscles with a reflex hammer to test nerve function. Laboratory tests are sometimes essential to distinguish metabolic and organic causes of symptoms.

Circumferential Measurements

Muscle atrophy can be detected by measuring the circumference of the calf muscles and thigh muscles. Differences between the right and left legs of more than two centimeters could indicate that the patient has a neurological impairment.

Reflex Tests

In the **ankle jerk reflex test**, the doctor strikes the Achilles tendon with a rubber hammer to test the reflexes related to the L4-L5 disks and the S1-S2 disks. A diminished ankle jerk reflex is indicative of sciatic nerve entrapment.

In the **Babinski test**, the examiner runs a pointed object along the bottom of the patient's foot. The great toe extends when the foot is stroked. If the toe flexes backward, it can indicate a lesion.

In the **patellar reflex test**, the examiner strikes the patellar tendon for reflex indications of femoral nerve problems at the L2, L3, and L4 levels.

Clinical Tests of Function or Performance

There are several tests and signs used to help determine the cause of back pain. Lasègue's sign, Linder's sign, and knee flexion tests are used to help determine whether disk herniation is causing the pain. Fabere's sign is used to determine whether the patient's arthritis is in the hip.

In **Lasègue's sign**, also known as the straight-raised-leg (SRL) test, the examiner performs the test with the patient lying supine (on his or her back). Each leg is tested individually by raising the straight leg until the patient complains of pain or tightness in the back or back of the leg. The examiner slowly and carefully lowers the leg until the pain subsides. If the examiner cannot raise the leg through the normal ranges without pain, then the test is considered positive for a lumbar nerve root compression that would indicate a disk herniation. Variations to the straight leg test involve flexing the foot and knee in different directions to help diagnose the problem more specifically. For example, with sciatica, flexion of the hip is painful with the knee extended but not with the knee flexed.

In **Linder's sign**, with the patient supine and legs fully extended, the examiner flexes the neck upward toward the patient's chest. Pain in either the leg or the lumber area is a positive sign of irritation of the sciatic nerve.

In the **knee flexion test**, the patient stands and bends forward to touch his or her toes. If the patient bends the knee on the affected side while forward flexing the spine, the test is positive for sciatic spinal nerve root compression.

In **Fabere's sign** (also known as **Patrick's test**), with the patient supine, the knee is flexed with the outside of the ankle resting on the knee of the opposite leg and the knee depressed. Pain would indicate arthritis in the hip.

Tests for Symptom Magnification or Fabrication

There are a few tests designed to detect patients who are exaggerating or fabricating their symptoms. These tests may involve simulations that give the impression that a particular exam is being performed when in fact it is not. Some simulations should not produce pain even in patients who have anatomical problems. Other exams work by distracting the patient and then indirectly observing them for symptom magnification. Examiners also look for overreactions. Examples include a patient who grimaces, holds his or her breath, tightens his or her muscles, or excessively verbalizes pain. The Hoover test, Burns test, sitting root test, and Waddell tests are examples of tests used for detecting symptom magnification or exaggeration.

In the **Hoover test**, the patient lies supine. The examiner places one hand under each heel while the patient's legs remain relaxed on the examining table. The patient is then asked to lift one leg off the table, while keeping the knees straight. Normally attempts to elevate one leg are accompanied by downward pressure by the opposite leg. A patient who does not lift the leg, or tries to lift the leg but the examiner does not feel pressure on the opposite heel from the other leg trying to "help" the weaker one, is probably not trying.

In the **Burns' test**, the patient is asked to kneel on a chair and then bend forward to touch the floor with the fingers. The test is positive for symptom magnification if the patient is unable to perform the test or the patient overbalances.[23]

The **sitting root test** is sometimes used to catch the patient unaware. In this test, the patient sits while the examiner extends the knee, pretending to examine the foot. Patients with true sciatic pain arch backward and complain of pain into the buttock, posterior thigh, and calf when the leg is straightened, indicating a positive test for tension on the sciatic nerve.[24]

The **Waddell tests** use five categories for assessing symptom magnification:

1. Tenderness
2. Simulation
3. Distraction
4. Regional disturbances
5. Overreaction

If the patient tests positive in three of the five categories, then the patient is magnifying symptoms. As mentioned earlier, there are various motivations for claimants to exaggerate injuries and disabilities.

An example of a simulation test is an **axial loading test**. In this test, the examiner places his or her hands on the patient's shoulders (usually while the patient is standing) and lightly presses down. If the patient reports low back pain, the patient is magnifying symptoms because, even for patients with true disk problems, this maneuver would not cause low back pain.

Waddell's straight leg exam is an example of an exam in the distraction category. Similar to the sitting root test mentioned previously, the examiner looks for improvement in the patient's ability to function while the patient is distracted performing other tests that appear to be unrelated to the low back. For example, a positive result in this category would be a patient who claims to be unable to touch his or her toes while standing, but who can easily grab his or her ankles while seated on the exam table.

Diagnostic Imaging

As mentioned in Chapter 2, diagnostic imaging includes use of a variety of technologies to make a diagnosis. These tests can be used to determine physical causes of low back pain. Because of managed care protocols and increased patient awareness of potential risks related to imaging, the Agency for Health Care Policy and Research (AHCPR) recommends that providers wait four weeks before performing diagnostic imaging, unless the provider has noted "red flags" (potential indicators of serious anatomical problems) in the patient history or physical examination. By waiting, more than 90 percent of patients will recover spontaneously. Besides avoiding the need for unnecessary procedures, waiting also reduces the potential for falsely labeling age-related changes as the cause of low back pain, and exposing patients unnecessarily to risks.

At other times, the provider may prescribe diagnostic tests to rule out serious problems that would need to be addressed immediately. When claim representatives receive bills that do not appear to be accident-related or necessary, it is permissible and even expected for claim representatives to ask providers for an explanation. For example, a doctor might order a series of tests on the patient's kidney because of the unusual amount of back pain experienced by the patient. The purpose of this is to rule out a problem with the kidney. Claim representatives may balk at paying for kidney tests since kidney problems are not accident-related. However, if the provider provides an appropriate explanation for why the test was needed, the claim representative should consider it compensable. If the claim representative encounters unnecessary or unreasonable tests that are not explained, the claim representative should request an explanation. If the explanation is unclear or unsatisfactory, then the claim representative should contact a medical consultant to review the tests' appropriateness.

The most commonly used diagnostic imaging tests for acute low back pain are:

- Plain film radiography (X-rays)
- Computed tomography (CT), including computerized axial tomography (CAT)
- Myelography
- Radionuclide imaging (bone scans)
- Magnetic resonance imaging (MRI)
- Electromyogram (EMG)

These technologies were discussed in Chapter 2. Less commonly used diagnostic imaging tests include discography and thermography.

Exhibit 5-10 shows a comparison of the ability of the various medically accepted techniques to identify and define low back pain causes. The number of "+" signs indicates the relative ability of the technique to identify the problem (for example, tension of the sciatic nerve) and determine the anatomical defeat (for example, a herniated disk in the L4-L5 region).

Exhibit 5-10
Ability of Different Techniques To Identify and Define Cause of Low Back Pain

Technique	Identify Injury/Illness	Define Anatomical Defect
Patient History+	+	
Straight leg raising test	++	+
Circumference measurements	+	+
Reflexes	++	++
X-rays	0	+*
Myelography	0	++++*∇
Bone scans	+++*	++*
CT	0	++++*∇
MRI	0	++++∇
EMG	+++	++

+ Indicates the relative ability of the technique to identify the problem and determine the anatomical defect

0 Indicates that the technique is not effective for the corresponding purpose

* Indicates risk of complications from infection or radiation (higher for myelography than for X-rays, bone scan or CT)

∇ Indicates false-positive diagnostic findings of up to 30% of people without symptoms

Adapted from Wilbert Fordyce, *Back Pain in the Workplace* (Seattle: International Association for the Study of Pain, 1995), p. 50.

X-Rays

X-rays, like other imaging techniques, are not recommended for routine evaluation of patients with acute low back pain within the first four weeks unless a "red flag" is noted by the health-care provider during the clinical examination.[25] The routine use of X-rays unnecessarily exposes individuals to radiation. Recently, the value of X-rays has come into question in diagnosing acute low back pain because X-rays do not detect lumber nerve root impingement, herniated disks, or spinal stenosis. Only 1 out of 2,500 X-rays detects something that would affect patient care that could not be determined from reviewing the medical history or conducting a physical examination.[26]

Computerized Tomography

Spinal *computerized tomography* (CT) involves a computer synthesis of an X-ray of a cross-sectional plane of the back. CT can be used to reveal problems such as:

- Herniated disks
- Tumors
- Nerve root or spinal cord compression

- Congenital problems
- Cervical or lumbar spondylolysis and degenerative arthritis

Myelography

Myelography involves the injection of radio-opaque dye into the spinal column. The dye settles in the spinal column so that X-rays can outline the spinal cord and nerves. The result is called a mylegram. This procedure must be done in a hospital because it sometimes produces moderate to severe side effects, including nausea, vomiting, and intense headaches.

A myelogram shows:

- Herniated disks
- Tumors and inflammations in the spinal structure
- Congenital deformities

The invasive nature of using contrast agents (injections of dyes) and their possible unpleasant side effects are the major disadvantage of this type of test.

Bone Scans

Bone scans, or **radionuclide imaging**, involve injecting radioactive compounds that adhere to bones. These compounds settle into areas where the bone is fractured or deteriorating. A gamma camera creates an image that shows the problem areas. Bone scans can detect problems that cannot be detected by X-rays.

Magnetic Resonance Imaging

Magnetic resonance imaging (MRI) can detect soft tissue injuries and herniated disks by providing a detailed image of the body's interior. This prevents patients from having to undergo more invasive and painful testing technologies such as myelography.

Electromyogram

An electromyogram (EMG) is a graphic representation of the electric currents associated with muscular action. EMGs are useful for detecting herniated disks and the source of nerve root irritation. The EMG is accompanied by nerve conduction tests that determine how motor and sensory impulses move through nerve roots. This is an invasive procedure that is not typically used by itself to make a diagnosis.

Discography

Discography is an extremely invasive procedure that involves injecting an imaging dye directly into the nucleous pulposus of the disk. There are two diagnostic objectives to this technique: (1) to evaluate the extent of disk damage and (2) to evaluate the patient's pain response when the dye is injected.

A degenerative disk will disperse the dye in an abnormal pattern. This is a painful test and is not recommended for assessing patients with acute low back pain. Discography is most effectively used to determine which lumbar vertebra should be fused for those patients requiring surgery.[27]

Thermography

Thermography, measuring the surface temperature of the skin to detect injured areas, is still sometimes used. Claim professionals should not rely on the objective findings of thermography because they are widely derided in the medical community as being inaccurate and unreliable.

Treatment of Low Back Pain

After reviewing the medical history and the results of the physical examination and diagnostic tests (if required), the health-care provider should have a definitive diagnosis on which to base treatment.

Back sprains are normally treated conservatively with measures such as limited bed rest, ice packs, heat (beginning forty-eight hours after injury), and anti-inflammatory drugs. Studies show that bed rest should be limited to three days because longer duration of rest can lead to slower recovery and increased disability.[28] Many individuals with uncomplicated low back injuries do not miss work. Two weeks is commonly the maximum amount of time a person would be off work for a low back injury.[29] Although 90 percent of individuals with low back pain recover within four to eight weeks, the remaining 10 percent account for as much as half of the treatment costs.[30]

Conservative Clinical Care Methods for Low Back Pain[31]

In the absence of complications, the initial treatment for low back pain is similar for most patients. Examples of common conservative clinical care treatment are:

- Patient education
- Medication
- Physical treatments

The purposes of these treatments are to:

- Reduce pain, swelling, and inflammation
- Increase motion, flexibility, and endurance

Patient Education

Treatment of low back pain can be thought of as a triangle, each side representing a different aspect of treatment:

1. Medications
2. Physical treatments and surgery
3. Patient motivation

This third side is as important as the first two. For this reason, patient education is needed to achieve a complete and effective treatment.

The U.S. Department of Health and Human Service's patient guide booklet, "Understanding Acute Low Back Problems," is available from AHCPR by mail or over the Internet at www.ahcpr.gov.

Information about the AHCPR and its guidelines for the treatment of acute low back pain is in Appendix 5-A of this chapter.

Patient education is an underrated and overlooked form of treatment. Patient education includes explaining issues such as expected recovery time, methods for controlling symptoms, safe activities, the effectiveness and risks of various diagnostic tests, and what further treatment could be considered if the back does not heal in the normal period. Many doctors and employers use booklets that explain the various low back problems, treatment techniques, and ways to avoid future low back problems. Doctors who do not adequately explain the normal recovery period can cause patients to seek advice and treatment elsewhere in order to try to relieve symptoms.

One example of patient education is the "back school." Some employers have begun formal education of employees suffering from low back pain. The purpose of these classes is to teach employees about anatomy, the common causes of low back pain, and the importance of diet, exercise, and posture. The results of these formal classes vary by company.

Overall, patient education reduces stress by making the individual aware of treatment and diagnostic options and reduces misconceptions such as the need for complete inactivity. If patients know that some moderate level of activity after two days is better than complete bed rest, they may have fewer reservations about returning to some form of work. Studies consistently show that patient education reduces the use of medical resources, decreases patient apprehension and emotional tension, and helps to speed recovery.

Medication

Acetaminophen, ibuprofen, and aspirin are the most common and most effective medications for relieving back pain. Ibuprofen and aspirin are nonsteriod anti-inflammatory drugs (NSAIDs). Over-the-counter NSAIDs include Advil, Aleve, and Naprosin. Tylenol is an example of an over-the-counter acetaminophen. Tylenol is usually prescribed for the first twenty-four hours after an injury, because aspirin and ibuprofen thin the blood and can increase bruising during this period. Acetaminophen, ibuprofen, and aspirin are inexpensive, low-risk drugs for alleviating pain and avoiding impairment.

Muscle relaxants, a traditional medication used for treatment of low back pain, are now less preferred because they cause drowsiness and are no more effective than other medication. For workers who could become injured because of this side effect, muscle relaxants are normally avoided. Although there is no proven benefit in taking muscle relaxants, such as Flexiril, with NSAIDs, these drugs are commonly prescribed together with the purpose of helping the healing process by dulling the pain.

Steroids and anti-depressants are used occasionally for low back pain, but their benefit in the treatment of *acute* low back pain is questionable. The steroid Medrol with its "dose pack" treatment is used to reduce swelling and help patients sleep better, and sleep is important in nerve regeneration.

In contrast to acute back pain, anti-depressants are often prescribed for people who experience *chronic* low back pain. This is because anti-depressants address psychological factors (especially depression) that may accompany chronic low back pain.

Physical Treatments

Physical treatments for low back pain traditionally include physical therapy, spinal manipulation, ice, heat, traction, ultrasound, and electrical stimulation. Chiropractors and physical therapists are usually the health-care providers who use physical treatments. Osteopaths, who are medical doctors, also prescribe physical treatments. These treatments are the most controversial because research has not conclusively proven their benefits to patients and because they are the most commonly abused form of treatment. As discussed in Chapter 1, the controversy related to back care can be attributed in part to the differences between the goals of palliative care and restorative care. Most of the research cited in this chapter uses the standard of restorative care to judge the effectiveness of physical treatments.

One recent example of research, published in the *New England Journal of Medicine*, compared groups of patients receiving different treatments for low back pain. One group of patients was given an education booklet on low back pain but received no physical treatment for low back pain. The other two groups received chiropractic care or physical therapy. In terms of symptom reduction, time missed from work, and physical functioning, the study found only marginal advantages for the two groups receiving treatment compared to the group that was just given the booklet. However, 75 percent of the patients who received therapy rated their care as good or excellent compared to 30 percent for the patients who were only given the booklet.[32] This demonstrates an important point—the *perception* of care by the patient.

Insurance companies who wish to satisfy insureds treated under first-party coverages such as automobile medical payments, uninsured/underinsured motorist, and personal injury protection (PIP) need to recognize how patients perceive care. Employers, too, want to maintain employee morale and therefore rank perception of the quality of care as one of the top five most important outcomes they look for in measuring the success of a managed care program. In addition to the issue of perception, patients receiving physical treatments might experience other psychological benefits. Because psychological factors can influence the recovery of a significant percentage of patients, these benefits should not be dismissed. Therefore, even in an era of managed care, *limited* physical treatment might be justified even when the functional benefits are marginal or questionable. This does not mean that claim representatives must pay for unnecessary treatments.

Manipulation

The most well known type of physical treatment is probably spinal manipulation. **Manipulation** (referred to by chiropractors as adjustments) varies from gentle stretching of back joints to forceful rotation of the flexed spine using long or short levers (finger thrusts). Practitioners of manipulation claim that it "unlocks" or mobilizes a "jammed" facet, releases muscle spasms, and realigns subluxed joints. The concept behind manipulation is that by thrusting the joint past its normal range of motion, the joint will lose its tightness and return to its normal range of motion. Manipulation is usually performed by chiropractors. Osteopaths are also trained in manipulations. Many states permit physical therapists to perform manipulations, too.

Systematic reviews have concluded that spinal manipulation appears to be effective in some patients with low back pain.[33] Research indicates that manipulations are effective in reducing pain and improving functioning for patients who have had symptoms for longer than fourteen days but less than twenty-eight days. Most studies show no differences between the improvement in patients treated with manipulations before fourteen days or after twenty-eight days and improvement in patients who received no manipulations.[34] Evidence is insufficient to support the use of manipulations for patients with sciatica or for patients who have been treated for more than one month without improvement in symptoms.

Chiropractic manipulations and physical therapy for low back pain are still controversial. While manipulation may slightly reduce symptoms, the main benefit to manipulations (as with other physical treatments) appears to be increased patient satisfaction with their care. From the patient's perspective, practitioners using manipulation appear to be taking a more active role in treatment than practitioners who just prescribe medication and rest.

Manipulation is one of the few physical treatments recommended by AHCPR. AHCPR recommends stopping manipulations and re-evaluating the patient after thirty days if there has been no improvement.

Physical Agents

Physical agents such as ice, heat, ultrasound, TENS, and exercise are commonly used in an attempt to reduce pain and increase functioning. One common physical agent is transcutaneous electrical nerve stimulation (TENS). The TENS unit is a small battery-operated device worn by patients. It provides continuous pulses of electricity by way of surface electrodes. Presumably, TENS counters the nervous system and modifies pain. Several studies have been conducted on TENS, but there is no conclusive evidence that TENS is beneficial. TENS is not recommended by the AHCPR because it is not supported by research.[35]

Traction involves the application of force on the spine in an attempt to stretch the **paraspinal muscles** attached to spinal bones. Pelvic traction is the most commonly used form with low back pain. With pelvic traction, a snug girdle is placed around the pelvis and is tied to weights at the foot of the bed. The objective of this exercise is presumably to reduce pain. Studies show that traction is of questionable benefit.

Physical agents that have proven somewhat effective are shoe insoles for workers who spend prolonged periods of time on their feet and lumbar corsets (back belts) because they can reduce lost time for workers whose jobs require lifting. One study indicated that patients who performed back-strengthening exercises had better outcomes than patients who used other types of physical agents.[36]

Research, and controversy, continue on the use of physical treatments. These treatments are getting even more scrutiny now in the environment of managed care. The latest research indicates that there are few objective (restorative) benefits from physical treatments. However, many chiropractors argue that the research is too narrowly focused on functional improvements in the low back (to the exclusion of subjective benefits like temporarily reduced pain or increased sense of well-being). They argue for a more holistic view of results that takes into account the overall issues including the psychological factors of low back pain. Their argument is bolstered by research that shows placebo treatments can be effective for a significant minority of individuals. Support for alternative treatments, including chiropractic care, is growing in the United States. One study found 40 percent of adults with low back pain seek chiropractic treatment.[38] The approach currently taken by the majority of medical management guidelines is to allow physical/chiropractic treatment but to set reasonable limits on the type and number of treatments. Some states statutorily require workers compensation benefits to cover reasonable expenses for chiropractic care and other alternative forms of treatment. The Milliman and Robertson medical management guidelines recommend that a case manager review any uncomplicated low back injury claim if the claimant has more than seven visits to a chiropractor or physical therapist.[39]

Microscopic tears in the muscle fiber (muscle strains and sprains) should be treated conservatively. If the patient is not responding to these conservative treatments, a reevaluation of the diagnosis is needed. This may mean additional testing.

A patient went to a chiropractor for her back pain after finding no relief with the orthopedist. After three adjustments and a week of no symptoms, she had a follow-up visit with her orthopedist. Upon learning about the success of the chiropractor, the orthopedist stated, "That was the placebo effect." The patient responded, "If it works so well, why didn't you use it?"[37]

Treatment of Serious Disk Problems

Treatment of disk herniation is usually directed at pain relief and restoration of normal function. A support such as a corset may be prescribed to reduce pressure on the disk and surrounding nerves and to reduce or eliminate pain during activity. However, extended use of back supports increases the risk that the back and abdominal muscles will atrophy. Acute herniation is treated with bed rest, NSAIDs, and heat. With prolonged bed rest, irritation of the nerve root should be reduced and symptoms should subside.

Before continuing with more aggressive treatment, a reevaluation of the diagnosis may be needed. This may include additional diagnostic testing. More invasive and aggressive treatments may be used for herniated disks with nerve involvement or unstable ligaments or bony processes. Examples of more invasive and aggressive treatments are injection therapy and surgery.

Injection Therapy

Trigger point injections, including prolotherapy, epidural blocks, and facet joint injections, are the main types of injection therapy used with low back pain. Trigger point injections involve the injection of a local anesthetic and a steroid into the muscles near the tender points in the back. The purpose of this injection is to relax the back muscles and allow healing to occur. The theory that "trigger points" cause low back pain is controversial and disputed by many experts.

Prolotherapy ligamentous injection, also known as trigger injection of ligament and tendon (TILT), involves injecting a substance (usually sugar water) directly into several interspinal ligaments in an attempt to form new cells to strengthen weak tendons and ligaments. Proponents of prolotherapy suggest that tendons and ligaments stretched and weakened by injury cause pain. The goal of prolotherapy is to restore the tissue to its normal length and strength. Before undergoing prolotherapy, a patient should have completed other more conventional forms of treatment. Prolotherapy should be used with a well-designed rehabilitation program.[40]

Epidural blocks are used for patients with positive indications for herniated disks. This treatment involves injections into the spinal canal near the point where the disk herniation is pressing against the nerve.

Facet joint injections involve injecting anesthetics or corticosteroids into or around facet joints of the lumbar spine. If this relieves pain, the facet is recognized as the source of pain and denervation of the facet joint would be recommended to treat the back problem. Facet joint injection is also a controversial treatment.

Injections are invasive procedures and are not generally recommended by the AHCPR for acute low back pain because of the lack of evidence to support their benefits and because of the potential risk of nerve damage, infection, and hemorrhaging.

Back Surgery

Surgery is commonly discussed with patients that have unresolved back symptoms. Surgery is an expensive and often ineffective treatment and is not advisable for most low back pain sufferers. The two most common types of low back surgery are discectomy and fusion.

Discectomy and Laminectomy

During **discectomy**, the disk material is excised (cut out), the space is explored, and any disk fragments are removed. A laminectomy is often required in order to gain access to the disk. A **laminectomy** is the removal of a portion of the bony process of the vertebral bodies.

Spinal Fusion

A spinal fusion is the fixing of one vertebra to another with a bone graft. Fusions are most commonly performed at the L4-L5 level, fusing these vertebrae with the sacrum. The sacrum is scraped to prepare it for bone graft material, which is obtained from the ilium. The graft material is packed along the sides of the vertebral bodies. The fusion solidifies during the six months after surgery.

Surgical Considerations

Patients with acute back pain alone, with *no* suspicious findings of nerve root compression, do not normally need surgical consultation for a possible herniated disk.[41] Surgery is indicated only for patients who have a sudden loss of function of lower limbs, or bowels, who do not respond well to conservative treatment, or who suffer repeated severe sciatica. According to the AHCPR, the treating physician may consider referral for surgical consultation when all of the following conditions are met:

1. Symptoms of sciatica persist without improvement.
2. The sciatica is severe and disabling.
3. There is clinical evidence of nerve root compromise.

According to *Medical Disability Advisor* (MDA), in cases of severe or progressive muscle weakness, surgery should not be delayed. In cases of mechanical instability (bone movement) that cannot be managed, bone fusion is indicated. Spinal fusions are controversial. Some doctors believe that most cases involving a disk problem require a spinal fusion, while others believe fusions should be used only as a last resort. The patient's lifestyle, occupation, and personal preference are important considerations. A manual laborer, who depends upon the strength and stability of his spine to perform his daily tasks, may benefit from a fusion, since it can prevent further degeneration and recurrent nerve root entrapment. In contrast, a patient with a relatively sedentary lifestyle may not require more than a disk excision.

Surgical Results

Lumbar discectomy may relieve symptoms faster than nonsurgical therapy, but the long-term outcomes (greater than four years) of discectomy are similar to conservative care. As with the length of disability related to low back pain, psychological factors have a significant affect on the outcome of surgery for a herniated disk. In fact, studies show that a high score on certain dimensions of the MMPI psychological exam is a better predicator of a favorable or unfavorable surgical outcome for a patient than the objective findings from imaging techniques.[42]

Tying It All Together

Exhibit 5-11 summarizes the process for treating low back pain. The role of the claim representative throughout the process is to evaluate compensability. This requires claim representatives to understand anatomy, trauma, diagnostic techniques, and treatments. This sometimes requires claim representatives to work with various medical professionals to make sure that all of the information is properly evaluated in making the compensability decision. Claim representatives, especially those in workers compensation, may be required to work with claimants, doctors, and claimants' employers in designing the most effective plan to return the claimant to a productive status.

Exhibit 5-11
Simple Algorithm for Treatment of Low Back Pain

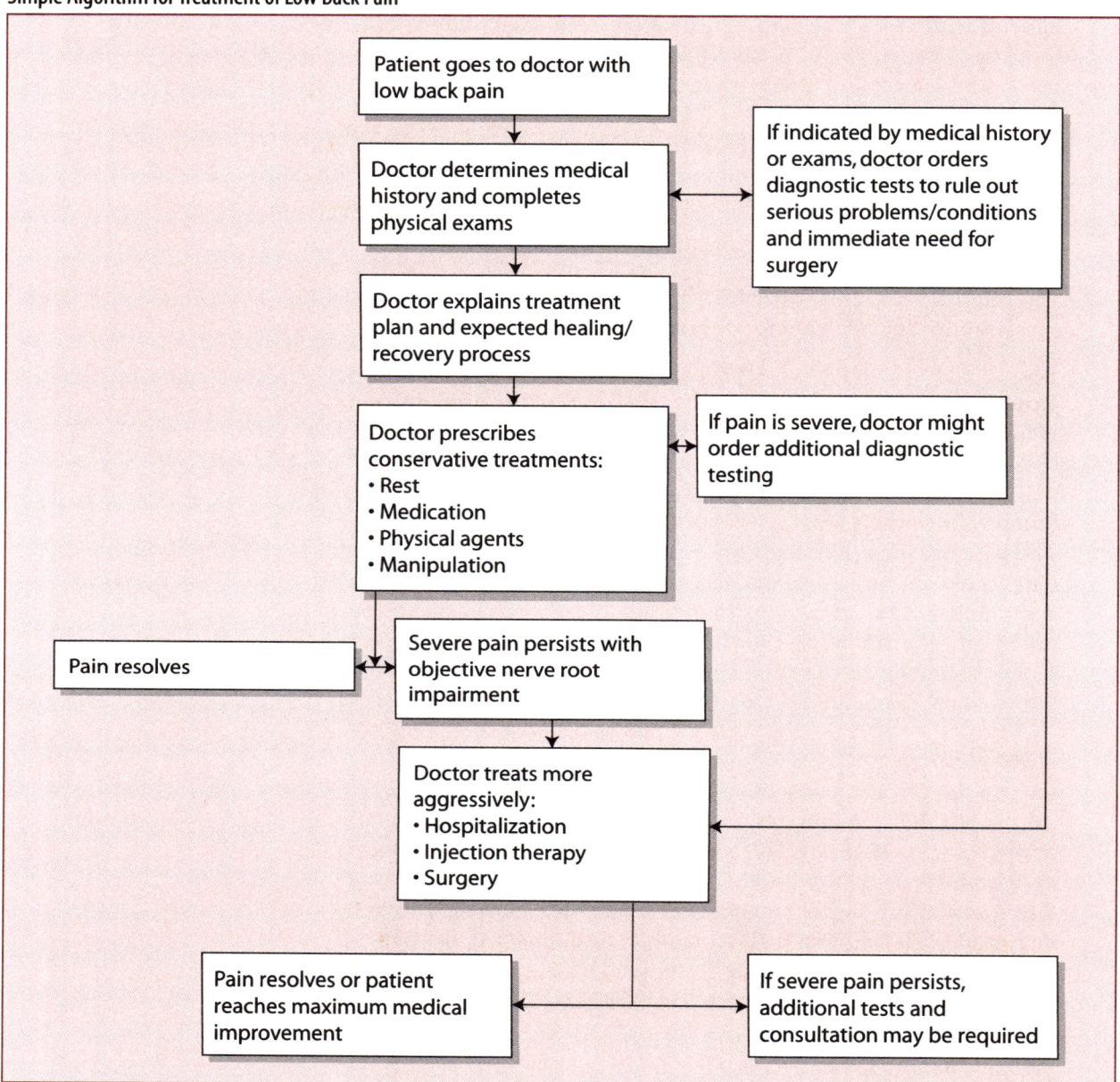

Case Study—Low Back Injury Claim*

At issue is whether a large right-sided posterolateral L5-S1 disk herniation is causally related to a broadside motor vehicle accident that occurred at an intersection.

*Adapted with permission from, Steven C. McAliley, "Evaluation of Herniated Disks," *Hippocrates Lantern*, vol. 5, No. 4., December 1998, p. 24.

Accident description: Mr. Roberts was the lap- and torso-belted, 32-year-old driver of a Nissan Pathfinder that was towing a boat and traveling northbound. The patient's Nissan Pathfinder entered an intersection and passed a stopped dump truck located on the westbound cross street. Simultaneously, a westbound Pontiac Grand Am two-door sedan pulled around the dump truck, entered the intersection, and broadsided the right side of Mr. Roberts' Nissan Pathfinder.

The Nissan Pathfinder was "totaled," and an independent engineer consultant inspected the damage and determined that the impact was severe enough to cause an injury.

Clinical evidence: Within seven hours of the accident, Mr. Roberts went to his family physician with chief complaints that included noticeable right lower lumbar and sacroiliac discomfort. The patient returned four days later to his family physician with new symptoms of right buttock and posterior right thigh pain without signs of seatbelt bruising or abrasion.

Two weeks after the accident, the patient again returned to his family physician with increased and constant low back and right hip pain that radiated into the buttock and posterior aspect of the right thigh. A trial of oral analgesic and anti-inflammatory medications was initiated in an attempt to abate the patient's symptoms. Two months after the accident, Mr. Roberts had not yet responded to the medication, and the doctor decided to initiate physical therapy.

The patient is an automotive technician, and he reported one week of disability immediately after the accident. Because Mr. Roberts' radiating right buttock symptoms did not remit with conservative physical therapy, he underwent low back surgery four months after the accident, followed by six months of disability.

Because of consistent and reproducible symptoms of right buttock pain, markedly positive right straight-leg raising with radiating pain down the posterior thigh, and an absent right ankle reflex, the patient's neurosurgeon suspected an L5-S1 disk herniation and diagnosed sciatica. A lumbar spine MRI indicated a large right posterolateral L5-S1 disk herniation causing S1 nerve root impingement. On the basis of remarkable clinical and imaging findings and recalcitrant symptoms consistent with sciatica, Mr. Roberts' neurosurgeon performed a right-sided microdiscectomy at the L5-S1 level with removal of numerous extruded disk fragments. After rehabilitation, Mr. Roberts showed significant improvement and was able to return to work.

Conclusions:

- The available medical evidence has supported to a reasonable degree of medical certainty that the patient's L5-S1 herniated disk could have occurred as a result of sheer forces produced by the lap belt during his forward and right lateral torso movement, even though there were no physical signs of contusions or abrasions.
- The accident severity exceeded that of a low-velocity collision, so the possibility of disk herniation caused by a single traumatic event could not be denied.

- From the accident date, through all of the exam, up until the time of surgery, Mr. Roberts' symptoms were consistent with having a right-sided L5-S1 disk lesion impinging on the S1 nerve root. The chronology and consistency of symptoms would indicate that the injury was caused by the accident.
- The absent right-sided Achilles reflex was consistent with an S1 nerve root compression.
- The lumbar MRI confirmed a structural neurologic lesion that correlated with the patient's symptoms.
- The operative report confirmed a herniated disk.
- The patient responded positively to the surgery with significant improvement of symptoms and was able to return to work.
- No pre-accident medical records or imaging studies indicated a preexisting condition. Even if the patient had a prior asymptomatic disk lesion, the nature of the accident was clearly at a level of severity capable of aggravating a concealed condition and precipitating pain and nerve impingement in a predisposed individual.
- Based on this information, a logical causal relationship exists between the accident and the patient's disk herniation, and the patient's need for surgery.

Chapter Notes

1. Wilbert Fordyce, *Back Pain in the Workplace* (Seattle: International Association for the Study of Pain, Task Force on Pain in the Workplace, 1995), p. 1.
2. John Mendez, M.D., "New Treatments for Low Back Pain," *Claims Magazine*, October 1997, p. 32.
3. R.A. Sternbach, "Survey of Pain in the United States: The Nuprin Pain Report," *Clinical Journal of Pain*, 1986, pp. 49-53.
4. National Safety Council, *Accident Facts*, 1996, p. 58 and *Accident Facts*, 1993, p. 42.
5. Insurance Research Council, *Paying for Auto Injuries* (Oak Brook, IL: Insurance Research Council, 1994), p. 6.
6. Insurance Research Council, *Auto Injuries: Claiming Behavior and Its Impact on Insurance Costs* (Oak Brook, IL: Insurance Research Council, 1994), p. 38.
7. Jury Verdict Research, *Current Trends In Premises Liability* (Horsham, PA: LRP Publications, 1997), p. 23.
8. Jury Verdict Research, p. 24.
9. E. Volinn, D. Van Koevering, and J. Loeser, "Back Sprain in Industry: The Role of Socioeconomic Factors in Chronicity," *Spine*, vol. 16, 1991, pp. 542-548.
10. Insurance Research Council, *Auto Injuries: Claiming Behavior and Its Impact on Insurance Costs*, p. 61.
11. Insurance Research Council, *Fraud and Buildup in Auto Injury Claims* (Wheaton, IL: Insurance Research Council, 1996), p. 27.
12. Scott Haldeman, David Chapman-Smith, and Donald Peterson, *Guidelines for Chiropractic Quality Assurance and Practice Parameters* (Burlington, CA: Proceedings of a Consensus Conference commissioned by the Congress of Chiropractic State Associations, 1992), p. 133.

13. Judith Willis, "Back Pain: Ubiquitous, Controversial," *FDA Consumer*, November 1983, p. 1.
14. W. Spitzer and F. LeBlanc, "Scientific Approach to the Assessment and Management of Activity-Related Spinal Disorders," *Spine*, 12:7S, supplement 1, 1987, pp. S1-S59.
15. B. Vallfors, "Acute, Subacute and Chronic Low Back Pain: Clinical Symptoms, Absenteeism and Working Environment," *Journal of Rehabilitation Medicine*, supplement 11, 1985, p. 11.
16. Stanley Bigos, M.D., Michelle Battie, Ph.D., Dan Spengler, M.D., Lloyd Fisher, Ph.D., Wilbert Fordyce, Ph.D., Tommy Hansson, M.D., Ph.D., and Alf Nachemson, M.D., "A Prospective Study of Work Perceptions and Psychological Factors Affecting the Report of Back Injury," *Spine*, vol. 16, 1991, p. 1.

    And, J.D. Troup, "The Perception of Back Pain and the Role of Psychophysical Tests for Lifting Capacity," *Spine*, vol. 12, 1987, pp. 645-647.
17. Bigos, Battie, Spengler, Fisher, Fordyce, Hansson, and Nachemson, p. 5.
18. Robert Jamison, B.S., Ph.D., Denise Matt, B.S., and Winston Parris, M.D., "Treatment Outcome in Low Back Pain Patients: Do Compensation Benefits Make a Difference?," *Orthopaedic Review*, December 1988, pp. 1210-1215.
19. L. Cameron, E. Leventhal, and H. Leventhal, "Symptom Representation and Affect as Determinants of Care Seeking in Community-Dwelling: Adult Sample Population," *Health Psychology*, vol. 12, 1993, pp. 171-179.
20. Randall Neumann, *Orthopedic Secrets* (Philadelphia: Hanley and Belfus, 1995), pp. 197-201.
21. Presley Reed, M.D., *Medical Disability Advisor: Workplace Guidelines For Disability Duration* (Horsham, PA: LRP Publications, 1994), p. 472.
22. David Magee, *Orthopedic Physical Assessment*, 3d ed. (Philadelphia: Wallace Saunders, 1997), p. 364.
23. Magee, pp. 400-401.
24. D.M. Spengler, *Low Back Pain: Assessment and Management* (Orlando, FL: Grune and Stratton, 1982), p. 32.
25. Steven Bigos, O. Bowyer, and G. Braen, *Acute Low Back Problems In Adults: Clinical Practice Guideline No. 14 AHCPR Publication No. 95-0642* (Rockville, MD: Agency for Health Care Policy and Research, United States Department of Health and Human Services, 1994), p. 68.
26. Bigos, Bowyer, and Braen, pp. 71-72.
27. Bigos, Bowyer, and Braen, pp. 79-81.
28. Bigos, Bowyer, and Braen, p. 52.
29. Reed, p 49.
30. California Workers Compensation Institute, "Medical Treatment of Lower Back Injuries," CWCI research notes, December 1996, p. 1.
31. Bigos, Bowyer, and Braen, pp. 23-58
32. Daniel C. Cherkin, Richard Deyo, Michele Battie, Janet Street, and William Barlow, "A Comparison of Physical Therapy, Chiropractic Manipulation, and Provision of an Educational Handbook for the Treatment of Patients With Low Back Pain," *New England Journal of Medicine*, October 8, 1998, p. 339.
33. W.J.J. Assendelft, B.W. Koes, G.M.G. van der Heijdam, and L.M. Bouter, "Spinal Manipulation for Low Back Pain: An Updated Systematic Review of Randomized Clinical Trials," *Spine*, vol. 21, 1996, pp. 2860-2861.
34. R.S. MacDonald, and C.M. Bell, "An Open Controlled Assessment of Osteopathic Manipulation in Non-Specific Low Back Pain," *Spine*, May 1990, 15 (5): 364-370.

35. R.A. Deyo, N.E. Walsh, D.C. Martin, L.S. Schonfield, and S.A. Ramurthury, "A Controlled Trial of Transcutaneous Electrical Nerve Stimulation (TENS) and Exercise for Chronic Low Back Pain," *New England Journal of Medicine*, June 7, 1990, pp. 322-334.
36. C. Manniche, G. Hesselsoe, L. Bentzen, I. Christensen, and E. Lundberg, "Clinical Trial of Intensive Muscle Training for Chronic Low Back Pain," *Lancet*, December 1988, 24-31;2 (8626-8627), pp. 1473-1476.
37. R.D. Mootz, "Chiropractic Models: Current Understanding of Vertebral Subluxation and Manipulable Spinal Lesions," *Chiropractic Family Practice: A Clinical Manual*, ed. J.J. Sweere (Gaithersburg, MD: Aspen Publishers, Inc., 1992), p. 2.
38. Nancy C. Elder, Amy Gillcrist, Rene Minz, "Use of Alternative Health Care by Family Practice Patients," Archives of Family Medicine, March 1997, pp. 181-184.
39. Milliman-Robertson, *Health Care Management Guidelines: Workers Compensation*, vol. 7, May 1997, p. 5.22.
40. K. Dean Reeves, "Technique of Prolotherapy," *Psychiatric Procedures* (Philadelphia: Hanley and Belfus, Inc., 1995), pp. 57-70.
41. Bigos, Bowyer, and Braen, p. 82.
42. Bigos, Bowyer, and Braen p. 84.

Appendix 5-A

Excerpt from the AHCPR's Acute Low Back Problems in Adults: Clinical Practice Guideline No. 14

The Agency for Health Care Policy and Research (AHCPR) was established in December 1989 under Public Law 101-239 (Omnibus Budget Reconciliation Act of 1989) to enhance the quality, appropriateness, and effectiveness of health care services and access to these services. AHCPR carries out its mission by conducting and supporting general health services research, including medical effectiveness research, facilitating development of clinical practice guidelines, and disseminating research findings and guidelines to health care providers, policymakers, and the public.

The legislation also established within AHCPR the Office of the Forum for Quality and Effectiveness in Health Care (the Forum). The Forum has primary responsibility for facilitating the development, periodic review, and updating of clinical practice guidelines. The guidelines will assist practitioners in the prevention, diagnosis, treatment, and management of clinical conditions.

Other AHCPR components include the following. The Center for Medical Effectiveness Research has principal responsibility for patient outcomes research and studies of variations in clinical practice. The Center for General Health Services Extramural Research supports research on primary care, the cost and financing of health care, and access to care for underserved and rural populations. The Center for General Health Services Intramural research uses large data sets for policy research on national health care expenditures and utilization, hospital studies, and long-term care. The Center for Research Dissemination and Liaison produces and disseminates findings from AHCPR-supported research, including guidelines, and conducts research on dissemination methods. The Office of Health Technology Assessment responds to requests from Federal health programs for assessment of health care technologies. The Office of Science and Data Development develops specialized databases and enhances techniques for using existing databases for patient outcomes research.

Guidelines are available in formats suitable for health care practitioners, the scientific community, educators, and consumers. AHCPR invites comments and suggestions from users for consideration in development and updating of future guidelines. Please send written comments to Director, Office of the Forum for Quality and Effectiveness in Health Care, AHCPR, Willco Building, Suite 310, 6000 Executive Boulevard, Rockville, MD 20852.

Clinical Practice Guideline
Number 14

Acute Low Back Problems in Adults

Stanley J. Bigos, MD (Chair)
Rev. O. Richard Bowyer
G. Richard Braen, MD
Kathleen Brown, PhD, RN
Richard Deyo, MD, MPH
Scott Haldeman, DC, MD, PhD
John L. Hart, DO
Ernest W. Johnson, MD
Robert Keller, MD
Daniel Kido, MD, FACR
Matthew H. Liang, MD, MPH
Roger M. Nelson, PT, PhD
Margareta Nordin, RPT, DrSci
Bernice D. Owen, PhD, RN
Malcolm H. Pope, DrMedSc, PhD
Richard K. Schwartz, MS, OTR, FSR
Donald H. Stewart, Jr., MD
Jeff Susman, MD
John J. Tirano, MA, DC
Lucius C. Tripp, MD, MPH, FACPM
Dennis C. Turk, PhD
Clark Watts, MD, JD
James N. Weinstein, DO

U.S. Department of Health and Human Services
Public Health Service
Agency for Health Care Policy and Research
Rockville, Maryland

AHCPR Publication No. 95—0642
December 1994

Guideline Development and Use

Guidelines are systematically developed statements to assist practitioner and patient decisions about appropriate health care. This guideline was developed by an independent multidisciplinary panel of private-sector clinicians and other experts convened by the Agency for Health Care Policy and Research (AHCPR). The panel employed explicit, science-based methods and expert clinical judgment to develop specific statements on acute low back problems in adults.

Extensive literature searches were conducted and critical reviews and syntheses were used to evaluate empirical evidence and significant outcomes. Peer review and field review were undertaken to evaluate the validity, reliability, and utility of the guideline in clinical practice. The panel's recommendations are primarily based on the published scientific literature. When the scientific literature was incomplete or inconsistent in a particular area, the recommendations reflect the professional judgment of panel members and consultants.

The guideline reflects the state of knowledge, current at the time of publication. Given the inevitable changes in the state of scientific information and technology, periodic review, updating, and revision will be done.

We believe that the AHCPR-assisted clinical guidelines will make positive contributions to the quality of care in the United States. We encourage practitioners and patients to use the information provided in this *Clinical Practice Guideline*. The recommendations may not be appropriate for use in all circumstances. Decisions to adopt any particular recommendation must be made by the practitioner in light of available resources and circumstances presented by individual patients.

Clifton R. Gaus, ScD
Administrator
Agency for Health Care Policy and Research

Publication of this guideline does not necessarily represent endorsement by the U.S. Department of Health and Human Services.

Abstract

Findings and recommendations on the assessment and treatment of adults with acute low back problems—activity limitations due to symptoms in the low back and/or back-related leg symptoms of less than 3 months' duration—are presented in this clinical practice guideline. The following are the principal conclusions of this guideline:

- The initial assessment of patients with acute low back problems focuses on the detection of "red flags" (indicators of potentially serious spinal pathology or other nonspinal pathology).

- In the absence of red flags, imaging studies and further testing of patients are not usually helpful during the first 4 weeks of low back symptoms.

- Relief of discomfort can be accomplished most safely with nonprescription medication and/or spinal manipulation.

- While some activity modification may be necessary during the acute phase, bed rest >4 days is not helpful and may further debilitate the patient.

- Low-stress aerobic activities can be safely started in the first 2 weeks of symptoms to help avoid debilitation; exercises to condition trunk muscles are commonly delayed at least 2 weeks.

- Patients recovering from acute low back problems are encouraged to return to work or their normal daily activities as soon as possible.

- If low back symptoms persist, further evaluation may be indicated.

- Patients with sciatica may recover more slowly, but further evaluation can also be safely delayed.

- Within the first 3 months of low back symptoms, only patients with evidence of serious spinal pathology or severe, debilitating symptoms of sciatica, and physiologic evidence of specific nerve root compromise corroborated on imaging studies can be expected to benefit from surgery.

- With or without surgery, 80 percent of patients with sciatica recover eventually.

- Nonphysical factors (such as psychological or socioeconomic problems) may be addressed in the context of discussing reasonable expectations for recovery.

This document is in the public domain and may be used and reprinted without special permission. AHCPR will appreciate citation of the source, and the suggested format is provided below:

Bigos S, Bowyer O, Braen G, et al. *Acute Low Back Problems in Adults. Clinical Practice Guideline No. 14.* AHCPR Publication No. 95-0642. Rockville, MD: Agency for Health Care Policy and Research, Public Health Service, U.S. Department of Health and Human Services. December 1994.

Panel Members

Stanley J. Bigos, MD, Chair
University of Washington
Seattle, Washington
Orthopedic Surgeon

Reverend O. Richard Bowyer
Fairmont State College
Fairmont, West Virginia
Consumer Representative

G. Richard Braen, MD
University of New York
Buffalo, New York
Emergency Medicine Physician

Kathleen Brown, PhD, RN
University of Alabama
Birmingham, Alabama
Occupational Health Nurse

Richard Deyo, MD, MPH
University of Washington
Seattle, Washington
General Internist

Scott Haldeman, DC, MD, PhD
University of California at Irvine
Santa Ana, California
Neurologist/Chiropractor

John L. Hart, DO
Still Regional Medical Center
Columbia, Missouri
Physiatrist

Ernest W. Johnson, MD
Ohio State University
Columbus, Ohio
Physiatrist

Robert Keller, MD
Maine Medical Assessment
  Foundation
Belfast, Maine
Orthopedic Surgeon

Daniel Kido, MD, FACR
Washington University
  Medical Center
St. Louis, Missouri
Radiologist

Matthew H. Liang, MD, MPH
Harvard Medical School
Boston, Massachusetts
Rheumatologist

Roger M. Nelson, PT, PhD
Thomas Jefferson University
  College of Allied Health Sciences
Philadelphia, Pennsylvania
Physical Therapist

Margareta Nordin, RPT, DrSci
Hospital for Joints Diseases
New York, New York
*Physical Therapist/
  Orthopedic Researcher*

Bernice D. Owen, PhD, RN
University of Wisconsin
Madison, Wisconsin
Community Health Nurse

Malcolm H. Pope, DrMedSc, PhD
University of Vermont
Burlington, Vermont
Orthopedic Researcher

Richard K. Schwartz, MS, OTR, FSR
San Antonio, Texas
Occupational Therapist

Donald H. Stewart, Jr., MD
Arlington, Virginia
Neurosurgeon

Jeff Susman, MD
University of Nebraska
 Medical Center
Omaha, Nebraska
Family Physician

John J. Triano, MA, DC
Texas Back Institute
Plano, Texas
Chiropractor

Lucius C. Tripp, MD, MPH, FACPM
General Motors-Henry Ford Hospital
 Rehabilitation Center
Warren, Michigan
Neurosurgeon/Occupational Medicine Specialist

Dennis C. Turk, PhD
University of Pittsburgh School of
 Medicine
Pittsburgh, Pennsylvania
Psychologist

Clark Watts, MD, JD
University of Texas Health Sciences
 Center
San Antonio, Texas
Neurosurgeon

James N. Weinstein, DO
University of Iowa Hospitals
Iowa City, Iowa
Orthopedic Surgeon

Appendix 5-B

Positional Terms

Claim representatives should know common positional terms without using a medical dictionary. The following **positional terms** identify areas of the body and the position of an injury or body part relative to another part of the body.

Superior refers to a position that is near the head or the highest place on the body. For example, the superior vena cava is the principal vein carrying blood from the upper part of the body.

Inferior refers to a position that is away from the head or on the lower part of the body. For example, the inferior vena cava is the principal vein carrying blood from the lower part of the body.

Anterior refers to a position near the front of the body. For example, the kneecap is located on the anterior surface of the leg.

Posterior, opposite of anterior, refers to a position near the back of the body. For example, the shoulder blades are located on the posterior body surface.

Medial identifies a position close to the midline (or vertical axis) of the body. For example, the breastbone is located in the medial portion of the chest.

Lateral identifies a position that is away from the midline of the body. For example, the ears are lateral to the nose.

External means outside the body (usually on the skin).

Internal means within the body. For example, internal hemorrhaging is bleeding on the inside of the body.

Proximal identifies a location close to the torso of the body. For example, an upper arm (humerus) fracture close to the shoulder would be called a proximal fracture of the humerus.

Distal is the opposite of proximal. It identifies a position away from the torso. For example a fracture of the upper arm close to the elbow would be called a distal fracture of the humerus.

Introduction to Case Studies

"The best sermon is a good example."

Chapters 1 through 5 familiarized the student with the legal and medical knowledge necessary to handle bodily injury claims. Chapters 6 through 8 each contain a case study that demonstrates how to apply that knowledge. The cases provide examples of how bodily injury claims can be managed.

The cases are not intended to be medical references but rather to provide students with an analytical framework to handle any type of bodily injury claim and to understand how to use the references rather than memorize medical terms.

Developing investigative skills, problem-solving abilities, and innovation are the educational objectives of these case studies. These skills are normally developed from experience, but claim representatives are increasingly expected to become productive quickly. These cases help to accelerate learning and to quickly prepare students to handle challenging bodily injury claims.

The Case Construction

Each of the cases addresses different investigative issues and different injuries that are based on claims frequently encountered by claim professionals. Students should read the chapters that contain cases in the order they appear in this text so that they can build an understanding of these investigative issues and the anatomy related to each of the bodily injury claims. Chapter 6 introduces the medical investigation process. This process can be applied to most bodily injury claims. Chapter 7 deals with the investigation and settlement of claims that have a questionable cause of injury. Chapter 8 covers the biomechanics of an injury and the use of case management in handling a disability claim.

The chapters that contain cases have less text than traditional chapters because the student is expected to spend more time reviewing the exhibits, which include medical bills and reports, letters, and other documents that would be included in claim files.

The characters in the cases represent various members of a claim department. They illustrate important legal and medical investigative issues. The job titles and number of employees vary depending on the resources and the structure of a company's claim department. For example, some companies have in-house medical or legal consultants, while others use outside consultants. Some insurers use third-party administrators or independent adjusters instead of staff claim representatives. These cases do not intend to suggest how a company should use its claim personnel. The characters are used solely for illustrating medical and legal points.

Preparation for Case Studies

A basic knowledge of medical references and terminology is necessary for bodily injury claim handling. This section introduces medical references and terminology that are used throughout Chapters 6 through 8. (Appendix 5-B, which defines positional terms, also serves as a reference for the cases.)

Medical References

In addition to the company consulting nurse or case manager, a wide variety of medical references can assist claim representatives in assessing injury, treatment, and disability. Most of the following references are available in electronic versions that allow a claim representative to access the reference while working on a claim at a computer.

- ***International Classification of Diseases (ICD-9-CM)*** provides a comprehensive list of injury and disease codes and describes injuries and diseases and the treatments for each. This reference also lists codes identifying the type of accident causing the injury. Doctors and hospitals use this book worldwide.
- ***Current Procedural Terminology (CPT)*** explains the codes that identify the specific medical and surgical procedures used by health-care providers.
- ***Taber's Medical Dictionary*** defines medical terminology found in medical documents.

- **Health Care Financing Common Procedure Coding System (HCPC)**, often pronounced as "hicpics," explains codes for medical and surgical supplies, injections, and prescriptions.
- ***The Medical Disability Advisor (MDA)*** explains common treatments and prognoses of injuries and provides general guidelines on the duration of disabilities resulting from a given injury. This reference is not intended to refute the diagnosis or treatment of a physician. Claim personnel should refer questions regarding the diagnosis or treatment to claim management personnel to determine whether an independent medical exam (IME) should be used to review the diagnosis or treatment.
- **Milliman-Robertson *Health Care Management Guidelines*** provides information on treatment, medical case management, and disabilities for common injuries. This reference is based on comprehensive research of health-care providers but is not intended to be used as the sole reason for limiting or denying treatments recommended by a physician. The purpose is to help establish guidelines and assist reviewers in determining when treatments may require additional explanation or an independent medical exam.

Basic Terminology

Claim representatives can consult *Taber's Medical Dictionary* or other medical references when they encounter medical terms with which they are unfamiliar. However, claim representatives should know some basic medical terms that are frequently encountered in bodily injury claims.

Medical reports often indicate the need for conservative treatment. **Conservative treatment**, especially when used with sprains and strains, means treatment with **R.I.C.E.**:

Rest

Ice

Compression (applying pressure to injury using bandages)

Elevation (raising injured part of body above the heart)

An acronym often seen in medical reports is HEENT, which refers to the examination of the:

Head

Eyes

Ears

Nose

Throat

When claim representatives conduct a medical investigation involving a preexisting injury or condition, they often encounter the terms *recurrence*, *aggravation*, and *exacerbation*. In this text, the term **recurrence** means a preexisting condition that becomes worse as a normal or reasonably expected consequence of the original injury, and the term **aggravation** refers to a preexisting condition that worsens as a result of an insured event even if the preexisting condition makes the person more susceptible to subsequent injuries or disabilities. The term exacerbation has no uniform meaning in the medical community. Claim representatives should ask providers who use the term exacerbation to clarify what they mean.

The terms recurrence and aggravation are sometimes erroneously used interchangeably. For this reason, claim representatives should seek clarification from a provider that uses these terms. The issue that claim representatives must resolve is whether the preexisting condition or symptoms worsened as a result of the insured event or whether the condition or symptoms worsened as a normal progression for the condition. Just because a condition worsens at or near the same time as an insured event does not necessarily make it related to the event.

The term "lighted-up" has appeared in recent medical literature as a way of addressing the confusion between the terms recurrence and aggravation. **Lighted-up** is usually synonymous with aggravation as used in this text, but claim representatives need to clarify how the provider uses the term.

Roots in Medical Terminology

A familiarity with roots commonly used in medical terms is helpful to those who handle bodily injury claims. Exhibit I-1 lists the definitions of roots along with examples of words that use the roots and their definitions. Students will not be tested on these roots but rather can use this section as a reference when performing their jobs.

Each root always has the same meaning. Some roots typically come at the beginning of a word; others, at the end.

Exhibit I-1
Word Roots Common in Medical Terms

The following roots are typically found at the beginning of words.

Root	Definition	Example	Definition
A-, Ab-	Away from, lack of	Abduction	Movement away from the body
A-, An-	Absence of	Asepsis	Absence of infection
Ad-	To, toward, near	Adrenal	Near the kidney
Ambi-	Both	Ambidextrous	Having dexterity in both hands
Ante-	Before	Antenatal	Before birth
Anti-	Against	Antiseptic	Against infection
Arth-	Joint	Arthritis	Inflammation in a joint
Auto-	Self	Autolesion	Self-inflicted injury
Bi-, Bin-	Two	Binocular	Pertaining to both eyes
Brachi-	Arm	Brachialis	A muscle of the forearm
Brachy-	Short	Brachydactylia	Having short fingers or toes
Bronch-	Windpipe	Bronchiectasis	Dilation of the bronchial tubes
Carcin-	Cancer	Carcinogenic	Causing cancer
Cardio-	Heart	Cardiologist	A heart specialist
Cephal-	Head	Cephalgia	Headache

Root	Definition	Example	Definition
Chondr-	Cartilage	Chondritis	Inflammation of the cartilage
Circum-	Around	Circumocular	Around the eyes
Contra-	Against	Contra-indication	Any condition making the use of a remedy inadvisable
Costa-	Rib	Costal	Relating to ribs
Cranio-	Skull	Craniotomy	A hole cut into the skull
Crypto-	Hidden	Cryptogenic	Of unknown origin
Cut-	Skin	Cutaneous	Relating to the skin
Cysto-	Sac or bladder	Cystitis	Inflammation of the bladder
Cyto-	Cell	Cytology	Study of the cell
Derma-	Skin	Dermabrasion	Abrading of the skin to reduce scars
Di-	Two	Diplopia	Double vision
Dis-	Apart	Disarticulation	Taking a joint apart
Dys-	Impaired	Dyspepsia	Difficulty in digestion
Em-, En-	In	Encapsulated	Inside a capsule
Encephalo-	Of the brain	Encephalitis	Inflammation of the brain
Endo-	Within	Endothelium	Layer of cells inside the heart and blood vessels
Entero-	Intestine	Enteritis	Inflammation of the intestine
Epi-	Over or upon	Epidermis	Top layer of skin
Eu-	Well	Euphoria	Feeling of well-being
Ex-, E-	Out	Excretion	Waste products leaving the body
Exo-	Outside	Exocrine	Excreting outward
Extra-	Outside	Extramural	Outside of a wall
Febri-	Fever	Febrile	Having a fever
Gastr-	Stomach	Gastritis	Inflammation of the stomach
Glyco-	Sugar	Glycosuria	Sugar in the urine
Gyneco-	Woman	Gynecologist	Physician specializing in the care of women
Hem-	Blood	Hematuria	Blood in the urine
Hemi-	Half	Hemisphere	Half of a sphere
Hepat-	Liver	Hepatitis	Inflammation in the liver
Hetero-	Other	Heterosexual	Pertaining to the opposite sex
Hist-	Tissue	Histology	The study of tissue
Homo-	Same	Homosexual	Pertaining to the same sex
Hydr-	Water	Hydrocephalic	Having water accumulated around the brain
Hyper-	Above, excess, elevated	Hyperactive	Overactive
Hypo-	Deficiency of	Hypoglycemia	Low blood sugar
Hyster-	Uterus	Hysterectomy	Removal of the uterus
Idio-	Self	Idiopsychologic	Ideas developed in one's mind, independent of external suggestion
Im-	Not	Immature	Not mature
In-	In	Innate	Occurring within
Infra-	Below	Infraorbital	Below the orbit
Inter-	Between	Intermuscular	Between the muscles

Continued on next page.

Root	Definition	Example	Definition
Intra-	Within	Intramuscular	Within the muscle
Leuko-	White	Leukemia	An excess of white blood cells
Macro-	Large	Macroblast	Abnormally large red cell
Mast-	Breast	Mastectomy	Removal of a breast
Micro-	Small	Microbiology	Study of small organisms
My-	Muscle	Myalgia	Pain in a muscle
Necro-	Dead	Necrosis	Death of tissue
Neo-	New	Neonatal	Newly born
Nephro-	Kidney	Nephritis	Inflammation of a kidney
Neuro-	Nerve	Neuron	Nerve cell
Ophthalmo-	Eye	Ophthalmometer	Instrument to measure the eye
Ortho-	Straight	Orthograde	Walking straight
Oss-, Osteo-	Bone	Osseous	Pertaining to bone
Ot-	Ear	Otorrhea	Discharge from the ear
Para-	Around	Paradenitis	Inflammation of the tissues around or adjacent to a gland
Patho-	Disease	Pathology	The study of disease
Ped-, Pedo-	Foot	Pedograph	Imprint of the foot
Ped-, Pedi-	Child	Pediatrics	Child specialist
Per-	Through	Perutaneous	Through the skin
Peri-	Around	Periapiocal	Surrounding the root of a tooth
Phleb-	Vein	Phlebitis	Inflammation of a vein
Poly-	Many	Polyarthritis	Arthritis in many joints
Pre-	Before	Prenatal	Before birth
Post-	After	Postpartum	After birth
Procto-	Rectum	Proctology	Study of the rectum
Pseudo-	False	Pseudoangina	False angina
Pyo-	Pus	Pyorrhea	Discharge of pus
Retro-	Backward	Retrovision	Turning backward
Rhin-	Nose	Rhinorrhea	Discharge from the nose
Steno-	Narrow	Stenosis	In a narrowed state
Super-	Above	Superacute	Excessively acute
Supra-	Above, upon	Suprarenal	Above the kidney
Sym-, Syn-	With, together	Symphysis	Growing together
Tachy-	Fast	Tachycardia	Fast heart rate
Uni-	One	Unilateral	Affecting one side
Vaso-	Vessel	Vasodilator	Something that dilates a vessel

The following roots are typically found at the end of words.

Root	Definition	Example	Definition
-algia	Pain	Cephalalgia	Pain in the head
-asis, -osis	Affected with	Leukocytosis	An increase in the number of leukocytes
-asthenia	Weakness	Neurasthenia	Nerve weakness
-cele	Tumor or hernia	Enterocele	Hernia of the intestine

-ectasis	Dilation	Angiectasis	Dilation of a blood vessel
-ectomy	Excision	Appendectomy	Removal of the appendix
-esthesia	Sensation	Anesthesia	Lacking sensation
-itis	Inflammation	Iritis	Inflammation of the iris
-lysis	Loosening, dissolution	Hemolysius	Destruction of red blood cells
-malacia	Softening	Chondromalacia	Softening of cartilage
-oma	Tumor	Neuroma	Tumor on a nerve
-ostomy	Creation of an opening	Colostomy	Opening in to the colon
-otomy	Cutting into	Osteotomy	Cutting into bone
-penia	Lack of	Leukopenia	Lack of white blood cells
-pexy	To fix	Proctopexy	Repair of rectum
-phagia	Eating	Polyphagia	Excessive eating
-phasis	Speech	Aphasia	Inability to speak
-ptosis	A falling	Enteroptosis	Falling of the intestine
-rhoia	Flow	Ororrhea	Discharge from the ear
-rhaphe	Seam	Herriorrhaphy	Surgical repair of a hernia
-taxis	Order, coordination	Ataxia	Lack of coordination
-uri	Urine	Hematuria	Blood in the urine

Approaching the Cases

As mentioned earlier, the purpose of the cases in Chapters 6 through 8 is to apply knowledge learned in previous chapters. Some of the most important information from Chapters 1 through 4 is repeated in the cases. For a more detailed explanation of the information, students should review the related sections found in the previous chapters.

Gathering, organizing, and understanding medical documents are at the center of the cases presented in Chapters 6 through 8. For this reason, students should review the medical documents presented in Chapter 2 and consider how they might be helpful in the cases. Several of the cases mention diagnostic tests, such as MRIs and X-rays. These were also covered in Chapter 2.

It is important to look beyond standard medical documents in conducting an investigation of a bodily injury claim. Claim representatives should consider the entire claim file as potential documentation for the injury investigation. Often, important nonmedical documents help prove or disprove an injury claim. The claim file example shown in Exhibit I-2 briefly illustrates how the entire claim file can be used in an injury investigation. Not all of the illustrated documents are found in every claim file. The documents contained in a claim file might be paper, electronic, or a combination of both.

Fraud and Insurance Abuse

The vast issues related to fraud and insurance abuse are beyond the scope of the three cases presented in Chapters 6 through 8. However, fraud and insurance abuse are important issues in many bodily injury claims. For this reason, Chapter 2 includes the National Insurance Crime Bureau's "Indicators for Casualty and Workers Compensation Fraud" as well as a list of investigative questions and suggested investigative activities for claims with a questionable causation.

Exhibit I-2
Claim File Documents Used in an Injury Claim

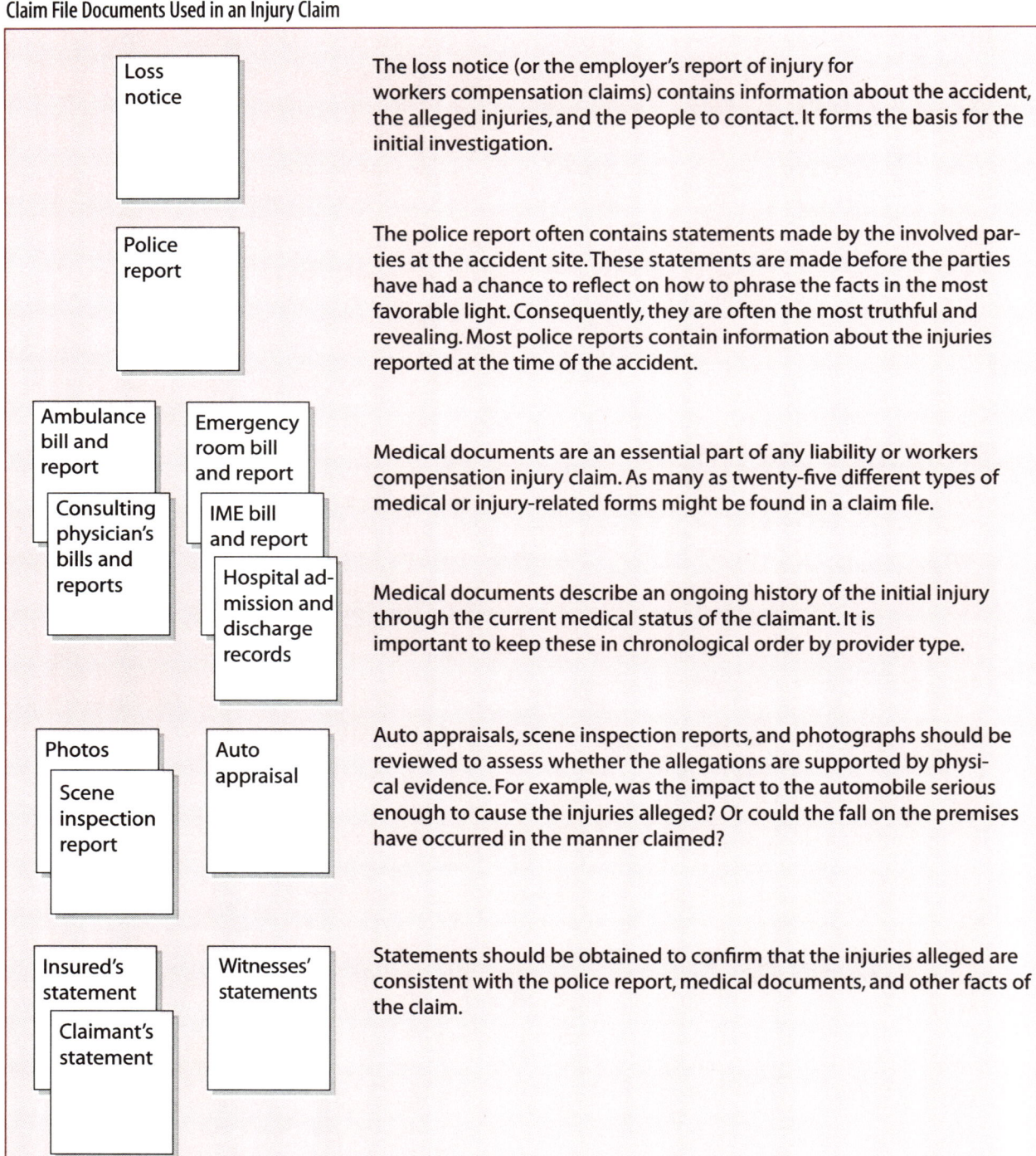

The loss notice (or the employer's report of injury for workers compensation claims) contains information about the accident, the alleged injuries, and the people to contact. It forms the basis for the initial investigation.

The police report often contains statements made by the involved parties at the accident site. These statements are made before the parties have had a chance to reflect on how to phrase the facts in the most favorable light. Consequently, they are often the most truthful and revealing. Most police reports contain information about the injuries reported at the time of the accident.

Medical documents are an essential part of any liability or workers compensation injury claim. As many as twenty-five different types of medical or injury-related forms might be found in a claim file.

Medical documents describe an ongoing history of the initial injury through the current medical status of the claimant. It is important to keep these in chronological order by provider type.

Auto appraisals, scene inspection reports, and photographs should be reviewed to assess whether the allegations are supported by physical evidence. For example, was the impact to the automobile serious enough to cause the injuries alleged? Or could the fall on the premises have occurred in the manner claimed?

Statements should be obtained to confirm that the injuries alleged are consistent with the police report, medical documents, and other facts of the claim.

Chapter 6 — Case Study

Medical Investigation Process (The Arm Injury)

Mary Jansen is a workers compensation claim trainee for Superior Ventures Insurance (SVI). Mary's experience had been limited to processing workers compensation claim payments for claim representatives until her supervisor, Karen Moore, decided that Mary was ready to progress in her training and presented her with a new claim.

Karen: Mary, we've discussed the claim process and how to conduct a medical investigation, so I'm going to give you a chance to apply some of that knowledge. I'm giving you a file to handle from start to finish. I don't see any coverage or compensability problems with this case. It looks pretty straightforward.

Karen handed Mary a file with an injury report.

Claim Process

The claim process, shown in Exhibit 6-1, begins with the notice of a loss and the assignment of the claim. Coverage determination is normally the second step. Mary's supervisor pointed out that, in this case (as in most workers compensation cases), policy coverage was not an issue. Based on the employer's report of injury, compensability did not appear to be an issue either. However, the fourth step in the claim

Exhibit 6-1
Claim Process

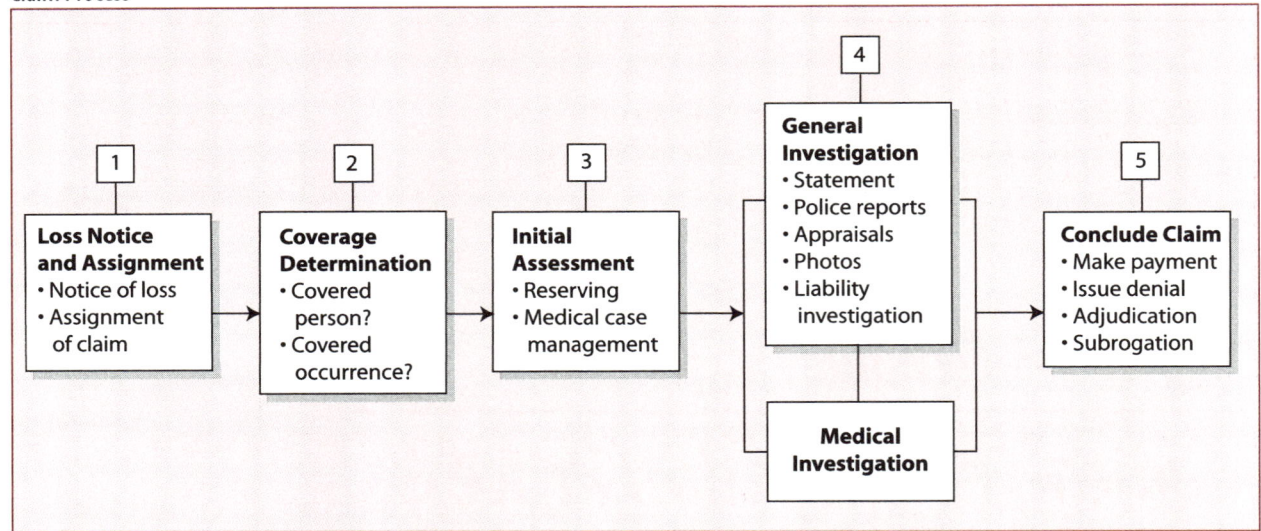

process, the general investigation, sometimes uncovers compensability issues, especially in third-party liability cases. For practical purposes, this case skips the coverage determination step.

Notice of Loss

Mary began the claim process by reviewing the employer's report of loss, shown in Exhibit 6-2. She noted that the claimant, Bill Jenkins, was treated at Quality Park Medical Center. She wondered whether he was taken to the hospital by ambulance.

 *What factors should be considered in initial assessment?*

Initial Assessment

The initial assessment is an important stage of the claim process because it sets the parameters for the investigation and alerts management of potentially serious claims. Mary set up an initial reserve and assessed the need for medical case management in Bill's claim.

At the outset, the claim representative must establish rapport with the claimant, explain the claim process, and discuss the duties of all involved parties. Information gathered from the initial contact with the claimant, the claimant's employer (for workers compensation claims), the doctor (if permitted), and witnesses forms the basis for the initial claim assessment. Mary reviewed the injury report of Bill Jenkins, an employee of Quality Corporation. She obtained information about Bill's specific job tasks from Bill's employer. She learned that Bill was a supervisor who spent at least half of the time lifting boxes and doing other physically demanding tasks. This information helped in the assessment of Bill's impairment and formed the basis for reserving

---

Factors Indicating the Need for Immediate Medical Case Management

- Head injuries
- Spinal cord injuries
- Psychiatric/stress diagnosis
- Significant trauma
- Multiple fractures and crushing-type injuries
- Vision or hearing loss
- Serious burns
- Loss of consciousness
- Neonatal injury
- Possible substance abuse
- Previous injuries or disabilities
- Questionable injury causation
- Pending layoff of employee
- Pending strike by union
- Amputation

Exhibit 6-2
Employer's Report of Injury

LIBC-344 (8/89)

COMMONWEALTH OF PENNSYLVANIA
DEPARTMENT OF LABOR AND INDUSTRY
BUREAU OF WORKERS' COMPENSATION
1171 SOUTH CAMERON STREET, ROOM 103
HARRISBURG, PENNSYLVANIA 17104-2501
TELEPHONE 783-5421
LONG DISTANCE (TOLL FREE) 800-482-2383

EMPLOYER'S REPORT OF OCCUPATIONAL INJURY OR DISEASE

INJURED'S SOCIAL SECURITY NUMBER: 401-73-2911
EMPLOYER'S UC REPORTING NUMBER:
INSURANCE POLICY NUMBER:

DATES
1. DATE OF REPORT: 3/4/97
2. DATE OF INJURY AND TIME: 3/4/97 ☒ AM ☐ PM
3. NORMAL STARTING TIME: 8 ☒ AM ☐ PM
4. IF EMPLOYEE BACK TO WORK GIVE DATE:
5. AT SAME WAGE? ☐ YES ☐ NO
6. IF FATAL INJURY, GIVE DATE OF DEATH:
7. DATE EMPLOYER KNEW OF INJURY: 3/4/97
8. DATE DISABILITY BEGAN: 3/4/97
9. LAST FULL DAY PAID - DATE: 3/3/97

EMPLOYER
10. EMPLOYER: Quality Corporation
11. PERSON MAKING OUT THIS REPORT: Mike Simpson
12. ADDRESS - INCLUDE COUNTY AND ZIP CODE: 1421 E. Main Street   Oakton, CT
13. EMPLOYER TELEPHONE NUMBER (INCLUDE AREA CODE): (610) 244-2100
14. MAILING ADDRESS - IF DIFFERENT THAN ABOVE:
15. NATURE OF BUSINESS - TYPE OF MFG., TRADE, CONSTRUCTION, SERVICE, ETC.:

EMPLOYEE
16. EMPLOYEE: FIRST: Bill MIDDLE: LAST: Jenkins
17. ☒ MALE ☐ FEMALE
18. EMPLOYEE TELEPHONE NUMBER (INCLUDE AREA CODE): (610) 849-2349
19. ADDRESS - INCLUDE COUNTY AND ZIP CODE: 129 W. Springfield Ave.
20. MARRIED: ☐ YES ☐ NO
21. NUMBER OF CHILDREN UNDER 18:
22. DATE OF BIRTH:
23. AGE: 37
24. IF UNDER 18, CERTIFICATE NUMBER:
25. OCCUPATION FOR WHICH ISSUED: Maintenance Supervisor
26. OCCUPATION: Supervisor
27. DEPARTMENT OR DIVISION REGULARLY EMPLOYED: Maintenance
28. HOW LONG EMPLOYED: 5 years

OCCURRENCE
29. PLACE OF INJURY: EMPLOYER'S PREMISES ☒ YES ☐ NO
30. IF NO - EXACT LOCATION - STREET, CITY, COUNTY, AND STATE:
31. WHAT WAS EMPLOYEE DOING WHEN INJURED? (BE SPECIFIC, IF USING TOOLS OR EQUIPMENT OR HANDLING MATERIAL - NAME THEM AND TELL WHAT HE WAS DOING WITH THEM.)

Employee fell climbing down from fork lift

32. HOW DID INJURY OCCUR? (DESCRIBE FULLY THE EVENTS WHICH RESULTED IN INJURY OR DISEASE. TELL WHAT HAPPENED AND HOW IT HAPPENED. NAME ANY OBJECTS OR SUBSTANCES INVOLVED AND TELL HOW THEY WERE INVOLVED. GIVE FULL DETAILS ON ALL FACTORS WHICH LED OR CONTRIBUTED TO INJURY OR DISEASE.)

Employee fell head first off of fork lift on to concrete floor in warehouse
Broke his fall with left arm

DID INJURY OR DISEASE OCCUR BECAUSE OF —
33. MECHANICAL DEFECT ☒ NO ☐ YES (DESCRIBE ABOVE)
34. UNSAFE ACT ☒ NO ☐ YES (DESCRIBE ABOVE)
35. CHECK IF AMPUTATION ☐

INJURY OR DISEASE
36. NATURE AND LOCATION OF INJURY OR DISEASE (DESCRIBE FULLY, INCLUDING PARTS OF BODY AFFECTED.)
Injured left arm
37. ATTENDING PHYSICIAN AND ADDRESS (IF HOSPITAL INVOLVED - INDICATE)
Quality Park Medical Center

DO NOT WRITE IN THIS COLUMN:
- DATE
- HOURS WORKED
- REPORT LAG
- DISABILITY
- INDUSTRY
- SEX
- AGE
- OCCUPATION
- COUNTY
- ACCIDENT TYPE
- OCCUPATIONAL DISEASE
- UNSAFE ACT
- MECHANICAL DEFECT
- NATURE
- LOCATION
- INSURANCE
- PAYMENT LAG
- COMPENSATION RATE

EMPLOYER INSTRUCTIONS AND WAGE INFORMATION ON REVERSE SIDE

DISTRIBUTION OF THIS REPORT:
1. ORIGINAL MUST BE SENT IMMEDIATELY TO WORKMEN'S COMPENSATION INSURANCE CARRIER
2. COPY TO BUREAU - SEE INSTRUCTIONS
3. EMPLOYER'S COPY - RETAIN AS RECORD
4. MEDICAL COPY MUST BE SENT IMMEDIATELY TO TREATING PHYSICIAN OR DELIVERED BY INJURED EMPLOYEE
5. CHANGE OF STATUS REPORT - SEE INSTRUCTIONS
6. INJURED EMPLOYEE'S COPY

Mike Simpson
SIGNATURE OF PERSON IN 11 ABOVE

Maintenance Manager
OFFICIAL POSITION

Distributed by: BSC LITHO
WORKERS' COMPENSATION SERVICE
P.O. BOX 1321, HARRISBURG, PA 17105

Bill's disability claim. Other factors affecting Bill's disability claim are discussed later in this chapter.

Age is always an important factor to consider. If, for example, Bill was older and his job required fine hand movements, his period of temporary disability might be lengthened. Physical rehabilitation would be used to help reduce the disability caused by this injury.

As discussed in Chapter 4, several factors indicate the need for immediate medical case management. Mary reviewed this list to ensure that she had not overlooked any reason why this claim might require immediate case management. This step is crucial for controlling claim costs. At that point, nothing indicated the need for early medical case management. Claim representatives should reevaluate the need for medical case management after an analysis of the injury and treatment.

Medical Investigation

As indicated in Exhibit 6-1, the medical investigation usually runs concurrently with the general investigation. The investigative issues of the general investigation for workers compensation claims are covered in Assignment 5 of *Principles of Workers Compensation*. This case focuses on the *medical investigation*. Exhibit 6-3 illustrates the medical investigation process.

Exhibit 6-3
Medical Investigation Process

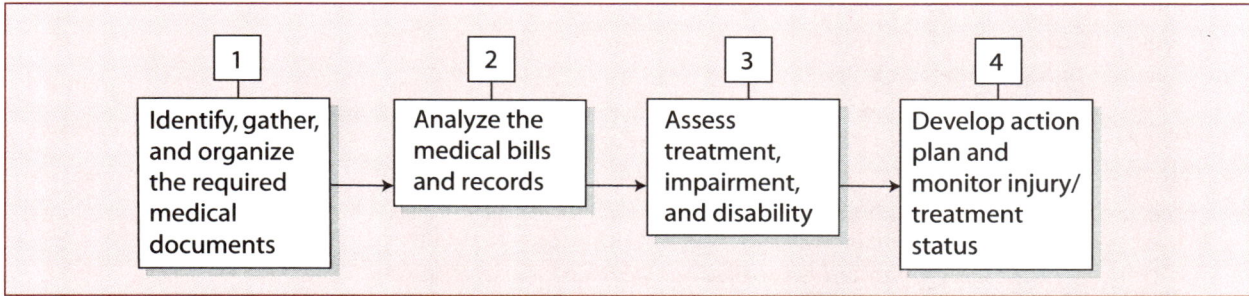

Step 1—Identify, Gather, and Organize Medical Documents

Step 1 of the medical investigation involves identifying, gathering, and organizing the medical bills and reports. Normally the medical bills arrive before any other medical documents, and often they come without requesting them. The claim representative should use the bills to begin the analysis of the injury and treatment and to identify what other medical bills and records need to be gathered.

Identify and Gather Medical Bills and Reports

The process that Mary's company follows is:

1. Identifying all of the health-care providers who will be billing

2. Obtaining those bills
3. Determining what other bills or medical records should be gathered

Mary learns from Bill's supervisor that he was taken to Quality Park emergency room (ER) by ambulance.

 **What medical bills would an ambulance trip to the emergency room for a fracture usually generate?**

The following medical bills relate to the medical treatment that Bill received:

- HCFA-1500 ambulance bill
- UB-92 Quality Park ER bill
- HCFA-1500 W.C. Yu radiology group bill
- HCFA-1500 J.P. Osecasse, M.D. bill for ER consulting on orthopedic care
- Orthopedic follow-up bills

When emergency transportation is used, the ambulance service bills for the transportation and treatment at the accident site. Ambulance services are often slower to bill than other health-care providers.

The ER department bills for the use of its emergency room, supplies, and medication. In this case, Bill's arm was broken, so an X-ray was required. The hospital would charge for the use of the X-ray machine. The radiology group that produced the X-rays would also bill separately. Often the ER doctor brings in an on-call orthopedic doctor to set a fractured bone, as was the case with Bill's ER visit. The on-call doctor, as the consulting physician, would bill separately. Emergency trauma teams also bill separately from the emergency room medical facility. In Bill's case, the trauma team was not activated. Frequently, the emergency room physician bills separately. In Bill's case, that fee was included in the hospital bill.

Health-Care Provider Billing Forms

Medical bills are one of two forms:
- UB-92
- HCFA-1500

The UB-92 (Uniform Billing) form is used by hospitals. The HCFA-1500 (Health Care Financing Administration) form is used by individual physicians, chiropractors, outpatient rehabilitation facilities, radiology groups, and ambulance services. The HCFA-1500 form is approved by the American Medical Association and published by the federal government. The UB-92 and the HCFA-1500 forms are used to establish a uniform billing for all health-care providers.

Continued on next page.

> Claim representatives should not accept patient invoices in lieu of the UB-92 or HCFA-1500 forms because patient invoices do not show the ICD-9-CM, CPT, or HCPS codes (explained later in this chapter) and sometimes show charges from services unrelated to the claim.

Mary reviewed a list of medical documents (refer to Chapter 2) and decided that she needed the following medical reports:

- Ambulance report
- Emergency room report
- Radiology report
- Orthopedic consultation ER report
- Follow-up reports from orthopedist's office

Although the insurer is generally authorized to obtain medical records under state workers compensation laws, many health-care providers resist sending out medical information without an authorization from the patient on file. Many health-care providers now require patients to give limited authorizations to allow for the release of medical records related to their medical bills. To avoid delays, Mary obtained a medical authorization from Bill when she first spoke with him (see Exhibit 6-4). The medical authorization for this claim permitted access to prior medical documents as well as to those starting on the accident date.

Exhibit 6-4
Medical Authorization

> I authorize any doctor, hospital, employer, health-care organization, or other person to whom a signed photocopy of this authorization is delivered to furnish any information, reports, or records that are requested by the Superior Ventures Insurance (SVI) Company, Inc., or its representatives.
>
> Claim Number: 36-498-1224   Insured: Quality Corporation
>
> Patient Name: William Jenkins
>
> Date of birth: 1/29/60
>
> Social Security Number: 499-74-2911
>
> Address: 129 W. Springfield Ave., Rockville, CT 88411
>
> Date: 3/5/97
>
> Patient Signature: *William Jenkins*

? *How should medical documents be organized?*

Organize the Medical Documents

The last part of the initial step is organizing the medical documents. Mary sorted and marked the documents by provider. This can be done either electronically with imaged documents or manually with paper files. She then arranged them chronologically. This method of organization is recommended because it enables the claim representative to recreate the chain of medical evidence in the order that the claimant received medical care. This method also allows the claim representative to easily follow the progression of the injury and treatment and to analyze whether the patient's complaints are related to the accident. (The importance of following this progression will become more evident in Chapters 7 and 8, in which the injured parties in the cases receive care from multiple providers over extended periods.) Organizing the records as they are received from the providers is also efficient. In this case, Mary organized the records as follows:

1. Ambulance bill
2. Emergency room bill
3. Radiology bill
4. Consulting physician bill
5. Orthopedic follow-up bills
6. Ambulance report
7. Emergency room records (with face sheet)
8. Radiology report
9. Orthopedic consultation ER report
10. Follow-up reports from orthopedist's office

> **Technical Note**
> The same systematic approach to organizing medical documents can be used with electronic imaging technology.

This is the preferred method of organizing the file, but this is not necessarily the order in which documents arrive.

Although Mary was responsible for gathering and organizing the medical records, she delegated these tasks to a claim technician. A claim technician is a claim support person who assists the claim representative with the more routine tasks involved in the claim process. The role of the claim technician is becoming more prevalent in claim departments. Claim technicians are also known as claim handlers, medical processors, and medical expediters, depending on the company.

Step 2—Analyze Medical Bills and Reports

In addition to the amount charged, bills provide useful information about the injury and treatment to those who understand how to read them. The information in the ER bill and the consulting physician's ER bill is so useful that, in many minor claims, the records are not required to conclude the claim. Bills should be reviewed with the same diligence as other medical documents. Codes that do not match up might indicate that the injury treatment is unrelated, unnecessary, or unreasonable.

Mary received the consulting physician's ER bill (an HCFA-1500) first and began analyzing it. Exhibit 6-5 shows the consulting physician's bill with annotations.

6-8 / Managing Bodily Injury Claims

Exhibit 6-5
HCFA-1500 Consulting Physician's ER Bill

Items 12 and 13 are normally typed "Signature on File." This gives the health-care provider authorization to release medical records to the insurance company. The authorization for release is not as comprehensive as the authorizations that insurance companies obtain from claimants. It only gives authorization to release records that support the medical bills.

Items 14 and 24A show date of occurrence and the date of service, respectively. If there is a gap between the two dates, then there is a possibility of a preexisting condition, and an explanation is needed.

Item 21 has the ICD-9-CM diagnosis code (in this case 813.41).

Item 24D gives the CPT procedure codes that explain patient treatment.

Item 24F shows the charge for the treatment.

Item 31 shows the name of the doctor who performed the service.

Item 32 shows the facility where the patient was treated.

HEALTH INSURANCE CLAIM FORM

1. MEDICARE / MEDICAID / CHAMPUS / CHAMPVA / GROUP HEALTH PLAN / FECA BLK LUNG / OTHER
1a. INSURED'S I.D. NUMBER (FOR PROGRAM IN ITEM 1)

2. PATIENT'S NAME (Last Name, First Name, Middle Initial): Jenkins, William B.
3. PATIENT'S BIRTH DATE: 1/29/60 SEX: M
4. INSURED'S NAME: Quality Corp.

5. PATIENT'S ADDRESS (No., Street): 129 West Springfield Ave.
6. PATIENT RELATIONSHIP TO INSURED: Self [X]
7. INSURED'S ADDRESS: 1421 E. Main

CITY: Rockville STATE: CT
8. PATIENT STATUS: Married [X]
CITY: Oakton STATE: CT

ZIP CODE: TELEPHONE: ( )
Employed [X] Full-Time Student / Part-Time Student
ZIP CODE: 88143 TELEPHONE: (610) 849-2349

9. OTHER INSURED'S NAME:
10. IS PATIENT'S CONDITION RELATED TO:
11. INSURED'S POLICY GROUP OR FECA NUMBER

a. OTHER INSURED'S POLICY OR GROUP NUMBER
a. EMPLOYMENT? (CURRENT OR PREVIOUS) [X] YES [ ] NO
a. INSURED'S DATE OF BIRTH SEX

b. OTHER INSURED'S DATE OF BIRTH SEX
b. AUTO ACCIDENT? [ ] YES [X] NO PLACE (State)
b. EMPLOYER'S NAME OR SCHOOL NAME: Quality Corp.

c. EMPLOYER'S NAME OR SCHOOL NAME: Quality Corporation
c. OTHER ACCIDENT? [X] YES [ ] NO
c. INSURANCE PLAN NAME OR PROGRAM NAME: Superior Ventures Inc.

d. INSURANCE PLAN NAME OR PROGRAM NAME
10d. RESERVED FOR LOCAL USE
d. IS THERE ANOTHER HEALTH BENEFIT PLAN? [ ] YES [X] NO

12. PATIENT'S OR AUTHORIZED PERSON'S SIGNATURE
SIGNED: Signature on File DATE: 3/4/97
13. INSURED'S OR AUTHORIZED PERSON'S SIGNATURE
SIGNED: Signature on File

14. DATE OF CURRENT ILLNESS/INJURY/PREGNANCY: 3/4/97
15. IF PATIENT HAS HAD SAME OR SIMILAR ILLNESS
16. DATES PATIENT UNABLE TO WORK: FROM 3/4/97 TO 3/4/97

17. NAME OF REFERRING PHYSICIAN OR OTHER SOURCE: Quality Park Medical Center
17a. I.D. NUMBER OF REFERRING PHYSICIAN
18. HOSPITALIZATION DATES

19. RESERVED FOR LOCAL USE
20. OUTSIDE LAB? [ ] YES [ ] NO $ CHARGES

21. DIAGNOSIS OR NATURE OF ILLNESS OR INJURY:
1. 813.41
22. MEDICAID RESUBMISSION CODE / ORIGINAL REF. NO.
23. PRIOR AUTHORIZATION NUMBER

24.
DATE(S) OF SERVICE From / To	Place of Service	Type of Service	PROCEDURES, SERVICES, OR SUPPLIES CPT/HCPCS / MODIFIER	DIAGNOSIS CODE	$ CHARGES	DAYS OR UNITS	EPSDT Family Plan	EMG	COB	RESERVED FOR LOCAL USE
3 4 97	23	3	99284	813.41	182.00					
3 4 97	23	2	25600	813.41	787.00					

25. FEDERAL TAX I.D. NUMBER
26. PATIENT'S ACCOUNT NO.: 490472
27. ACCEPT ASSIGNMENT? [ ] YES [ ] NO
28. TOTAL CHARGE: $ 969.00
29. AMOUNT PAID: $
30. BALANCE DUE: $ 969.00

31. SIGNATURE OF PHYSICIAN OR SUPPLIER: Jean Paul Osecasse, M.D.
32. NAME AND ADDRESS OF FACILITY: Quality Park Medical Center
33. PHYSICIAN'S, SUPPLIER'S BILLING NAME, ADDRESS, ZIP CODE & PHONE #: Quality Park Medical Center

> **? What do the CPT and ICD-9-CM codes indicate about this patient?**

Item 21 shows an ICD-9-CM code of 813.41. Mary consulted the *International Classification of Diseases (ICD-9-CM)* book and confirmed that the billing was for a Colles' fracture with closed reduction. Closed reduction means that no surgery was required to align the bone fragments. Mary looked up **Colles' fracture** in *Taber's Medical Dictionary* and determined that the extent of the fracture and any complications resulting from it would have to be determined by reviewing the medical reports that Mary had requested.

In *Taber's Medical Dictionary*, Mary also reads the definition of the radius, the body part injured, and learned that the radius is a bone in the lower part of the arm.

ICD.9.CM

813.4 Lower end, closed
    Distal end
    813.40   Lower end of forearm, unspecified
    813.41   Colles' fracture
                 Smith's fracture
    813.42   Other fractures of distal end of radius (alone)
                 Duypuytren's fracture, radius
                 Radius, lower end
    813.43   Distal end of ulna (alone)
                 Ulna: Ulna:
                 head   lower epiphysis
                 lower end styloid process
    813.44   Radius with ulna, lower end

Taber's Definition

Colles' fracture. The transverse fracture of the distal end of the radius (just above wrist) with displacement of hand backward and outward.

NURSING IMPLICATIONS: The emergency room nurse assesses patient for pain, swelling, mobility, and any obvious deformity of the distal forearm, observes the extremity above the fracture site, and palpates the extremity to determine the presence of pulse and sensation distal to the fracture. Skin color and temperature distal to the fracture site are also evaluated. The affected extremity should be, as ordered, temporarily immobilized with a splint, and a radiograph should be taken.

Item 24D in Exhibit 6-5 lists two CPT codes, 25600 and 99284. Mary looks up these codes in the *Current Procedural Terminology (CPT)* book. The code 25600 offers an explanation of the treatment given. The treatment also matches the description of the injury—a broken arm reported by the employer. Code 99284 indicates the type of medical exam given. It also gives examples of exams that fall into this category. If the description of the exam that was given does not match with the codes, the claim representative must ask the provider for an explanation. In the case of Bill Jenkins, the codes match the type of medical exam given (that is, a "moderate" exam).

After reviewing one medical bill, Mary had enough information to reevaluate the reserve set during the initial assessment. Mary could also reevaluate the decision on medical case management made during the initial assessment. She was also in a better position to assess how detailed of an investigation she needed to conduct. She continued with her analysis by reviewing the next medical bill she received, the ER bill (a UB-92 form). As previously mentioned, the ER bill covers only the services, equipment, and supplies of the medical center. Exhibit 6-6 shows Bill's hospital ER UB-92 bill with annotations.

After analyzing the bills, Mary reviewed the ER and consulting physician's reports, shown in Exhibits 6-7 and 6-8, to ensure that the treatments billed for matched the treatments given.

Step 3—Assess Treatment, Impairment, and Disability

After determining the claimant's injury, the claim representative must then assess the claimant's treatment, impairment, and disability. Understanding the injury and the anatomy of the injured body part is essential to assessing the treatment, impairment, and disability of the claimant. In Bill's case, Mary had to learn about fractures and the anatomy of the arm to assess the claim.

Fractures and the Anatomy of the Arm

Fractures, or broken bones, are a common accidental injury. The seriousness of a broken bone depends on which bone is involved, how it is broken, and the patient's age, health, and occupation. Forces that are powerful enough to break bones usually cause damage to the surrounding soft tissues. In addition, improper healing of a broken bone can cause nerve damage, loss of function, and "shortening" of bone causing misalignment in the affected bones.

Fractures vary widely depending upon the type of trauma that causes them. A **closed fracture**, or **simple fracture**, is a fracture where the skin has not been punctured by the bone. An **open fracture**, or a **compound fracture**, is a fracture where the skin has been punctured by the bone. Closed and open fractures should not be confused with closed and open reduction, which are methods of treating fractures. Compared to simple fractures, compound fractures take longer to treat and heal and have a greater potential for permanent impairment and infection. Fortunately, in this case, Bill suffered a simple fracture.

> Fractures account for 14.3 percent of all workers compensation claims[1] and 13 percent of auto *injury* claims.[2] The average claim payment for a fracture is $5,528 per claim for workers compensation and $31,543 per claim for auto bodily injury liability.

Exhibit 6-6
UB-92 Quality Park Medical Center

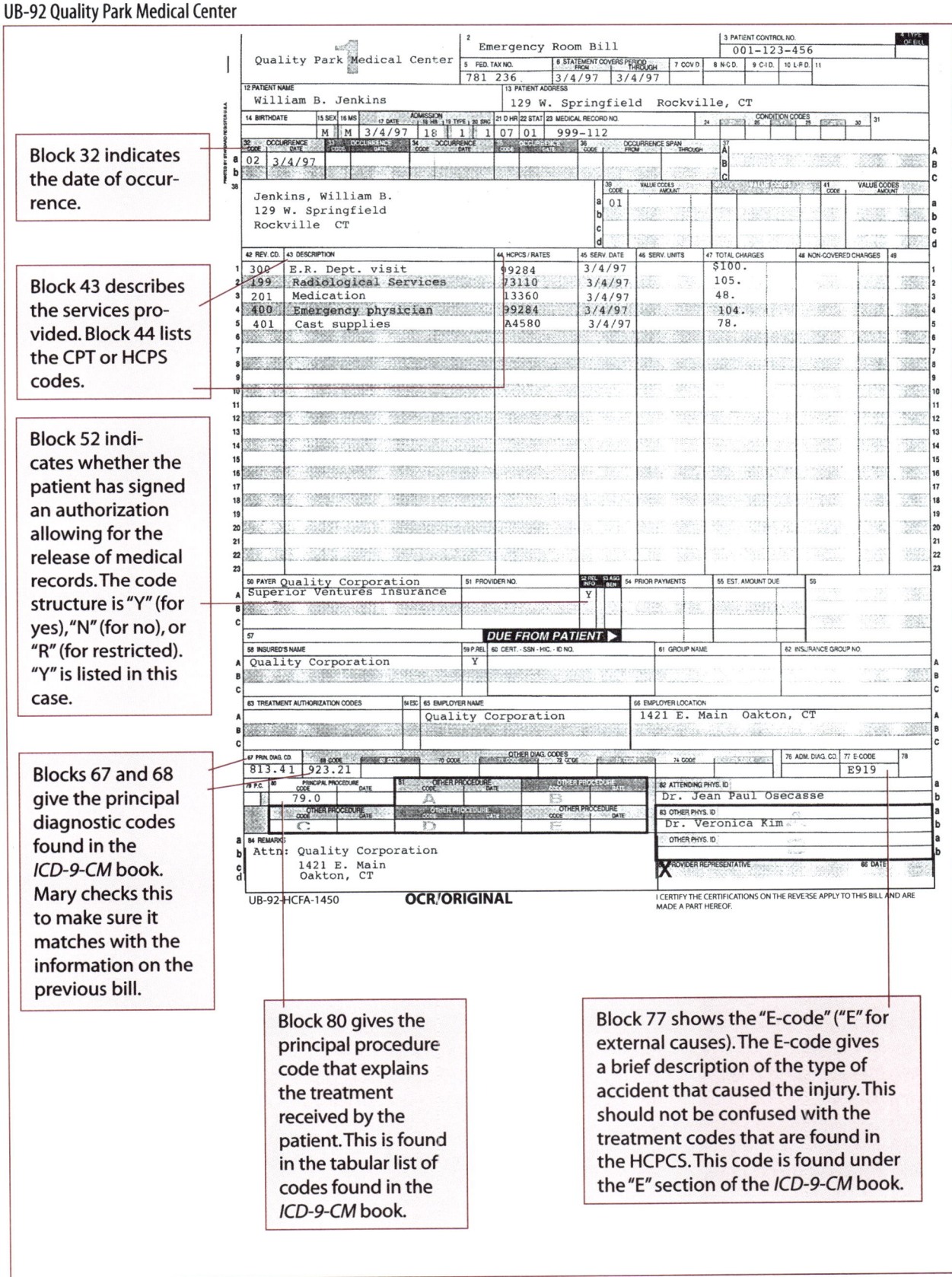

Block 32 indicates the date of occurrence.

Block 43 describes the services provided. Block 44 lists the CPT or HCPS codes.

Block 52 indicates whether the patient has signed an authorization allowing for the release of medical records. The code structure is "Y" (for yes), "N" (for no), or "R" (for restricted). "Y" is listed in this case.

Blocks 67 and 68 give the principal diagnostic codes found in the *ICD-9-CM* book. Mary checks this to make sure it matches with the information on the previous bill.

Block 80 gives the principal procedure code that explains the treatment received by the patient. This is found in the tabular list of codes found in the *ICD-9-CM* book.

Block 77 shows the "E-code" ("E" for external causes). The E-code gives a brief description of the type of accident that caused the injury. This should not be confused with the treatment codes that are found in the HCPCS. This code is found under the "E" section of the *ICD-9-CM* book.

Exhibit 6-7
Emergency Room Physician's Report

EMERGENCY ROOM REPORT

Quality Park Regional Medical Center
2000 Quality Rd.
Quality Park, CT 88413

DD: 3-4-97 11:45   Veronica Kim, M.D.
PATIENT: William B. Jenkins
DOB: 1-29-60
ADMISSION DATE: 3-4-97
DISCHARGE DATE: 3-4-97
EMERGENCY DEPARTMENT RECORD
FAMILY PHYSICIAN: None given.
CHIEF COMPLAINT: Work accident.
HISTORY OF PRESENT ILLNESS: A 37-year-old white male presents after a work accident wherein he fell off a forklift onto the concrete floor of a warehouse. The patient is a maintenance supervisor for Quality Corporation. He fell head-first and tried to brace himself with his left arm, falling onto his left arm. The patient stated that other than having the injured left arm, he had no other complaints.
MEDICAL HISTORY: The patient denies any surgeries, hospitalizations, or other medical problems.
MEDICATIONS: None. The patient had a tetanus shot about three years ago.
ALLERGIES: Erythromycin
SPECIAL HISTORY: The patient reports history of smoking three packs a day for 22 years. Reports occasional alcohol use. Denies street drug use.
PHYSICAL EXAMINATION: Temperature is 98.6. Pulse is 72. Respiration is 18. Blood pressure is 138/92. The patient presents as a well-developed, well-nourished white male who is alert and oriented at times three and in mild distress. He was presented to the emergency department by the local ambulance company on a stretcher in a cervical collar.
HEENT: Normocephalic and atraumatic. Eyes: pupils are equal, round, and reactive to light in accommodations. Ears: normal. Mouth and throat: clear. Face: found to be stable.
NECK: The patient has equal range of neck motion to the right and to the left, and the neck is found to be non-tender. He has no jugular venous distention.
CARDIOVASCULAR: Regular rate and rhythm without murmurs, heaves, or rubs.
LUNGS: Clear to auscultation bilaterally with equal breath signs bilaterally. Chest wall is non-tender to palpation. Bowel sounds are present. Abdomen is soft and non-tender in all quadrants.
PELVIS: Non-tender to pelvic rock and compressions.
MUSCULAR SKELETAL: Patient is complaining of severe pain in the left wrist. Left hand is swollen and somewhat discolored and painful to the touch. The wrist is warm to the touch and both radial and ulnar pulses are present and equal to that of the right hand. Mr. Jenkins is unable to flex or extend his left wrist. His fingers are pink, warm, and dry, and all digits and thumb blanch to pressure with capillary refill within two seconds. All digits and palm of the left hand are sensitive to both one and two point discrimination. Patient able to oppose left thumb as well as abduct left thumb. Typical dinner fork deformity of the left wrist is noted.
IMPRESSION: Simple Colles' fracture of left wrist revealed per radiographic findings. Minimal dorsally displaced/non-comminuted fracture of the left distal radius. Physical exam reveals medial nerve intact.
PLAN: Closed reduction left wrist with application of dorsal-palmar above the elbow plastered slab. Dr. Osecasse, orthopedic surgeon, called in for closed reduction in the emergency room department cast room. See consultation notes.
DIAGNOSIS: Simple Colles' fracture at the left wrist.
CONDITION ON DISCHARGE: Stable. Signed Veronica Kim, M.D.

> Oriented at times three means the patient can answer 3 questions:
> 1. Who are you?
> 2. Where are you?
> 3. What time is it?

Exhibit 6-8
Orthopedic Consultation-ER Report

CONSULTATION REPORT

Quality Park Regional Medical Center
2000 Quality Road
Quality Park, CT 88413
807-503-2000

PATIENT: William B. Jenkins
DICTATED BY: Jean Paul Osecasse
DATE OF BIRTH: 1-29-60
ACCOUNT NUMBER: XA53221170
MEDICAL RECORDS NUMBER: 30021598
ADMISSION DATE: 3-4-97
DATE OF CONSULTATION: 3-4-97
EMERGENCY ROOM PHYSICIAN: Veronica Kim, M.D.
CONSULTING PHYSICIAN: Jean Paul Osecasse, M.D.
ADMITTING DIAGNOSIS: Rule out left Colles' fracture.
HISTORY OF PRESENT ILLNESS: The patient is an otherwise healthy 37-year-old white male who was in his usual state of good health until approximately two hours ago while at work. At that time, the patient, who works as a maintenance supervisor for Quality Corporation, was getting off a forklift and fell. He tried to catch himself by extending both his left and right arms. He fell striking his left arm harder than his right onto the concrete floor. The patient immediately noticed pain and deformity of the left wrist. He was brought by the ambulance to the hospital emergency department for evaluation.
PAST MEDICAL HISTORY: Non-contributory.
SURGERY: None.
MEDICATIONS: None.
PHYSICAL EXAM (Limited orthopedic): The patient is found to have a left wrist that is swollen and somewhat discolored. Mr. Jenkins describes it as painful to the touch. Mr. Jenkins is unable to flex or extend his left wrist. It is noted by this examiner that the wrist is warm to the touch with both the radial and ulnar pulses being present. The medial nerve dermatome distribution was found to be intact and sensitive to both one- and two-point discrimination. The patient was able to oppose the thumb as well as to abduct his left thumb. The patient has a typical "dinner fork" deformity of the left wrist indicating probable Colles' fracture.
IMPRESSION: Radiographs of the left wrist reveal simple Colles' fracture minimally displaced on the dorsal aspect; non-comminuted fracture.
PLAN: Closed reduction of left wrist with application of dorsal palmar above the elbow plaster slab.
PROCEDURE: Pre-procedural diagnosis: simple Colles' fracture of left wrist. Post-procedure diagnosis: Colles' fracture of left wrist. The patient was given a sedative of 10 mg Diazepamim and this was tolerated well. Vital signs were stable: Temperature 98.6. Pulse 72. Respiration 18. Blood pressure 138/92. An 18 gauge jelco was started in the patient's rt. antecubital fossa with 500 cc lactated ringers TKO. 5 mg Diazepamim was given IV push. Light sedation was immediately obtained.

With the patient lying supine on the orthopedic table in the emergency department cast room, manual traction was applied by the examiner approximately to the left forearm to immobilize it. The thenar eminence of the practitioner's hand pressed the radial fragment posturally, causing ulnar deviation. The radial fragment was slipped into place and the forearm was pronated. The practitioner's hand took a new grip and the radial fragment was pushed ulnarly. The forearm was then casted in a dorsal palmar above the elbow plaster cast, leaving all digits freely mobile.

The patient tolerated the procedure well and was able to move all fingers and make a fist. Post reduction X-rays revealed the left wrist positioned anatomically in 15 degrees of flexion and 15 degrees of ulnar deviation. The patient was given prescriptions of Tylenol #3, #40 Q 4 to 6 hours PO PRN for left wrist pain and a sheet of cast instructions. He was advised to call the office for a follow-up visit in one week. Patient was also advised to keep the left arm elevated for the next 24 hours with an ice pack applied to the dorsal cast over the fracture site.

The patient was dismissed with family to drive him home. The patient was advised to return to the emergency department if he experienced any extreme swelling or pain of the left forearm. The patient will be off of work through the weekend. He is scheduled to be seen on Monday and at that time should be evaluated for temporary physical restrictions.

Jean Paul Osecasse, M.D.   Quality Park Regional

The "*dorsal palmar*" refers to a cast that extends from the bottom of the fingers to above the elbow. The back (dorsal) part of the hand is where most of the casting material is placed with much thinner material covering the palm of the hand.

A **nondisplaced fracture**, or an **undisplaced fracture**, is a fracture where the bone is still aligned. A **displaced fracture** is one where the bone moves out of alignment.

An incomplete fracture is a fracture in which the line of the fracture does not include the whole bone. A complete fracture is one in which the bone is completely broken into two or more pieces.

Exhibit 6-9 compares an undisplaced, simple fracture with two types of displaced compound fractures. Exhibit 6-10 describes some types of fractures, and Exhibit 6-11 illustrates some types of fractures.

Exhibit 6-9
Undisplaced Versus Displaced Fractures

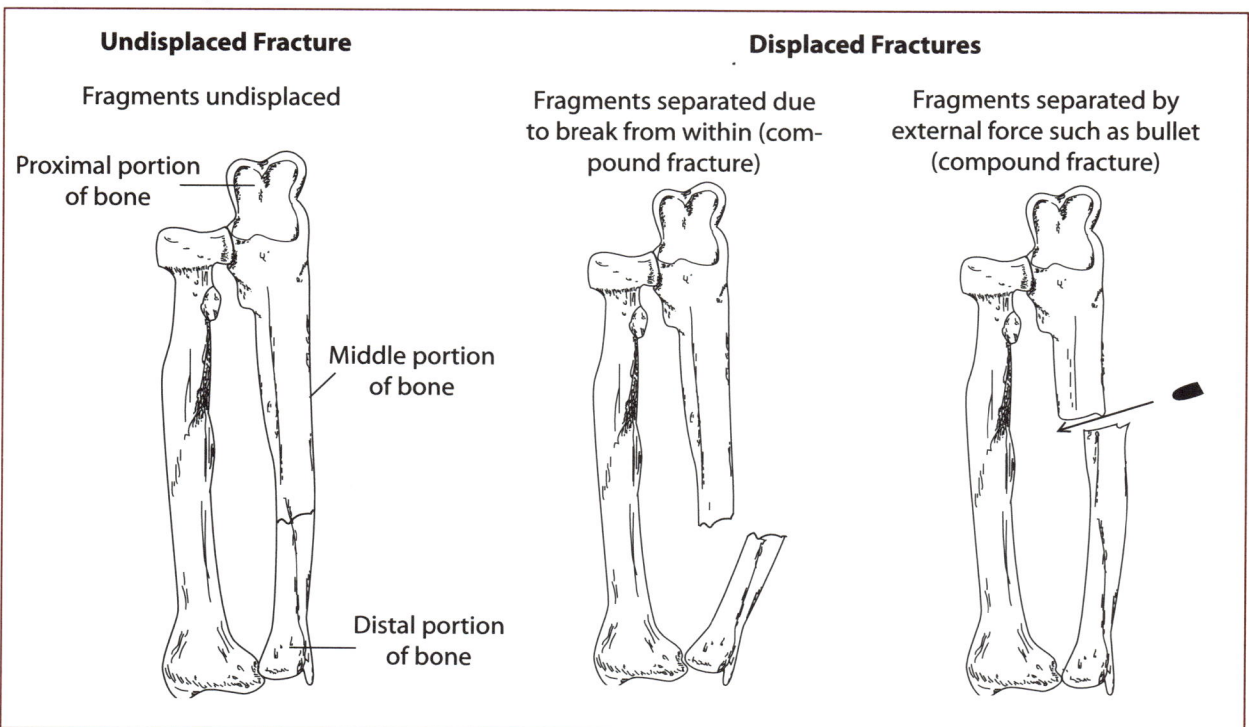

Exhibit 6-10
Types of Fractures

Types of fractures	Description of fracture
Hairline fracture	A simple fracture that involves only a line or crack in the bone.
Comminuted fracture	The bone is broken into more than two pieces. Open reduction (surgery) is required to repair this type of fracture.
Impacted fracture	The bone is forced towards its midsection. These fractures usually occur in the lower legs as a result of landing heavily on the feet.
Spiral fracture	The break twists around the bone as a result of an injury from a twisting motion.
Greenstick fracture	The bone looks like a broken green branch; there is no complete break, and one side of the bone appears "torn" or "shredded."
Complicated fracture	The bone is broken and has injured some internal organ (for example, a broken rib puncturing a lung).

Exhibit 6-11
Common Types of Fractures

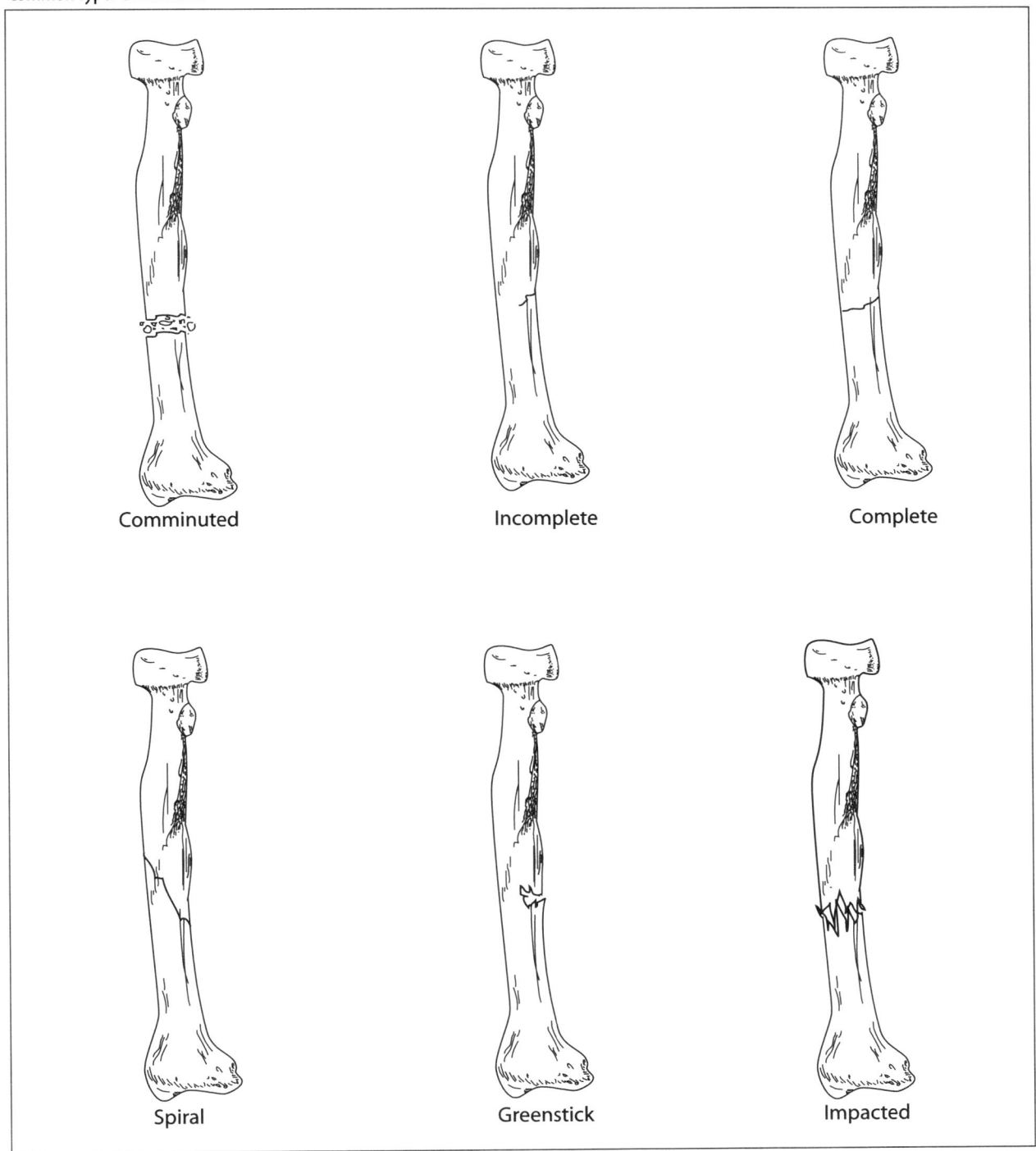

The most common type of fracture to the radius is a Colles' fracture, named after the nineteenth-century surgeon who first described its characteristics. A Colles' fracture, shown in Exhibits 6-12 and 6-13, looks like a dinner fork. The **radius** is a bone that lies on the thumb side of the forearm. The head of the radius articulates with (fits into) the distal end of the humerus (upper arm bone) and with the side of the ulna. At the lower, or distal, end of the humerus are smooth surfaces that articulate with the radius and ulna of the lower arm. The **ulna**, on the little finger side of the forearm, is a slender bone that fits into the humerus. The distal end of the ulna does not directly articulate with the wrist bones. A disk of fibrous cartilage cushions the space between the ulna and the wrist. The **styloid process**, at the distal end of the ulna, can also be broken when a Colles' fracture occurs because of tension of the ligament pulling on that portion of the bone. Although common, this did not occur in Bill's case.

Exhibit 6-12
Colles' Fracture

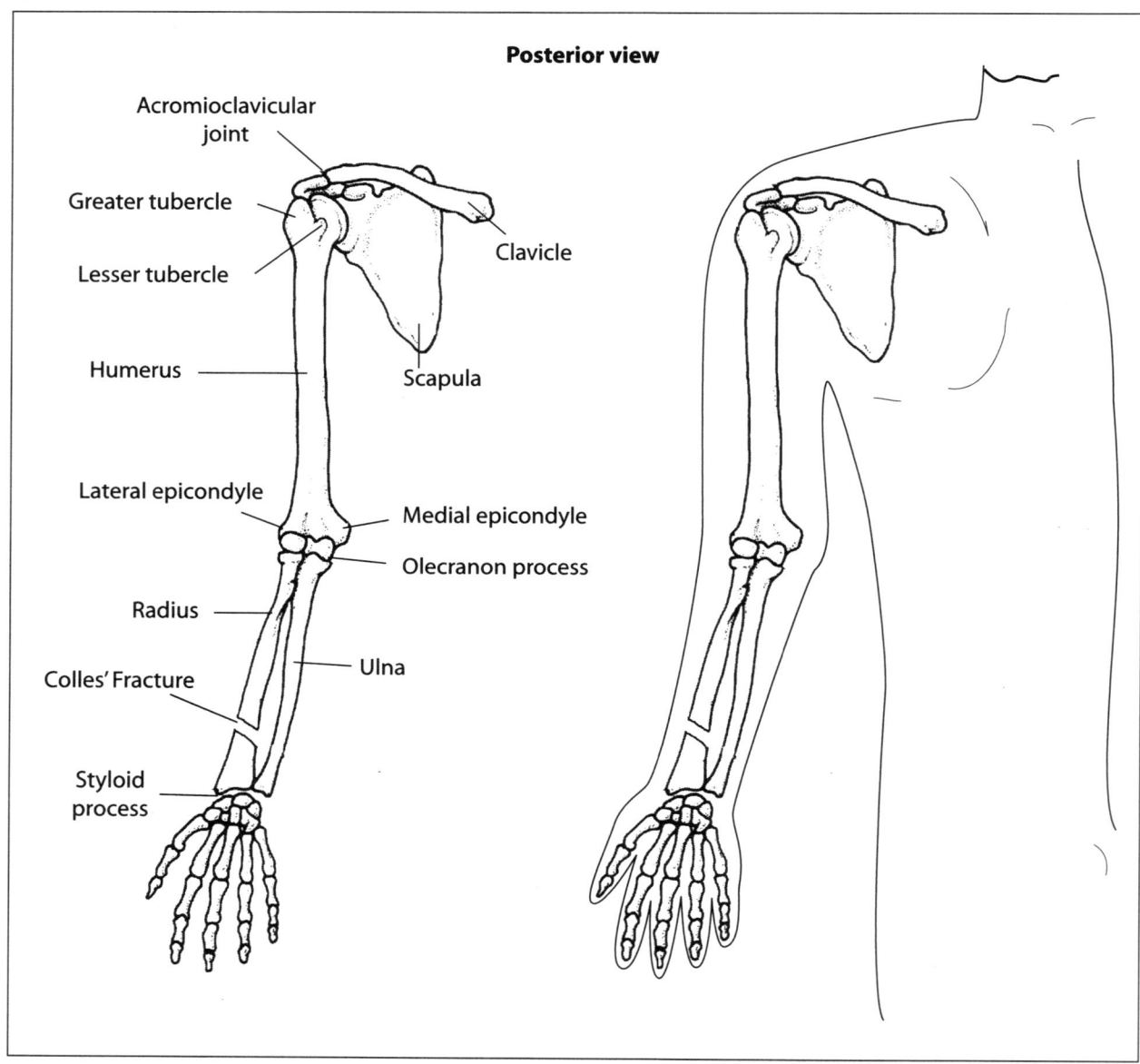

Exhibit 6-13
Dinner Fork Break

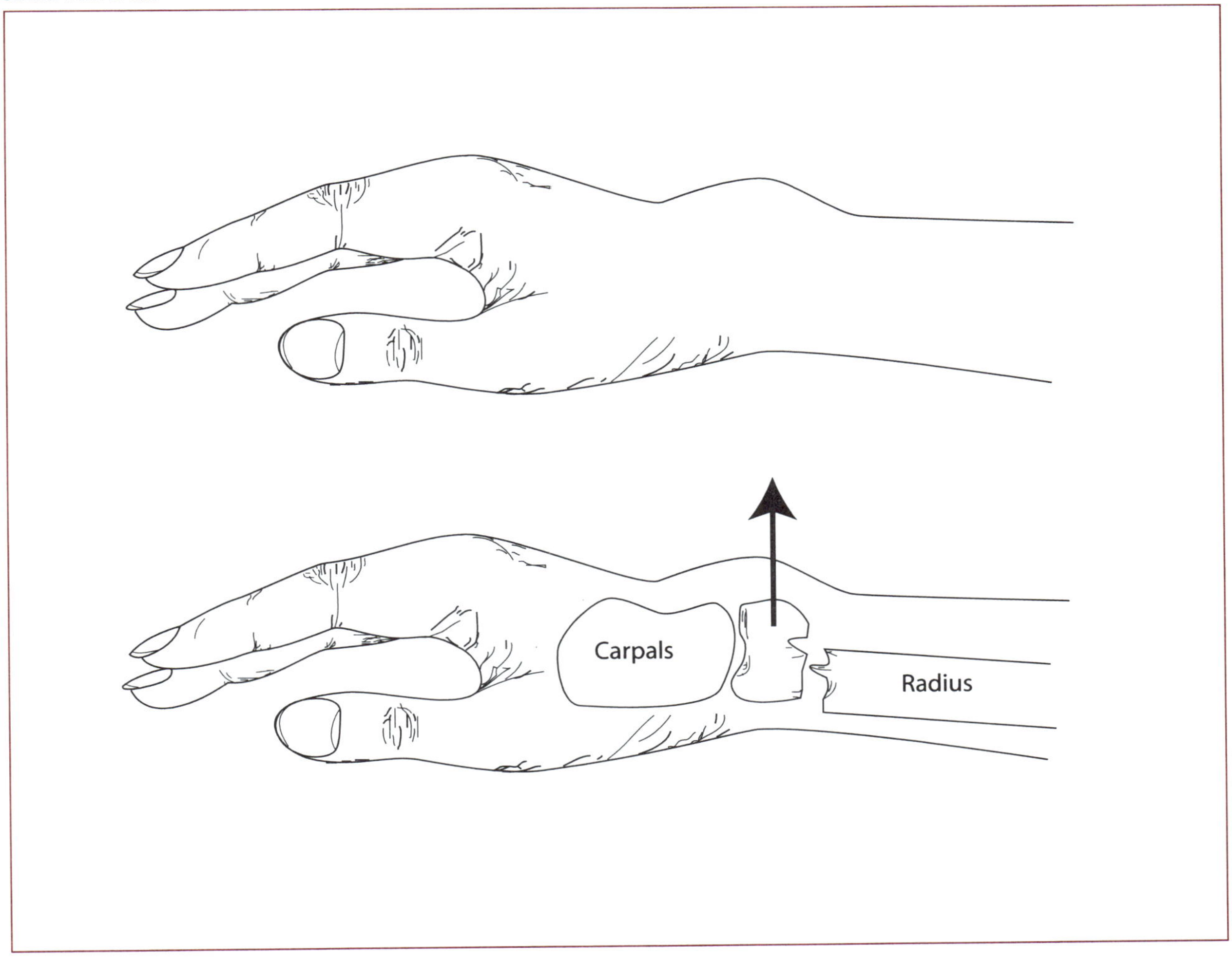

Impairment and Disability

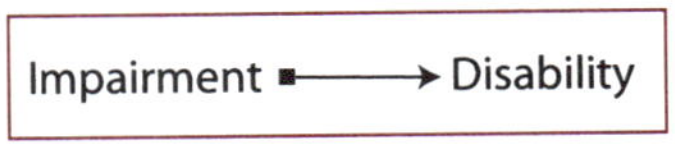

An *impairment* is a loss of, loss of use of, or derangement of any body part, system, or function. Impairments can, but do not always, lead to disabilities. A *disability* is an inability to meet personal, social, or occu-pational demands because of an impairment. Impairments and disabilities can be temporary (as in the case of a strained muscle) or permanent (as in the case of an amputated hand), and a claim's reserve should re-flect those exposures. Disabilities range from partial to total.

Assessing the impairment and disability is essential to proper claim evaluation because the impairment and disability directly relate to the value (potential cost) of the claim. To determine the value of Bill's claim, Mary evaluated the extent of Bill's impairment and its potential affect on his disability.

Impairment ■⟶ Disability

> *What is the length of time that the claimant will be unable to work?*

First, Mary determined Dr. Osecasse's prognosis for Bill. A **prognosis** is a prediction of when the problem will end and an estimate of the chance of recovery. What restrictions has Dr. Osecasse placed on Bill? How will these restrictions affect Bill's ability to perform his job? How long will Bill's arm be in a cast?

Mary received a follow-up report from Dr. Osecasse and learned that the cast would be on for at least six weeks. Until that time, Bill was restricted from lifting with his left hand. Mary wondered how much time it would be after the cast is removed before Bill would be able to use his left arm. Physical therapy would probably be required after the cast was removed because of muscle atrophy (loss of muscle strength).

Mary consulted *The Medical Disability Advisor (MDA)* to help estimate the length of time of disability for this type of injury. She used the ICD-9-CM code 813.41 (the code for a Colles' fracture) for estimating the disability time. (She also could have used the injury description, but Mary has *MDA* on her computer, so she can quickly access the applicable sections with the ICD-9-CM code.) If the disability time stated in the reference differed significantly from the doctor's prognosis, Mary should have requested an explanation from Dr. Osecasse if he had not already provided one. According to the *Medical Disability Advisor*, the typical length of disability for "medium work" ranges from nine to twenty-one weeks for a fractured radius (see Exhibit 6-14).

Exhibit 6-14
Estimated Disability

	Distal Radius: Code [813.41]		
Job Classification	**Minimum Expectancy**	**Optimum**	**Maximum Expectancy**
Sedentary work	7 Days	14 Days	28 Days
Light work	14 Days	21 Days	91 Days
Medium work	63 Days	91 Days	147 Days
Heavy work	119 Days	182 Days	238 Days
Very heavy work	119 Days	182 Days	273 Days

Reprinted with permission from *The Medical Disability Advisor: Workplace Guidelines for Disability Duration*, Third Edition (1997), Presley Reed, MD. © Reed Group, Ltd. Boulder, CO. (800) 347-7443. All rights reserved. http://www.rgl.net.

MDA defines "medium work" as occasionally lifting 50 pounds, and/or frequently lifting 20 pounds, and/or lifting 10 pounds constantly. This definition most closely describes Bill's job requirements.

After reviewing the pertinent medical documents, Mary had a good understanding of Bill's impairment. She knew the type, location, and severity of the injury. She also knew that the doctor was expecting a full recovery and that the estimated time that Bill would be out of work was nine to twenty-one weeks. *MDA* explained that the most common complications related to Bill's injury were residual pain and stiffness and limitations in the movement of the wrist. Joint movement with a Colles' fracture generally returns slowly, with little permanent impairment. After reviewing the records, Mary felt confident that she fully understood Bill's injury and how it would affect his ability to perform his job. She met again with Karen.

Mary: Karen, I think I've got everything I need to evaluate the Jenkins claim and come up with a reasonable assessment of the injury and disability.

Mary goes through the information she has gathered and explains her assessment of the claim. Karen looks over the file.

Karen: You've done a good job of gathering and analyzing the medical documents on this, and I compliment you on the way you've organized this. It makes it a lot clearer to understand. Before we move on, I'd like to review some of the factors that will affect our decision. These are things you need to keep in mind when dealing with fractures. Let's take a look and make sure we've got these figured in.

Mary and Karen reviewed the medical documents keeping in mind the following factors that affect the extent of impairments:

1. The type and location of the injury
2. The degree and direction of displacement
   - The degree of comminution (bone pieces)
   - The type of reduction used (open versus closed) and its effectiveness
   - The severity of surrounding soft tissue injury (including tendons and ligaments)
3. The age of claimant
4. Preexisting conditions (for example, diabetes, AIDS, prior injuries, bone disease)
5. Medical complications particular to the injury
6. Lifestyle issues (smoking, alcohol use, drug use, obesity)

In addition to a claimant's impairment, what factors could affect the length of a disability?

Karen: We've discussed a lot factors that affect the impairment, but how is this impairment going to affect Bill's ability to work? First of all, Mary, was Bill's dominant arm injured? [Mary shrugs her shoulders.] You'll need to know that in evaluating how this will affect his ability to work. Are these lifting restrictions going to keep him from doing his job?

Mary: I'm not sure whether he'll be able to go back to the maintenance job immediately. I assume that they'll find him some light duty work.

Karen: I'm familiar with Quality Corporation's operations from previous claims that we've handled in this office. One obstacle that we're going to face on this is finding **light duty** work for Mr. Jenkins.

Light duty means an alternative job that is less physically demanding than the one held by the claimant at the time of the accident. Many union contracts preclude the use of light duty jobs for return-to-work programs. In this case, Karen is suggesting that Mary examine the tasks performed by the claimant and see whether his job can be modified to accommodate his restrictions. Unions usually have fewer limitations for job modifications than for alternative jobs.

Their union policy precludes putting employees at another job on light duty status. If his existing job can't be modified to accommodate his impairment, he may end up on disability longer. Talk to Quality and see if they can modify his job. He's a supervisor, so they might be able to do that.

Another thing that you ought to be aware of is that the union and Quality are in a contract dispute right now. Did you get the sense from talking with Bill that he might have an adversarial relationship with Quality?

Motivation is a key to getting people back to work. You'll also need to think about motivation from Bill's supervisor's perspective. If his supervisor doesn't want Bill back, you're going to have an additional challenge in returning him to work.

Mary: I hadn't considered those issues.

Karen: You'll find out as you progress in your career that you'll have to look beyond just the physical impairment in order to determine the disability.

Besides the impairment, several factors can affect the length of disability. Those factors include the following:

1. *The job tasks the claimant must perform.* How does the impairment affect the claimant's ability to perform the required job task? (For example, a broken finger would have a significantly different disability for a concert pianist than for a Dallas Cowboy lineman.)
2. *Personal characteristics of the claimant.* This relates to the adaptability and motivation of the claimant. Motivation affects how well the patient will cooperate with the treating physician and affects his or her willingness to return to work. Secondary gains to the claimant that can influence motivation include the following:
   a. Financial gains resulting from the claimant's extending the length of the disability. An example is a claimant who is receiving more income after taxes from workers compensation than from wages. Another example is a claimant who wants to build up his or her "specials" (out-of-pocket expenses) to increase the value of a third-party claim.
   b. Psychological gains to claimants who view disability as a way to escape boring or strenuous work.
3. *Ability to direct and manage claimant care.* This is an important tool of the claim representative. This is affected by:
   a. Type of claim. Claim representatives can usually manage workers compensation claims and first-party claims better than third-party claims.
   b. Jurisdiction of the claim. Some states allow employers to choose the physicians who treat injured workers.
4. *Ability to return claimant to work in the shortest possible time.* This depends on:

a. Availability of modified or light duty work. This can vary by company.
b. The opportunity and ability of the claimant to be re-trained. This relates to the transferability of the claimant's skills. This also depends on the local job market at the time.
c. The union status of the claimant. Union contracts may preclude the employee from returning to light duty work. The union might also be in a labor dispute with the employer that taints the employee's relationship with the employer and consequently the claim representative.

5. *Attorney involvement.* Claimants with attorneys often have cases with higher disability reserves. This is true because:
   a. Claimants are more likely to hire attorneys on more serious cases.
   b. Attorneys can cause a claim to become more expensive because of the adversarial relationship that often develops between the claimant and the employer or insurer, which causes delays and additional administrative expenses.

Step 4—Develop Action Plan and Monitor Injury/Treatment Status

After assessing Bill's treatment, impairment, and disability, Mary was ready to develop an action plan and monitor the injury and treatment.

Develop Action Plan

The action plan for Bill consists of a return-to-work program and rehabilitation. Mary consulted with Karen about how to proceed.

Karen: We need to find ways to return Bill to work as soon as possible. Since Bill's injury is serious, I'm concerned that there might be some problem. If his progress isn't what it should be, you'll need to get an explanation from his doctor. We might even need a hand specialist to review the orthopedic doctor's prognosis. Keep me posted on any developments.

Bill will probably require some physical therapy after the cast comes off, so you should arrange that, too. I'll give you a list of rehabilitation specialists to choose from. According to the *MDA*, this type of injury would normally require physical or occupational therapy three times per week for six to eight weeks.

You've also got some loss control issues that need to be addressed. Why did Bill fall? The last time I was at the warehouse where Bill works, the people were hurrying around because they were trying to make a deadline to get their incentive bonuses. I've also read about some problems with the forklifts used at the warehouse coming out of gear. At any rate, there are some safety, and possibly some *subrogation*, issues to address. Make sure the loss control people know about this accident. They might also want to look

> *Subrogation* refers to the right to seek reimbursement from the responsible parties. In this case, if a problem with the design or functioning of the forklift caused Bill to fall off of it, then the workers compensation payor, in this case Superior Ventures Insurance, would be entitled to be reimbursed for what it pays on this claim.

into the loss frequency patterns to see if they are related to these incentive bonuses.

Monitor Injury/Treatment Status

Finally, Mary needed to monitor Bill's healing process and advise Karen if any complications arose. The physical rehabilitation specialist assisted with monitoring the healing process. If Bill did not improve within the estimated disability time frame of four to eight weeks, then Mary would have needed to get an explanation from his doctor. To monitor the medical aspects of this claim, Mary needed an understanding of the healing process of fractures and the possible complications that could arise.

Healing Process of Fractures

A membrane containing bone-forming cells surrounds each bone. These cells are dormant until a bone has been fractured. When a fracture occurs, these cells are activated to create new bone. Blood vessels are broken and form clots around the fracture. The bone-forming cells begin to grow in the clot, forming fibrous tissue. Blood vessels surrounding a fracture site feed this tissue and begin to form callus. **Callus** is a bony material that hardens into permanent bone. Activity may cause stiffness and swelling for a few weeks. Rest and elevation of the hand may be necessary.

Possible Complications With the Healing of Fractures

A firm union of a broken bone will usually occur in three to four months after the fracture. However, several adverse results may occur. Mary reviewed the following so that she would know what could go wrong. Mary would need to alert her supervisor if any of the following problems arose:

1. *Improper union of bones.* If bone fragments do not unite properly, they can heal in a position that results in loss of function. Fractures to certain bones, such as collarbones or ribs, do not require perfect alignment.

   In some severe cases, a rod can be inserted to bear weight and to provide stability. If this is not possible, the patient may suffer a shortening of the extremity. This can occur when damaged bone must be removed and the remaining pieces attach to each other. Some examples include the following:

   a. **Partial union.** This occurs when the callus does not grow over the entire fractured area, leaving portions of the fragments separated.

   b. **Fibrous union.** This occurs when the callus does not harden.

   c. **Mal-union.** This occurs when the fragments unite in a position that renders the bone far less functional than normal or when the fragments unite with another bone.

   d. **Non-union.** This occurs when the bone does not heal and the fragments are held together only by tissue.

2. *Nerve damage.* If the bone shatters, a bone fragment can easily lacerate a nerve. If a nerve becomes involved with the callus while

> One factor in this case that could complicate the healing process is Bill's heavy smoking, indicated in the ER report. Studies have indicated that heavy smoking reduces the flow of oxygen to tissues, which in turn slows the healing process.[3]

it is hardening, it may be pinched, resulting in a loss of sensation or movement. A fracture to the humerus can damage the radial nerve, which controls movement in the entire arm. In Bill's case, the ER report stated that there was no damage to the medial nerve.

3. *Vascular damage.* Blood vessels adjacent to the fracture may be damaged.
4. *Infection.* Infection often occurs with open fractures. *Osteomyelitis* is an infection of the bone that causes a buildup of pus in the bone. The bone or surrounding tissues might die leading to loss of a limb or patient death if not properly treated.
5. *Complex regional pain syndrome* is a disorder that causes an irritation to the nerves at the site of the injury. The nerves react in a way that damages the tissue and ultimately the bone. An example of this is reflex sympathetic dystrophy syndrome (RSDS). This kind of disorder can occur after a wrist fracture. Tendon ruptures may also be a late complication.

Case Conclusion

Dr. Osecasse's office report indicated that the claimant could return to work two weeks after the accident with a temporary restriction of "no lifting, right hand work only." Two weeks are less than MDA indicated because the work was being modified. Bill returned to modified job duties after two weeks. He was able to perform his normal administrative duties as supervisor, but the physical demands were limited while his arm healed.

His employer supported the need for Bill to continue to work even if his productivity was reduced. They had learned from experience that sometimes workers who took off for several weeks, waiting until they reached maximum medical improvement, would have a difficult time making the psychological adjustment to working full time.

SVI's loss control experts visited Bill's employer. They could find no product defect with the forklift, but they identified a pattern of injuries that correlated with incentive bonus deadlines. A cost-benefit analysis showed that the money they saved in filling orders rapidly was lost in additional workers compensation premium as a result of their poor loss experience.

Case Evaluation

The claim representative was required to assess an injury for the following reasons:

- Estimating the claimant's disability
- Establishing reserves
- Determining the need for medical case management

This assessment requires the claim representative to perform a medical investigation. The medical investigation is a four-step process:

1. Identify, gather, and organize medical documents
2. Analyze medical bills and reports
3. Assess treatment, impairment, and disability
4. Develop an action plan and monitor the injury/treatment status

The two most important aspects of the medical investigation are:

1. Understanding the investigative process
2. Knowing how to use the available medical resources to analyze the anatomy, the injury, and the treatment

Fractures can be simple or compound, displaced or undisplaced, and complete or incomplete. Some fractures include the following:

- Hairline
- Comminuted
- Complicated
- Greenstick
- Impacted
- Spiral

The type of fracture affects the degree of impairment, which in turn affects the length of disability. Several considerations must be weighed in estimating the potential for impairment. They are:

1. The type and location of the injury
2. The degree and direction of displacement
3. The age of the claimant
4. Preexisting injuries or conditions
5. Medical complications particular to the injury
6. Lifestyle issues

Factors affecting the degree of disability are:

1. The impairment to the claimant
2. The job tasks the claimant must perform
3. Personal characteristics of the claimant
4. Ability of the claim representative to direct and manage claimant care
5. Ability of the claim representative to return the claimant to work in the shortest possible time
6. Attorney involvement

To monitor the status of injuries, the claim representative must understand the potential for complications related to specific injuries. Some possible complications that can occur with fractures are:

- Improper bone union
- Nerve damage
- Vascular damage
- Infection
- Complex regional pain syndrome

The major steps in the medical investigation should remain constant. The activities of the claim team members may vary depending on the circumstances of the accident, injury, and treatment. Exhibit 6-15 shows the activities in the claim process and the medical investigation process as well as the claim personnel who perform the activities.

Exhibit 6-15
Claim Process and Medical Investigation Process and Activities

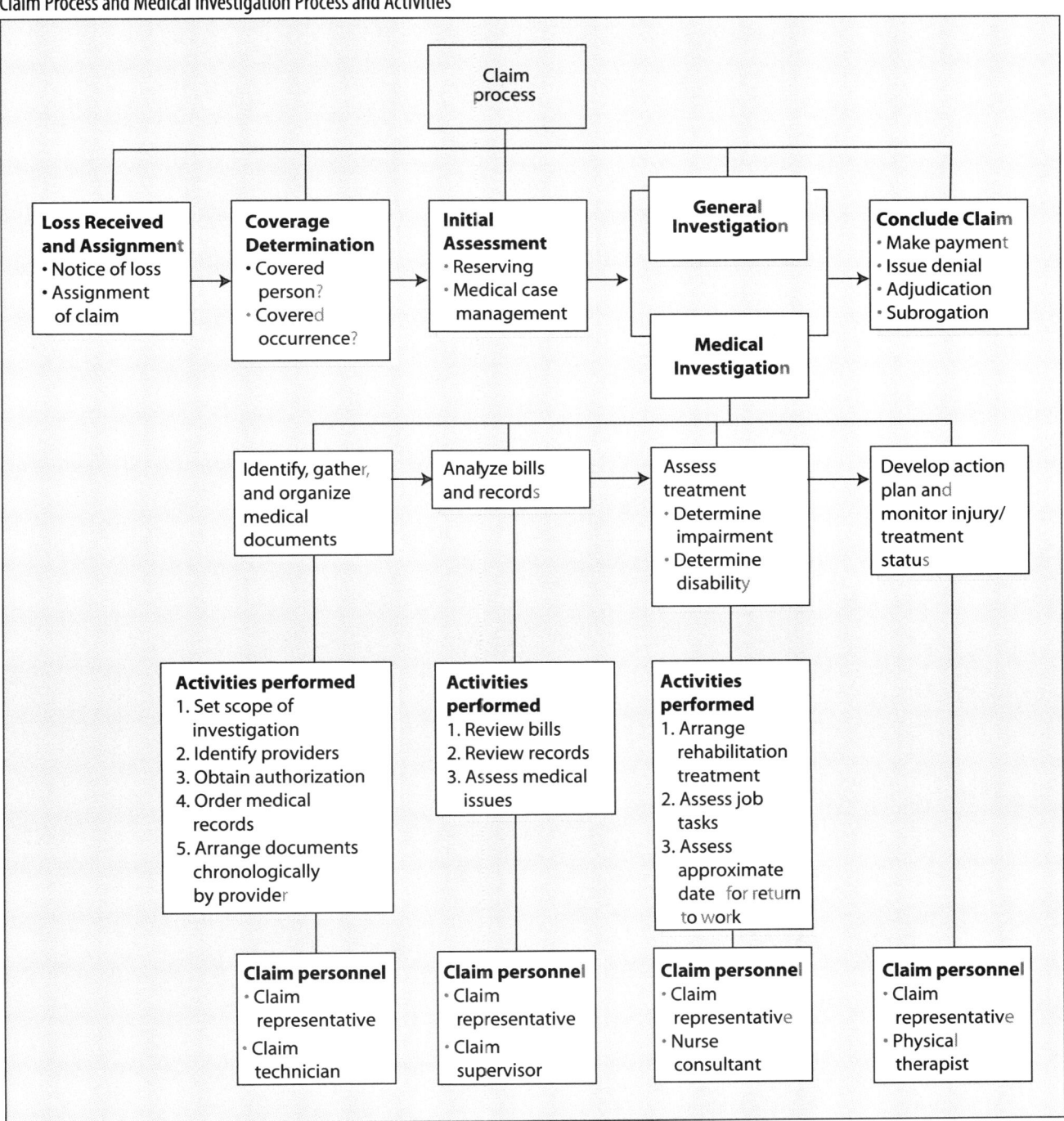

Chapter Notes

1. National Safety Council, "Accident Facts" (Itasco, IL: National Safety Council, 1998), p. 57.
2. Insurance Research Council, "Auto Injuries: Claiming Behavior and its Impact on Insurance Costs" (Oak Brook, IL: Insurance Research Council, 1994), p. 38.
3. T.C. Kwiatkowski, E.N. Hanks Jr., and W.K. Ramp, "Cigarette Smoking and Its Consequences," *American Journal of Orthopedic Medicine* (September 25, 1996), pp. 590-597.

Chapter 7—Case Study

Investigation of Causation (The Hip and Lower Extremities)

This case study involves a case with questionable causation. The claimant in this case, Mr. Thomas, was involved in a motor vehicle accident caused by an insured of Best Insurance Company. Paul, the claim representative for Best Insurance, verified coverage and liability for the accident based on the police report and the claimant's and insured's statements.

At first the claim seemed straightforward, involving only minor property and bodily injury damage. Paul received an estimate to repair Mr. Thomas's car and an emergency room (ER) bill for treatment of a sprained ankle and a contusion to the knee. Paul was prepared to pay the claim based on these documents and any follow-up medical bills with no further investigation, as is customary with uncomplicated claims.

Two weeks after the accident, Paul received a letter from Dr. Baker, Mr. Thomas's orthopedist. A brief moment of panic ensued as Paul read Dr. Baker's letter. Dr. Baker claimed that the accident caused Mr. Thomas to sustain a hip injury. Paul shook his head in disbelief; this was the first he had known of a hip injury. He could not believe he had misjudged Mr. Thomas's liability claim so completely. Exhibit 7-1 shows Dr. Baker's letter.

Exhibit 7-1
Letter From Claimant's Physician

ORTHOPEDIC Consultants
Kevin Baker, M.D.—Don Hur, M.D.
American Board of Orthopaedic Surgery

September 30, 1996

Paul Robinson
Best Insurance Company
2000 Industrial Drive
Kempshire, PA 19033

Re: Allen Thomas
DOI: 9-16-96

> **MVA** is a motor vehicle accident.

Dear Mr. Robinson:

Today I saw Allen Thomas. As you are aware he was involved in a MVA on 9-16-96. At that time he was taken by ambulance to General Hospital and treated for a sprain to his right ankle.

He complains today of serious pain in his left hip and decreased sensation in the left leg. After an exam, it was determined that he did not have an acute fracture of the left femoral neck but he may have suffered impaction of the femoral head, which already had severe degenerative changes secondary to his avascular necrosis.

During examination, he had exquisite pain in the L. hip radiating to his L. groin and L. buttock. The patient was unable to move hip due to pain. I attempted passive range of motion evaluation beginning with Faber's, but the patient was unable to tolerate flexion of left hip beyond 30°.

Obviously, Mr. Thomas had an injury to his left hip secondary to his MVA. Mr. Thomas is now totally disabled. He takes Percocet tabs for pain and has been instructed on crutch walking. He can bear no weight on the lower left extremity. He is scheduled for a total hip arthroplasty for next week.

> **Hip arthroplasty** is an expensive operation that may require the replacement of the hip joint with a prosthesis, or artificial hip joint.

Sincerely,

Kevin Baker, M.D.

Medical Investigation

 *What investigative issues does this letter prompt?*

When Paul had last talked to Mr. Thomas, his only complaint was a sprained right ankle. He reviewed the letter again to make sure that he had not missed anything.

He noted the following:

- The date of the letter from Dr. Baker (the orthopedic doctor) was September 30, 1996, and the accident date was September 16, 1996.
- Mr. Thomas did not have an acute (sudden) fracture of the femoral neck (where the leg meets the pelvis), but the femoral neck may have been wedged into the pelvis.
- Mr. Thomas had severe deterioration of the leg secondary to (caused by or related to) avascular necrosis.
- In Dr. Baker's opinion, Mr. Thomas is totally disabled secondary to his motor vehicle accident.
- Mr. Thomas is having a total hip arthroplasty next week.

> **Taber's Definitions**
>
> **Avascular**: Lacking in blood vessels or having a poor blood supply.
>
> **Necrosis**: Death of areas of tissue or bone surrounded by healthy parts; death in mass as distinguished from necrobiosis, which is gradual deterioration. Term is usually applied to bone destruction or small areas of tissue, while gangrene is applied to larger areas.
>
> **ETIOL**: Insufficient blood supply; physical agents such as trauma, radiant energy, chemical agents acting locally or inserted into wrong tissues.

ETIOL is short for etiology, which refers to the causes of diseases.

Paul considers the following causation issues:

1) Is there an intervening cause for Mr. Thomas's hip injury?
2) Is the hip injury a preexisting injury from a previous accident or possibly a chronic problem unrelated to trauma? (Is this operation required as a result of the accident or is it a recurring problem unrelated to the accident?)

Intervening Cause

To determine whether there was an intervening cause of the hip injury, Paul ran a bodily injury index check to see whether Mr. Thomas had been involved in any accidents since the September 16 accident. The index check showed no "hits" (no recorded claim activity). Paul set aside the possibility of an intervening cause and continued to search for another explanation.

Paul decided to get some direction in investigating these issues. He took the case to his supervisor, Al Gorman.

Paul: Al, I've got an auto liability claim here where the claimant is preparing to have a hip operation. He wants us to authorize payment for the operation. I know we don't normally do that, but there is clear liability on the part of our insured, and there is a possibility that we can manage this claim if we authorize this. I'm just not sure that the injury is accident-related. I was thinking we should probably set up an independent medical exam to see whether the hip injury is related to the covered accident or even necessary. I know I need to coordinate that with Jennie [the nurse consultant] and Phil [the litigation manager], but I wanted to run it by you first.

Al: [Thumbing through the medical documents.] Before we get an independent medical exam, I'd like to have a better understanding of what we are talking about. It looks like we've skipped a few steps. Why don't you put these medical records in order and string together a time line to give us a better understanding of the sequence of events? I'll call Jennie and Phil and set up a meeting with them for tomorrow. Go over the file material and give us a brief report on the issues involved.

Paul returned to his desk and began preparing for tomorrow's conference. The letter from Dr. Baker had prompted Paul to begin assessing the impairment and disability to Mr. Thomas. As his supervisor pointed out, Paul had skipped a few steps of the medical investigation process. Before assessing Mr. Thomas's treatment, impairment, and disability (Step 3 in the medical investigation process), Paul should identify, gather, and organize the medical documents (Step 1) and then analyze them (Step 2). In addition to medical documents, claim representatives should also examine police reports and statements. These may contain information about the injury or accident that clarifies the cause of the injury. In this case, a police report was written immediately after the accident, and Mr. Thomas's statement was taken on September 21.

Preexisting Conditions

Although an intervening cause for Mr. Thomas's hip injury seemed unlikely, a preexisting condition was still a possibility. Paul reviewed the file material chronologically to see whether he had failed to gather any documents. He realized that he needed to order a few medical documents that might help piece things together. The claim file contained the following documents:

1. September 16—Police report stating that Mr. Thomas complained of soreness to the right ankle and left knee and was taken to General Hospital by ambulance
2. September 16—General Hospital medical bill for treatment of sprained right ankle and contusion on left knee
3. September 21—Claimant's statement confirming pain in his right ankle and left knee after the accident (no other complaints)
4. September 30—Dr. Baker's letter claiming that Mr. Thomas's hip injury was caused by the September 16 MVA and that Mr. Thomas was scheduled for hip replacement surgery the following week

Until Paul received Dr. Baker's letter on September 30, Mr. Thomas's claim seemed logical and straightforward—the type of claim that could be settled without gathering and analyzing more medical documents. Because Dr. Baker's letter did not logically follow, Paul requested the following medical documents:

- Ambulance report
- ER report (with admission face sheet)

- Dr. Baker's office notes on Mr. Thomas for six months before the accident

Paul requested the ER report and the admission face sheet by phone and received them immediately by fax.

> **What information contained in the emergency room records could help clarify the issues in this claim?**

As stated in Chapter 6, the ER admission face sheet accompanies the ER report. It contains personal data about the patient, such as name, address, employer, Social Security number, and health insurance carrier, if there is one. The admission face sheet for Mr. Thomas, shown in Exhibit 7-2, indicated that he had no health insurance.

Next, Paul began to analyze the ER report, shown in Exhibit 7-3. The HISTORY OF PRESENT ILLNESS indicated that the claimant was unemployed. During the ER examination, Mr. Thomas complained about his right ankle and his left knee. The report indicated no other complaints.

The MEDICAL HISTORY indicated that, in 1992, Mr. Thomas had been diagnosed with a crack in the neck of the femur caused by a fall. This required surgery that Dr. Kevin Baker had performed. Paul made a note to request medical records related to the surgery.

The DIAGNOSIS indicated a Grade II sprained right ankle and a contusion to the left knee. Again, no injury to the hip was indicated. Paul wondered what the natural progression of a "pinned" hip would be, four years after the fact. Would Mr. Thomas have needed surgery on the left hip eventually without the motor vehicle accident?

After analyzing the ER report and face sheet and reviewing the other contents of the claim file, Paul became increasingly convinced that the hip injury was a preexisting condition unrelated to the auto accident. Based on this assessment, Paul began to prepare a claim status report to present to his supervisor, the nurse consultant, and the litigation manager.

Legal and Medical Issues

At the meeting, Paul's claim status report prompted some discussion of legal and medical issues.

> *Paul:* Here's a quick summary of the Thomas claim. The insured ran a red light and struck the claimant's car, causing around $1,200 in property damage. The police report indicates that Mr. Thomas complained of soreness in his right ankle and left knee. The claimant was taken to the emergency room from the scene of the accident by ambulance. The ER report states he was treated for a sprain to his right ankle and a contusion to his left

Exhibit 7-2
Emergency Admissions Face Sheet

GENERAL HOSPITAL EMERGENCY DEPARTMENT RECORD

HOSPITAL # 17209	ADMISSION DATE: 16 September 96	TIME: 1534	ARRIVED: Ambulance
NAME: Allen Thomas [X] MALE [ ] FEMALE	MEDICAL PROVIDER Hess/Baker		
ADDRESS: 410 South Street	ALLERGIES: N/K/A		
CITY: Pleasantville STATE: PA			
ZIP CODE: 19029			
PHONE HOME: 367-9543 WORK: 993-4908			
D.O.B.: 5-15-47 AGE: 49			
SOCIAL SECURITY # 593-984-8575	HOME MEDICATIONS: Aldomet 125 ml bid		
NEXT OF KIN: Dean RELATIONSHIP: Son			
FAMILY PHYSICIAN: none			
INSURANCE: none			
EMPLOYER: none	MEDICATIONS GIVEN IN ER: none		
HT: 6'2" WT: 229			
LAST TETANUS: 10 years			
T 98.6 P 68 R 18 BP 150/90			

MEDICAL ORDERS: X-rays left knee, left hip, right ankle

NURSES NOTES:

49-year-old admitted to ER per gurney by Atlantic EMT. VSS.

Known hypertensive taking medication. Complained of pain to left knee and right ankle.

No other complaints offered.

Dr. Hess in to see patient.

Dr. with patient

Patient to X-ray per cart

Patient from X-ray per cart

Dr. in to see patient

Discharge instructions and RX given; ACE to r. ankle.

Instructed on crutches. Weight bear to tolerance r. side

Verbalizes all his instructions

Dismissed per w/c to car with family member

DISCHARGE TIME: 1849   DISPOSITION: Home   CONDITION ON DISCHARGE: Good   HOME INST.: X

NURSE SIGNATURE: *Keena Freeman*

knee. The report indicates no other complaints. The claimant's statement, taken on September 21, confirms the ER report, stating that Mr. Thomas had pain in his right ankle and left knee and had no other complaints. Two weeks after the accident I received a letter from Mr. Thomas's doctor stating that he's scheduled for a left hip replacement. Dr. Baker, Mr. Thomas's doctor, claims the accident caused the hip injury. At no time before did the claimant mention a hip problem. The ER report indicates that he had surgery on his

Exhibit 7-3
Emergency Room Report

DD: 9-16-96   3:34P
ADMISSION DATE: 9-16-96
DISCHARGE DATE: 9-16-96
PATIENT: Allen J. Thomas

Carolyn Hess, M.D.

<u>EMERGENCY DEPARTMENT RECORD</u>

FAMILY PHYSICIAN: None given
CHIEF COMPLAINT: Motor vehicle accident

HISTORY OF PRESENT ILLNESS: 49-year-old white male presents after an auto accident where his auto collided with second auto at an intersection. Patient states he was unrestrained at time of accident. Patient is a machine operator but is currently unemployed. Patient states that right ankle was depressed on brake pedal and that impact caused his right ankle to turn outward. Complains of soreness to top of left knee that impacted with lower dashboard. No other complaints.

ALLERGIES: None

MEDICATIONS: Advil on occasional basis.

MEDICAL HISTORY:
Patient states that in 1992 he was diagnosed with a crack in the neck of the left femur. He underwent surgery with Dr. Kevin Baker, which patient states was a bone graft and a pin in the femur.

SOCIAL HISTORY: He has smoked two packs of cigarettes a day for the past 30 years. He stopped using alcohol two years ago. Before that he was a moderate-heavy drinker for over 30 years.

EXAMINATION: Vital signs as follows: blood pressure 150/90; Height: 6'2"; weight: 229 lbs.

> **HEENT** stands for:
> Head
> Eyes
> Ears
> Nose

HEENT: Head is a traumatic and normal cephalic. Eyes: The pupils are equal and rounded and reacted to light. Extraocular movements are intact. Ears, nose, and throat are normal.

NECK: Supple/no meningeal signs. No thyromegaly. Carotids are without bruits. Cervical range of motion is normal.

CHEST: Clear to auscultation and percussion. No rhonchi, rales, or wheezes.

HEART: Regular rate and rhythm and normal S1 and S2. No S3 or S4. No heaves, clicks, or murmurs.

MUSCULAR SKELETAL: Both hip flexion and extension reveal decreased range of motion on the left side compatible with left hip repair. Radiograph left hip W/N/L. Left knee contusion. Right ankle swollen. X-rays W/N/L.

ASSESSMENT: Sprain to right ankle. Contusion left knee.

PLAN: Tylenol tab 2 Q4 h for the 1st 24 hours for pain then switch to Ibruprofen 800 mg QID po. Rest. Wrap R. ankle in Ace bandage. Elevate R. ankle above level of heart.
Ice to R. ankle for swelling. Walk with crutches only, R. foot bearing partial weight.
Follow up with Kevin Baker, M.D., orthopedist, in 2 days.

DIAGNOSIS: 1) S/P 1992 hip repair   3) Sprain r. ankle (Grade II)
                2) Hypertension   4) Contusion l. knee

CONDITION ON DISCHARGE: Good, ambulatory with crutches, partial weight bearing, prescriptions and instructions given.

Signed, Dr. Carolyn Hess, M.D.

left femur with this same doctor in 1992. I have ordered a report on the femur surgery as well as Dr. Baker's office notes on the claimant for the six months before the accident.

The claimant has $300,000 liability limit, so we have a significant coverage exposure. I think we need to get an IME on Mr. Thomas. I'm just not sure which doctor to use and when we should do it.

Jennie [nurse consultant]: You said he was taken away by ambulance. What did the ambulance EMTs [Emergency Medical Technicians] find? They usually do a pretty good job of triage at the scene, and if Mr. Thomas had a complaint, that probably would have been noted. What does the ambulance report say?

Paul: I knew you were going to ask me that. I've ordered that but I haven't gotten it yet. When I receive the ambulance report, I'll check to see whether it mentions any pain in the left hip. For now, we need to discuss whether we should order an IME. Mr. Thomas is scheduled for hip replacement surgery next week, so if we want to use the IME report to determine if this is accident-related, we need to act fast.

Al: Are we even sure that he needs a hip replacement? I was thinking we should get an IME to make sure that's even necessary.

Phil [legal consultant]: Wait a minute. I think the courts in this state are only going to give you one shot at an IME, and you'll probably want to save that until after the operation to see what his final disability will be.

Al: Are you sure that we can't get a limited IME just to determine whether the surgery is required? We're not even sure that it's necessary.

Phil: I don't think so. The court of appeals in this state just ruled against that. Have you approached the patient about getting a second opinion on whether this surgery is necessary? It seems like he would voluntarily want to do that. What's his attorney saying?

Paul: I forgot to mention, he's unrepresented so far as I can tell. I talked to Mr. Thomas after I got the letter and asked him if he was going to get a second opinion about the operation, but he said that he was going to do whatever Dr. Baker told him to do.

Al: Send a letter to Mr. Thomas confirming that we will pay for a second opinion. Explain that we are still investigating this and can't commit to any payment for the hip injury at this point.

Jennie: [Thumbing through some medical records] My guess is that he probably does need a hip replacement. The ER report says the claimant smoked two packs a day for thirty years. That affects the healing process. It also says that he used to be a heavy drinker, and alcoholism is another risk factor for bone degeneration.

Paul: The admission sheet says that he has no health insurance to cover this. I think we might have a case of a sympathetic doctor trying to shift the cost of this hip replacement over to us. I think we should pay for the sprained ankle but deny the hip injury claim. The guy had all these problems beforehand.

Phil: Let me play the devil's advocate. The law says we have to take the claimants as we find them. If this accident aggravated his condition then we're going to owe for that aggravation.

Al: But we only owe to get him back to the condition he was in before the accident, and at this point we're not sure what that condition was.

Paul: What if I write a letter to his doctor asking for an explanation as to how and to what extent the accident caused this?

Al: You should do that, but I'm not sure that Dr. Baker will be able to give you an objective opinion. Get together with Jennie and Phil and come up with a high quality orthopedic surgeon to perform an IME on the claimant. If we can't get the IME twice then set it up for after the surgery. Phil, check with our legal counsel to make sure that the orthopedic surgeon you pick can present well to a jury if this goes to trial. Paul, work with Jennie on drafting a letter to Dr. Baker asking for the necessary information to evaluate this claim. Thank you all for your time. [The conference breaks up.]

Jennie: Phil, you know Dr. Geller, don't you? He's got good credentials. He's done some IMEs for us before. I know he's really personable because I've had claimants call me after some of his IMEs and ask if they could use him as their treating physician. That's got to help with getting these settled.

Phil: Yeah, and he makes a good appearance in court, too.

[Phil approaches Paul after the meeting] *Phil:* Hey Paul, there were a couple of other things I thought about. What about the police report? Did it mention injuries?

Paul: It said that he complained of soreness to the right ankle and left knee.

Al: Now, as I remember, he told you in his statement that his right ankle and left knee hurt, right?

> **Biomechanics** refers to the science that integrates physics and human anatomy. It is used to help determine whether an impact is severe enough to have caused an alleged injury.

Paul: That's right. On 9-21 he told me that he had sprained his right ankle and the left knee was just bruised.

Phil: What does the damage to the two cars look like? What direction were the cars headed when they collided? We've won some cases on **biomechanics** issues. If you've got photos of very minor vehicle damage to show the jury, I think it gets to the credibility issue.

Paul: The claimant had an estimate for $1,200 that we paid. At the time, I didn't think we needed to send an appraiser out for that amount. The insured doesn't have collision coverage so we didn't photograph that damage either. Anyway, the damage was serious enough for him to get a sprained ankle.

Phil: [Turning to Paul] If the claimant needs a hip replacement because of the accident, I'd like to see photos showing the impact damage to the cars.

Paul: I'll see if the cars are still available to be inspected.

Questioning Claimants' Doctors

Medical consultants or company medical personnel are good resources for claim representatives when questioning claimants' doctors. A nurse consultant can help delineate the issues and potential problems in a bodily injury claim. Claim representatives should consult a staff medical expert when drafting letters to claimants' doctors.

In the Thomas case, Jennie suggests that Paul include the following in a letter to Dr. Baker:

A. Questions:
1. What are the history and nature of this hip injury? (There are many types of hip injuries, each having its own treatment and prognosis.)
2. How did this accident aggravate the hip injury specifically?
3. To what degree did the accident aggravate this hip injury based on the facts of this accident?
4. What is Dr. Baker's professional opinion on whether this operation would have been required, irrespective of the accident, and when it would have been required?

B. Documents requested (based on the patient's authorizing the release of documents):
1. Prior office notes
2. Hospital admission history and physical examination report from 1992 hip "pinning" operation
3. Operative report from 1992
4. X-ray report
5. Pathology report
6. Discharge summary
7. History from 1992 to current of hip-related problems

Mr. Thomas had the left hip arthroplasty on October 4. He retained an attorney when Paul suggested that he submit to an independent medical exam (IME).

Independent Medical Exams

In this case, the court limited the insurer to one IME, which Paul and Al opted to use after the hip operation to determine the claimant's impairment. Others might rightfully believe that it should have been used before the surgery, as this would have been the best opportunity to show a causal connection or lack of it. It would be perhaps the only opportunity to assess whether the procedure was needed. The necessity of a procedure is difficult to argue after the procedure has already been performed.

The limitation of one IME varies by jurisdiction, and claim representatives should understand its consequences. The timing of the IME is based on several medical and legal factors, and the appropriate personnel should be consulted when planning an IME. A mistimed IME is a serious disadvantage to the insurance company.

Because insurers are often limited to one IME per claim, it is important that the doctor performing the IME has the necessary information before the exam. Nurse consultants can help draft the IME request letter to ensure that the necessary information is included. That assistance ensures that:

- The proper medical background is given.
- The purpose and scope of the IME are properly defined.
- Complete medical documentation is included with the request.
- Questions are properly phrased for the examiner/reviewer.

The selection of an IME doctor is equally important to the claim. The selection criteria for IME doctors were covered in Chapter 2. In this case, Dr. Geller was selected to perform the IME. Jennie helped Paul write the IME request letter to Dr. Geller. The IME request letter is shown in Exhibit 7-4, and Dr. Geller's letter stating the results of the IME is shown in Exhibit 7-5.

Negotiation and Mediation

Dr. Geller had difficulty getting some medical records from Mr. Thomas and his physician. The medical records should be marked for **discovery**, should the case proceed to litigation.

Dr. Geller examined Mr. Thomas two-and-one-half months after the hip operation. He seemed to be recuperating well but had not reached maximum medical improvement (MMI) regarding his hip. Dr. Geller pointed out later in his report that he had reached MMI with respect to the right ankle sprain and the left knee contusion. The most important part of Dr. Geller's findings was that the left hip condition was not related to the accident on September 16, 1996. Dr. Geller

---

In legal terms, **discovery** is a process sanctioned by the court requiring the disclosure of facts, documents, and other evidence by one litigant to another. Some methods of discovery include:

- Depositions
- Interrogatories
- Requests for production of documents

Exhibit 7-4
Letter Requesting the IME

December 13, 1996

Samuel Geller, M.D.
Atlantic Medical Orthopedics
Atlantic Medical Center
101 Historic Way
Philadelphia, PA 19016-4273

Re: Allen Thomas
    Claim #: 2653013-A
    DOI: 9-16-96

Dear Dr. Geller:

The above-captioned claimant, Allen Thomas, has an appointment to be examined by you for a second opinion on 1/8/97. The primary purpose of this examination is for you to review all clinical data and accident facts and determine the nature and extent of Mr. Thomas's MVA-related injuries and what treatment protocol and time frames are necessary for him to achieve MMI.

The accident facts are as follows: Mr. Thomas, a 49-year-old, unemployed machinist was the seat-and-shoulder-restrained driver (although the ER report indicated he was unrestrained) of a 1980 Oldsmobile Delta 88. A 1992 Chevrolet Corsica driven by our insured struck him in the rear bumper. The damage to the Oldsmobile was approximately $1,200, but the vehicle was driven from the scene. Photos of Mr. Thomas's vehicle are enclosed. No photos of the Corsica are available.

Mr. Thomas was listed as injured on the police report and was evaluated at the scene by Atlantic Emergency Transport, and determined to have sustained a contusion to the left knee from striking the dashboard, and a sprained right ankle. He was transported to General Hospital Emergency Department where he was treated and released with instructions to follow up with his orthopedist, Kevin Baker, M.D., on or around 9-18-96.

Best Insurance Company had no indication that Mr. Thomas followed up with Dr. Baker, nor any other physician, until 9-30-96. At that time, Dr. Baker concluded Mr. Thomas suffered an injury to his left hip secondary to the 9-16-96 MVA and needed a total left hip replacement.

Please examine Mr. Thomas and review all the enclosed accident facts, vehicle photos, and clinical data from the 9-16-96 MVA, including Mr. Thomas's prior orthopedic history of his left hip. Please send a full report of your findings to me answering the following questions as outlined within all degree of reasonable medical certainty:

1. According to the accident facts and clinical data, what injuries did Mr. Thomas sustain as a direct result of the 9-16-96 MVA?

2. What clinical data and accident facts substantiate that Mr. Thomas sustained injury to his left hip as a direct result of the 9-16-96 MVA?

3. In your opinion, was the need for Mr. Thomas's left hip arthroplasty of 10-4-96 a result of the 9-16-96 MVA? What clinical data and accident facts support or refute this opinion?

4. What permanent physical restriction(s), if any, did Mr. Thomas sustain as a result of the 9-16-96 MVA?

5. In your opinion, what period of time would Mr. Thomas have been unable to work as a direct result of the 9-16-96 MVA? Please specify time frames.

6. Is Mr. Thomas at MMI with regard to any MVA-related injuries that he sustained on 9-16-96?
    A. If so, on what date did Mr. Thomas achieve MMI?
    B. If not, what specific treatment protocol and time frames would he require in order to attain MMI?
7. In your opinion, for what period of time, if any, would Mr. Thomas have been unable to perform his avocational and/or daily living activities as a direct result of any MVA-related injury(ies) sustained on 9-16-96?

Thank you for seeing Mr. Thomas. Should you need to order any diagnostic tests on Mr. Thomas in order to complete this evaluation, please know that this letter serves as authorization for you to do so. Please contact me at the number listed below if you need additional information or have any questions regarding this letter.

Sincerely,

Paul Robinson, Claim Rep.
Best Insurance Company

Enclosures

Exhibit 7-5
Results of the IME

Atlantic Medical Center

Samuel Geller, M.D.
Keith Goldstine, M.D.
101 Historic Way
Philadelphia, PA 19016

January 8, 1997

Paul Robinson
Best Insurance Company
2000 Industrial Dr.
Kempshire, PA 19033

Re: Allen Thomas
DOI: 9-16-96

Dear Mr. Robinson:

I performed an independent medical exam at Atlantic Medical Center on Allen Thomas. I derived the following history from the patient. Mr. Thomas did not bring all of the medical records, but he did bring X-rays taken one week before the September 16, 1996, accident. Before Mr. Thomas's exam, I made repeated attempts to contact Dr. Baker at his office regarding the claimant's records, but without response.

I did review all accident facts and clinical data that you sent with your December 13, 1996, letter.

His history is remarkable for avascular necrosis of the left hip s/p total hip replacement in October 1996. The patient had no significant difficulties in his recuperation phase of the total hip replacement. He did not attend formal physical therapy. He is not doing any exercises at home.

Continued on next page.

Mr. Thomas's work history reveals that he had worked as a machine operator at Morgan Glass for ten years. He was recently laid off. His family history reveals his parents are deceased from cancer, his wife is alive, and they have three children. Social history reveals he smokes two packs of cigarettes per day. He was a moderate to heavy drinker for thirty years but stopped drinking two years ago. He completed high school. His systemic review is negative.

On examination, this is a tall, well-nourished, 49-year-old white male who walks with a slight limp on the left side without the use of a cane. His height is 6'2"; weight is 229 pounds, blood pressure 150/90. He is able to toe and heel walk. Reflexes, sensation, strength, and circulation of the upper extremities are normal.

Motions of the hips, ankles, and feet are normal and painless. Straight leg raising left at 90 degrees causes pain in the back of the left lower thigh. Patellar and Achilles reflexes, right and left, are normal. Sensation, strength, and circulation of the lower extremities are normal. Romberg, Clonus, and Babinski tests are negative.

The prognosis for Mr. Thomas is fairly good. The patient is now about two-and-one-half months post total left hip replacement. He is walking with a slight limp on the left and uses no cane.

The patient's medical condition and/or problems with his left hip are preexisting. His treatment to date has been appropriate and necessary. Future therapy is probably not needed. The patient will be able to do light duty or medium work in about one month. The patient has not yet reached MMI regarding his left hip.

ASSESSMENT:
1. Left hip arthroplasty
2. Hypertension
3. Resolved right ankle sprain
4. Resolved left knee contusion

I shall answer the questions posed to me in your December 13, 1996, correspondence. The answers to these questions, as well as my examination of Mr. Thomas, are given within all degree of reasonable medical certainty:

1. Review of all clinical data and accident facts substantiates that Mr. Thomas sustained a right ankle sprain and contusion to the left kneecap as a direct result of the 9/16/96 MVA.

2. There is no evidence that the MVA of 9/16/96 in any way caused or aggravated Mr. Thomas's preexisting left hip condition.

3. No. The prior clinical data from 1992 indicated that Mr. Thomas would eventually need a total hip replacement as Dr. Baker's first follow-up post operative report of Mr. Thomas stated on 4/4/92: "I explained to the patient that because of his young age (44) and activity level, the hip pinning was a temporary fix and that arthroplasty, including total left hip replacement, would be probable within the next 5 years." X-rays taken on 9/9/96 indicated avascular necrosis.

4. None. Mr. Thomas has no permanent physical restrictions as a result of the 9/16/96 MVA.

5. In my opinion, Mr. Thomas would have been precluded from work activity as a direct result of the MVA-related injuries from MVA date, 9/16/96, until 9/30/96. Dr. Baker's findings on 9/30/96 obviously relate to Mr. Thomas's preexisting condition, which in my opinion was not aggravated by the MVA.

6. In my opinion, Mr. Thomas attained MMI with regard to both his contused left knee and right ankle sprain on 9/30/96.
    a. as answered above
    b. as answered above

7. In my opinion, Mr. Thomas would have possibly needed help mowing the lawn and may have needed to be driven places by his wife or others from the date of the MVA, 9/16/96, until 9/30/96.

If there are any further questions, please feel free to call me.

Very truly yours,

Samuel Geller, M.D.

refers to X-rays taken one week before the accident that indicate aseptic necrosis. He also refers to a medical report that he received from Dr. Baker that stated that the hip pinning that Mr. Thomas received in 1992 was only a temporary fix lasting up to five years and that eventually the claimant would need a total left hip arthroplasty.

Armed with the information from Dr. Geller, Paul called the claimant's attorney. Paul offered to pay the special damages (including the ambulance and ER visit) and general damages (pain and suffering) related to the sprained right ankle and bruised left knee.

Unfortunately, the claimant's attorney was not convinced by Dr. Geller's findings and stated that Dr. Baker was still willing to testify that, in his medical opinion, the accident aggravated the left hip problem. Dr. Baker did not indicate how or to what extent this had occurred. A few days passed and the claimant's attorney called back asking whether Paul would be willing to go to **mediation**.

Mediation is an alternative to litigation. It can be thought of as a conference with a referee, the mediator. The mediator's role is not to decide the case but instead to facilitate discussions and to try to get the two sides to reach an amicable agreement.

What could each side gain from mediation in this case?

Paul decided to take the claim to his supervisor to get his opinion on how to proceed.

Paul: Al, I haven't been able to settle the Thomas claim. His attorney doesn't accept Dr. Geller's findings. He says that Dr. Baker will testify that the accident aggravated the left hip problem. Dr. Baker hasn't provided a written explanation of how and to what extent this occurred. The attorney asked me if I would mediate this. I'm not sure what benefit mediation would be since we've already made a fair offer based on what we know.

Al: Well, I'm willing to try anything, short of overpaying the claim, to avoid litigation. Actually my experience with mediation has been great, especially for cases like this. With all of the medical testimony and the discovery issues involved in this case, it would be expensive to take to trial. I'm sure his attorney realizes this too and is willing to take a chance on mediation. There's also the possibility that he has a client-control problem. He might be having a hard time convincing Mr. Thomas that this claim isn't worth a fortune. Maybe he's thinking that if Mr. Thomas sees everything laid out in front of him and hears the mediator point out the weaknesses in the case, he'll become a little more reasonable. Probably wishful thinking, but if the alternative is going to trial, I think it's worth trying mediation. Another benefit is that you'll get a chance to see what kind of witness the claimant would make. Mediation can give you a chance to see what ammunition they really have. If Baker comes through for them, then we'll have to reevaluate our position. You'll need to do a good job of organizing your presentation. You should become familiar with each of the injuries, the arthroplasty procedure, and the anatomy of the injured parts, so that you can talk intelligently about them. I recommend you mediate this. It works!

The major point of contention in the case is whether the accident aggravated the injury. The settlement value of the claim would change dramatically if the accident aggravated the preexisting condition. The burden of proof in this case would be on Mr. Thomas to prove that his condition actually changed for the worse because of this accident.

Anatomy, Trauma, Treatment, and Disability

Paul prepares for mediation, as Al suggested, by familiarizing himself with the anatomy and trauma facts related to this claim. Paul reviews the sprained ankle injury information first.

The Sprained Ankle

A sprain occurs when a muscle, tendon, or ligament moves past its normal range of motion and stretches or tears. **Ligaments** are tough bands of dense fibrous tissue that connect bones to other bones. **Tendons** differ from ligaments in that they connect muscles to bones. Because the blood supply to ligaments and tendons is limited and because ligaments and tendons have fewer nerve endings than other types of tissue, injuries to ligaments and tendons heal extremely slowly. They are also extremely painful because the affected areas generally play such an important part in the movement of the extremities.

In Mr. Thomas's case, the **talofibular ligament** (the ligament connecting the talus and the fibula) was stretched.

The **talus** is the anklebone. The **fibula** is the long, slender bone on the lateral aspect of the lower leg. The fibula bears only 5 percent of the weight of the body. The **tibia**, or shinbone, is the large bone of the lower leg. The wide, smooth base (bottom) of the tibia connects to the talus and the fibula, but the head (top) of the tibia does not connect to the fibula. Exhibit 7-6 shows the lower leg and ankle.

Treatment of Sprains

Sprains are graded on a scale of I to III. Grade III sprains, when the ligament actually tears, normally require surgical repair. Grade I and II sprains, where the ligament is stretched or partially torn, can normally be treated conservatively with good results.

Exhibit 7-6
The Lower Leg and Ankle

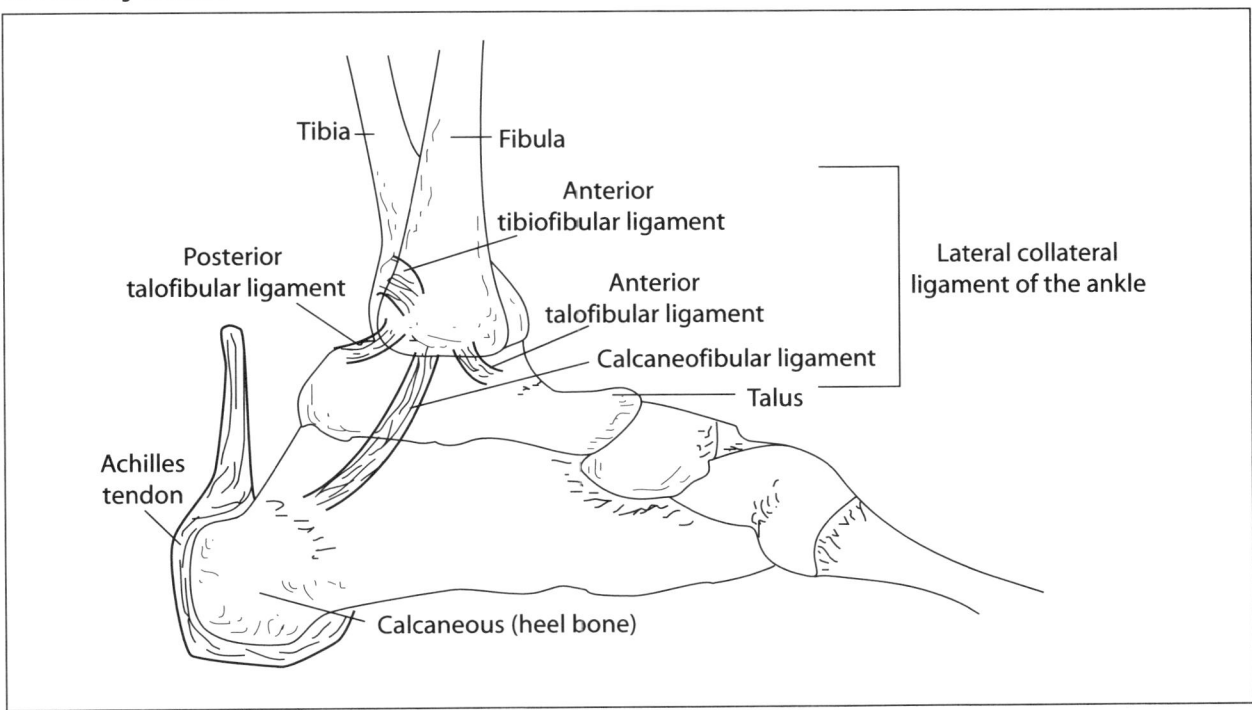

Conservative treatment includes resting, taking mild pain relievers, wrapping the injured area with an Ace bandage, elevating (above the heart) the affected area, and icing the area with cold packs to alleviate the edema (swelling). Heat should be avoided during the first forty-eight hours as it will increase the swelling.

After the swelling has decreased, a cast may be applied. The type and duration of the cast depend on the location of the torn ligament and the activity level of the patient. If a non-weight-bearing cast is used, it can be replaced with a walking cast after three to four weeks. When the walking cast is removed, an air splint may be worn for an additional three to nine weeks. An air splint limits joint mobility. Rehabilitation, including physical therapy, will often follow to restore strength and range of motion.

Disability Related to Sprains

For mild to moderate sprains (Grades I and II), the disability should rarely exceed four weeks and is usually much less. *The Medical Disability Advisor* lists the expected disability length according to job classification, as shown in Exhibit 7-7. Any diagnosis of a sprain without a torn ligament diagnosis in which symptoms persist for more than one month requires an additional explanation. The affected patient may be suffering from a recurring sprain or may have a more serious problem that has not been properly diagnosed or treated. In this case, the opinion of Dr. Geller (the physician who performed the IME) was that the claimant had MMI on September 30, two weeks after the accident.

Exhibit 7-7
Disability Related to Ankle Sprains

First or second-degree (mild to moderate) sprain or strain. May not be disabling.			
Job Classification	**Minimum Expectancy**	**Optimum**	**Maximum Expectancy**
Sedentary work	1 Day	7 Days	14 Days
Light work	1 Day	7 Days	14 Days
Medium work	7 Days	7 Days	14 Days
Heavy work	14 Days	21 Days	42 Days
Very heavy work	14 Days	21 Days	42 Days
Third-degree (severe) sprain or strain (other than Achilles tendon rupture).			
Job Classification	**Minimum Expectancy**	**Optimum**	**Maximum Expectancy**
Sedentary work	1 Day	3 Days	7 Days
Light work	1 Day	21 Days	42 Days
Medium work	14 Days	28 Days	56 Days
Heavy work	28 Days	56 Days	112 Days
Very heavy work	28 Days	56 Days	112 Days

Reprinted with permission from *The Medical Disability Advisor: Workplace Guidelines for Disability Duration*, Third edition (1997), Presley Reed, M.D. © Reed Group, Ltd. Boulder, CO. (800) 347-7443. All rights reserved. http://www.rgl.net

The Hip Injury

In Dr. Baker's opinion, the MVA aggravated Mr. Thomas's hip joint injury. To determine whether the accident could have caused or aggravated the hip joint injury, Paul must understand the anatomy of the hip joint.

As shown in Exhibit 7-8, the hip joint is the junction between the femur and its socket in the pelvis. The **femur**, or the thighbone, is one of the strongest bones in the body, bearing the weight of the entire upper body. The base of the femur connects with the head of the fibula. The upper, or proximal, end of the femur has a rounded head supported by a narrow neck. The head fits into the **acetabulum**, the cup-shaped socket of the hipbone. When the neck of the femur is fractured, the injury is often referred to as a broken hip. The original letter from Mr. Thomas's doctor referred to the injury of the femur. At the top of the shaft of the femur on the lateral surface is a large protuberance called the **greater trochanter**.

As shown in Exhibit 7-9, the pelvis consists of two hipbones, each of which includes a ball and socket joint. The ball is the head of the femur and the socket is the acetabulum, into which the head of the femur fits. A coating of cartilage and a lubricating agent called **synovial fluid** reduces friction in the hip joint, as in any joint. The flared upper portion of each hipbone is called the ilium. A wedge of this portion of the hipbone is sometimes used as bone graft in spinal vertebrae fusions.

Exhibit 7-8
The Lower Extremities

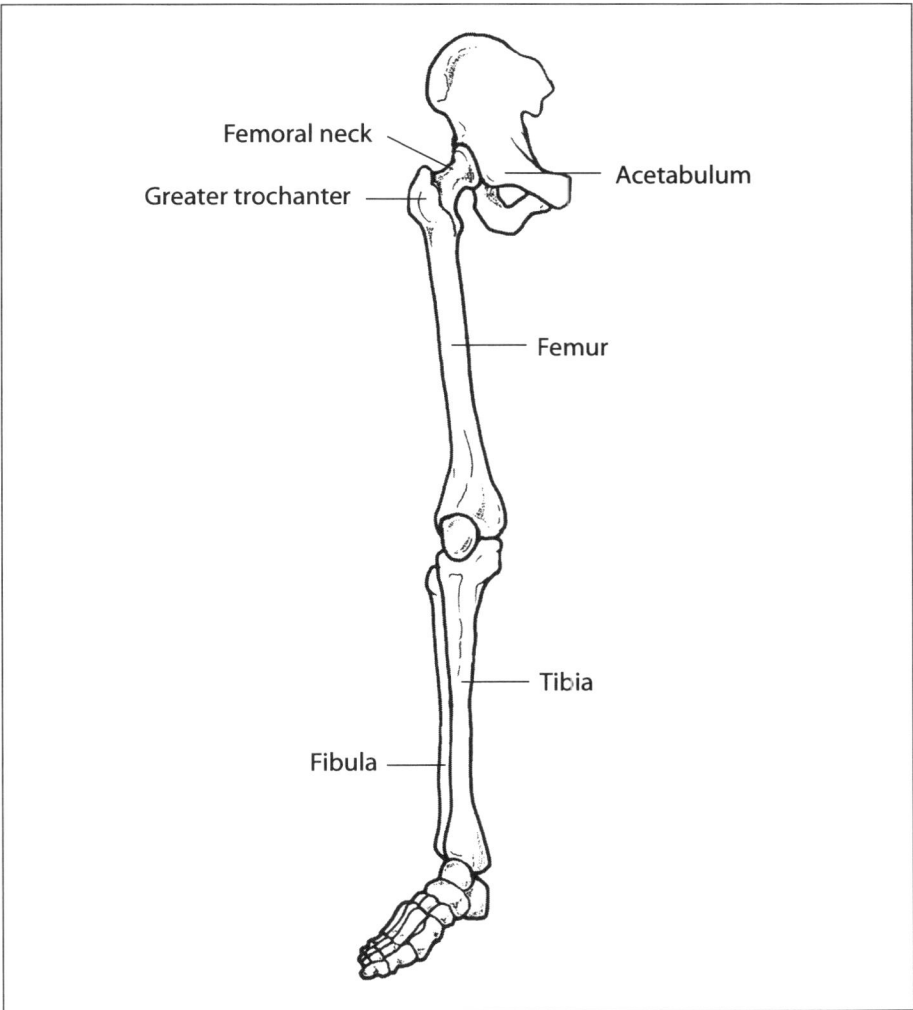

The ischium is the bottom portion of each hipbone. The ischium supports the body in a sitting position. The anterior portion of each hip is called the pubis, which is made up of two bars of bone that meet in a flat body to the front. The bars themselves, referred to as rami, are frequent sites of pelvic fractures.

After reviewing the anatomy, Paul better understood the parts of the body and the claimant's injury.

Hip Joint Replacement

Mr. Thomas is diagnosed with avascular necrosis. Avascular necrosis is one of several reasons for hip replacements. Hip joint replacement can be either total, involving replacement of all surfaces of the joint, or partial, involving replacement of one side of the joint. Mr. Thomas required a total hip replacement. Paul continued his review of the case by studying the surgical procedure of the total hip arthroplasty—replacement of the hip joint with a prosthesis.

> More than 200,000 people in the United States undergo hip joint replacement each year. This number is expected to increase as the population of the U.S. ages.

Exhibit 7-9
The Pelvis

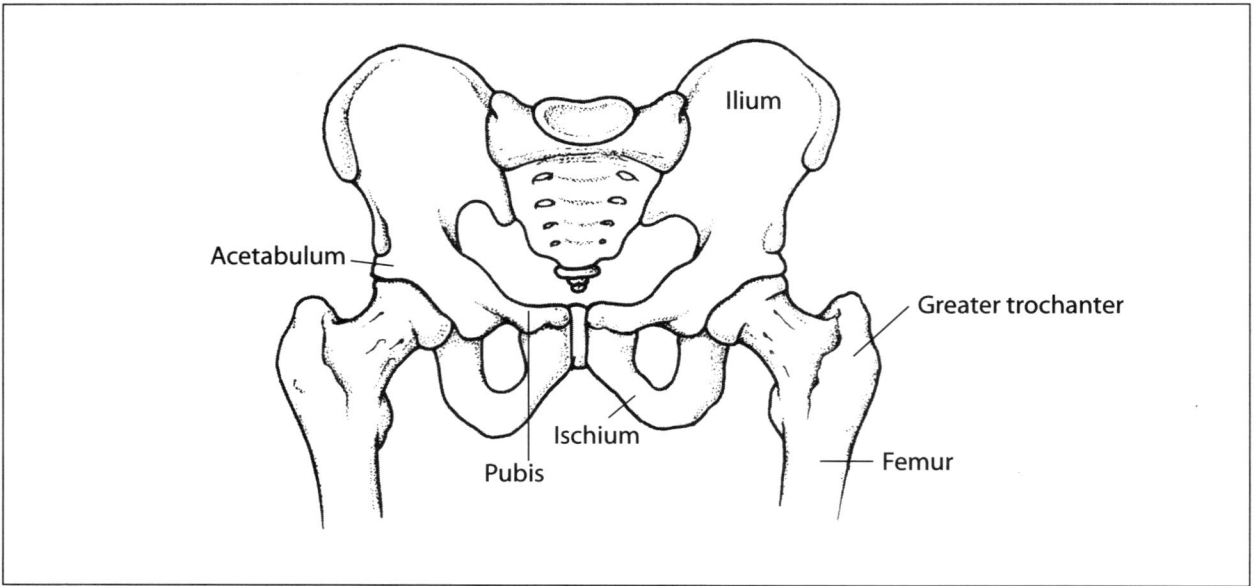

Before hip joint replacement surgery, the patient is given antibiotics to treat any present infections and to prepare the acetabulum for the prosthesis (artificial replacement).

A metal alloy cup with a high-density plastic lining is secured inside the acetaulum. The metal stem of the prosthesis is inserted into the shaft of the femur. Depending on the patient's needs, the stem may be cemented in place with bone cement. Exhibit 7-10 shows the components of a hip joint replacement.

The expected life of hip arthroplasty is not more than ten years. Some of the potential complications include:

- Loosening of the prosthesis
- Rejection or allergic reaction to the replacement material
- Damage to the prothesis
- Mechanical freezing of the joint
- Disintegration of joint material because of the patient's weight, disease, or normal decomposition

Disabilities Related to Hip Replacement

According to *The Medical Disability Advisor*, the claimant's job activity level would fall into the sedentary work category; therefore, the disability period for a hip replacement would range from twenty-eight to eighty-four days after the operation with the average at sixty-three days (see Exhibit 7-11). The treatment would last for about six months. During recovery, the patient would be expected to have physical therapy treatments three times a week for about six to eight weeks.

Exhibit 7-10
Hip Joint Replacement Components

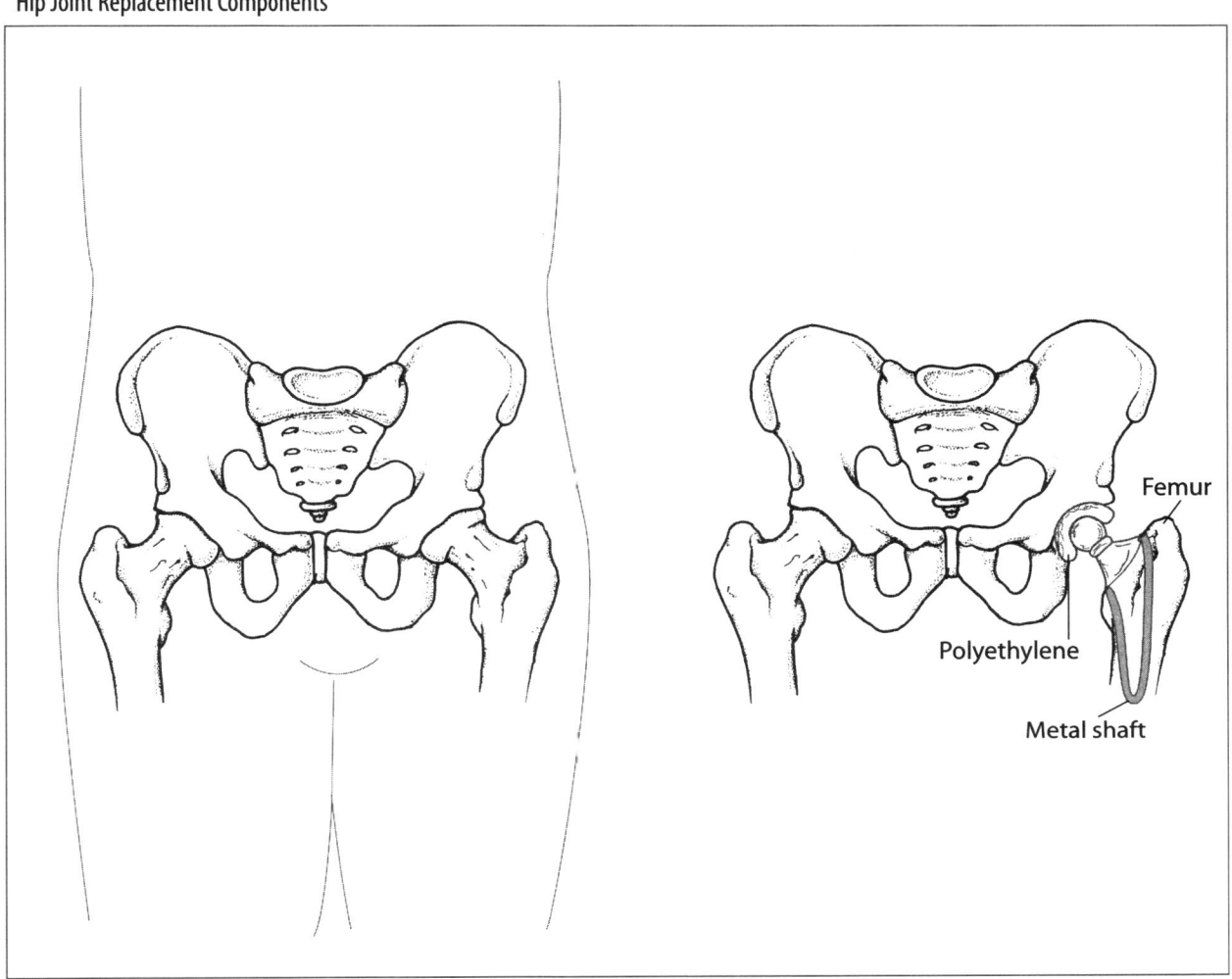

Exhibit 7-11
Disability Related to Hip Joint Replacement

Sedentary and light work can be performed sooner if done sitting. Hip replacement is not compatible with heavy work. Disability may be permanent.			
Job Classification	Minimum Expectancy	Optimum	Maximum Expectancy
Sedentary work	28 Days	63 Days	84 Days
Light work	42 Days	112 Days	140 Days
Medium work	84 Days	112 Days	182 Days
Heavy work	Indefinite	Indefinite	Indefinite
Very heavy work	Indefinite	Indefinite	Indefinite

Reprinted with permission from *The Medical Disability Advisor: Workplace Guidelines for Disability Duration*, Third edition (1997), Presley Reed, M.D. © Reed Group, Ltd. Boulder, CO. (800) 347-7443. All rights reserved. http://www.rgl.net

In this claim, the hip replacement and accompanying disability are unrelated to the accident according to the IME doctor; however, this is still a point of contention in the claim.

Case Conclusion

To Paul's disappointment, a lawsuit was filed shortly after the mediation. A few weeks later, Dr. Baker gave a deposition that was not very convincing. He failed to explain how and to what extent the injury was aggravated by the accident. Near the end of his cross-examination, he admitted that he was unsure whether the accident had affected the ultimate outcome of Mr. Thomas's condition.

The next day, Mr. Thomas accepted a settlement for damages related to the repair of his car and the treatment of his sprained ankle and the contusion to his knee. The settlement included the following special damages: (1) ER and follow-up medical expenses for the ankle and knee injuries and (2) lost wages based on Dr. Geller's assessment of when Mr. Thomas reached MMI with respect to the sprained ankle. Mr. Thomas also collected general damages for pain and suffering caused by the ankle and knee injuries.

Chapter 8—Case Study

Assessing Treatments and Disability (The Knee Injury)

Rob Hanson is a claim representative with River City Insurance, a small regional insurance company. Rob has five years of experience handling auto injury cases. Most of Rob's experience is with minor, neck and back, soft tissue injury claims. A complication arose on one of Rob's workers compensation claims when the claimant-employee, who was receiving treatment for minor cervical trauma, reported that his chiropractor had discovered a knee problem. The claimant, a professional house painter, had been involved in a motor vehicle accident that occurred during the course of employment. Rob wondered whether the motor vehicle accident had caused the knee injury.

Because of Rob's inexperience with knee injury claims and because of the potential liability exposure related to the knee injury, Rob took the claim to his supervisor for guidance. His supervisor, Joanne Moore, arranged for him to meet with Nolan Lanam, an experienced senior claim representative who has handled claims with similar injuries.

Rob: Nolan, I have a workers compensation claim where the claimant was rear-ended. I thought it was a typical soft tissue neck injury claim, but yesterday I received a call from the claimant telling me that he had a knee injury and was going to be off from work for some time. I was hoping you could give me some direction. I understand you've handled a lot of knee injuries.

Nolan: Do you know what kind of knee injury he has?

Rob: I'm not sure what type of injury it is, but the chiropractor said that he tore something. The chiropractor mailed the medical documents, but I haven't received them yet.

Nolan: First of all, it's unusual for a chiropractor to diagnose a knee injury. You'll obviously need an orthopedist's diagnosis. Second, knee injuries are not all the same. Knee tears could involve ligaments, tendons, muscles, or cartilage. How much do you understand about the anatomy of the knee?

Rob: Well, I know there are ligaments, tendons, and a knee cap that's called a patella, but that's about the extent of my knowledge of the knee.

Nolan: Well, let's get you up to speed with the anatomy of the knee first. When you get the medical information, we can then determine exactly what type of knee injury the claimant has.

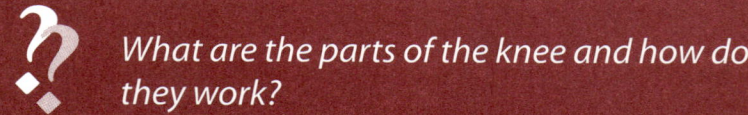

What are the parts of the knee and how do they work?

Knee Injuries

Exhibit 8-1 illustrates the important muscles, bones, and tendons of the knee.

Four bones form the knee:

- The lower end of the femur (thigh bone)
- The upper end of the tibia (shin bone)
- The upper end of the fibula (slender bone of the lower leg)
- The patella (kneecap)

The hamstring muscles, a group of muscles that cover the back of the thigh and connect the pelvis to the tibia, flex and extend the thigh. The **quadriceps femoris muscle** (a group of muscles that cover the front of the thigh) flex and extend the knee. The quadriceps merge into a common tendon (the patellar tendon). The patella is embedded into the quadriceps tendon and glides over the surface of the femur as the knee is flexed and extended.[1]

Exhibit 8-1
The Anatomy of the Knee

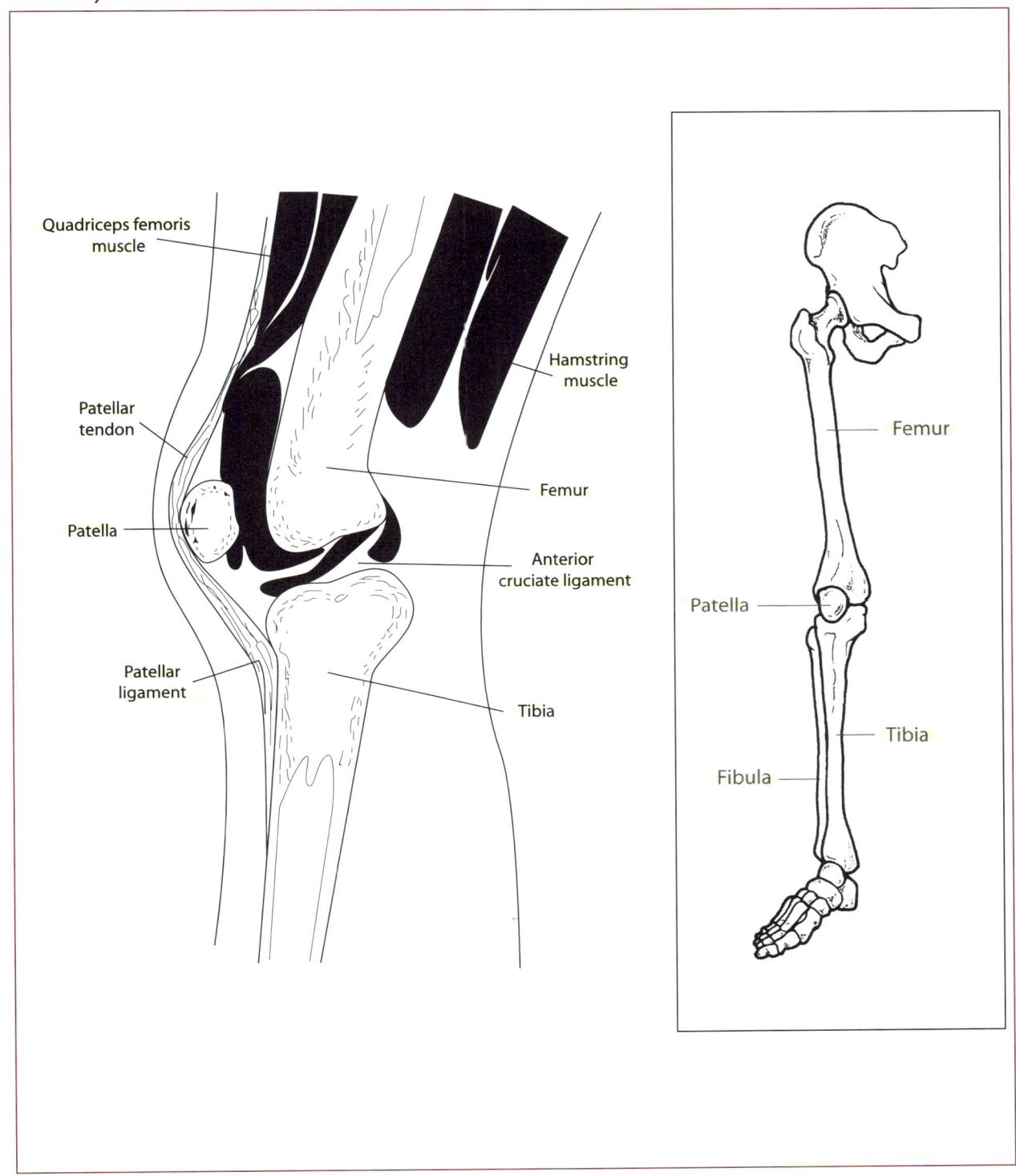

> **What are the roles of ligaments and menisci in the knee?**

Knee Ligaments and Menisci

The ligaments in the knee, shown in Exhibit 8-2, are strong fibrous tissues that bind the knee. Muscles and tendons that surround the knee assist the ligaments in binding the knee. The knee has four major ligaments. The **medial collateral ligament** and the **lateral collateral ligament** limit and stabilize the side-to-side movement of the knee. The other two, the **anterior** and **posterior cruciate** (crossing) **ligaments**, crisscross inside the knee. The cruciate ligaments prevent abnormal forward and backward movement of the knee. Most knee sprains involve the medial collateral and/or the anterior cruciate ligaments. Severe sprains involving torn ligaments may require surgery. Exhibit 8-3 lists some indicators of knee ligament injuries.

Exhibit 8-2
The Ligaments and Menisci of the Knee

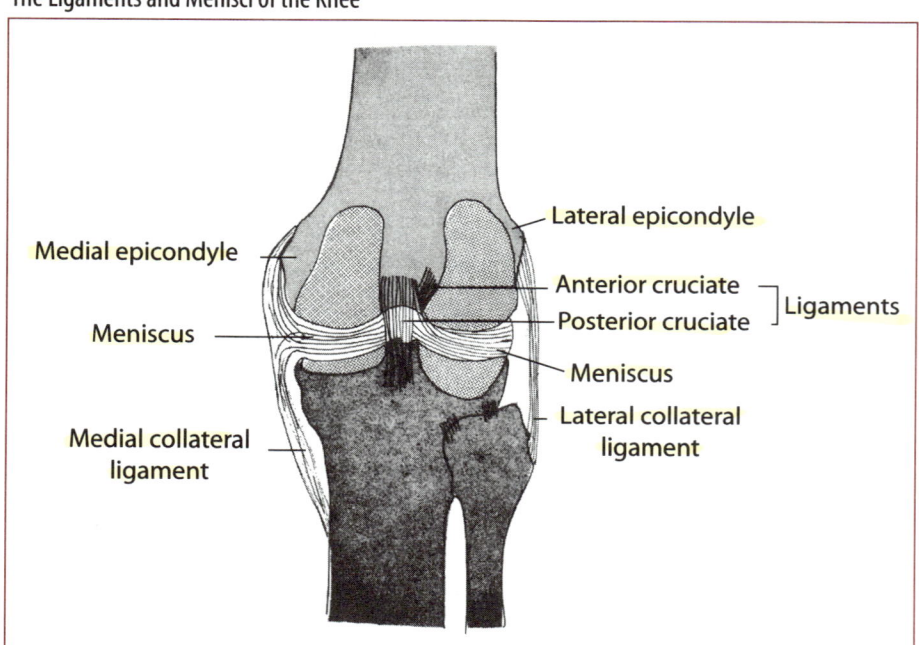

Adapted from Rene Calliett, M.D., *Knee Pain and Disability*, 2d ed. (Philadelphia: F.A. Davis Co., 1993), p. 21.

In addition to ligaments, the knee requires cartilage to bind and cushion the ends of the femur and the tibia. The knee cartilage is called **menisci** (the plural of meniscus). The medial meniscus helps guide the shinbone into place when the leg bends. Exhibit 8-4 illustrates several types of meniscus tears.

Medical Alert

Sometimes people who suffer knee injuries are reluctant to see a doctor and assume that the injury will heal (or at least not worsen) in time. Some premium-conscious employers may "suggest" that an injured worker wait before making a claim. This can lead to a permanent impairment. Often the best surgical repairs for ligament injuries are made within the first week or two of the injury. After that, the repair may become more difficult and the outcome more uncertain. Allowing an unstable knee to go untreated for a prolonged period may lead to further degeneration, scarring, and osteoarthritis. Because of the importance of identifying these types of injuries early, people suffering knee injuries should be strongly encouraged to seek immediate medical attention.[2]

Sometimes a torn meniscus causes the knee to lock up. The injured person should seek medical attention immediately. If the knee stays in a locked position for too long, the meniscus can permanently lose its elasticity and can become displaced from its normal position in the knee.[3]

Exhibit 8-3
Indicators of Potential Knee Ligament Injuries

Symptoms	Possible Injury Indicated
The knee gives way, or collapses.	Instability is the major indicator of a complex ligament injury.
The knee pops when the injury occurs.	A distinct pop could indicate a torn anterior cruciate ligament.
The injury occurs while the person is slowing down rather than speeding up.	An injury occurring while slowing down is usually associated with a ligament injury.
The injury was caused by an impact with an automobile dashboard.	Impact with a dashboard often results in a posterior cruciate ligament injury.
The knee flexed beyond its normal range (hyperflexion).	Hyperflexion often results in an anterior cruciate ligament injury.

 *What does "mechanism of injury" mean?*

Mechanism of Injury

The **mechanism of injury** refers to the specific motions and forces involved in causing an injury. This is especially important in claims that might have other injury causes unrelated to the covered accident. A detailed statement should include questions related to the mechanism of injury.

Nolan: Do you know the mechanism of injury for this claim? For example, did his knee hit the dashboard straight on or was his leg turned when he hit? If you have a detailed enough statement about

Exhibit 8-4
Types of Meniscus Tears

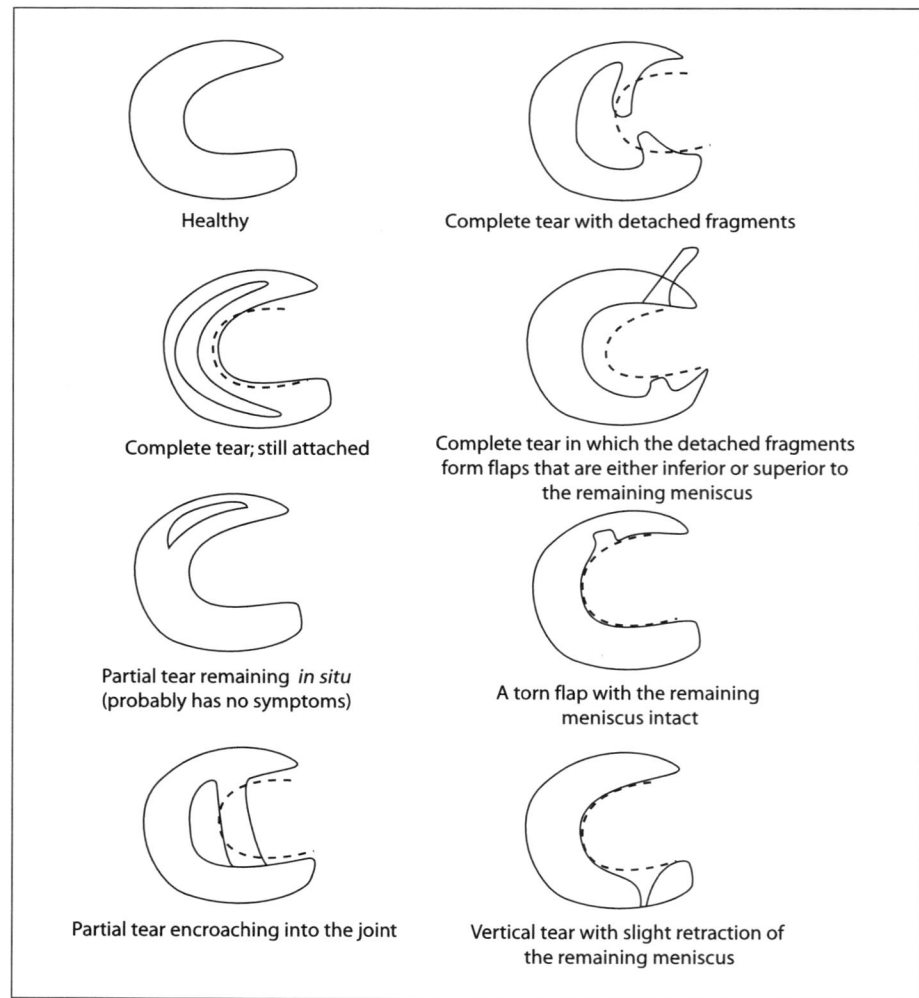

the circumstances of the injury, you can sometimes determine the type of injury.

Rob: Since I didn't know about this knee problem upfront, I didn't get a detailed statement. But I'm not sure what you mean by the mechanism of injury.

Nolan: Well, if the knee injury wasn't immediately apparent and the claimant was able to walk then it's probably not a torn ligament because a torn ligament would mean severe, immediate disability. A torn quadriceps tendon would also be immediately disabling. He might have a mild to moderate ligament problem. On the other hand, a torn meniscus, by itself, would be like having a foreign body caught in the knee. It might not cause immediate instability. A torn meniscus would be my guess in this case.

Rob: What would cause a meniscus to tear? If he banged his knee on the dash, would that cause it?

Nolan: Usually it takes a little more than a straight-on blow like that.

What is the mechanism of injury for meniscus tears?

The following mechanisms of injury can injure the meniscus:[4]

- A direct blow to the side of the knee while the knee is turned. The blow can be to either the medial or the lateral ligament. This kind of motion occurs in sports when the knee is hit from the side while it is flexed and then extended. Usually the medial meniscus tears because it is less mobile than the lateral meniscus; therefore, athletic activities place great stress on it. Often a severe impact causes both the collateral ligament and the meniscus to tear at the same time.
- The knee twists inward or outward while the person is picking up an item.
- The knee twists beyond the knee's normal range while the person is carrying an object.

Rob: What's the length of disability for something like this? I need to update the reserve for this claim.

Nolan: Well, I'd really like to know what the injury is. As I said before, all knee injuries are not the same. We can't wait too long to increase the reserve, but if you're going to have the medical documents in the next couple of days, I'm sure that Joanne [their supervisor] won't mind if, by waiting, we can set a more accurate reserve.

The following day the police report and medical documents arrived, and Rob and Nolan reviewed the documents in chronological order. Exhibit 8-5 lists the significant findings in the reports.

Nolan and Rob were convinced that the knee injury was related to the accident because (1) the injury was immediately reported at the scene, (2) the emergency room noted the knee condition, and (3) the chiropractor's initial examination, three days after the accident, mentioned the knee complaint even though the seriousness of the injury was initially underestimated.

Exhibit 8-5
Chronological List of Document Findings

Document	Important Finding
Police report—3/14/98	The claimant reported injuries to neck and knee to police officer at the time of accident.
Emergency room report—3/14/98	The attending physician's diagnosis included cervical trauma and acute traumatic right knee subluxation with edema.
Chiropractor's report—3/17/98	Chiropractic examination, three days after the accident, indicated that the right knee was tender and swollen on the medial side. The chiropractor's X-rays indicated posterolateral subluxation of the tibia upon the fibula.
MRI report—4/30/98	The chiropractor stated that the MRI indicated a Grade III tear (on a scale of I to III) of the posterior horn of the medial meniscus.*
Orthopedic surgeon's report—5/4/98	The orthopedic surgeon recommended arthroscopy (with meniscus repair or meniscectomy depending on damage).

*Under most circumstances, an overread (review) by a board-certified radiologist and/or orthopedic surgeon would be recommended for MRIs in order to verify the diagnosis.

What investigative steps may have been overlooked in this case?

Nolan and Rob probably should have investigated causality more thoroughly. No clinical profile had been investigated for this claimant. The claim representative in this case should have requested information about the claimant's medical history related to the knee and leg. Information about prior accidents, surgeries, or blows to the knee or leg should have been included as part of the assessment process. Also, a medical records review or an independent medical exam (IME) from a physician is needed to complete the claim file. The causality report would document the following:

1. The relationship between the injury and the mechanism of injury.
2. The role of chronic diseases related to the present injury site. (The claimant's job makes chronic, repetitive injuries more likely.)
3. The role of medications in this injury. (Some medications induce muscle-skeletal problems.)
4. The role of the claimant's weight in causing the injury.

How would the treatment and disability duration differ between a meniscectomy and a meniscus repair?

Treatment of Meniscus Injuries

The orthopedic surgeon's report confirmed the diagnosis and compared the prognosis for the two surgical procedures—meniscus repair and meniscectomy. Rob reviewed the two possibilities to help understand the potential disabilities of each. A second opinion would normally have been generated to confirm the diagnosis.

The Meniscectomy

The term **meniscectomy** (or **meniscus removal**) is somewhat misleading. It is not the *complete* removal of the meniscus cartilage. Instead, it is the selective trimming of torn "flaps" on the outer layer of the meniscus. This procedure is used to repair a partial tear of the outer layer of the meniscus. The goal is to leave intact as much of the meniscus as possible.

Meniscectomy is performed on an outpatient basis. The patient is normally off from work for two weeks, followed by two to four weeks of light duty work (if available) and subsequent return to full duty at four to six weeks after surgery.

Meniscus Repair

The formal **meniscus repair** is more serious than a meniscectomy. This procedure is used to repair a serious tear that extends through the deepest layers of the meniscus. Because this procedure involves suturing the meniscus, a longer healing period is required after surgery. The chance of finding a repairable meniscus is about 10 percent, and the chance of a successful repair is about 50 percent.

Rob: The MRI said that there is a Grade III tear, which is pretty serious. I guess that the claimant will have to have the meniscus repair rather than just snipping off the rough edges.

Nolan: Maybe so, but the doctor really won't know for sure until he does an **arthroscopy** and sees the extent of the damage. It also depends on where the tear is on the meniscus. Some locations are more disabling than others.

Arthroscopy permits the surgeon not only to look directly at the injury but also to remove any "flaps" protruding from the meniscus with a blunt hook.

 *What are the estimated medical expenses, duration of treatment, and length of disability for knee injuries?*

Disability Related to Knee Injuries

Exhibit 8-6 shows the estimated duration of treatment and return-to-work expectations for a meniscus injury.

As indicated, for 75 percent of claims, medical treatment will conclude within fifty-six days for a meniscus removal and within eighty-four of a meniscus repair. The amount of time that a person is expected to be off work varies from seven to seventy-seven days after surgery depending on the individual, the job, and the type of injury treatment given.

Exhibit 8-6
Treatment Duration and Return-to-Work Expectations

Injury Treatment	Duration of Treatment (for 75% of claims)	Return-to-Work Expectations (Work Activity Level 2)
Meniscectomy	56 days	7–42 days
Meniscus repair	84 days	42–77 days

Adapted with permission from Millman-Robertson, *Health Care Management Guidelines: Utilization Review and Case Management Template, Workers Compensation*, vol. 7, May 1997, p. 5.126.

The level of work activity affects the length of disability and the restrictions and accommodations that must be made. This claimant's job as a painter would probably be considered at a Level 2 because he climbs ladders. (See Exhibit 8-7.) It would also be helpful to supplement this with a physical capacity evaluation—a form that details what the patient can and cannot do for work.

Exhibit 8-7
Work Activity Levels

Ankle, Lower Leg, Foot, Toe, Knee, Hip, Pelvis, and Upper Leg Injuries			
Activity	**Level 1**	**Level 2**	**Level 3**
Standing	Up to 10 min/hr	Up to 50 min/hr	Unlimited
Walking 1: smooth surface	Crutches with limited pressure on the foot	Walking up to 1,000 ft/hr carrying up to 25 lbs	Unlimited
Walking 2: irregular surface	None	Walking up to 1,000 ft/hr carrying up to 25 lbs	Unlimited
Climbing stairs	None	Climbing up to 8 flights/hr carrying up to 50 lbs	Unlimited
Climbing ladders	None	**Climbing up to 50 rungs/hr carrying up to 25 lbs**	**Unlimited**
Activities requiring balance	None	Up to 40 min/hr; able to work with two hands without assistance for balance	Unlimited
Applying strength against bent knee (pedaling, squatting, kneeling, etc.)	None	Up to 60 times/hr	Unlimited
Special needs	Elevate 50% of time: may need to be immobilized	May need brace for uneven ground or ladders	May need work break, and occasional elevation

Adapted with permission from Millman-Robertson, *Health Care Management Guidelines: Utilization Review and Case Management Template, Workers Compensation*, vol. 7, May 1997.

Rob: I'll need to find out whether he needs a meniscus removal or a repair. But it looks as if he could be out for several months.

Nolan: Maybe there's a light duty job that would keep him off the ladders so he could return to work while he's healing—something like painting the trim or assisting other painters in some way.

The Need for Case Management

Traditionally, knee surgery patients were told not to walk for four weeks and were allowed to start placing weight on the leg after six weeks. More recently, patients have been instructed to gradually place weight on the knee after a few weeks, depending on the patient's ability to tolerate the pain. Doctors believe that gradually bearing weight helps the rehabilitation process. Rehabilitation is used to build up the muscles supporting the knee. In this claim, the orthopedic doctor's prognosis was that the claimant should be able to return to full duty work in nine to twelve weeks after the meniscus repair, if no complications arose. According to Milliman-Robertson's disability guidelines, more than 75 percent of patients with similar work activities will return to work within seventy-seven days. It would be appropriate for a claim representative to require an explanation of why the prognosis for a claimant is longer. The availability of light-duty work could significantly reduce the length of time that the claimant is off work.

Rob: What kind of medical rehabilitation would normally be involved with this?

Nolan: Physical therapy would include heat packs, electrostimulation, and a knee brace. You should expect three to six weeks of physical therapy followed by an exercise program at home.

Rob: What kind of outcome would you expect to see on this?

Nolan: The outcome is usually good. He may not even have a partial permanent disability. A couple of things to watch for are osteoarthritis and rheumatoid arthritis. These can cause joint inflammation, but that's rare. Another possibility is that the doctor overlooked knee ligament damage. That happens sometimes. I think the most serious potential problems on these type claims are nonmedical. If the claimant doesn't get along with his employer or doesn't like his job, the length of disability and wage loss could become a problem. If you get that impression or if physical therapy lasts more than six weeks, you should involve a case manager.

Case Conclusion

Unfortunately, Nolan's prediction for a good outcome did not occur. The claimant continued to complain of knee pain and swelling after six weeks. He complained about the pain so much that his treating physician sent him to a pain management clinic. Complicating matters, the claimant slipped (but did not fall) while on a ladder three months after he returned to work. He claimed that he slipped because his knee gave out. Despite the apparent lack of any physical condition that would have caused his knee to fail, the claimant refused to work. He said that his slip had caused him to lose confidence and he now had a fear of climbing ladders. He also continued to complain of pain, and his doctor stated that there was "functional overlay" (psychological factors) involved in his disability. The claimant's doctor permanently restricted him from using ladders. The claimant retained an attorney and, at a workers compensation hearing, was given a 40 percent permanent partial disability rating. This rating was partly due to the doctor's diagnosis that the claimant was suffering from a phobia and partly due to the pain disorder. Rob and Nolan were unprepared to argue this aspect of the claim.

Chapter Notes

1. Presley Reed, M.D., *Medical Disability Advisor*, 3d ed. (Horsham, PA: LRP Publications, 1994), p. 743.
2. Presley Reed, M.D., *Medical Disability Advisor*, 2d ed. (Horsham, PA: LRP Publications, 1993), p. 490.
3. Rene Calliett, M.D., *Knee Pain and Disability*, 3d ed. (Philadelphia: F.A. Davis Co., 1993), p. 97.
4. David Magee, *Orthopedic Physical Assessment*, 3d ed. (Philadelphia: Wallace Saunders, 1997), p. 509.

Chapter 9
Psychological Injuries and Conditions

Claims for injuries and conditions that are purely psychological in nature are comparatively rare but are increasing in frequency. Yet psychological injuries and conditions frequently accompany or preexist physical injuries, thereby complicating them. The psychological aspect of a case is significant in the investigation, control, and settlement of every claim. Whether they realize it or not, claim representatives must deal with the psychological conditions and problems of claimants. Some cases explicitly involve claims for psychological injury. In other cases, the psychological dimension is important even if the claim is not explicitly made for a psychological condition.

Sometimes claim representatives encounter the term **functional overlay** in physician notes. This means that the provider believes psychological factors involved in the patient's symptoms are interwoven with the physical condition.

This chapter begins with descriptions of the usual psychological responses to physical injuries. The next sections of the chapter describe how to evaluate psychological injury claims with comprehensive criteria for diagnosing these injuries. All treatment and discussion of psychological conditions should be based on such standard diagnoses. The diagnostic criteria make clear that judgment and clinical skill play an important part in psychological diagnosis.

Claims involving some of these disorders are frequently not compensable for various reasons that will be discussed in this chapter. Claim representatives must therefore develop a working understanding of the behaviors and symptoms associated with these disorders and be able to identify the indicators of fraud or abuse associated with psychological injury claims. Claim representatives must also be able to investigate preexisting conditions or other causes of claimants' psychological conditions.

Psychological Response to Physical Injury

This section describes certain psychological responses that are commonly associated with physical injury and how such responses should be considered in the evaluation of claims. Injuries to the body can create psychological responses. In general, the severity of the psychological response corresponds to the severity of the injury: trivial injuries can be expected to produce trivial responses, and massive injuries are likely to produce massive psychological responses. However, the level of response to a given injury may vary greatly. Differences in psychological makeup, levels of personal support, and occupational demands affect how people respond to the stress of physical injury.

Beyond the predictable responses described in this section, most psychological conditions are *not* caused by physical injury. Thus, a claim for a psychological condition based on accidental physical injury should be scrutinized. Most psychological conditions are found to be the predictable response to injury, conditions that preexisted the accidental injury, or the result of causes unrelated to the physical injury.

Injured individuals frequently experience pain, stress, anxiety, and depression in response to a physical injury. Most individuals also cope with their suffering through defense mechanisms.

Pain

Pain is both physically and psychologically produced. It is directly related to tissue damage and thus serves the important purpose of withdrawal or retreat from the cause of harm. However, the reality and extent of pain are related to numerous other factors, including personality, expectations, age, and sociocultural background.[1]

Health professionals have observed a wide range of reactions to pain. Some patients are stoic in response to injuries that usually cause great pain; other patients complain loudly, bitterly, or theatrically about injuries that are usually not severely painful. Yet the subjective reality of their suffering cannot be denied. The presence and extent of pain cannot be objectively proven or disproven.

Pain can cause anxiety and anxiety can increase pain. Likewise, chronic pain can cause depression, and depression can make a patient highly sensitized to pain. This interaction of pain with depression and anxiety shows that psychological reactions to physical injury can reinforce and complicate one another. Pain may be simultaneously "real" and "psychological." "Psychological" pain is also referred to as "functional," "psychogenic," or "psychosomatic" pain.

Pain can usually be effectively managed with medications, although psychological treatment may also be necessary for psychologically caused pain. Properly managed, pain-relief medications should not normally result in addiction. Claimants who abuse narcotics are likely to have medical, psychological, or personality problems that complicate settlement of the claim.

Anxiety and Stress

Anxiety is a feeling of apprehension, tension, dread, or uneasiness. It may be caused by specific external threats such as fear of losing one's job or by internal psychological conflicts. Anxiety not connected to a specific cause is unfocused and diffuse (sometimes called free-floating). Anxiety causes physiological responses including increased blood pressure, heartbeat, and sweating; changes in the rate and depth of breathing; changes in blood chemistry; and suppression of the immune system.

The term "stress" is frequently used synonymously with anxiety. However, stress also refers to the causes of anxiety. Stressors may be internal or external. The American Psychiatric Association requires that sources and levels of stress be included as part of the information in a complete diagnosis of psychological disorders. The American Psychiatric Association also suggests that all of the following types of stress be considered: conjugal, parenting, other interpersonal, occupational, living circumstances, financial, legal, developmental, physical injury or illness, and other.[2] An injury that is the subject of an insurance claim or lawsuit creates several of these types of stress, including financial, legal, physical, and possibly occupational and conjugal. Thus, because injuries cause stress and stress causes anxiety, it can be expected that claim-related injuries create a great deal of anxiety. Anxiety is not considered a psychological disorder unless it is excessive, unrealistic, and irrational.

Depression

Depression is both a diagnosis (such as major depressive disorder, dysthymia) and a symptom. As a diagnosis, it is addressed in the following section of this chapter. As a symptom and in its mild form, it is as nearly a universal human experience as anxiety.

Mild forms of depression are described as sadness and grief. More serious and lasting forms of depression are described as a loss of pleasure and interest in life and feelings of complete hopelessness, helplessness, and emptiness. Depression may be accompanied by weight loss or gain, change in appetite, insomnia or excessive sleepiness, decreased energy, psychomotor agitation or retardation, poor concentration, indecisiveness, feelings of worthlessness, and suicidal thoughts.

Physical injury can readily cause symptoms of depression since it results in loss, loss of control, and helplessness. Frustration with recovery and the social isolation and insecurity accompanying injury can worsen symptoms of depression.

Defense Mechanisms

A **defense mechanism** is any reaction that serves to protect against something harmful. Psychological defense mechanisms are unconscious behaviors that resolve or conceal anxieties. Defense mechanisms may serve the useful purpose of protecting against overwhelming anxiety. Some defense mechanisms such as humor are very important social skills. Other defense mechanisms create problems when they become a chronic means of avoiding anxiety-related situations. Some defense mechanisms that may be used to fight the stress of physical injury and illness that are commonly encountered in insurance claims are the following:

- Denial
- Displacement
- Isolation
- Projection
- Repression

The following are descriptions of these defense mechanisms and an explanation of how they affect claim handling.

Denial—The person does not acknowledge some aspect of reality. Denial is a normal stage in the gradual adjustment to permanent injury, but it is an unhealthy long-term response. Denial can also delay necessary treatment of acute problems if the person refuses to recognize the seriousness of an injury.

Displacement—Emotionally significant feelings are directed away from their real source or object toward some other object. For example, a claimant may become furious at the doctors or claim representative for not being more helpful, rather than at the person who caused the accident, or a claimant might blame a product for his injury even though the injury was due solely to the claimant's failure to follow safety precautions.

Isolation—The person can separate thoughts about an event or situation from feelings. Patients who employ this mechanism can give highly detailed accounts of their accidents and injuries without evidence of any feelings on these matters. This could mislead claim representatives who might wrongly conclude that the person is coping well with a disability.

Projection—A person may attribute his or her own thoughts and feelings to another. For example, someone who has suffered a disfiguring injury might insist that his family members find him repulsive to look at.

Repression—Someone may try to forget an unpleasant, anxiety-producing event or emotion. Repression of accidents is very common.

Many victims of accidental injuries are completely unable to give an account of their accident, even though they were conscious throughout the incident. Claim representatives might mistake repression as an unwillingness to cooperate or as an indication that the person is concealing some incriminating fact about the accident.

Claim representatives must understand the psychological responses to physical injuries in order to effectively handle injury claims. A description of other defense mechanisms that claim representatives sometimes observe is found in the glossary of this chapter.

Evaluation of Psychological Injury Claims

Claim representatives are often unsure about how to handle ordinary psychological responses to physical injury. Should they ignore them? automatically pay for any treatment of them? resist payment for their treatment? No single answer fits all cases. The appropriateness of payment depends on several factors.

The evaluation should include a review of three fundamental questions. First, is there a diagnosable psychological disorder? A correct diagnosis is a crucial step in determining causation and treatment. Second, what caused the disorder? The issue of cause is crucial in determining legal liability or compensability under various insurance policies. Finally, what is the appropriate treatment? The fact that a disorder is genuine and was caused by an insured event does not mean that all types and amounts of treatment must be uncritically accepted. The issues raised by these questions are discussed below. Two important tools that are used in making a diagnosis are:

(1) The *Diagnostic and Statistical Manual of Mental Disorders* (DSM-IV)
(2) Psychological tests

Claim representatives cannot diagnose patients or disorders or administer psychological examinations, but they can review a clinician's report to determine how thoroughly and carefully the diagnosis was made and identify potential test problems that could influence test results.

Diagnostic and Statistical Manual of Mental Disorders (DSM-IV)

The identification, diagnosis, and description of psychological disorders are based on the *Diagnostic and Statistical Manual of Mental Disorders* (DSM-IV) of the American Psychiatric Association. This section describes how the current edition of DSM-IV works. The DSM-IV provides descriptions of and diagnostic criteria for hundreds of mental disorders. The American Psychiatric Association defines **mental disorders** as follows:

In DSM-IV, each of the mental disorders is conceptualized as a clinically significant behavioral or psychological syndrome or pattern that occurs in a person and that is associated with present distress (a painful symptom) or disability (impairment in one or more important areas of functioning) or with a significantly increased risk of suffering death, pain, disability, or an important loss of freedom. In addition, this syndrome or pattern must not be merely an expectable response to a particular event, e.g., the death of a loved one. Whatever its original cause, it must currently be considered a manifestation of a behavioral, psychological, or biological dysfunction in the person. Neither deviant behavior, e.g., political, religious, or sexual, nor conflicts that are primarily between the individual and society are mental disorders unless the deviance or conflict is a symptom of a dysfunction in the person, as described above.[3]

This definition makes clear that mental disorders are not simply an isolated response to an incident, but a syndrome or pattern of behavior that is a manifestation of some psychological dysfunction. In addition, mental disorders are not necessarily sharply distinguished from one another. Numerous disorders share many common symptoms or behaviors. While some diagnoses are mutually exclusive, most are not. Thus, a patient may be diagnosed with two or more disorders if all criteria are met.

For each disorder, the DSM-IV provides the following information when available.

General description. Each entry begins with a general description of the syndrome, including the most prominent symptoms and behaviors.

Associated features. These are features of a syndrome that are often, but not always, present.

Age at onset. Any characteristic pattern or the absence of a pattern is identified.

Course. The usual progression and resolution of symptoms, if any, is described.

Impairment. The usual occupational and social impairments that result from the disorder are identified.

Complications. Problems that may arise as a result of or in the course of the disorder are identified.

Predisposing factors. Characteristics of a person that may precede the disorder and make that person more vulnerable to the disorder are given.

Prevalence. The percentage of the population that at some time in their lives suffer from the disorder is noted.

Sex ratio. The frequency with which the disorder is diagnosed in men and women is identified.

Familial pattern. This is the frequency with which the disorder is found in close relatives versus the general population.

Differential diagnosis. Disorders that should be distinguished from the disorder in question are identified. Differential diagnoses generally share many of the same symptoms and behaviors as the disorder in question.

Diagnostic criteria. These are the criteria that must be met for the diagnosis to be made. In many instances, a certain number of criteria from a longer list is sufficient to make the diagnosis.

A good diagnosis should conform to the standards of the DSM-IV. A report explaining a diagnosis should describe all symptoms of the disorder as specified by the DSM-IV and explain how all relevant differential diagnoses have been made. Unless all characteristic symptoms have been identified and all relevant differential diagnoses have been made, a diagnosis cannot be accepted as accurate. Testimony or reports from a practitioner who asserts that the DSM-IV is irrelevant or optional would be subject to serious impeachment at a trial or hearing, if not excluded from evidence altogether. Claim representatives should not accept any report or bill from such a practitioner.

A correct diagnosis is a prerequisite to proper care and should be required by claim representatives before any psychological condition is accepted as compensable. A correct diagnosis prevents improper treatment of symptoms and controls therapist bias. Finally, the diagnosis of an identifiable disorder does not automatically mean the person is disabled.

Under the DSM-IV, a patient's diagnosis is based on five separate categories (called axes). These five axes help the clinician establish a plan of treatment and predict the likely outcome. The five axes are as follows:

> Axis I—Clinical Disorders (and other conditions that may be a focus of clinical attention)
>
> Axis II—Personality Disorders and Mental Retardation
>
> Axis III—General Medical Conditions
>
> Axis IV—Psychosocial and Environmental Problems
>
> Axis V—Global Assessment Functioning

This text will explain how each of the axes is used in making a DSM-IV diagnosis.

Axis I—Clinical Disorders

Axis I is used to identify most of the disorders set forth in the DSM-IV and most of the disorders that would be claimed in a casualty loss. Axis I disorders and conditions are listed below. They range from childhood conditions such as attention deficit disorders (under the Axis I category of Disorders Usually Diagnosed in Childhood) to Alzheimer's disease (under the Axis I category of Dementia).

Axis 1—Clinical Disorders

- Disorders usually diagnosed in infancy, early childhood, or adolescence
- Delirium, dementia, amnestic and other cognitive disorders
- Mental disorders due to a general medical condition
- Substance-related disorders
- Schizophrenia and other psychotic disorders

- Mood disorders
- Anxiety disorders
- Somatoform disorders
- Factitious disorders
- Dissociative disorders
- Sexual and gender identity disorders
- Eating disorders
- Sleep disorders
- Impulse-control disorders
- Adjustment disorders
- Other conditions that may be focus of clinical attention

The Axis I disorders that claim representatives are likely to encounter are as follows:

- Mood disorders
- Anxiety disorders
- Somatoform disorders
- Factitious disorders

Mood Disorders

A **mood** is a pervasive and sustained emotion that in the extreme can affect one's perception of reality. Examples of mood disorders include:

- Major depressive disorder
- Manic-depressive (or bipolar disorders)

The diagnostic criteria for these disorders are found in the glossary at the back of this chapter. The diagnostic criteria for mood disorders are broad enough to include patients having dramatically different disorder severity and, consequently, dramatically different impairments. For example, depression is characterized by persistent and pervasive despair often manifested as a lack of interest in life, and the diagnosis of major depressive disorder can be used to describe patients with relatively mild depression and little impairment characterized by fatigue, insomnia, and feelings of worthlessness, as well as to patients who are suicidal, have diminished ability to think or concentrate, and have significant disability even in performing simple physical tasks.[4]

The **manic-depressive** (or bipolar) mood is another well-known mood disorder. A manic episode is characterized by an unusually and persistently elevated, expansive, or irritable mood. When the mood is positive, it may seem cheerfully infectious to those who do not know the person. Yet manic episodes are genuine disorders that interfere with the person's occupational or social functioning and may even require hospitalization. Manic episodes may be accompanied by an inflated sense of self-esteem (even to the point of grandiose delusions), decreased need for sleep, talkativeness, flights of ideas, distractibility, increased activity or agitation, and involvement in pleasurable but dangerous activities such as buying sprees, reckless sexual behavior, or foolish investments.

Both manic and depressive episodes are classified by their severity, the presence of psychotic features (delusions and hallucinations), and the affected person's extent of remission (full or partial). Neither the manic nor the depressive mood is diagnosed if the symptoms can be accounted for by organic mood disorders or schizophrenia.

Anxiety Disorders

Anxiety disorders are associated with mental stress. Although there may be "stress claims," "stress" is not a medical diagnosis. Circumstances that feel stressful create psychophysiological responses. These responses may initiate, prolong, or worsen a physical ailment or may create separate psychological disorders.

Stress may aggravate existing psychological disorders, especially personality disorders. However, this is very different from causing such disorders, as evidenced by the fact that with the removal of stress, the disorder may be mitigated but does not disappear. Claim representatives should not accept a clinician's report that an accident caused a psychological disorder unless the clinician has ruled out the possibility of a preexisting problem. Exhibit 9-1 shows various life events and the level of stress associated with these events. Personal injuries are stressful for everyone as are other events.

Anxiety disorders are among the most frequently encountered psychiatric disorders. This category of disorders includes post-traumatic stress disorder, panic disorders, phobias, obsessions, compulsions, and generalized anxiety disorder. These disorders all include symptoms of anxiety or behaviors performed to relieve anxiety. The glossary contains a description of common anxiety disorders. Three anxiety disorders that claim representatives are likely to encounter are:

- Post-traumatic stress disorder
- General anxiety disorder
- Specific phobia

Following are descriptions of these disorders and explanations of some of the issues encountered in insurance claims:

Post-traumatic stress disorder may follow a stress that is so severe as to be beyond usual human experience. The disorder is characterized by persistent re-experiencing of the event, persistent avoidance of anything associated with the event or a general numbing of responsiveness, and persistent symptoms of arousal.

The DSM-IV acknowledges that "the classification of post-traumatic stress disorder is controversial since the predominant symptom is the re-experiencing of a trauma, not anxiety or avoidance behavior." The DSM-IV further notes, "However, anxiety symptoms and avoidance behavior are extremely common, and symptoms of increased arousal are invariably present."[5] Such arousal would be indicated by irritability,

Exhibit 9-1
Relative Stress Value of Life Events

Life Event	Mean Value
1. Death of spouse	100
2. Divorce	73
3. Marital separation from mate	65
4. Detention in jail or other institution	63
5. Death of a close family member	63
6. Major personal injury or illness	53
7. Marriage	50
8. Being fired at work	47
9. Marital reconciliation with mate	45
10. Retirement from work	45
11. Major change in the health or behavior of a family member	44
12. Pregnancy	40
13. Sexual difficulties	39
14. Gaining a new family member (e.g., through birth, adoption, moving in, etc.)	39
15. Major business readjustment (e.g., merger, reorganization, bankruptcy, etc.)	39
16. Major change in financial state (e.g., much worse off or much better off than usual)	38
17. Death of a close friend	37
18. Changing to a different line of work	36
19. Major change in the number of arguments with spouse (e.g., either many more or many less than usual regarding child-rearing, personal habits, etc.)	35
20. Taking out a mortgage or loan for a major purchase (e.g., for a home, business, etc.)	31
21. Foreclosure on a mortgage or loan	30
22. Major change in responsibilities at work (e.g., promotion, demotion, lateral transfer)	29
23. Son or daughter leaving home (e.g., marriage, attending college, etc.)	29
24. Trouble with in-laws	29
25. Outstanding personal achievement	28
26. Wife beginning or ceasing work outside the home	26
27. Beginning or ceasing formal schooling	26
28. Major change in living conditions (e.g., building a new home, remodeling, deterioration of home or neighborhood)	25
29. Revision of personal habits (dress, manners, association, etc.)	24
30. Trouble with the boss	23
31. Major change in working hours or conditions	20
32. Change in residence	20
33. Changing to a new school	20
34. Major change in usual type and/or amount of recreation	19
35. Major change in church activities (e.g., much more or much less than usual)	19
36. Major change in social activities (e.g., clubs, dancing, movies, visiting, etc.)	18
37. Taking out a mortgage or loan for a lesser purchase (e.g., for a car, TV, freezer, etc.)	17
38. Major change in sleeping habits (much more or much less sleep, or change in part of day when asleep)	16
39. Major change in number of family get-togethers (e.g., much more or much less than usual)	15
40. Major change in eating habits (much more or much less food intake, or very different meal hours or surroundings)	15
41. Vacation	13
42. Christmas	12
43. Minor violations of the law (e.g., traffic tickets, jaywalking, disturbing the peace, etc.)	11

Adapted from T.H. Holmes and R.H. Rahe: The Social Readjustment Rating Scale, *Journal of Psychosomatic Research* 1967; 11:213-218, as reprinted in Herbert Lasky, J.D., *Guidelines for Handling Psychiatric Issues in Workers' Compensation Cases* (Ranchos Palos Verdes, CA: Lex-Com Enterprises, 1988), pp. 167-168.

difficulty in sleeping and concentrating, hypervigilance, and an exaggerated startle response. Given that the American Psychiatric Association regards the diagnosis as controversial, claim representatives should not accept a diagnosis of post-traumatic stress disorder unless all criteria of the disorder have been clearly established.

The event that causes post-traumatic stress disorder must be one that is "outside the range of usual human experience and that would be markedly distressing to almost anyone."[6] Some of the examples given are rape, military combat, floods, earthquakes, airplane crashes, bombings, torture, and death camps. The DSM-IV acknowledges that "car accidents with serious physical injury" may be a cause, but notes that such a cause is likely to "produce it only occasionally."[7] Thus, the usual accidents and injuries that are the subjects of insurance claims are not normally considered "stressful enough" to cause post-traumatic stress disorder. Any allegation that an ordinary accident caused post-traumatic stress disorder would require a great deal of explanation.

Re-experiencing the traumatic event through flashbacks, dreams, or feelings that the event was recurring is essential to a diagnosis of post-traumatic stress disorder. The re-experiencing must be persistent. The required symptoms must persist for more than a month.

Exhibit 9-2 lists the DSM-IV criteria for post-traumatic stress disorder.

Generalized anxiety disorder is characterized by unrealistic and excessive anxiety manifested by a variety of physical and behavioral symptoms. Anxiety that is realistic and appropriate because it is based on an actual situation is *not* indicative of this disorder. The clinician must carefully assess what anxiety is realistic and appropriate and what is unrealistic and excessive. A claim representative should respect the skill of an experienced clinician who has thoughtfully considered the matter. However, a claim representative need not accept a diagnosis that is implausible because it fails to explain how or why a patient's anxiety is judged to be unrealistic and excessive, or one that does not identify physical symptoms required to support the diagnosis. In addition, this diagnosis is only made when the anxiety focuses on *two or more* circumstances and when most other possible causes of the symptoms have been ruled out. The claim representative should obtain an explanation of why other causes have been ruled out.

Specific phobias are marked and persistent, exaggerated fears of specific objects or situations. The object or situation causes distress or anxiety that the victim often recognizes as being unreasonable or excessive. Common phobias include a fear of spiders, snakes, dogs, closed spaces, air travel, and heights. A common phobia encountered in a claims situation is a dog phobia. This may occur after a person (often a child) has been bitten by a dog.

Somatoform Disorders

Somatoform disorders are characterized by the presence of physical symptoms suggesting a physiological disorder that has no organic basis. In the absence of physiological evidence and because of usually strong evidence of a psychological cause, these disorders are

Exhibit 9-2
Post-Traumatic Stress Disorder

A. The person has been exposed to a traumatic event in which both of the following were present:
   (1) The person experienced, witnessed, or was confronted with an event or events that involved actual or threatened death or serious harm
   (2) The person's response involved intense fear, helplessness, or horror.
   Note: In children, this may be expressed instead by disorganized or agitated behavior.

B. The traumatic event is persistently re-experienced in one (or more) of the following ways:
   (1) Recurrent and intrusive, distressing recollections of the event, including images, thoughts, or perceptions
   Note: In young children, repetitive play may occur in which themes or aspects of the trauma are expressed.
   (2) Recurrent, distressing dreams of the event
   Note: In children, there may be frightening dreams without recognizable content.
   (3) Acting or feeling as if the traumatic event were recurring (includes a sense of reliving the experience, illusions, hallucinations, and dissociative flashback episodes, including those that occur on awakening or when intoxicated)
   Note: In young children, trauma-specific reenactment may occur.
   (4) Intense psychological distress at exposure to internal or external cues that symbolize or resemble an aspect of the traumatic event
   (5) Physiological reactivity on exposure to internal or external cues that symbolize or resemble an aspect of the traumatic event

C. Persistent avoidance of stimuli associated with the trauma and numbing of general responsiveness (not present before the trauma), as indicated by three (or more) of the following:
   (1) Efforts to avoid thoughts, feelings, or conversations associated with the trauma
   (2) Efforts to avoid activities, places, or people that arouse recollections of the trauma
   (3) Inability to recall an important aspect of the trauma
   (4) Markedly diminished interest or participation in significant activities
   (5) Feeling of detachment or estrangement from others
   (6) Restricted range of affect (e.g., unable to have loving feelings)
   (7) Sense of a foreshortened future (e.g., does not expect to have a career, marriage, children, or a normal life span)

D. Persistent symptoms of increased arousal (not present before the trauma), as indicated by two (or more) of the following:
   (1) Difficulty falling or staying asleep
   (2) Irritability or outbursts of anger
   (3) Difficulty concentrating
   (4) Hypervigilance
   (5) Exaggerated startle response

E. Duration of the disturbance (symptoms in Criteria B, C, and D) is more than one month

F. The disturbance causes clinically significant distress or impairment in social, occupational, or other important areas of functioning.

Adapted with permission from *Diagnostic and Statistical Manual of Mental Disorders*, Fourth Edition. Copyright 1994, American Psychiatric Association.

considered mental disorders. Unlike malingering or factitious disorders, somatoform disorder symptoms are not consciously created.

People with somatoform disorders do not usually initially consult a psychologist or psychiatrist. They typically go to one or more physicians who treat physical disorders. Because such physicians may not immediately think of somatoform disorders, or because they are reluctant to suggest that the illness is psychologically created, claim representatives who suspect a somatoform disorder should specifically request the doctor to address the possibility before diagnosing a physical disorder. Three common examples of somatoform disorders are:

- Hypochondriasis
- Somatization disorder
- Pain disorder

Following are descriptions of these three somatoform disorders.

Hypochondriasis is characterized by preoccupation with the fear of, or belief that one has, a serious illness. This fear or belief persists despite an absence of physical evidence and despite medical reassurance to the contrary.

Somatization disorder is characterized by multiple complaints over several years for which the person has sought medical attention. The reported symptoms are often vague, complicated, or dramatic and almost always include gastrointestinal problems, pain, cardiopulmonary symptoms, loss of function of a body part, or sexual complaints. This disorder is usually chronic, with symptoms appearing and disappearing. Doctor shopping, anxiety, and depression are often associated with this disorder.

Pain disorder often involves an injury that plays a major role in its onset. When the pain continues for months, impairing the victim's social and occupational functioning and becoming the major focus of the person's life, it becomes a disorder. Unemployment, marital discord, and substance abuse are frequently encountered with chronic pain disorders (lasting more than six months). The diagnostic criteria for a pain disorder are shown in Exhibit 9-3.

Other Disorders

Because of the seriousness of the disorder, claim representatives should have a basic understanding of schizophrenia. **Schizophrenia** is one of the major psychotic disorders. This psychotic disorder is characterized by an inability to recognize or respond to external reality; instead, the patient creates and responds to a separate psychological (or internal) reality. The disorder may have an early phase and residual phases characterized by social isolation or withdrawal, impaired functioning, peculiar behavior, a lack of personal hygiene, a blunted or inappropriate affect, incoherent speech, odd or magical beliefs, unusual perceptions, or lack of initiative. (An "affect" is the external manifestation of emotional "tone" or mood, usually as associated with a thought.) During the course of the illness, the ability to perform social, occupational, and

Exhibit 9-3
DSM-IV Diagnostic Criteria for Pain Disorder

- A. Pain in one or more anatomical sites is the predominant focus of the clinical presentation and is of sufficient severity to warrant clinical attention.
- B. The pain causes clinically significant distress or impairment in social, occupational, or other important areas of functioning.
- C. Psychological factors are judged to have an important role in the onset, severity, exacerbation, or maintenance of the pain.
- D. The symptom or deficit is not intentionally produced or feigned (as in factitious disorder or malingering).
- E. The pain is not better accounted for by a mood, anxiety, or psychotic disorder and does not meet criteria for dyspareunia.

Code as follows:

307.80 Pain Disorder Associated With Psychological Factors: Psychological factors are judged to have the major role in the onset, severity, exacerbation, or maintenance of the pain. (If a general medical condition is present, it does not have a major role in the onset, severity, exacerbation, or maintenance of the pain.) This type of pain disorder is not diagnosed if criteria are also met for somatization disorder.

Specify if:

Acute: duration of less than 6 months

Chronic: duration of 6 months or longer

307.89 Pain Disorder Associated With Both Psychological Factors and a General Medical Condition: Both psychological factors and a general medical condition are judged to have important roles in the onset, severity, exacerbation, or maintenance of the pain. The associated general medical condition or anatomical site of the pain (see below) is coded on Axis III.

Specify if:

Acute: duration of less than 6 months

Chronic: duration of 6 months or longer

Note: The following is not considered to be a mental disorder and is included here to facilitate differential diagnosis.

Pain Disorder Associated with a General Medical Condition: a general medical condition has a major role in the onset, severity, exacerbation, or maintenance of the pain. (If psychological factors are present, they are not judged to have a major role in the onset, severity, exacerbation, or maintenance of the pain.) The diagnostic code for the pain is selected based on the associated general medical condition if one has been established or on the anatomical location of the pain if the underlying general medical condition is not yet clearly established—for example, low back (724.2), sciatic (724.3), pelvic (625.9), headache (784.0), facial (784.0), chest (786.50), joint (719.4), bone (733.90), abdominal (789.0), breast (611.71), renal (788.0), ear (388.70), eye (379.91), throat (784.1), tooth (525.9), and urinary (788.0).

The DSM-IV multiaxial diagnosis for Mr. B would be

Axis I: 307.89 Pain Disorder Associated With Both Psychological Factors and a General Medical Condition, Chronic

Axis II: Dependent personality features

Axis III: 715.9 Postlumbar laminectomy

Axis IV: Loss of job and inability to work in chosen field

Axis V: GAF = 45

Adapted with permission from *Diagnostic and Statistical Manual of Mental Disorders*, Fourth Edition. Copyright 1994, American Psychiatric Association.

personal tasks becomes seriously impaired. Schizophrenia is marked by such characteristic psychotic features as delusions (false beliefs) and hallucinations (inaccurate perceptions). Bizarre delusions, such as the belief that one's thoughts are being broadcast to the world, and auditory hallucinations are characteristic symptoms. Other symptoms include incoherent speech, dissociation, and a flat or grossly inappropriate affect. Catatonic behavior, also characteristic of schizophrenia, is a psychomotor disturbance such as excitement, posturing, rigidity, or stupor without an organic basis. In making a diagnosis during an acute psychotic episode, the clinician must be careful to distinguish schizophrenia from organic brain disorders and substance abuse problems. Schizophrenia is not diagnosed if symptoms have been present for fewer than six months or if the predominant aspect of the problem is a mood disturbance.

Axis II—Personality Disorders and Mental Retardation

Personality traits that are inflexible and maladaptive, that cause significant impairments or distress to the person, and that become chronic patterns of behavior are called personality disorders. Personality disorders typically develop over many years. Claim representatives are likely to encounter people with personality disorders, but these disorders are not usually compensable in casualty losses. However, personality disorders can complicate the evaluation and settlement of a claim. The glossary contains a list of Axis II disorders and a description of each. Some of the recognizable examples of personality disorders include:

- Antisocial personality disorder
- Borderline personality disorder
- Narcissistic personality disorder
- Obsessive-compulsive personality disorder
- Paranoid personality disorder
- Passive-aggressive personality disorder

This section defines these disorders and explains the significance of personality disorders in claim handling and the difficulty in diagnosing personality disorders.

Examples of Personality Disorders

Antisocial personality disorder is characterized by a pattern of socially irresponsible, truant, cruel, and often deviant behavior for which the person generally feels no remorse. This disorder is especially noteworthy in claims as an indicator of malingering. The presence of an antisocial personality disorder and the legal context of a claim are two indicators of malingering. This disorder is usually fairly easy to spot from the patterns of personal, occupational, and legal problems in the person's life.

Borderline personality disorder is characterized by a pervasive pattern of instability of self-image, mood, and interpersonal relations. Identity problems may be related to issues of career choice, long-term goals, sexual orientation, types of friends, or values. Relationships tend to be unstable and intense as the person exhibits mood swings, inappropriate anger, chronic feelings of emptiness, and impulsiveness. The person may threaten suicide and engage in self-mutilation.

Narcissistic personality disorder is characterized by simultaneous feelings of grandiosity and hyper-sensitivity; there is also a lack of empathy. The affected person believes he or she is special and feels entitled to the attentions of and special treatment from others. Narcissistic individuals also exploit other people and are preoccupied with fantasies of unlimited success, power, brilliance, and beauty; yet they also envy others. They are typically less dramatic than the histrionic personalities, are better integrated than the borderline personalities, and are not as irresponsible as individuals with the antisocial personality; yet each of these disorders can coexist with narcissism. People with this disorder make difficult claimants.

Obsessive-compulsive personality disorder is characterized by perfectionism and inflexibility, but not necessarily by the more obvious obsessions and compulsions of the obsessive-compulsive disorder discussed earlier. A person with an obsessive-compulsive personality disorder is preoccupied by details and procedures and rigidly expects things to be done his or her way. He or she is devoted to work to the exclusion of leisure, yet an excessive focus on details and procedures interferes with task completion. This sort of person appears stiff and rigid, is usually stingy with gifts or compliments, and is overly scrupulous about matters of morality.

People with a **paranoid personality disorder** chronically interpret the actions of others as deliberately demeaning or threatening. They expect to be exploited and harmed, and continually question, without justification, the loyalty of friends, associates, spouse, or lover. They distort the meaning of innocent remarks and events, are easily slighted or enraged, and bear grudges. They characteristically engage in projection as a defense mechanism. People with paranoid personality disorder appear cold and serious. They are very apt to begin litigation.

Passive-aggressive personality disorder is characterized by anger that is expressed indirectly by resisting expected social and occupational performance. For instance, instead of saying, "I am angry with you," or "I am unhappy about this," the passive-aggressive individual will express dissatisfaction by sulking, dawdling, forgetting, or being intentionally incompetent. The person with this disorder believes that the demands on him or her are unreasonable and that his or her performance is better than others judge it to be. He or she resents suggestions and refuses to do his or her share of a task.

The Significance of Personality Disorders in Claims

Because personality disorders develop over a lifetime, they cannot be attributed to a single accidental injury, the usual subject of insurance claims. Claim representatives should *never* accept a diagnosis of a personality disorder or its treatment as the result of an accidental injury. It is likely that the disorder existed before the injury. Since approximately 6 to 10 percent of the general population could be diagnosed with a personality disorder,[8] it is inevitable that personality disordered individuals will be among the population of claimants. Indeed, it is estimated that a much higher percentage of workers compensation claimants are personality-disordered than is the general population. It is also estimated that among claimants with purely psychological injuries, the incidence of personality disorders may be approximately 50 percent.[9] These findings are not surprising in that personality disordered individuals tend to be inflexible, are less able to cope with stress, and often tend to blame others for their problems.[10]

Persons with personality disorders make difficult claimants. The physical, emotional, financial, occupational, and legal stress of making an insurance claim and/or pursuing a lawsuit brings out the worst in these individuals. By definition, these individuals chronically display maladaptive behavior toward the external environment. Added stress causes even more pronounced maladaptive behavior.

Most personality disorders feature clinical symptoms that also appear in Axis I disorders. Neither claim representatives nor clinical professionals should confuse the exacerbation of a personality disorder with a separate Axis I disorder. The indicated treatment of and legal compensability for personality disorders differ from the Axis I disorders. The treatment of personality disorders is often unsuccessful. Only with extended psychotherapy and then only with certain personality disorders is there likely to be any hope for change. As noted above, personality disorders are not legally compensable since they are not caused by accidental injuries. Therefore, the existence of a personality disorder and its role must be established in every case. The failure to note the presence of a personality disorder constitutes an inadequate diagnosis, which cannot serve as a basis for treatment. Claim representatives should not pay for a course of treatment based on such a diagnosis.

Diagnosis of Personality Disorders

Personality disorders are diagnosed only when the person in question shows a pervasive pattern of a certain behavior as well as numerous characteristics of the prototype. Many people show some characteristics of a prototypical personality disorder but would not be diagnosed with the disorder because they do not share enough of the characteristics or their behavior is not pervasive enough for the diagnosis. Personality disorders are among the most difficult of mental disorders to diagnose; even when a personality disorder is diagnosed, that diagnosis is among the most unreliable of the various mental disorders.

Because they represent a lifetime of maladaptive behavior, personality disorders can only be properly identified with a thorough and accurate history. Such histories are often unavailable. The person in question may be unwilling or unable to cooperate in giving a history. Records from school, military service, and work can be helpful and should be investigated in any claim involving a substantial psychological injury.

Because personality disorders share many symptoms with Axis I disorders, a differential diagnosis can often only be made by a clinician who obtains a careful and accurate account of the course and patterns of symptoms. If the clinician fails to do so, the claim is open to criticism.

Axis II also includes the diagnosis for mental retardation. Other developmental disorders such as childhood learning disabilities are included in Axis I.

Axis III—General Medical Conditions

The claimant's medical history should be carefully reviewed for possible causes of psychological disorders. Indeed, a thorough medical review should be a precondition to any psychological diagnosis. An enormous number of psychological symptoms and conditions may be caused by physical illnesses and disorders. Perhaps the most common physical cause is traumatic brain injury (TBI). Brain injuries can lead to a wide variety of psychological conditions. Before confirming a claim for a serious psychological disorder or disability, a claim representative should consider spending the money necessary for a complete physical exam and tests, including blood work, metabolic studies, and brain scans. A defense psychiatrist attuned to organic causes of psychological problems can provide valuable assistance in identifying cases that need a complete physical workup. The psychiatrist is especially useful in this type of case because he or she is also a medical doctor.

Axis IV—Psychosocial and Environmental Problems

Axis IV is for reporting psychological, social, and environmental problems that may affect the diagnosis, treatment, or prognosis of mental disorders. These problems are placed in the following categories:

- Problems with family (death of a family member, divorce, child neglect)
- Problems related to the social environment (death of a friend, discrimination, moving away from friends)
- Educational problems (illiteracy, academic problems, discord with teachers or classmates)
- Occupational problems (unemployment, job loss, stressful work, job dissatisfaction, discord with co-workers or boss)
- Housing problems (homelessness, living in an unsafe neighborhood, discord with neighbors)
- Economic problems (poverty, inadequate finances)
- Problems with access to health-care services
- Problems with legal system/crime (arrested, jailed, involved in litigation, victim of a crime)
- Other problems (exposure to war, natural disasters)

These problems are included because they can affect a person's mental health.

Axis V—Global Assessment Functioning (GAF)

Axis V is for reporting the clinician's judgment of the individual's overall level of functioning. The GAF scale goes from 0 to 100 with 100 being the highest level of functioning. A person with a GAF score of 70 would have mild symptoms (depressed mood, mild insomnia) or some difficulty in social, occupational, or school functioning (household theft, truancy). A GAF score of 40 would indicate a person who has some impairment in communication (illogical speech) or a major impairment is several areas of school, work, or family relations (child abuse, failing at school or work). A GAF score of less than 20 would indicate a person who poses some danger to himself or others or a person who fails to maintain personal hygiene or speaks incoherently. Sometimes it is useful to examine GAF scores at different points in time during treatment to track the progress in social and occupational disability rehabilitation.

Cautionary Statement

The introduction to DSM-IV concludes with a cautionary statement.

> The specified diagnostic criteria for each mental disorder are offered as guidelines for making diagnoses, since it has been demonstrated that using such criteria enhances agreement among clinicians and investigators. The proper use of these criteria requires specialized clinical training that provides both a body of knowledge and clinical skills.[11]

There are three important points to keep in mind when using the DSM-IV.

1. The proper application and use of the diagnostic criteria require clinical experience. Claim representatives or others who might use the DSM-IV as a reference should never consider substituting their judgment for that of an experienced clinician.

2. The disorders identified in the DSM-IV are not the only legitimate subjects of treatment. However, any clinician treating a disorder that is allegedly outside the DSM-IV should explain why DSM-IV criteria cannot be applied.

3. DSM-IV criteria do not necessarily determine legal matters. For example, the criteria for insanity in a criminal matter are established by court cases. However, the fact that the DSM-IV does not determine legal matters does not mean it is irrelevant to legal matters. The DSM-IV establishes standards for practice in psychiatry and psychology and is essential to the resolution of factual medical issues that may arise in legal and claims matters.

Psychological Tests and Problems Related to Psychological Tests

Psychological tests can be invaluable aids in diagnosing mental disorders. A clinical evaluation alone is not nearly as reliable as an evaluation supplemented by testing. Using psychological tests, the clinician can compare a patient to population norms and identify abnormalities. However, psychological tests are not foolproof. Claim representatives should realize that these tests can be inappropriately and incorrectly applied, administered, and interpreted.

Types of Tests

Tests can be categorized by type and format. The most common types of tests are intelligence, personality, and neuropsychological. The format can be objective, in which the subject can answer in only a few ways, or projective, in which the subject can answer in any manner.

The most common intelligence test is the Wechsler Adult Intelligence Scale-Revised (WAIS-R). The WAIS-R is an objective test containing ten subtests, five verbal subtests and five performance subtests. The WAIS-R yields both verbal and performance IQs and a full-scale IQ. In addition, the results from many of the subtests provide valuable clues about levels of education, neurological problems, cultural and social judgment and background, and ability to concentrate.

The most widely used personality test is the Minnesota Multiphasic Personality Inventory (MMPI). The MMPI is an objective test that yields ten clinical scales and four scales regarding the validity of the testing. The clinical scales measure personality tendencies such as hypochrondriasis, hysteria, paranoia, and introversion. The scales regarding the validity of the test measure tendencies to lie, to exaggerate, or to be defensive. Malingering can often be detected using these scales. These scales must be interpreted in light of one another. The MMPI subscores are not independently meaningful as are the subscores of the WAIS-R. These are considered objective tests.

Two popular projective tests of personality are the Rorschach Inkblot Test and the Thematic Apperception Test (TAT). In the Rorschach, the subject views ten standardized inkblots in sequence and describes what he or she sees. The test administrator records the subject's responses and the timing and emotion of the responses. In the TAT, the subject views several illustrations of ambiguous scenes and is asked to make up a story about each scene. Although the content of the TAT illustrations is more structured than the Rorschach inkblots, the subject is encouraged to interpret the scenes. The administration and scoring of these projective tests are more difficult than for the objective tests. In addition, the emotional stress of taking these tests makes them inappropriate for severely disturbed individuals.

A frequently used neuropsychological test is the Halsted-Reitan Battery. This battery includes the WAIS-R, the MMPI, and various other tests designed to detect brain abnormalities. Administering this battery is expensive and time-consuming.

Testing Problems[12]

Although testing can be a valuable supplement to clinical evaluation, it has numerous problems. There are literally hundreds of psychological tests, and the validity and reliability of many have not been established. Test results for the same subject vary from test to test and from examiner to examiner. Claim representatives presented with psychological testing evidence from tests they have never heard of should consult an expert. Many tests are not valid: they have not been shown to measure what they purport to measure.

Aside from problems of validity and reliability, tests may be inappropriately or incorrectly administered. Most psychological tests are "normed" against white, middle-class Americans. Using such a test for someone who is not a white, middle-class American may be inappropriate and meaningless. This problem has been corrected to a great extent in the most recent edition of the MMPI but persists in many other tests.

Some psychological tests are normed such that they yield an unusually high percentage of "false positive" results. This means that the subject is identified as having an abnormality or pathology when neither exists. Tests that tend to yield such results are favorites among plaintiff attorneys.

All valid psychological tests have strict guidelines for administration. An expert hired by a claim representative to review psychological testing should always investigate and critique the circumstances under which the test is administered and scored. Many test results are highly sensitive to environmental factors. Scoring cannot be assumed to be accurate. A defense expert should always obtain the raw data of test administration.

Tests prove nothing about causation. An injury and a mental abnormality shown by testing cannot be connected unless both "before" and "after" tests show a clinically significant difference between pre-accident and post-accident states of mind. Even then, other potential causes would have to be examined and eliminated.

Most important, the majority of psychological tests have been designed under the assumption that test subjects will honestly answer questions on the test and will have no motives other than providing accurate data to the test administrator. Because of the number of false or exaggerated claims, this assumption is often untrue. The claim representative should therefore question the validity of almost all psychological tests of claimants, especially those not given in a controlled environment (for example, the claimant is given a test to take home and complete), or if the tests given were only projective tests. Although the MMPI has certain internal checks of validity, it is not foolproof, and most other tests have no such safeguards. It is obvious to many claimants how to fake deficits on an intelligence test. Neurological deficits are more difficult to fabricate, but giving answers to create the appearance of being impaired will invalidate all results of a test.

Investigating Causation Issues

Physical injuries do not normally cause psychological disorders. Purely psychological disorders do not usually have simple causes. These two facts should cause claim representatives to be skeptical and critical of all claims they receive for psychological injury.

A causal relationship between physical injury and psychological disorder is generally limited to cases of head trauma with resulting brain injury and organic brain disorders. A competent neurologist can review and comment on such cases. A neuropsychologist may be needed to explain the functional consequences of specific injuries.

Once a claim representative has determined that an identifiable psychological disorder actually exists, the cause of the disorder should be examined. Potential defenses related to causation include the following:

- Other causes for the psychological condition exist.
- The condition preexisted the injury.
- The condition is part of the natural progression of, or an aggravated form of, a preexisting condition.

Causation in Fact

To be compensable, treatment of any kind must be for an injury or condition that was actually caused by the compensable accident. Sometimes there is even a question as to whether the physical injury occurred as a result of a compensable accident. This is especially true of claims in which the accident was not witnessed. Psychological injury claims based on uncertain circumstances require thorough investigations.

Anxiety and depression may be normal responses to a physical injury, or they may be a response to a divorce, elderly parents who are dying, or even difficult teenage children. If this person is found to be anxious or depressed following a physical injury, the insurer should only be responsible for the physical injury—not for psychological treatment created by factors unrelated to the injury.

Resolving such problems depends on complex factual medical issues that claim representatives are not competent to address. Yet a claim representative may be the only one involved in a claim who asks critical questions about alternative causes. While physicians generally try to be conscientious in their observations and conclusions, they often base their conclusions on information from the claimant that they have accepted at face value. Claim representatives should investigate alternative causes for claimants' symptoms.

Preexisting Conditions and Other Causes

The National Institute of Mental Health estimates that approximately one person in five has a diagnosable mental disorder.[13] Many of these people become claimants. As a matter of probability, a significant minority of claimants can be expected to have mental disorders. This fact does not mean that the injury or event that is the subject of the claim was the cause of the mental disorder. One of the most common failures of plaintiffs' psychological experts is the failure to consider and report preexisting psychological problems.

A preexisting mental disorder can only be detected through a complete history and review of records. The following topics and information should be considered:

- Family history, including infancy and childhood experiences
- Education and scholastic performance (GPA, class rank, courses taken, Stanford Achievement Tests or Otis-Lennon test scores, enrollment in special education or individualized educational program (IEP) classes)

- Psychosocial functioning before injury (marital status, two or more divorces, arrests, financial distress)
- Occupation (earnings, the level of occupational functioning before the injury, discipline problems, spotty employment history)
- Military service (dishonorable discharge)
- Medical records (dyslexia, learning disabilities, attention deficit disorder, pediatric records)
- Drug and alcohol use (DUI driving convictions, blood work, liver dysfunction, prescriptions with side effects)
- Previous psychological treatment

In addition to obtaining a complete history, the clinician should get documentation on the claimant's academic, occupational, medical, legal, and military records. Many allegedly recent emotional difficulties and intellectual deficits may actually have a long history.

Substance abuse is another potential cause of psychological conditions. Any psychoactive substance except for nicotine and caffeine may become the object of dependence or abuse. One substance abuse disorder that should be considered is dependence on and abuse of psychoactive substances.

Psychoactive substances include alcohol, amphetamines, caffeine, cannabis, cocaine, hallucinogens, inhalants, nicotine, opium, phencyclidine (PCP), and barbiturates. Dependence on and abuse of psychoactive substances are not considered a mental disorder. However, dependence on or continuing abuse of these substances despite adverse consequences is recognized as a psychological problem and can cause organic changes.

> The term organic means a condition that is associated with observable or detectable changes in an organ or tissues of the body. When the term is used with substance abuse, it refers to chemical changes caused in the brain.

Continued use alone is not considered dependence. **Clinical dependence** means that the user consumes increasing amounts of a substance over a longer period of time than he or she had intended; that the user wishes to but has not reduced, or has unsuccessfully tried to reduce, usage; that an increasing amount of the user's time is devoted to obtaining and using the substance; that the user's social, occupational, or recreational activities are impaired as a result of use; that the user has developed a physical tolerance for the substance; that the user is experiencing a characteristic withdrawal from the substance; or that the user takes more of the substance to relieve withdrawal symptoms.

Among the disorders caused by psychoactive substance abuse are intoxication, withdrawal, delirium, hallucinosis, amnestic disorders, dementia, delusional disorders, and mood disorders. Intoxication that does not bother the person or anyone else around him is not considered a mental disorder.

Progression or Aggravation of a Preexisting Condition

Many psychological disorders are characterized by periods of exacerbation and remission. An exacerbation of a preexisting psychological disorder that coincides with an accidental physical injury or some other event cannot necessarily be attributed to that injury or event. In addition, some psychological disorders become progressively worse. The occurrence of a physical injury in the course of a psychological illness does not mean that the injury caused the disorder to get worse; it would have done so anyway.

Certain psychological disorders may be aggravated by a physical injury or another event that is the subject of a claim. Such aggravation is usually relieved as soon as the injury heals or the event in question ceases. If an event aggravates a condition, it does not mean that the claimant should be compensated for the entire condition. Once the condition has returned to its pre-injury status, the responsible party has no further liability for the future of the condition.

Conscious Symptom Production

Symptoms of both physical and mental disorders are sometimes fabricated by people who wish to be treated as sick. Two common intentional disorders are factitious disorders and malingering. The different motives for such behavior distinguish between those who suffer from factitious disorders and those who are malingering. In both conditions, the person consciously controls the symptoms.

Although these disorders do have specific diagnostic criteria, they are not considered compensable disorders. Although not compensable, a diagnosis of a factitious disorder or malingering can help give claim representatives direction in handling the claim.

Factitious Disorders

A person suffering from a **factitious disorder** has a psychological need to assume the sick role. Although the symptoms may be voluntarily created, the motivation to do so is typically rooted in some unconscious need to be sick.

It is thought that a history of true illnesses during childhood or adolescence may predispose a person toward this disorder, as might significant contact with the medical community through employment or a personal relationship with a physician. Substance abuse, especially with analgesics and sedatives, is common, as is a history of abdominal surgeries.

People with factitious disorders often "doctor shop" from one community to the next as their behavior is discovered. They present their symptoms dramatically but are vague and inconsistent about details.

A factitious psychological illness is quite difficult to diagnose. A clinician must eliminate all other possibilities, but should note the presence of uneven cooperation from the client. A factitious disorder must often be inferred from the fact that the collection of symptoms reported by the person is clinically meaningless.

Malingering

Malingering differs from factitious disorders in that the motive for creating the symptoms is external, such as impending job change or a trial. Malingering is commonly referred to as fraud or insurance abuse. Technically, this is not accurate because the definitions for fraud or insurance abuse are not codified, but malingering has a specific medicolegal definition described in the DSM-IV. The consequences are the same for the claimant—a noncompensable claim. The fact that a claimant has symptoms with no organic basis does not necessarily mean that person is malingering. There may be a somatoform or factitious disorder.

The DSM-IV advises that malingering should be strongly suspected if any combination of the following are present:

1. Medicolegal context
2. Marked discrepancy between the person's claims and the objective findings
3. Lack of cooperation during evaluation or treatment
4. Antisocial personality disorder[14]

Insurance claims with no objective evidence of injury automatically meet two of these criteria. However, a claimant should never be accused of malingering unless there is definite evidence that symptoms are voluntarily produced. Such evidence would include surveillance films or eyewitnesses' testimony showing the claimant behaving in ways that would be incompatible with his or her alleged disorder.

When alert to the possibility of malingering, physicians can usually detect it. Malingering patients do not know as much about disorders as physicians and tend to overstate or misstate the symptom pattern they are trying to mimic. Most physicians agree that the following six clinical criteria are most useful for detecting malingering:

- Weakness to manual testing not seen in other activities
- Disablement disproportionate to objective findings
- Pain not following an organic pattern
- Endorsing suggestions of false symptoms
- Cogwheel weakness (diffuse weakness)
- Overreaction during examination

Malingering of psychological symptoms can usually be detected through clinical assessment and psychological testing. The Minnesota Multiphasic Personality Inventory, the Rorschach inkblot test, and the Bender-Gestalt tests are regarded as helpful for this purpose. Malingered intellectual deficits are fairly easy to detect since the person is rarely able to present a consistent and meaningful pattern of intellectual deficit.

Treatment

Even when a psychological disorder is genuine and is caused by an accident or event of a claim, the claim representative does not have to accept treatment that seems to be inappropriate or excessive in duration or cost.

Assuming that causation is established, there should be no problem in providing compensation for treatment of the ordinary psychological responses to physical injury. The symptoms are very real, and their treatment can generally be effective and appropriate. Nevertheless, if the symptoms are ordinary responses to physical injury, the focus of treatment should be on healing the physical injury. Under this assumption, recovery from physical injuries should simultaneously relieve the accompanying psychological problems.

If treatment focuses primarily or solely on the psychological problems, the claim representative must assume that (1) the claimant is being treated inappropriately or (2) the claimant suffers from a distinct psychological disorder, the cause of which cannot be assumed to be the accidental physical injury.

Psychological Injury Treatment Methods

Following are brief descriptions of the major forms of treatment and some parameters for proper treatment.

Psychotherapy

Psychotherapy is the treatment of emotional, behavioral, personality, and psychiatric disorders based primarily on verbal and nonverbal interaction between patient and therapist (or clinician), not on the use of chemical and physical treatments. Unlike psychoanalysis, which is based on the Freudian model of treatment and in which the therapist (psychoanalyst) does little interacting, most current psychotherapy involves the therapist to a much greater degree. Psychoanalysis is typically a long-term treatment. Psychotherapy can range anywhere from a few months to a number of years, depending on the nature of the disorder, the goals of the patient, and the style of the therapist. Each session is typically fifty minutes or one hour long.

Psychotherapy requires a certain level of cooperation from the patient. The patient ordinarily must be functional and have enough psychological strength to endure the sometimes stressful nature of treatment. Psychotherapy is not the best choice when immediate symptom relief is required for the well-being of the patient or those around him or her.

Medications

Psychopharmacology, the use of medication to treat psychological illness, has greatly improved in recent years. A wide range of drugs are available to treat various problems, especially the symptoms of schizophrenia, affective disorders, and anxiety disorders. Symptom relief may range from slight to substantial. The biggest drawback of drug therapy is side effects, which can range from unpleasant to dangerous. Any form of drug therapy should be preceded by a thorough physical and be carefully monitored.

Placebos provide relief from pain in a significant minority of cases. Placebos are agents such as saline solution or sugar pills that have no pharmacological effect. They are inert substances that would be expected to do nothing, yet they have a very real effect. Because placebos can relieve both "organic" and "psychological" pain, their effectiveness cannot be seen as an indicator that pain is only "psychological."

Behavior Modification

Behavioral therapists are often at odds with psychotherapists' methods of effecting change. Behavioral therapists emphasize making changes in behaviors and thinking, not the value of insight into emotions. Behavioral therapy is based on conditioning through which new behaviors or responses are learned. Some therapists may use behavioral techniques with disorders such as compulsions or substance abuse or for the relief of depression or anxiety.

Hospitalization

Hospitalization is indicated when the patient is completely out of touch with reality or cannot control behavior to the extent that he or she is a danger to himself or herself or others. Hospitalization may also be necessary when the patient's entire environment must be controlled, as during the administration of a complex drug regimen or during withdrawal from an addictive substance. Otherwise, hospitalization is probably no more effective than outpatient forms of treatment; it is also much more expensive.

Utilization Review Services

Utilization review services of psychiatric and psychological services are available. The American Psychiatric Association has a division devoted to utilization review and case management. Utilization review services are more expert than claim representatives at analyzing psychological conditions. Claim representatives or their managers should develop guidelines on when utilization review services should be consulted. Many insurers have utilization review guidelines applicable to claims in general. They should be reviewed to see whether they are appropriate for psychiatric cases. Claim representatives should bring psychological injury treatment issues to managers in the following situations:

- The cost of psychiatric or psychological treatment exceeds several thousand dollars.
- Disability is alleged.
- The diagnosis does not appear to match the symptoms.
- An attorney referred the claimant to the provider.
- The claimant has had multiple providers in a short period of time.
- The treatment frequency and severity do not match the injury diagnosis.
- The treatment is family or marriage counseling rather than psychotherapy.
- The provider has a subordinate perform the therapy.
- The provider has a longstanding relationship with the claimant's attorney.

Treatment Problems

Common treatment problems relate to treatment of symptoms only and to therapist bias.

Treatment of Symptoms

Clinicians should treat disorders, not symptoms. A disorder is one of the conditions documented in the DSM-IV. Unless a disorder has been properly identified, the clinician can only respond to symptoms. Treatment would therefore be inappropriate because a given symptom may be characteristic of a number of disorders, each of which is treated in a different way. For instance, the DSM-IV lists twenty-one disorders with depressed mood as a characteristic, twenty-one disorders with fatigue as a characteristic, and thirty-four disorders with some impairment in occupational functioning as a characteristic. In addition, a symptom such as irritability is frequently attributed to psychological causes, yet it can be caused by any of at least twenty-one medical conditions or any of at least twenty-six medications.

Therapist Bias

The claim representative must consider **therapist bias** because it can influence the validity and compensability of a claim. Therapist bias is the failure of the therapist to be adequately critical of a patient's statements. That is, the therapist fails to be objective about or to appropriately analyze a patient's statements and behavior, thereby drawing inappropriate conclusions about the patient's state of mind as it relates to a given accident or injury. For instance, if a patient tells a therapist that he or she has been anxious since an automobile accident or if the patient exhibits symptoms of anxiety, the therapist should not assume that the auto accident caused this state of mind.

Therapist bias usually stems from the therapist's attempt to create an atmosphere of trust. Since trust is essential to successful therapy, the therapist must be able to establish trust by acknowledging the patient's statements while realizing that the patient may be disguising an issue (or his or her feelings), falsifying an issue, avoiding an issue, or acting and speaking in such a way that is clinically significant, but not necessarily "true" in the sense that the words or behavior do not represent reality. A good therapist will distinguish between what is "true" for the patient and what is true in reality.

Careful use of DSM-IV criteria can help a therapist avoid bias. A therapist who conscientiously applies the DSM-IV criteria must carefully address whether each required characteristic or behavior is present and must rule out every relevant differential diagnosis. Inconsistencies in the patient's statements, behavior, demonstrated moods, and test results would be apparent. Although therapists can be misled by difficult and unusual patients, careful use of diagnostic criteria minimizes the extent to which misinformation from the patient causes such problems.

Challenges in Handling Psychological Injury Claims

Because of the nature of psychological injury claims and their relatedness to physical injury claims, it is often difficult to separate and assess the pain and suffering damages associated with psychological injury claims. Furthermore, disability—an important component of serious injury claims—is often difficult to assess in psychological injury claims.

General Damages With Physical Injuries Versus Specific Psychological Injury Damages

Psychological problems that are normal responses to physical injury should not be regarded as separate injuries in a liability claim. Such psychological problems are part of general damages, which are damages for all intangible losses such as pain and suffering. The ordinary psychological responses to physical injury are exactly what general damages are designed to compensate.

While treatment of the ordinary psychological responses to physical injury may be perfectly appropriate, such treatment does not increase the value of general damages in liability claims. Attorneys for claimants will argue that the treatment provides strong proof of the existence of general damages, so the award for general damages should be higher. The appropriate response to this argument is that the existence of general damages is taken for granted. Further proof is unnecessary and does not increase the value of general damages. Indeed, it can be argued that treatment for psychological problems should make the value of general damages less, as the treatment should have relieved the problems.

Assessing Disability

Many individuals with psychological disorders are working and functioning in society. The existence of a disorder does not automatically result in disability. Total disability caused by psychological problems is generally limited to the most severe cases. However, some degree of occupational impairment is a common characteristic of many disorders. Disability must be analyzed in terms of the relationship between the impairment and the job requirements. This is also true of alleged psychological disabilities. Because many jobs require minimal social or intellectual skills and involve minimal stress, disability cannot be assumed even in the presence of fairly substantial psychological disorders.

Chapter Notes

1. Hoyle Leigh, MD, and Morton F. Reiser, *The Patient: Biological, Psychological, and Social Dimensions of Medical Practice*, 2nd ed. (New York: Plenum Medical Books Co., 1985), p. 210.
2. American Psychiatric Association, *Diagnostic and Statistical Manual of Mental Disorders (DSM-IV)*, 4th ed. (Washington, DC: American Psychiatric Press, 1992), pp. 29-30.
3. *DSM-IV*, p. xxi.
4. Allen Frances and Ruth Ross, *DSM-IV Case Studies* (Washington, DC: American Psychiatric Press, 1996), p. 110.
5. *DSM-IV*, p. 427.
6. *DSM-IV*, p. 428.
7. American Psychiatric Association, *Diagnostic and Statistical Manual of Mental Disorders (DSM-III)*, 3rd ed. (Washington, DC: American Psychiatric Press, 1987), p. 248.
8. Robert Cooper, MD and Glen Repko, MD, "The Disability Due to Personality Disorder," reprinted in Herbert J. Laskey, *Guidelines for Handling Psychiatric Issues in Workers Compensation Cases* (Rancho Palos Verdes, CA: Lex-Com Enterprises, 1998), p. 278.
9. Cooper and Repko, p. 278.
10. Cooper and Repko, pp. 308-309.
11. Adapted from *DSM-IV*, p. xxvii.
12. Material is adapted from Paul R. Lees-Haley, Ph.D., "Confronting Neuropsychological Testing," *For the Defense*, May 1990, p. 27.
13. As cited in Paul Lees-Haley, Ph.D., "A Checklist for Defending Psychological Testing Claims," *Claims Magazine*, December 1989, p. 49.
14. *DSM-IV*, p. 683.

Glossary

Anxiety disorders—Dysfunctional behaviors performed to relieve anxiety.

Anxiety—A feeling of apprehension, dread, or uneasiness. Causes physiological changes such as increased blood pressure, sweating, and increased rate and depth of breathing.

Arthroscope—Instrument used to look directly at joint injuries (for example, a knee injury) and perform operations.

Behavior modification therapy—The treatment of disorders based on behavioral conditioning through learning new behaviors and responses.

Clinical dependency—Occurs when the user consumes increasing amounts of a substance, the user cannot reduce consumption, and an increasing amount of the user's life is devoted to obtaining and using the substance.

Collateral ligaments—Stabilize the side-to-side movement of the knee.

Cruciate ligaments—Prevent forward and backward movement of the knee.

Defense mechanism—Any reaction that serves to protect against something harmful Psychological defense mechanisms are unconscious behaviors that resolve or conceal anxieties.

Denial—A person does not acknowledge some aspect of reality.

Depression—A medical diagnosis of a mood disorder characterized by persistent and pervasive despair usually accompanied by loss of interest in life. Can also mean a mood expressed as sadness or grief.

Diagnostic criteria—Criteria that must be met for a diagnosis to be made.

Differential diagnosis—Distinguishing one disorder from another.

Displacement—Feelings are directed away from their real source toward some other source.

Factitious disorder—When a person has a psychological need to assume the sick role. The person creates a situation to make himself or herself sick.

Generalized anxiety disorder—Unrealistic and excessive anxiety characterized by a variety of physical and behavioral symptoms.

Hamstring muscles—A group of muscles that cover the back of the thigh and connect to the upper ends of the tibia and fibula.

Hypochondriasis—Characterized by a preoccupation with the fear that one has a serious illness.

Intelligence tests—Designed to assess verbal, arithmetic, and spatial aptitudes, social judgment, ability to concentrate, general knowledge of a person.

Isolation—Separating thoughts from feelings about an event or situation.

Malingering—Motivated by an external reason, the person fabricates or exaggerates an injury or condition. There are specific criteria used to make this determination.

Mechanism of injury—Specific motions and forces involved in causing an injury.

Meniscectomy—The partial removal of meniscus cartilage.

Meniscus (Menisci)—Cartilage that binds and cushions the ends of the femur and tibia.

Meniscus repair—A repair of a serious tear that extends through the deepest layers of the meniscus.

Mental disorder—A manifestation of a psychological dysfunction characterized by a pattern of behavior associated with a present distress or disability.

Mood disorders—A dysfunctional pervasive and sustained emotion that in the extreme can affect a person's perception of reality.

Neurological tests—Used to identify brain abnormalities.

Pain disorder—When pain continues for months and impairs the person's social and occupational functioning and becomes a major focus of the person's life.

Patella—The kneecap.

Personality disorder—Personality traits that are inflexible, maladaptive, and cause significant impairment or distress for the victim. Typically developed over a period of many years.

Personality tests—Measures personality characteristics relevant to functioning at work, in a family, and with others. Identifies problems that may affect interactions with others, job functioning, and emotional distress.

Phobias—Marked, persistent, exaggerated fear of a specific object or situation.

Post-traumatic stress disorder—Follows a stress that is beyond normal human experience and is characterized by persistent reexperiencing of the event, persistent arousal, and avoidance of anything associated with the event.

Projection—The attribution of one's own thoughts or feelings to another.

Projective tests—Subjective tests that must be interpreted by the test administrator. An example is the Rorschach Inkblot Test.

Psychoactive substance disorders—Use or misuse of substances such as alcohol, amphetamines, cannabis, cocaine, opium, barbiturates, and phencyclidine (PCP) that lead to delirium, hallucinations, dementia, delusions, and mood disorders.

Psychopharmacology—The use of medication to treat psychological illness.

Psychotherapy—Treatment of disorders based primarily on verbal and nonverbal interaction between patient and therapist.

Quadriceps—A group of muscles covering the front of the thigh that extend the knee.

Repression—The forgetting of an unpleasant, anxiety-producing event or emotion.

Somatization disorder—Characterized by multiple complaints over several years for which the person has sought medical attention. The symptoms are often vague, complicated, or dramatic.

Somatoform disorders—Characterized by the presence of physical symptoms suggesting a physiological disorder for which there is no true physical cause.

Stress—Frequently used to mean anxiety or the cause of anxiety. For example, a loss of job would be a stress that causes anxiety.

Therapist bias—The failure of the therapist to be adequately critical of a patient's statements and behavior.

Index

Page references in bold refer to the definitions of Key Words and Phrases. Page references in italics refer to exhibits.

A

ADA (Americans with Disabilities Act), 3-9, 3-13–3-14
    employment and, 4-31
AMA (American Medical Association), impairment
    guide of, 3-15–3-19
Acetabulum, **7-18**, *7-19*
Acetaminophen, 5-28
Achilles tendon, *7-17*
Acromioclavicular joint, 6-16
Activity modification, **1-24**–1-25
Acute, **5-3**
Adjustments, chiropractic, 5-29–5-30
Admission records, *2-28*
Admissions face sheet, emergency, 7-6
Affect, 9-13
Aggravation, **I-3**–I-4
Ambulatory care records, **2-29**–2-30
American Medical Association (AMA), impairment
    guide of, 3-15–3-19
American Psychiatric Association, 9-27
Americans with Disabilities Act (ADA), 3-9, 3-13–3-14
    employment and, 4-31
Ankle jerk reflex test, **5-21**
Ankles
    anatomy of, *7-17*
    sprained, 7-16–7-18

Annulus fibrosis, rupture of, 5-14
Anterior, **5-46**
Anterior cruciate ligament, **8-4**
Anti-depressants, 5-29
Antisocial personality disorder, **9-15**
Anxiety, **9-3**
Anxiety disorders, **9-9**–9-11
Aptitude tests, 4-34
Arm, bones of, 6-15–6-16
Arthritis
    hip, 5-22
    spinal, 5-18
Arthroplasty, hip, 7-2, 7-19–7-22
Arthroscopy, **8-9**
Artificial limbs, 4-7
Aspirin, 5-28
Assessment, **5-3**
Assurance, quality, 4-14
Atlas, 5-7
Attending physicians, **4-6**
Audiologists, **4-7**
Audits
    hospital bill, 1-15–1-16
    medical bill, 1-14
Auto accident fraud, *2-18–2-19*
Auto bodily injury claims, 1-33
Avascular, **7-3**
Axial loading test, **5-23**

B

Babinski test, **5-21**
Back, anatomy of, 5-6–5-10
Back injuries
    claims for, 5-2–5-6
        case study of, 5-34–5-36
        diagnostic testing for, 5-20–5-27
        treatment of, 5-27–5-33, 5-34
        types of, 5-10–5-20
Backbone. *See* Vertebral column.
Behavior modification, 9-27
Billing forms, provider, 6-5–6-6
Biomechanics, **7-10**
Bipolar disorder, 9-8–9-9
Bodily injuries. *See* Injuries.
Bodily injury claim management. *See* Claim management.
Bone scans, **5-26**
Bones
    arm, 6-15–6-16
    knee, 8-2, 8-3
    leg, 7-19
    pelvic, 7-20
Borderline personality disorder, **9-15**
Buildup, **1-10**–1-11
    identification of, 2-16–2-17, 2-18–2-21
Burns' test, **5-23**

C

CPI (Consumer Price Index), medical care, 1-3
CPT (*Current Procedural Terminology*), **I-2**
    codes from, 6-10
CRCs (certified rehabilitation counselors), 4-10
CT (computerized tomography) scans, **2-7**, 5-25–5-26
CTT (computerized transverse axial tomography) scans, 2-7
Calcaneofibular ligament, 7-17
Calcaneus, 7-17
Capacity
Capitation, **1-21**
    earning, 3-29
    functional, 4-30
    hospital, 1-5
    physical, 3-25, 3-27, 3-28
Carpals, 6-17
Case management, 1-23, **4-10**, 4-26–4-30
    knee injuries and, 8-11
Case managers, **4-10**
Casualty claims
    cost controls in, lack of, 1-6–1-7
    disability and, 3-5–3-6
    fraud and, 2-18–2-19
    managed care in, 1-26

CAT (computerized axial tomography) scans, 2-7
Causation
    investigation of, 2-2–2-8
        case study of, 7-1–7-22
Causation in fact, 9-22
Causation issues of psychological injuries, investigating, 9-21–9-25
Central spinal canal, 5-19
Certified orthotists, **4-7**
Certified rehabilitation counselors (CRCs), 4-10
Cervical vertebrae, **5-7**
Chiropractic adjustments, 5-29–5-30
Chiropractic peer reviews, 2-34–2-36
Chiropractic records, 2-30
Chronic, **5-3**
Chronic medical conditions, 2-3
Circumferential measurements, 5-21
Claim files, documents in, I-8
Claim management
    direct intervention, 1-21–1-26
    disability, 1-23–1-26
    injury, equation for, 1-12
    prospective, 1-18–1-21
    reasons for, 1-2–1-12
    retrospective, 1-13–1-17
Claim process, 6-2
    medical, 6-4
Claim representatives, insurance rehabilitation and, 4-13–4-15
Claims, psychological injury, challenges in handling, 9-29
    evaluation of, 9-5–9-25
    significance of personality disorders in, 9-16–9-17
Clavicle, 6-16
Clinical dependence, **9-23**
Clinical disorders, under DSM-IV, 9-7–9-15
Clinical notes, 2-25
Clinical reports, 2-29
Clinical tests, back injury, 5-21–5-23
Clinical treatment, back injury, 5-27–5-31
Closed fractures, **6-10**
Coccyx, **5-7**
Collateral ligaments
    lateral, 8-4
    medial, 8-4
Colles' fracture, **6-9**, 6-15–6-16, 6-17
    disabilities from, 6-17–6-21
Comminuted fractures, 6-14, 6-15
Common tendon, 8-2, 8-3
Communications, disabilities and, 3-9–3-13
Complete fractures, 6-15
Complex regional pain syndrome, 6-23
Complicated fractures, 6-14
Compound fractures, **6-10**
Computerized axial tomography (CAT) scans, 2-7

Computerized tomography (CT) scans, **2-7**, 5-25–5-26
Computerized transverse axial tomography (CTT)
    scans, 2-7
Concurrent reviews, **1-21**, 1-21–1-22
Confidentiality, medical records and, 2-31–2-32
Congenital problems, back, 5-16–5-18
Conservative treatment, **I-3**
Consultation reports, *2-29*
Consulting physicians, **4-6**
Consumer Price Index (CPI), medical care, *1-3*
Contrast agents, 2-7
Cost shifting, **1-11**–1-12
Counselors, certified rehabilitation, 4-10
Cruciate ligaments
    anterior, 8-4
    posterior, 8-4
Current Procedural Terminology (CPT), **I-2**
    codes from, 6-10

D

DSM-IV (*Diagnostic and Statistical Manual of Mental
    Disorders*), 9-5–9-19
Damages
    general, 3-5–3-6
    special, 3-5–3-6
Defense mechanism, **9-4**
Defensive medicine, **1-5**
Definitive diagnosis, **4-26**
Degenerative disk disease, 5-18–5-19
Degenerative disorders, back, 5-18–5-20
Denial, **9-4**
Depression, 9-3–9-4
    disabilities and, 3-8
Diagnoses, 2-3–2-7, **5-3**
    back injury, 5-2–5-4, 5-20–5-27
    definitive, 4-26
    presumptive, 2-4, 4-26
    "rule-out", 2-4, 4-26
    working, 2-4, 4-26
Diagnostic equipment, cost of, 1-4–1-5
Diagnostic imaging, 5-24–5-27
Diagnostic tests, 2-7–2-8
Dinner fork fractures, 6-15–6-16, *6-17*
Direct intervention, **1-21**, 1-21–1-26
Disabilities, **3-3**–3-4
    age and, 3-21
    assessment of, 6-10, 9-29
    behavior effects of, 3-6, 3-8–3-9
    casualty claims and, 3-5–3-6
    Colles' fractures and, 6-17–6-18
    complications and, 3-22
    costs of, 3-14
    determination of, 3-14–3-20
    employment and, 3-13–3-14
    factors affecting, 6-20–6-21
    hip joint replacement and, 7-20–7-22
    human relations and 3-9–3-13
    knee injuries and, 8-9–8-11
    length of, complex claims and, 2-15–2-16
    motivation and, 3-23
    occupation and, 3-21
    preexisting conditions and, 3-22
    simulated, 3-13
    sprained ankles and, 7-17–7-18
    statements about, 2-13
Disability management, **1-23**–1-26
Discectomy, **5-32**, 5-33
Discharge planning, **1-21**
Discharge summary, *2-28*
Discography, **5-26**–5-27
Discovery, **7-11**
Disks, **5-8**
    degeneration of, 5-18–5-19
    herniation of, 5-13–5-15
        treatment of, 5-31–5-33
Dislocations, **5-16**
Disorder, factitious, **9-24**
    anxiety, **9-9**–9-11
    clinical, under DSM-IV, 9-7–9-15
    mental, 9-5–**9-6**
        under DSM-IV, 9-15–9-18
    mood, 9-8–9-9
    pain, **9-13**
    personality, diagnosis of, 9-17–9-18
        examples of, 9-15–9-16
        significance of in claims, 9-16–9-17
    psychological, medication for, 9-26–9-27
        treatment of, 9-25–9-28
    somatization, **9-13**
    somatoform, **9-13**
Displaced fractures, **6-14**
Displacement, **9-4**
Distal, **5-46**
Doctors. *See* Physicians.

E

EMG (electromyogram), 2-8, **5-26**
ER (emergency room) records, 2-27, 2-29–2-30, 6-8,
    6-11, 6-12, 6-13
Earning capacity, 3-29
Education, patient, 5-27–5-28
Educational achievement tests, 4-33
Electromyogram (EMG), 2-8, **5-26**
Emergency admissions face sheet, 7-6
Emergency room (ER) records, 2-27, 2-29–2-30, 6-8,
    6-11, 6-12, 6-13, 7-7

Employer liability, managed care and, 1-33–1-35
Employer's report of injury, 6-3
Employment
    Americans with Disabilities Act and, 4-31
    disabilities and, 3-13–3-14
    return to. *See* Vocational rehabilitation.
Environmental problems, under DSM-IV, 9-18
Epicondyle
    arm, 6-16
    knee, 8-4
Epidural blocks, 5-32
ETIOL (etiology), **7-3**
Exacerbation, I-3–I-4
Exaggeration, 1-10–1-11
    identification of, 2-16–2-17, 2-18–2-21
Expert reviews, 2-42–2-43
External, **5-46**

F

FFS (fee-for-service) system, **1-18**
Fabere's sign, **5-22**
Fabrication, symptom, tests for, 5-22–5-23
Face sheet, emergency admissions, 7-6
Facet, **5-9**
Facet joint impingement, 5-20
Facet joint injections, 5-32
Facet joint sprain, 5-20
Facet joints, osteoarthritis in, 5-18
Facet tropism, 5-16–5-17
Factitious disorder, **9-24**
Federal Privacy Act of 1974, 2-31–2-32
Fee schedules, 1-18–1-21
    state, 1-14–1-15
Fee-for-service (FFS) system, **1-18**
Femoral neck, 7-19
Femoral nerves, 5-22
Femur, **7-18**, *7-19*
Fibrosus, annulus, rupture of, 5-14
Fibrous union, **6-22**
Fibula, **7-16**, *7-19*
Food liability fraud, 2-19
Foramen, vertebral, 5-9
Forensic rehabilitation, **4-12**, 4-37–4-38
Fractures, 6-10, 6-14–6-17
    healing process of, 6-22–6-23
    impairment and, 6-19
    spinal, 5-10–5-11
Fraud, **1-10**–1-11
    identification of, 2-16–2-17, 2-18–2-21
Functional capacities, **4-30**
Functional overlay, **9-1**
Fusion, spinal, 5-32–5-33

G

GAF (global assessment functioning), under DSM-IV, 9-18–9-19
General damages, **3-5**–3-6
Generalized anxiety disorder, **9-11**
Global assessment functioning (GAF), under DSM-IV, 9-18–9-19
Goniometry, **3-16**, *3-17*
Greater trochanter, **7-18**, *7-19*
Greater tubercle, 6-16
Greenstick fractures, 6-14, *6-15*
Group health insurance, workers compensation versus, 1-27–1-29
Guide to the Evaluation of Permanent Impairment, 3-15–3-19

H

HCFA-1500, 2-25, 6-5–6-6, 6-8
HCPC (Health Care Financing Common Procedure Coding System), **I-3**
HMOs (health maintenance organizations), **1-20**, 1-20–1-21
Hairline fractures, 6-14
Halsted-Reitan Battery of psychological tests, 9-20
Hamstring muscles, 8-2, 8-3
Handicaps, 3-6
Health Care Financing Administration (HCFA), 2-25, 6-5–6-6, 6-8
Health Care Financing Common Procedure Coding System (HCPC), **I-3**
Health Care Management Guidelines, Milliman-Robertson, **I-3**
Health insurance, group, worker compensation versus, 1-27–1-29
Health maintenance organizations (HMOs), **1-20**, 1-20–1-21
Hearing loss, 4-7
Heel bone, *7-17*
HEENT (head, eyes, ears, nose, throat), **I-3**
Herniation, disk, 5-13–5-15, 5-31–5-33
Hip arthritis, 5-22
Hip injuries, 7-18–7-19
Hip joint replacement, 7-19–7-22
Hoover test, **5-23**
Hospital bill audits, **1-15**–1-16
Hospitalization, 9-27
Hospitals
    billing forms of, 6-5–6-6
    capacity of, 1-5
    records of, 2-26–2-27

Human relations, disabilities and, 3-9–3-13
Humerus, 6-15–6-16
Humpback, 5-10
Hypochondriasis, **9-13**

I

ICD-9-CM (*International Classification of Diseases*), **I-2**
   codes from, 6-9
IMEs (independent medical examinations), **1-22**,
     1-22–1-23, 2-38–2-42
   requests for, writing, 7-11, *7-12–7-13*
   temporary disabilities and, 3-19
Ibuprofen, 5-28
Ilium, *7-20*
Impacted fractures, 6-14, *6-15*
Impairments, **3-1**–3-3
   assessment of, 6-10
   behavior effects of, 3-6, 3-8–3-9
   Colles' fractures and, 6-17–6-18
   criteria of, 3-16–3-18
   earning capacity and, 3-29
   evaluation of, guide for, 3-15–3-19
   factors affecting, 6-19
   job analysis and, 3-24–3-25, *3-26*
   medical reports on, 3-18–3-19
   physical capacity and, 3-25, 3-27, *3-28*
   vocational rehabilitation and, 3-28–3-29
Incomplete fractures, 6-15
Independent medical examinations (IMEs), **1-22**–1-23,
     2-38–2-42
   requests for, writing, 7-11, *7-12–7-13*
   temporary disabilities and, 3-19
Infection, fractures and, 6-23
Inferior, **5-46**
Inflation, medical cost, 1-3–1-4
Injection therapy, 5-32
Injuries. *See also* Back injuries; Fractures.
   ankle, 7-16–7-18
   cause of, verification of, 2-2–2-8
   diagnosis of, 2-3–2-7
   hip, 7-18–7-19
   ligament, knee, 8-5
   mechanism of, 8-5–8-7
   meniscus, knee, 8-6, 8-9–8-11
   serious, 2-15
   wrist, 6-15–6-16, *6-17*
Injury, physical, psychological response to, 9-2–9-5
Injury claim management equation, **1-12**
Inpatient care, 4-27–4-28
Insurance rehabilitation, **4-1**–4-2, 4-9–4-12
   benefits of, 4-4
   claim representatives and, 4-13–4-15

   costs of, 4-4
   vendors for, 4-15–4-17
Intelligence tests, 4-33
Internal, **5-46**
International Classification of Diseases (ICD-9-CM), **I-2**
   codes from, 6-9
Intervening causes, 2-3, 7-3–7-4
Intervention, direct, 1-21–1-26
Intervertebral disks, **5-8**
   degeneration of, 5-18–5-19
   herniation of, 5-13–5-15
     treatment of, 5-31–5-33
Investigation
   causation, 2-2–2-8
   medical, 6-4
     case study of, 6-1–6-25
Ischium, 7-19, *7-20*
Isolation, **9-4**

J

JCAH (Joint Commission on Accreditation of Hospitals), 2-26–2-27
Job analysis, **4-30**, 3-24–3-25, *3-26*
Job development, **4-33**
Job modification, **4-31**
Job placement specialists, **4-17**
Job-seeking skills, **4-33**
Joint Commission on Accreditation of Hospitals
     (JCAH), 2-26–2-27
Joints
   acromioclavicular, 6-16
   facet
     impingement of, 5-20
     injections in, 5-32
     osteoarthritis in, 5-18
     sprains of, 5-20
   motion of, 3-16, *3-17*

K

Knee flexion test, **5-22**
Kneecap, 8-2, 8-3
Knees
   anatomy of, 8-2–8-4
   injuries of, 8-5–8-7
     disability and, 8-9–8-11
Kyphosis, **5-10**

L

LPN (licensed practical nurse), **4-7**
Labor market, **4-33**

Laboratory reports, 2-29
Laminae, **5-9**
Laminectomy, **5-32**, 5-33
Laseque's sign, **5-22**
Lateral, **5-46**
Lateral collateral ligament, **8-4**
Lateral epicondyle
    arm, 6-16
    knee, 8-4
Lateral nerve root exits, 5-19
Leg, anatomy of, *7-19*
Lesser tubercle, 6-16
Liability, employer, managed care and, 1-33–1-35
Liability claims
    disabilities and, 3-5–3-6
    insurance rehabilitation and, 4-24–4-25
Licensed practical nurse (LPN), **4-7**
Ligaments, **7-16**
    ankle, 7-16, *7-17*
    knee, 8-4–8-5
Light duty, **6-19**
Lighted-up, **I-4**
Limbs, artificial, 4-7
Linder's sign, **5-22**
Lordosis, **5-10**
Lost earnings fraud, 2-19
Low back injuries. *See* Back injuries.
Lumbar nerve root compression, test for, 5-22
Lumbar vertebrae, **5-7**
    sacralization of, 5-17
Lumbarization, 5-17

M

MDA (*The Medical Disability Advisor*), **I-3**, 2-10, 2-10–2-12
    Colles' fracture and, 6-18
MRI (magnetic resonance imaging), **2-7**–2-8, 5-26
MVAs (motor vehicle accidents), **7-2**
Magnification, symptom, 5-6, 5-22–5-23
Malingering, **9-24**–9-25. *See also* Magnification.
Malpractice, medical, insurance for, 1-5
Mal-union, **6-22**
Managed care
    casualty claims and, 1-26
    employer liability and, 1-33–1-35
    health maintenance organizations and, 1-20–1-21
    preferred provider organizations and, 1-19–1-20
    workers compensation and, 1-26–1-33
Managed care organizations (MCOs), **1-30**–1-33
Management
    case, 1-23, **4-10**, 4-26–4-30
        knee injuries and, 8-11
    direct intervention, 1-21–1-26
    disability, 1-23–1-26
    injury, equation for, 1-12
    prospective, 1-18–1-21
    retrospective, 1-13–1-17
Managers
    case, 4-10
    involvement of, 2-17
Manic-depressive mood, **9-8**–9-9
Manipulation, **5-29**–5-30
Market, labor, 4-33
Mechanism of injury, **8-5**–8-7
Medial, **5-46**
Medial collateral ligament, **8-4**
Medial epicondyle
    arm, 6-16
    knee, 8-4
Mediation, 7-11, **7-15**–7-16
Medical authorization, 2-32, 6-6
Medical bill audits, **1-14**
Medical bills, 2-24–2-25
    forms for, 6-5–6-6
Medical case management, 1-23, **4-10**, 4-26–4-30
    knee injuries and, 8-11
Medical chart records, 2-28–2-29
Medical conditions
    chronic, 2-3
    under DSM-IV, general, 9-18
Medical costs, higher-than-average, 1-3–1-7
Medical data, **2-32**
The Medical Disability Advisor (MDA), **I-3**, 2-10–2-12
    Colles' fracture and, 6-18
Medical fraud, 2-19
Medical investigation, case study of, 6-1–6-25
Medical investigation process, 6-4
Medical malpractice, insurance for, 1-5
Medical opinions, **2-32**–2-33
Medical records, 2-22, **2-23**
    analyzing, 6-7–6-10
    causation and, verification of, 2-6–2-7
    gathering, 6-4–6-6
    obtaining, 2-30–2-32
    organizing, 6-7
    purpose of, 2-23–2-24
    standards for, 2-24
    types of, 2-24–2-30
Medical reports, 2-25–2-26, 6-12, 6-13, 7-7
    impairments and, 3-18–3-19
Medical social workers, **4-8**
Medical terminology, I-3–I-4
    word roots in, *I-4*–*I-7*
Medication, back injury, 5-28–5-29
Medications, 9-26–9-27

Medicine
    defensive, 1-5
    occupational, 4-5
    orthopedic, 4-6
Medicolegal reports, **2-25**
Meniscectomy, **8-9**
Menisci, **8-4**, 8-6
Meniscus repair, **8-9**
Mental disorders, 9-5–**9-6**
Mental retardation, 9-15–9-18
Merck Manual, 2-8, 2-9–2-10
Milliman-Robertson *Health Care Management Guidelines*, **I-3**
Minnesota Multiphasic Personality Inventory (MMPI) psychological test, 9-20
Monetary influences, back injuries and, 5-5–5-6
Mood, **9-8**
    manic-depressive, **9-8**–9-9
Mood disorders, 9-8–9-9
Motor vehicle accidents (MVAs), **7-2**
Muscle relaxants, 5-28
Muscles
    leg, 8-2, 8-3
    paraspinal, 5-30
    strain of, 5-15
Myelography, **5-26**

N

Narcissistic personality disorder, **9-16**
Narrative reports, **2-25**–2-26
Necrosis, **7-22**
Negotiation, 7-11, 7-15–7-16
NSAIDs (nonsteroid anti-inflammatory drugs), 5-28
Nerve damage, fractures causing, 6-22–6-23
Nerve root compression, lumbar, 5-22
Nerve root exits, lateral, 5-19
Nerves
    femoral, 5-22
    sciatic, 5-21, 5-22, 5-23
    spinal, 5-8
Neurologists, **4-6**
Neurology, **4-6**
Neurosugeons, **4-6**
Neurosurgery, **4-6**
Nondisplaced fractures, **6-14**
Nonphysical factors, back injuries and, 5-5–5-6
Nonsteroid anti-inflammatory drugs (NSAIDs), 5-28
Non-union, **6-22**
Nurses
    licensed practical, 4-7
    records of, 2-28
    registered, 4-7

O

Obsessive-compulsive personality disorder, **9-16**
Occupation, disabilities and, 3-21
Occupational medicine, **4-5**
Occupational therapy, **4-5**–4-6
Olecranon process, 6-16
Open fractures, **6-10**
Opinions, **2-32**–2-33
Organic, explanation of, 9-23
Orthopedic medicine, **4-6**
Orthopedic surgeons, **4-6**
Orthotists, certified, 4-7
Osteoarthritis, 5-18
Osteomyelitis, 6-23
Outpatient care, 4-28–4-30

P

PM&R (physical medicine and rehabilitation), **4-4**
PPOs (preferred provider organizations), **1-19**–1-20
    managed care organizations and, 1-32–1-33
Pain, **9-2**–9-3
Pain disorder, **9-13**
Palliative care, **1-17**
Paranoid personality disorder, **9-16**
Paraspinal muscles, **5-30**
Partial disabilities, 3-4
Partial impairments, 3-2–3-3
Partial union, **6-22**
Passive-aggressive personality disorder, **9-16**
Patella, 8-2, 8-3
Patellar ligament, 8-3
Patellar reflex test, **5-22**
Patellar tendon, 8-2, 8-3
Pathologists, speech, 4-7
Pathology reports, 2-29
Patrick's sign, **5-22**
Pedicles, **5-9**
Peer reviews, **1-16**
    chiropractic, 2-34–2-36
    physical therapy, 2-36–2-37
Pelvis, anatomy of, 7-18–7-19, 7-20
Permanent disabilities, 3-4
Permanent impairments, **3-2**–3-3, 3-25, 3-27, 3-28
    criteria of, 3-16–3-18
    earning capacity and, 3-29
    evaluation of, guide for, 3-15–3-19
    job analysis and, 3-24–3-25, 3-26
    vocational rehabilitation and, 3-28–3-29
Permanent partial impairments, **3-2**–3-3
Permanent physical restrictions, **3-3**
Permanent total impairments, **3-3**

Personality disorders
    diagnosis of, 9-17–9-18
    examples of, 9-15–9-16
    significance of in claims, 9-16–9-17
Personality disorders and mental retardation, under DSM-IV, 9-15–9-18
Personality tests, 4-34
Phobias, specific, **9-11**
Physiatrists, **4-4**–**4-5**
Physiatry, 4-4–**4-5**
Physical agents, **5-30**
Physical capacity, 3-25, *3-27*, *3-28*
Physical injury, psychological response to, 9-2–9-5
Physical medicine and rehabilitation (PM&R), **4-4**
Physical restrictions, 3-3
Physical therapists, **4-5**
Physical therapy peer reviews, 2-36–2-37
Physical/psychosocial rehabilitation, **4-1**, 4-4–4-9
Physicians
    attending, 4-6
    consulting, 4-6
    cooperation of, 3-20
    primary, 1-20
    questioning of, 7-10–7-11
    records of, *2-28*
    surplus of, 1-7
Placebos, 9-26
Population, changes in, 1-7–1-10
Posterior, **5-46**
Posterior cruciate ligament, **8-4**
Post-traumatic stress disorder, **9-9**, *9-12*
Preadmission certification, **1-18**
Preadmission testing, **1-18**
Preexisting conditions
    back, 5-4–5-5
    case study of, 7-1–7-22
    causation and, verification of, 2-3–2-4, *2-6*
    disabilities and, 3-22
Preferred provider organizations (PPOs), **1-19**–1-20
    managed care organizations and, *1-32*–*1-33*
Presumptive diagnosis, 2-4, **4-26**
Primary physicians, **1-20**
Privacy, medical records and, 2-31–2-32
Process
    olecrannon, *6-16*
    spinous, 5-9
    styloid, *6-16*
    transverse, 5-9
Products liability fraud, *2-19*
Projection, **9-4**
Prolotherapy, 5-32
Prospective management, **1-18**–1-21
Prosthetists, **4-7**
Providers. *See also* Nurses; Physicians.
    billing forms of, 6-5–6-6
    rehabilitation, 4-4–4-9
Proximal, **5-46**
Psychiatric and psychological services, utilization review services for, 9-27–9-28
Psychiatrists, **4-8**
Psychological conditions, preexisting, 9-22–9-24
    medication for, 9-26–9-27
    treatment of, 9-25–9-28
Psychological factors, back injuries and, 5-5–5-6
Psychological injury, treatment of, 9-25–9-28
    evaluation of, 9-5–9-25
Psychological injury claims, challenges in handling, 9-29
Psychological response to physical injury, 9-2–9-5
Psychological tests and related problems, 9-19–9-21
Psychologists, **4-8**
Psychometric tests, 4-33–4-34
Psychopharmachology, 9-26
Psychosocial adjustment, 4-11–4-12, 4-35–4-37
Psychosocial and environmental problems, under DSM-IV, 9-18
Psychosocial problems, under DSM-IV, 9-18
Psychosocial rehabilitation, **4-1**, 4-4–4-9
Psychotherapy, 9-26
Pubis, 7-19, *7-20*

Q

Quadriceps femoris muscles, **8-2**, 8-3
Quality assurance, **4-14**

R

RN (registered nurse), **4-7**
RSDS (reflex sympathetic dystrophy syndrome), 6-23
Radiographs, 2-7, 5-25
Radionuclide imaging, **5-26**
Radius, **6-15**
Rami, 7-19
Records reviews, 1-16–1-17
Recreational therapists, **4-8**
Recurrence, **I-3**–I-4
Reflex sympathetic dystrophy syndrome (RSDS), 6-23
Reflex tests, 5-21–5-22
Registered nurse (RN), **4-7**
Rehabilitation
    candidates for, identification of, 4-21–4-25
    forensic, 4-12, 4-37–4-38
    insurance, 4-1–4-2, 4-9–4-12
        benefits of, 4-4
        claim representatives and, 4-13–4-15
        costs of, 4-4
        vendors for, 4-15–4-16
    medical case management and, 4-26–4-30

need for, 4-2–4-4
   physical/psychosocial, 4-1, 4-4–4-9
   vocational, 4-10–4-11, 4-30–4-35
      impairments and, 3-28–3-29
Rehabilitation counselors, certified, 4-10
Rehabilitation process, *4-19*, 4-18–4-21
Rehabilitation providers, **4-4**–4-9
Release to work, **4-30**
Repression, **9-4–9-5**
Restorative care, **1-17**
Retrospective management, **1-13**–1-17
Retrospective reviews, **1-16**–1-17, 2-33–2-34
Return-to-work initiatives, **1-25**
Reviews
   concurrent, 1-21–1-22
   expert, 2-42–2-43
   peer, 1-16
      chiropractic, 2-34–2-36
      physical therapy, *2-36–2-37*
   records, 1-16–1-17
   retrospective, 1-16–1-17
   utilization, 1-13, *2-41–2-42*
R.I.C.E. (rest, ice, compression, elevation), **I-3**
Roentgenograms, 2-7, 5-25
Rorschach Inkblot Test, 9-20
"Rule-out" diagnosis, 2-4, **4-26**

S

SRL (straight-raised-leg) test, 5-22
Sacralization, 5-17
Sacrum, **5-7**
   lumbarization of, 5-17
Scapula, *6-16*
Schizophrenia, **9-13**
Sciatica, **5-15**, 5-22, 5-23
Scoliosis, **5-10**, 5-18
Self-referral, **1-10**
Shinbone, 7-16, *7-19*
Short stay records, *2-29*
Simple fractures, **6-10**
Simulated disability, 3-13
Sitting root test, **5-23**
Slip-and-fall fraud, *2-19*
SOAP notes, 2-30
Social services reports, *2-29*
Social workers, **4-8**
   medical, 4-8
Somatization disorder, **9-13**
Somatoform disorders, **9-11–9-13**
Special damages, **3-5–3-6**
Specialists. *See specific entries, such as* Orthopedic
   surgeons.
Speech pathologists, **4-7**

Spina bifida, 5-17
Spinal canal, central, 5-19
Spinal column, 5-7–5-10
Spinal cord, 5-8
Spinal fractures, 5-10–5-11
Spinal fusion, 5-32–5-33
Spinal injuries. *See* Back injuries.
Spinal nerves, 5-8
Spinal stenosis, 5-19–5-20
Spine, 5-6–5-10, **5-7**
Spinous process, **5-9**
Spiral fractures, 6-14, *6-15*
Spondylolisthesis, **5-11**–5-13
Spondylolysis, **5-11**–5-13
Sprains
   ankle, 7-16–7-18
   back, 5-15
State fee schedules, **1-14**–1-15
Stenosis, spinal, 5-19–5-20
Steroids, 5-28
Straight leg exam, Waddell's, 5-23
Straight-raised-leg (SRL) test, 5-22
Strains, back, 5-15
Stress, anxiety and, 9-3
Stress disorder, post-traumatic, **9-9**, 9-12
Stress value of life events, *9-10*
Styloid process, **6-16**
Subluxation, **5-16**
Superior, **5-46**
Supervisors, involvement of, 2-17
Surgeons
   neurological, 4-6
   orthopedic, 4-6
Surgery
   back, 5-32–5-33
   knee, 8-9
Surgical instruments, cost of, 1-4–1-5
Surplus, physician, 1-7
Swayback, 5-10
Symptom fabrication, 5-22–5-23
Symptom magnification, 5-6, 5-22–5-23
Symptoms, conscious production of, 9-24–9-25
   treatment of, 9-28
Synovial fluid, **7-18**

T

Taber's Medical Dictionary, **I-2**
Tailbone, 5-7
Talofibular ligament, **7-16**, *7-17*
Talus, **7-16**, *7-17*
Technology, medical, cost of, 1-4–1-5
Temporary disabilities, 3-4
   age and, 3-21

complications and, 3-22
determination of, 3-19
motivation and, 3-23
occupation and, 3-21
preexisting conditions and, 3-22
Temporary impairments, **3-2**
Temporary partial impairments, **3-2**
Temporary physical restrictions, **3-3**
Temporary total impairments, **3-2**
Tendons, **7-16**, *7-17*
knee, 8-2, 8-3
TENS, 5-30
Test, psychological, related problems and, 9-19–9-21
Thematic Apperception Test (TAT), 9-20
Therapeutic equipment, cost of, 1-4–1-5
Therapist bias, 9-28
Therapists
physical, 4-5
recreational, 4-8
Therapy, occupational, 4-5–4-6
Thermography, 2-8, **5-27**
Thigh bone, 7-18, *7-19*
Thoracic vertebrae, **5-7**
Tibia, **7-16**, *7-19*
Tomography, computerized, 2-7, 5-25–5-26
Total disabilities, 3-4
Total impairments, 3-2, 3-3
Traction, **5-30**
Training, vocational, 4-35
Transitional work, **4-31**
Transverse process, **5-9**
Traumatic brain injury (TBI), 9-18
Treatment
alternative, 2-12–2-13
ankle sprain, 7-16–7-17
assessment of, 6-10
back injury, 5-27–5-33, 5-34
conservative, **I-3**
fracture, 6-22–6-23
future, 2-13
hip injury, 7-19–7-20
meniscus injury, 8-9
necessity of, 2-8–2-13
redundancy of, 2-12
Treatment guidelines, **1-16**–1-17
Trigger point injections, 5-32
Trochanter, greater, 7-18, *7-19*
Tropism, facet, 5-16–5-17
Tubercle, *6-16*

U

UB-92, 2-25, 6-5–6-6, *6-11*
UCR (usual, customary, and reasonable charge), **1-15**
URs (utilization reviews), **1-13**
workers compensation claims and, *2-41–2-42*
Ulna, **6-16**
Undisplaced fractures, **6-14**
Usual, customary, and reasonable charge (UCR), **1-15**
Utilization reviews (URs), **1-13**
workers compensation claims and, *2-41–2-42*

V

Vascular damage, fractures causing, 6-23
Vertebrae
cervical, 5-7
lumbar, 5-7
thoracic, 5-7
Vertebral column, **5-7**–5-10
Vertebral foramen, 5-9
Vocational evaluation, **4-33**–4-35
Vocational rehabilitation, **4-10**–4-11, 4-30–4-35
impairment and, 3-28–3-29

W

Waddell tests, **5-23**
Waddell's straight leg exam, **5-23**
Wechsler Adult Intelligence Scale-Revised (WAIS-R) psychological test, 9-20
Work, 4-31
Work disabilities. *See* Disabilities.
Work evaluators, **4-16**-4-17
Work hardening, **4-31**
Work samples, **4-34**–4-35
Workers compensation
fraud and, *2-20–2-21*
group health insurance versus, 1-27–1-29
insurance rehabilitation and, 4-22–4-24
disability and, 3-5
managed care networks in, 1-26–1-33
Working diagnosis, 2-4, **4-26**
Wrist, anatomy of, 6-15–6-16

X

X-rays, **2-7**, 5-25